THE MURDERS AT
WHITE HOUSE FARM

Carol Ann Lee is the highly acclaimed author of ten books, including *Roses from the Earth: The Biography of Anne Frank* and *The Hidden Life of Otto Frank*. Her true crime books include *One of Your Own: The Life and Death of Myra Hindley*, *Witness: The Story of David Smith* and *A Fine Day for a Hanging: The Real Ruth Ellis Story*. She lives in Yorkshire with her son.

Also by Carol Ann Lee

Non-Fiction

Roses from the Earth: The Biography of Anne Frank

The Hidden Life of Otto Frank

A Friend Called Anne
(co-written with Jacqueline van Maarsen)

Anne Frank's Story

Anne Frank and the Children of the Holocaust

One of Your Own: The Life and Death of Myra Hindley

Witness: The Story of David Smith,
Chief Prosecution Witness in the Moors Murder Case
(also published as Evil Relations*)*

A Fine Day for a Hanging: The Real Ruth Ellis Story

Fiction

Come Back to Me

The Winter of the World

Carol Ann Lee

THE MURDERS AT WHITE HOUSE FARM

PAN BOOKS

First published 2015 by Sidgwick & Jackson

First published in paperback 2016 by Pan Books

This edition first published 2020 by Pan Books
an imprint of Pan Macmillan
The Smithson, 6 Briset Street, London EC1M 5NR
Associated companies throughout the world
www.panmacmillan.com

ISBN 978-1-5290-1331-3

1 3 5 7 9 8 6 4 2

A CIP catalogue record for this book is available from the British Library.

Typeset by Palimpsest Book Production Ltd, Falkirk, Stirlingshire
Printed and bound by CPI Group (UK) Ltd, Croydon, CR0 4YY

'People generally see what they look for,
and hear what they listen for.'

Harper Lee, *To Kill A Mockingbird* (1960)

'Somebody in this case is lying, and lying their heads off.'

Anthony Arlidge QC, closing speech at the Bamber trial,
22 October 1986

Contents

Family Tree *viii*

Floor Plans of White House Farm, 7 August 1985 *x*

Preface *xiii*

Prologue *1*

1: SOWING
29 December 1891 to 31 December 1984
9

2: GROWTH
1 January 1985 to 6 August 1985
109

3: HARVEST
7 August 1985 to 29 September 1985
161

4: WINTER
30 September 1985 to July 2015
331

Epilogue *404*

Appendix I: A reconstruction of events at
White House Farm on 7 August 1985 *410*

Appendix II: A message from Colin Caffell *417*

Acknowledgements *419*

Bibliography *422*

Notes and References *426*

Index *463*

The Bamber Family Tree

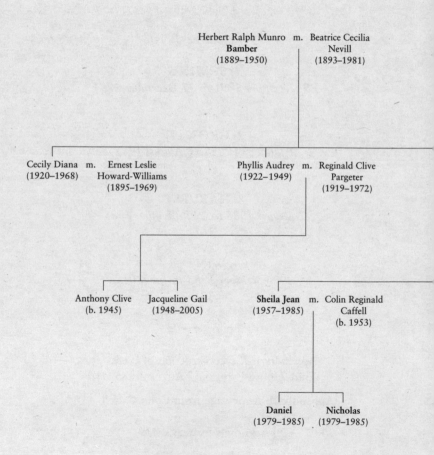

Herbert Ralph Munro   m.   Beatrice Cecilia
Bamber   Nevill
(1889–1950)   (1893–1981)

Cecily Diana   m.   Ernest Leslie   Phyllis Audrey   m.   Reginald Clive
(1920–1968)   Howard-Williams   (1922–1949)   Pargeter
                            (1895–1969)   (1919–1972)

Anthony Clive   Jacqueline Gail   Sheila Jean   m.   Colin Reginald
(b. 1945)   (1948–2005)   (1957–1985)   Caffell
                                                                              (b. 1953)

Daniel   Nicholas
(1979–1985)   (1979–1985)

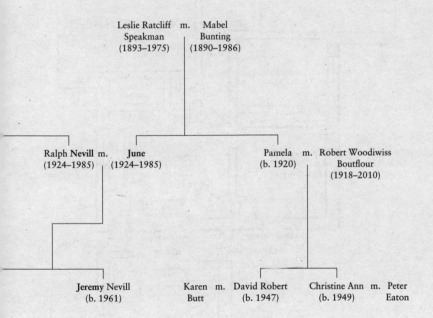

Leslie Ratcliff   m.   Mabel
Speakman   Bunting
(1893–1975)   (1890–1986)

Ralph **Nevill** m.   **June**   Pamela   m.   Robert Woodiwiss
(1924–1985)   (1924–1985)   (b. 1920)   Boutflour
                                                       (1918–2010)

Jeremy Nevill   Karen   m.   David Robert   Christine Ann   m.   Peter
(b. 1961)   Butt   (b. 1947)   (b. 1949)   Eaton

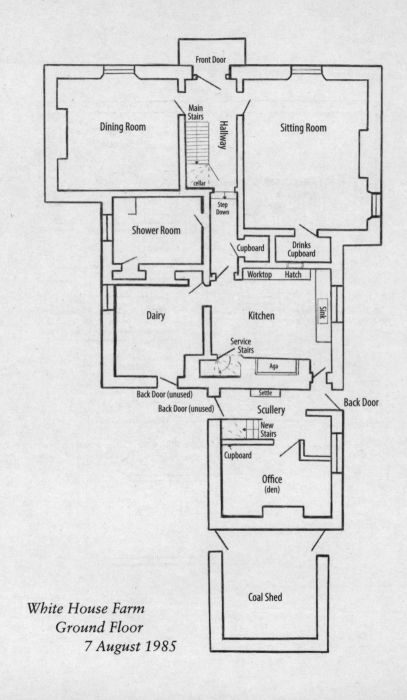

Front Door

Main
Stairs

Dining Room

Hallway

cellar

Sitting Room

Step
Down

Shower Room

Cupboard

Drinks
Cupboard

Worktop   Hatch

Sink

Dairy

Kitchen

Service
Stairs

Aga

Back Door (unused)

Settle

Back Door (unused)

Back Door

Scullery

New
Stairs

Cupboard

Office
(den)

Coal Shed

White House Farm
Ground Floor
7 August 1985

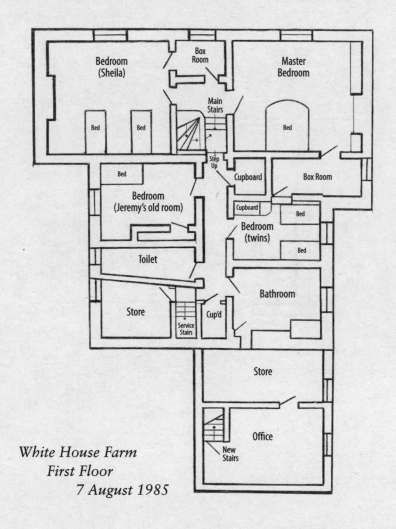

Bedroom
(Sheila)

Bed   Bed

Box
Room

Master
Bedroom

Bed

Main
Stairs

Step
Up

Bed

Bedroom
(Jeremy's old room)

Cupboard

Cupboard

Box Room

Bed

Bedroom
(twins)

Bed

Toilet

Store

Service
Stairs

Cup'd

Bathroom

Store

White House Farm
First Floor
7 August 1985

Office

New
Stairs

Preface

'Suicide Girl Kills Twins and Parents' bellowed the *Daily Express* headline on 8 August 1985. Beside a hauntingly beautiful photograph of the young woman and her two smiling children the article began: 'A farming family affectionately dubbed "the Archers" was slaughtered in a bloodbath yesterday. Brandishing a gun taken from her father's collection, deranged divorcee Sheila Bamber, 28, first shot her twin six-year-old sons. She gunned down her father as he tried to phone for help. Then she murdered her mother before turning the automatic .22 rifle on herself.'

Twenty-four-year-old Jeremy Bamber had raised the alarm shortly before 3.30am on Wednesday, 7 August 1985. He told police that he had just received a phone call from his father to the effect that Sheila had 'gone berserk' with a gun. Officers met him at the family home, White House Farm in Tolleshunt D'Arcy, Essex; Jeremy worked there but lived alone three miles away. Firearms units arrived but it wasn't deemed safe to enter the house until 7.45am. They found sixty-one-year-old Nevill Bamber in the kitchen, beaten and shot eight times; his wife June, also sixty-one, lay in the doorway of the master bedroom, shot seven times; Sheila's six-year-old twin sons, Nicholas and Daniel, had been repeatedly shot in their beds, while Sheila herself lay a few feet from her mother, the rifle on her body, its muzzle pointing at her chin and a Bible at her side. The two bullet wounds in her throat caused some consternation, but the knowledge that she suffered from schizophrenia, coupled with Nevill's call to his son and the apparent security of the house, convinced police that it was a murder-suicide.

For weeks to come, the tabloids gorged themselves on salacious stories about 'Hell Raiser Bambi', the 'girl with mad eyes', whom they claimed had been expelled from two schools before becoming a 'top model' with a wild social life that resulted in a £40,000 drug debt linking her to a string of country house burglaries. June Bamber, too, was condemned as a religious fanatic with little else to her character. When journalist Yvonne Roberts visited Tolleshunt D'Arcy that September for a more restrained article in London's *Evening Standard*, one local told her: 'What upsets us is that the whole family's life has been reduced to a series of newspaper headlines. And none of them has got it right.'

Jeremy Bamber's surviving relations believed the police hadn't got it right either. They informed officers that Sheila had lived for her children and had no knowledge of firearms, while the medication she took to control her illness left her physically weak and uncoordinated. The rifle's magazine was stiff to load and the killer had done so at least twice in order to disgorge twenty-five shots, all of which had found their mark. The killer had also overpowered Nevill Bamber, who was six feet, four inches tall and physically very fit.

Furthermore, the dissenting relatives told how they had located the rifle's silencer (technically known as a sound moderator) in a cupboard at the farm on the Saturday after the murders. It bore red paint which forensic experts linked to scratches on the mantelpiece above the Aga where Nevill had been found, and blood inside the baffles was identified as belonging to Sheila's blood group. Since the first wound to her throat was incapacitating and the second immediately fatal, it followed that she could not have gone downstairs after shooting herself to put away the silencer; nor did she have the reach to pull the trigger when the silencer was attached to the weapon.

The Bambers were a wealthy family. Soon after the murders, Jeremy began selling antiques from the farmhouse and his sister's flat in London, ostensibly to raise funds for the death duties he would be required to pay on his inheritance. But a few weeks later his ex-girlfriend Julie Mugford came forward with an extraordinary story: fuelled by jealousy and greed, Jeremy had been plotting to kill his family for at least eighteen months and had hired an assassin to carry out the murders for £2,000. Detectives quickly established that the alleged hit man (a local plumber) had a solid alibi and concluded that Jeremy had committed the murders himself; he had already admitted to stealing almost £1,000 from the family caravan site six months earlier 'to prove a point'. In her testimony, Julie stated that Jeremy had ended their relationship when she became too upset at having to conceal the truth about the shootings. He dismissed her claims as the bitter fulminations of a jilted woman – she was enraged that he had left her for someone else. But seven weeks after the murders, he was charged with killing his family.

'It comes down to this: do you believe Julie Mugford or do you believe Jeremy Bamber?' declared the judge at Chelmsford Crown Court in October 1986. The jury deliberated the question overnight and by a 10–2 majority found Jeremy guilty. Told that he would serve a minimum of twenty-five years in prison, in 1988 his tariff was increased to whole life.

'Too forgettable,' was Madame Tussauds' verdict one month after the trial, when asked by a *Today* reporter if they would be installing a wax mannequin of Jeremy Bamber in the Chamber of Horrors. But largely through his own efforts, Jeremy has remained in the public eye, steadfastly maintaining his innocence. Either he is truthful and the British justice system has meted out an appalling miscarriage of justice against a man already suffering an incalculable loss, or he is a callous, calculating killer whose attempts to gain freedom are another example of his psychopathy.

Since the failure of his first appeal in 1989, Jeremy has fastidiously worked his way through the case papers, putting forwards various scenarios absolving him of guilt. Although any of these have yet to result in an acquittal, he has seized the chance to distribute sections of the material to the media and other interested parties. As a consequence, virtually every news story about the murders originates from him via his legal team and campaigners.

One commentary on the case describes this 'repeated overlaying of detail through the production of new evidence' as having the effect of 'dilating rather than clarifying the story and making the violence at its core even harder to grasp'. A detailed examination of *all* the issues raised by Jeremy Bamber and his successive lawyers in their attempts to overturn his conviction falls outside the scope of this book; indeed, it would fill a book of its own. The list of sources includes those websites where more information can be found, but every issue put forward since the trial has been considered by various administrations, including the Police Complaints Authority, the City of London Police, the Criminal Cases Review Commission (CCRC) and the Appeal Court itself. None have been upheld. Likewise, reports commissioned from experts by Jeremy's lawyers since his case last reached the Appeal Court in 2002 have failed to convince the CCRC that there is any new evidence or legal argument capable of raising a real possibility of quashing his conviction.

Nonetheless, there are puzzling aspects to the case, such as how a guilty Jeremy managed to overcome three adults and why they met their deaths at the particular spots in which they were found. A possible 'solution' is presented here, in Appendix I, based on the known evidence and following consultation with experts who worked on the case originally. Jeremy's own solution is simple: he did not do it. The difficulties with that scenario are the reasons he remains in prison.

Opinions of Jeremy Bamber are profoundly contradictory. Those who believe in his innocence are voluble about his courage, strength and compassion, while those certain of his guilt detest him with equal vehemence, describing a man who never accepts responsibility for any wrongdoing and is swift to dispense with friendships that no longer serve a purpose to his campaign. The disparities make his personality difficult to pin down with authority.

'I will give you access to the truth,' Jeremy pledged in an early letter to me, after I wrote to him via his then lawyer Simon McKay. Naturally, he is willing to cooperate with anyone whom he believes will at the very least give him a fair hearing, which I have tried to do. His first letter, dated 24 May 2012, began: 'I have read your book *Roses from the Earth* as part of my research as a guide with the Anne Frank exhibition, it was put on at this prison a couple of years ago and for two weeks I showed people around . . . I was also lucky enough to attend a talk by two local Ausvich (spelling, sorry) survivors, being able to share coffee and a one on one conversation with them during this Anne Frank fortnight. I have since read at least 30 different books about the horrors of these hideous places – how did anyone endure such awfulness, is it clinging to hope no matter what? My experience in no way compares and I feel shame for trying to even understand the motivation – but I think hope is what makes the difference in me between life and death. Not for freedom, but for the truth to be acknowledged by the courts.'

From then on, I wrote to him with my questions and he

would reply promptly in his trademark capitals. His letters varied in length from a couple of pages to fifteen or more sides of A4 paper. Very often he would highlight areas of his case which he felt deserved closer scrutiny, especially when he was working on submissions to the CCRC, enclosing various documents with his letters. As a prisoner claiming a miscarriage of justice, he is allowed access to the voluminous material on his case, including crime scene photographs. Some documentation is kept in files inside his cell but much of it is housed elsewhere in the prison and he has to put in a request for those items he wishes to view.

In July 2012, he wrote that he was sifting through the papers on his case again – some three-and-a-half-million pages 'fitted together like a jigsaw' – that had been placed on a database and 'without getting too excited, we now have the key to the gate . . . If we can find verifiable proof of life in the house when I'm outside with the coppers then the case has to collapse immediately – it has to be confirmed proof of life to be a slam dunk point – well I have found that evidence – it was edited from the original case papers on the orders of the Dep. Director of Public Prosecutions in 1985 . . .' This related to an alleged sighting of a figure at a window just hours before the murders were discovered. At the same time, he was examining the official logs of the police operation at White House Farm, declaring that what he had found moved his case into 'a new and exciting area . . . my guess is that this will unravel very, very quickly.' On 27 September 2012 he asserted: 'The DPP should be invited to step in and grant me immediate bail as the crown cannot sustain my conviction.'

Three days later he wrote again, aggrieved that his arguments were not being dealt with quickly enough. His letter reflected his low, angry mood as he turned to the subject of his murdered family:

I have no desire to see my name in print, I don't even care that you might actually write a book that's 100% championing my innocence – you're not going to tell me something I don't already know – so this is about my deceased family and setting the record straight for them, highlighting the

difficulties society has with mental illness and sympatheti-
cally dealing with the issues around women who kill . . .
Sheila doesn't have a voice to explain why or what she was
experiencing, or whether she even knew what she was
doing. I won't let anyone just prosecute her as some sort of
evil lunatic – I'm all she has to rely on to speak for her . . .
It's also important that mum and dad are portrayed properly
. . . no one has stood up for them, put them in a proper
light, again it's my duty to tell it as it was . . . As for the
boys, the only person who should decide on how they are
written about is their dad Colin . . . they are the ultimate
innocents and the greatest tragedy of all this . . . I owe it to
my family to speak for them. . . my relatives are keeping
silent as they are scared they'd let the truth out and then
have to give back all the money they have gorged on over
the years that was never rightfully theirs.

He apologized in his next letter 'for having a bit of a rant . . . If
I have an excuse it's that I get myself pretty frustrated at everything.' Usually he tended not to write until his depression had
passed, explaining in November 2012 that his lawyer had
advised him to hold back on the 'logs issue' until a decision
had been made about his Judicial Review: 'I've just had a period
of despondency and it's all to do with having found the evidence
which will set me free at last. I know if it was the other way
round arrests would be made – but the state doesn't want to fall
on its sword.' Often he wrote of his fury at the police officers
who had helped convict him ('He is going to hell in a handcart
– well, Belmarsh first . . . he is corrupt to the very rotten core')
and was disappointed when his lawyer told him that 'police
corruption' was 'never going to be accepted' in his case and that
new forensic evidence would give him a better chance of winning
an appeal.

Mostly he remained upbeat and open, writing occasionally
about other matters, such as the revelations about Jimmy Savile's
prolific sex abuse: 'The whole thing is just so vile it makes my
skin crawl. But I suppose that when they do a proper enquiry
into my case and the actions of Essex Police that other people

will feel the same way about what has been done to secure my conviction.'

He wrote in March 2013 to say that he had read virtually all 340,000 pages of PII [Public Interest Immunity] material, 'placing them in context with the 3 million plus pages of disclosed documents – then editing it all down to manageable files on each key issue. I completed the work at 2am this morning. In the last 18 months I've been to sleep before 2am on maybe ten occasions, most night I work until 2.30 to 3am. I was only allowed my laptop [an access to justice computer he was temporarily permitted to use] from lock up at 6.40pm, and 5pm Friday to Sunday.' In October 2013 he was pursuing 'a new legal angle' and the following month he mentioned 'doing some of the most amazing research which is producing a long series of new strands of evidence – shocking.'

Significant reforms were brought into force in prisons on 1 November 2013. Since then, reasonable behaviour is not enough to earn inmates their privileges; they are expected to work actively towards their own rehabilitation and some privileges have been permanently withdrawn. When Jeremy wrote again it was following the temporary loss of his enhanced privilege status: 'I've had a really tough time over the past 6 weeks – I'm not allowed to discuss it or this letter will be stopped.' His research, however, had taken a new turn and 'the reason I've just spent Christmas 29 in jail is because the truth of what happened at the farmhouse is so unbelievable that no one is going to accept this as the truth unless they see all the evidence.'

His letters tailed off. HMP Full Sutton is situated a little over three miles across farmland from my home, but a planned visit failed to materialize, with Jeremy stating that the stricter regulations meant that 'you won't get permission to see me while I'm in jail, not in a million years.' In April 2014 he wrote to say that he was still working on his appeal submission: 'Discoveries are numerous and I don't expect to be in prison too much longer.' Three months later he sent word that he would 'continue contact once my conviction is overturned' and in December he wrote for a final time to explain briefly that he could no longer write 'meaningful' letters about his case.

Not having met Jeremy has its advantages and disadvantages.

It makes it easier to be objective and largely negates accusations of having been taken in by him, but obviously it is difficult to form a solid opinion of someone without meeting them. In his letters, he is – or can affect that he is – charming, always person-able, solicitous, witty, and has a magpie mind for the minutiae of his case. But at the same time he seems arrogant and curiously shallow, fixated on revenge, and is undoubtedly manipulative, as most high-profile prisoners are.

Jeremy offered to 'fact check' this book 'either chapter by chapter or once you've written it – I would not change anything or urge you to do so, but simply correct any facts you've got wrong and provide verification on anything I suggest is wrong and should be changed . . . It'll annoy me if you get things wrong, not the evidence stuff – as you don't have an excuse for getting that wrong, but all the other info that makes the case have position and context.' He agreed with my reasons for declining, adding that he hoped to be out anyway before publi-cation, in which eventuality 'they'll want a book from *me*.' He has not seen any part of *The Murders at White House Farm* in any form, nor have his friends or campaign team.

Among the many interviews conducted for this book were several with leading figures from the 1985 enquiry, including a number of former police officers, pathologist Peter Vanezis, Sheila's psychiatrist Dr Hugh Ferguson and ballistics expert Malcolm Fletcher.

The sentiment of those retired officers who declined to be interviewed can be summed up in the words of one former detec-tive inspector: 'A long time has passed since this awful crime was committed and without documentation it can be a little danger-ous for anyone to completely rely on their memory for facts. Yes, some facts will never be forgotten but there is bound to be a little variance over time in some matters. There is likely to be further litigation and I wouldn't want to be party to any compromise of any investigation, enquiry, or judicial proceedings that may take place in the future.' Some offered their insights but wished to remain anonymous, with one ex-officer providing a more per-sonal explanation: 'I have reservations about revisiting what was a terrible time for me and rocked me to the core emotionally. Even writing this short email, I can feel my heart beating faster.'

I have also drawn on several thousand pages of unpublished documentation such as witness statements, police records, court documents, personal letters, notebooks and memoirs in an effort to write a balanced, comprehensive study of the case. To those who find endnotes a distraction, I apologize; the book can be read without referring to them, but for the sake of transparency and also to reflect where memories and opinions have altered with the passage of time, some explanation of sources is necessary.

Although there are no crime scene photographs in this book, readers should be aware that some of those which appear on the internet and elsewhere in print have been substantially re-touched. Likewise, several sources mention the statement of an electrician who visited White House Farm two days before the shootings, apparently fearing for his life after being confronted by Sheila shouting abuse at him. The encounter is fictitious; there is no record of anything resembling it and certainly no statement. Nor did Sheila make a hysterical visit to Tolleshunt D'Arcy monastery shortly before her death. Some sources also inaccurately recount statements; wherever possible, I have quoted directly from the originals in order to avoid any confusion.

A number of themes recur throughout the case, with money and morality thornily intertwined. On a superficial level, whether we believe Jeremy Bamber to be innocent or guilty, it is hard not to view him as a product of his time – Thatcher's Britain and the era of Loadsamoney, Yuppies, the Big Bang and Gordon Gekko's 'Greed, for the lack of a better word, is good' ethic. Most of those who knew Jeremy thought of him as the brash young chancer who believed he could and should have it all: a home of his own, a smart car, gadgets, designer clothes, holidays in the sun and a lively social life.

All those things, in short, which are now widely regarded as necessities in our flagrantly materialistic society. But thirty years ago, in the Bambers' proudly rural community, such aspirations were seen as a deliberate spurning of traditional values. English culture has long been suffused with nostalgic notions of the countryside and the honest tilling of the soil; when news of the murders broke, most reports followed the *Daily Express's* lead in mentioning that the Bambers were known locally as 'the Archers of D'Arcy', after the farming family in the popular Radio 4 drama. 'England is the country and the country is England', British Prime Minister Stanley Baldwin had declared in 1924. The underlying fear that metropolitan decadence would obliterate the English pastoral dream seemed somehow brutally realized with the Bamber killings.

At the heart of the story are familial bonds, ceaseless but volatile, leading to a savage end. And while no one, with the possible exception of Jeremy Bamber, can know exactly what happened inside White House Farm that August night, understanding each individual and their relationships within the family unit is key to making some sort of sense of the incomprehensible.

Prologue

Evening sunlight slanted across the countryside in a blaze of copper as the Volkswagen camper van rattled along the road to Tollesbury, village 'of plough and sail', whose inhabitants had long relied on harvests from land and sea. Weatherboard houses and modern bungalows disappeared as fields unfurled on every horizon; to the south was the Blackwater estuary, a wilderness of salt marshes, tidal mudflats and islands. It was an hour's drive from London, yet a world away.

The six-year-old twins fidgeted in the back of the van, aware that the journey was almost over. From the driver's seat, their father glanced at them anxiously through the mirror. The boys looked almost identical, with their delicate faces, slim limbs and blond hair, but there was tension in Daniel's expression. Nicholas, too, was quieter than usual. In the front passenger seat their mother sat silently, her grey-blue eyes impassive.

Where the road twisted sharply to the left, Pages Lane appeared on the right. A postbox stood like a scarlet sentinel against the uncut field to one side of the lane; on the other was a hedgerow stippled with creamy blossom, leading to a neat row of four farm cottages. The van rumbled down the lane, passing the cottages and turning right at a fork in the track, where a tall hedge on the left coiled past black timbered barns to a large yard flanked by outbuildings. The van pulled in, close to the back door of a handsome Georgian farmhouse. Somewhere within, inscribed on a beam under the eaves, was the date '1820'.

White House Farm, on the glittering seaward reaches of Tolleshunt D'Arcy, was the hub of a thriving business covering hundreds of acres, yet the building itself had a cloistered air. Hidden by trees and set in large gardens, the elegant grey frontage could only be glimpsed by walkers from the creek end of the lane.

Before the week was out, its timeless seclusion would be gone forever.

*

The crime about to take place in the Essex countryside would dominate the headlines for weeks to come. Until then, the main news stories included the success of Live Aid, a sixteen-hour music marathon that raised millions for starving Ethiopians and secured the biggest global audience in television history; Prime Minister Margaret Thatcher and her husband Dennis buying a Barratt Homes house in south London; the discovery that the small pimple removed from President Ronald Reagan's nose was cancerous; the dropping of charges of riot and unlawful assembly against seventy-nine miners arrested when 10,000 pickets converged on Orgreave coking plant; and twenty-seven-year-old Madonna topping the charts for the first time with 'Into The Groove' from the film *Desperately Seeking Susan*.

In 'Aids Threatens to Spread Rapidly', on 6 August 1985, *The Times* drew attention to the latest information about the aggressive new virus. The government's chief medical advisers announced that 'heterosexuals are also at risk from the disease normally associated with homosexuals' and predicted over 2,000 cases within two years, mostly in London. An editorial in the same paper asked: 'Can Youth Cope With Our Age?', warning that in a society obsessed by immediate gratification, young adults were being influenced 'more by their peers than their parents, by present opportunity more than past tradition'. While older people yearned for the principled 1940s, their children faced 'the threat of nuclear war, the prospect of mass unemployment, a world in which there are many more sticks than carrots'. Positive responses such as CND and Live Aid were undermined by 'the implosion of ambition' and the 'radical rejection of the diminished world' of parents and grandparents.

Nevill and June Bamber understood only too well the conflicts highlighted by the editorial. Married in 1949 and unable to conceive naturally, they had adopted two babies: a daughter, Sheila Jean, in 1958, and a son, Jeremy Nevill, in 1961. Ever since, they had striven to instil the values of the pre-war world into their children.

On Sunday, 4 August 1985, Nevill Bamber attended the early church service at Tolleshunt Major. The Frosts, whom he had known for years, caught up with him afterwards. 'He seemed his normal self,' Joan Frost recalled. 'I would describe the Bambers as a loving couple, fond of both their children, devoted to their grandchildren, very caring for the community, generous financially and [with] time for others.'[1]

June Bamber was at the 10.30am service in Tolleshunt D'Arcy, where she had been a churchwarden since Easter. She read the lesson and waited outside the church for Nevill after the service. His familiar blue pickup truck soon appeared and Eric Turner, the elderly canon, greeted him as he strode across the gravel. Rev. Bernard Robson heard Nevill remark that he and June were looking forward to having their daughter Sheila and her six-year-old twins Daniel and Nicholas stay for the week. Their former son-in-law, Colin Caffell, was driving them from London.

Until a few months earlier, the twins had lived primarily with their mother, although Colin had joint custody and saw them every week. But in March 1985, Sheila was diagnosed with schizophrenia and admitted to St Andrew's Hospital, a private psychiatric clinic in Northampton. June Bamber had twice received treatment there herself and shared a psychiatrist with her daughter, who had suffered a nervous breakdown two years before. Nicholas and Daniel moved in with their father and remained living with him after Sheila was discharged.

Despite their divorce, Sheila and Colin were on good terms; he had invited her to his housewarming party in Kilburn the night before the visit. She arrived early to help him tidy up and prepare food, explaining how unhappy she was with the treatment her parents had chosen, which involved monthly injections of an anti-psychotic drug whose side effects included a debilitating lethargy. When Colin offered to speak to Nevill and June on her behalf, Sheila readily agreed.

During the party she was quiet. Her brother Jeremy and his girlfriend Julie Mugford were there, along with Colin's partner, Heather. Sheila complimented Julie on her make-up and chatted to a few people, but seemed distracted. Jeremy asked his sister several times if she was okay. 'Sheila appeared vacant and confused and said she was very tired,' he later told detectives.[2] Colin confirmed: 'Sheila just sat there looking detached. She continuously kept staring out of the window.'[3]

Shortly before midnight, Sheila asked Colin to take her home.

Because he had been drinking he summoned her brother, who hadn't touched alcohol. Sheila seemed to shrink from the idea, but Jeremy and Julie saw her safely home, then returned to the party. They left in the early hours for the small village of Goldhanger, where Jeremy lived in a cottage three miles from White House Farm.

On Sunday morning the twins were fretful about the visit to their grandparents. Much as they loved Granny Bamber, they didn't like how she made them pray with her so often. Colin had already promised Sheila he would speak to his former in-laws about her medical care; now he told his sons that he would ask their grandmother not to be so strict about prayers. He also re-assured Daniel, who had recently become vegetarian, that he would have a word about mealtimes.

At half-past three, the twins climbed into the camper van, clutching the plastic Care Bears that accompanied them everywhere. Colin drove the short distance to Morshead Road in Maida Vale, where Sheila lived at the immediate end of an imposing Edwardian building of thirteen red brick apartments. She settled in the camper van's front seat. Once they were out of London and onto the A12, it was a fairly straight run to Tolleshunt D'Arcy. The sun emerged from a dense ridge of cloud as Colin attempted to make conversation with his ex-wife, but Sheila was lost in her own thoughts. Later he recalled that she 'never spoke' during the two-and-a-half-hour journey and seemed 'quiet and inward' but 'smiling and content'.[4]

In contrast, the twins kept up a steady stream of chatter about the party, school friends and a forthcoming holiday to Norway with their father. But as the van lumbered closer to Tolleshunt D'Arcy, Daniel began to grow agitated. Above the stuttering din of the Volkswagen engine, he shouted, 'You will speak to Granny about the prayers and everything, won't you, Daddy?'[5] Colin nodded, calling back that Mummy would make sure everything was fine. He glanced at Sheila, who stared at the road ahead, unresponsive. A knot of unease settled in his stomach.

As they reached the village, his disquiet increased. He couldn't fathom why, nor could he think of an excuse for heading back to London. Instead, he followed the road where it led to Pages

Lane, with its postbox and sign that read: 'Private Road: White House Farm and Wycke Farm Only.'

At Bourtree Cottage, Julie Mugford stood looking at the ladies' burgundy bicycle resting on its stand: it had a 'sit-up-and-beg' frame, white saddle and metal bell. When she had asked Jeremy about it that morning, he told her that it belonged to his mother. 'He had got it so I could use it,' Julie recalled. 'I had not previously asked him to get me a bike, although I think I might have suggested it might be handy sometime the previous summer.'[6]

Julie carried her belongings out to the silver Vauxhall Astra. As Jeremy emerged from the cottage, she frowned in disapproval at his hair, dyed the day before. She had bought him a brown shade from Boots in Colchester to hide ginger streaks from a previous home tinting, which looked odd against his naturally light brown hair, but the result was black as coal. She told him it looked like a wig. Jeremy shrugged off her criticism, unperturbed.

'Jeremy took me to Chelmsford railway station at about 7pm on Sunday, 4th August 1985 to catch the 7.50pm train to London,' Julie explained four days later.[7] Studying for an honours degree in education at Goldsmith's College, she lived in Lewisham, but spent holidays and most weekends with Jeremy in Goldhanger.

Julie hadn't seen June or Nevill for over a month. She was aware that Sheila was due at the farm that Sunday, and the next time she heard from Jeremy was 'by telephone at 9.50pm on Tuesday, 6th August 1985 . . .'

After that, nothing would ever be the same again.

Red roses bloomed on the trellis by the back door of White House Farm. June, a keen nature lover, had scattered bread on the bird table in the kitchen yard and filled the birdbath.

'We arrived there about 6.45pm,' Colin told the police in a miasma of grief and disbelief four days later. 'I stayed with the boys, Sheila and the Bambers until about 8.30pm.'[8] The twins gravitated to their father's side as soon as they were out of the van. Daniel and Nicholas were not naturally clingy and the knot of unease in Colin's gut tightened as they entered the farmhouse. He nudged the boys through the scullery and into the kitchen.

Every surface was crammed, from the Children's Society collecting boxes on the worktop to the magazine rack overflowing with the *Sunday Times* and *Farming News*. A Welsh dresser took pride of place, crowded with ornaments, postcards, books and decorative plates, one bearing the solemn homily, 'A Place for Everything and Everything in its Place'.

June made hot drinks and poured juice into the twins' orange beakers. Crispy, an irascible shih-tzu known as 'the Pest', got under everyone's feet until he was shooed into his basket beside the Aga. After pleasantries had been exchanged, Colin broached the subject of prayers. Nevill pulled up his favourite Windsor chair next to the mantelpiece to listen. June bristled slightly, but let Colin talk. Nevill reacted with customary humour to the news that Daniel was now vegetarian; wagging a finger, he warned his grandson he would never grow up big and strong if he didn't eat his meat, but tempered his words with a smile.

The one issue Colin did not raise was Sheila's medical treatment. His priority was the welfare of the twins and he hoped the Bambers would respect his entreaties if he left it there. Sensing that Sheila was upset by his lack of support, he avoided meeting her gaze. Colin stayed to supper at June and Nevill's request, but Sheila had retreated into her own world: 'Sheila was very quiet and appeared to be very vacant.' After the meal he stood to leave and once more felt the weight of her gloom as she cast him a disappointed look.

It was the twins' reaction to his departure that troubled him most. Daniel and Nicholas fell against him, clutching his clothes and burying tearful faces into his neck as he scooped them up. Their inexplicable distress was overwhelming: 'It would be difficult to express how tightly they hugged me to say goodbye. They had never acted like this before.'[9] Gently, he unfastened their grip.

A cool breeze stirred the leaves of the shrubbery as Colin put the Volkswagen into gear. He waved vigorously before turning into the lane, and in his mirror caught a last, fleeting glimpse of the family watching from the darkened garden. In a moment he was at the end of the track and looking back saw only the black, gathered trees.

In the months to come, he went over that night again and

again, remembering every detail. He became convinced that his sons had experienced some sort of premonition, as the memory of that final evening, together with a series of deeply disturbing drawings by Daniel, led him to conclude that there was 'more to all this than I could logically explain' and that, 'on some level, they knew they were going to die'.[10]

1: SOWING

29 December 1891 to 31 December 1984

1

It was the winds surging up the lane to the house from the sea that turned his mind, so the inquest was told.

Benjamin Page had lived at White House Farm all his life. His mother managed the place after his father died and Benjamin took over after marrying Elizabeth Ann Seabrook in 1864. Widely regarded as a practical farmer and a thorough business-man, in private he struggled with depression. Poor weather seemed to deepen his malaise: the winds that buffeted the house, shuddering the windows and rattling the doorknobs, inflicted particular torment.

On 29 December 1891, Benjamin's twenty-six-year-old daughter Florence heard him calling from his room. Rushing upstairs she found her father crouched over the washstand, vomiting and in severe pain. A glass and spoon and the wrapper from a bottle of poison lay nearby. Florence sent for the local physician, then gave her father water mixed with mustard and salt to oust the poison from his body. When Dr James arrived he asked if there was any madness in the family. No, Florence told him, none that she knew of.

Despite attempts to save him, Benjamin Page died on 5 January 1892, aged fifty-seven. The inquest jury returned a verdict of 'suicide while of unsound mind'.[1] It was a stark reminder of another relative's death five years before: in October 1887, scarcely a mile from White House Farm, the shot body of seventy-eight-year-old Orbell Page was discovered in his bedroom, the muzzle of the gun under his chin and a piece of string used to pull the trigger around his right foot. The inquest concluded temporary insanity and Orbell Page was laid to rest in Tolleshunt D'Arcy.

Benjamin Page's widow remained at White House Farm after his death, dividing management duties between her sons Frank and Hugh. They lived frugally until the Great War, when compulsory food production on British soil brought them modest prosperity. But the economic depression of the 1920s endured

into the 1930s, with the cost of agricultural land soaring after
the Second World War.

By then Elizabeth Page had passed away and Frank was head
of White House Farm. In June 1950, aged seventy-seven, he
suffered a nervous breakdown. When Hugh died the following
month, Frank told their younger sister Minnie that he felt
suicidal. In the early hours of 10 November 1950, she awoke
with a start and went across to Frank's room. His bed was
empty. After a frantic search, Frank's body was discovered in the
deep water tank in the yard. The tractor wheels he had used to
climb inside stood propped against it. A pathologist found signs
of chronic heart disease but no evidence of drowning. In 'Heart
Failed in Drowning Bid' on 17 November 1950, the *Essex
County Standard* explained: 'Death was caused by heart failure
through contact with the cold water . . . Page was dead before he
hit the surface.' An inquest in Witham confirmed that he had
killed himself.

Frank Page was buried at St Nicholas Church in Tolleshunt
D'Arcy, where his father Benjamin had been interred fifty-eight
years before. The grave of Orbell Page lay nearby, the gun beside
him in the coffin, in accordance with his wishes.

The first White House Farm was built in the early seventeenth
century. *Excursions in the County of Essex* (1819) refers to
'New-house, or White-house farm, in this parish . . . purchased
by the trustees of the charity of Henry Smith esq. in 1635.'[2]
Smith, a London salt merchant and philanthropist, died a child-
less widower in 1628. He left £2,000 in his will for the establishment of the Henry Smith (Kensington Estate) Charity. The
trustees bought White House Farm for rental value to assist the
poor, with a proviso that no funds were to be granted to 'any
persons given to excessive drinking, pilferers, swearers, or dis-
obedient'.[3] The present farmhouse was completed in the early
nineteenth century in a position some 350 acres from the sea.

The Bambers' history at White House Farm originated with
June's father, Leslie Speakman. Although both Nevill and June's
families would play an important role in events to come, it was
her lineage that tied them to the area. June's forebears were
hard-working local landowners with considerable social standing

and an established network of shared business interests.

Born in 1893, Leslie was the eldest child of Samuel Speakman and Florence Ratcliff, whose marriage united two farming dynasties. Leslie and his siblings enjoyed an idyllic life at St Clere's Hall, a red brick manor in Danbury, Essex. After leaving school, he worked for his parents as a farm labourer until the Great War, when he served in the Army, Navy and the nascent RAF. In 1919, aged twenty-six, he married Mabel Bunting, three years his senior.

Mabel was the only daughter of Essex landowners John and Sarah Bunting. She grew up at Jehew's Farm in Goldhanger with three elder brothers, John (Jack), George and Joshua, who became farmers themselves. In 1914, Jack's wife died within days of giving birth at their home on Osea Island and Mabel took care of his children, three-year-old Betty and newborn Alice (Binks). Bridesmaids at her wedding to Leslie Speakman five years later, Betty and Binks were unofficially adopted by the couple, who had two daughters of their own: Pamela, born on 25 October 1920, and June, born on 3 June 1924. Betty recalled that the four of them were brought up harmoniously, 'almost as sisters', secure in their parents' love.[4]

Home was Vaulty Manor Farm, a beautiful seventeenth-century house facing the Blackwater estuary, set in 100 acres on the outskirts of Goldhanger. Every Sunday, the family attended the local church with its candle-snuffer tower overlooking the meadows and creek beyond; several close relatives were church-wardens in the area. Goldhanger itself was a quiet, gorse-scented hamlet, with red-roofed cottages dotted about the lanes and a sixteenth-century inn, the Chequers.

From the age of five, the girls attended private schools and had extra tuition in tennis and hockey. Pamela and June were also pupils at Miss Betty Page's School of Dance in Witham and performed locally, often with other family members. Pamela was the more outspoken and confident of the two girls; June was quieter but schoolfriends remembered her happy-go-lucky nature.

At home, Mabel taught her daughters traditional skills such as cooking, sewing and managing a household. More unusually, she instilled in them the value of sound business acumen. In

1933, during a nationwide camping craze, Mabel invited families of fruit and pea pickers to pitch their tents among the grazing cattle on the land opposite Vaulty. Before long, hundreds of Londoners were regularly flocking there. Mabel was involved in every aspect of the site's development, from buying more plots to installing facilities. 'She was very straight-talking – she didn't beat about the bush,' her great-granddaughter Janie explains. 'She was very assertive. She was really lovely, very clever, very driven.'[5]

While his wife concentrated on establishing the Osea Road campsite, Leslie Speakman managed six farms. In addition to Vaulty, three were local: Gardener's Farm, Charity Farm and White House Farm, where he shared management duties with its sitting tenant, the ill-fated Frank Page, from 1937. Burnt Ash Farm and Carbonells lay thirty miles away in Wix. The four girls worked for both family businesses and never thought themselves above any task.

Binks was the first to leave home, moving to Kent after her marriage in 1939. Betty wed local farmer Thomas Howie the following year and settled at Chappel Farm in the lane behind Vaulty. June's departure was the most adventurous by far, although she could tell her family nothing about it. More than half a century later, even Pamela had no idea that her sister was once part of Churchill's secret army. June's file in the National Archives was set to remain closed until 2025 and only a fraction of her service records have survived; many documents were destroyed by fire at SOE's former headquarters on Baker Street in 1946. But the pages that remain shed new light on her character.

June's first job after leaving Maldon Grammar had been in the typing pool at the Fire Guard service headquarters in Colchester. One of her colleagues there was a young woman named Agnes Brown Barrie, who became a lifelong confidante. But the work itself was dull and June transferred to the War Office in London as a shorthand typist. In 1944, she was put forward for an interview with a branch of the First Aid Nursing Yeomanry (FANY) affiliated with the Special Operations Executive (SOE).

Established in 1940, the SOE had a secret network of training stations throughout England and Scotland. Potential agents were schooled in resistance and sabotage for deployment to occupied Europe, North Africa, India and the Far East. By 1944, approximately 10,000 men and 3,000 women were serving in the SOE, with many of the latter enlisted from FANY SU (Special Unit).

June's qualifications were typing, shorthand, French, first aid and home nursing, her interests swimming, tennis and reading. Recruited on the spot, she was 'put through the cards' by MI5 on 16 November 1944 with a view to becoming a wireless operator.[6] Following an introductory course at Chichley Hall near Newport Pagnell, she signed the Official Secrets Act. On 20 January 1945 she arrived at STS 52 at Thame Park in Oxfordshire for intensive wireless and security training, where the capacity to type phenomenally fast and accurately was essential. From there it was on to parachute training at RAF Ringway in Cheshire, where she learned to jump from aircraft and a barrage balloon, with one drop at night. She then moved on to finishing school, where agents learned the skill of 'looking natural and ordinary while doing unnatural and extraordinary things'.[7]

Only the basic details of June's deployment have survived, but they show that she sailed for India on 14 July. Working with the SOE mission in India, Ceylon and the Far East (Force 136), June was based at Meerut, north-east of New Delhi. In the searing heat she transmitted vital messages to and from SOE agents behind Japanese lines. On the day that American forces dropped a second atomic bomb on Japan, she received orders to proceed by train to Poona in the lush, wet hills above Bombay. She worked there for two weeks, sleeping in a hut under a mosquito net, before transferring to a wireless signal station in Calcutta on 24 August 1945.

Following Japan's formal surrender on 2 September, Force 136 began to disband. June left Calcutta for Poona Holding Centre on 25 November. In mid-December she travelled to Karachi and from there caught a flight to England, arriving at Vaulty Manor Farm just in time for Christmas.

Officially demobbed in February 1946, June consigned her wartime bravery to memory and returned to her old life in sleepy Essex. She was a bridesmaid at her sister Pamela's wedding to

Robert Woodiwiss Boutflour on 11 January 1947 in Goldhanger.
Robert was born in Preston, in 1918, the grandson of a master
mariner and cousin of Ann Davison, the first woman to sail
alone to America. After attending a Newport boarding school
with his brother and sister, he took a degree in agricultural
science at Durham University and won a scholarship to America.
Sea and soil were in Robert's blood; his father was principal of
the Royal Agricultural College in Cirencester. During the war,
Robert returned to England and joined the Agricultural Service.
As an advisor for the Dengie Hundred area, he visited Vaulty and
fell in love with Pamela, whose father offered them the tenancy
of both farms in Wix. They settled at Carbonells after the wedding and nine months later Pamela gave birth to a son, David.

During the summer of 1948, Robert asked his father to send
him a couple of reliable students to help with the harvest. Ralph
Nevill Bamber immediately caused a stir among the local girls.
Nevill, as he preferred to be known, was tall and sinewy, with
dark blond hair and a wide grin. His paternal grandfather was a
former Indian Army Officer and District Superintendent of the
salt chowkies (customs) in Bengal. His father, Herbert Ralph
Munro Bamber, was born in India in 1889 and became an officer
in the Royal Navy, serving on submarines during the Great War.
Nevill's mother, Beatrice Cecilia Nevill, was born in Kensington
in 1893, the daughter of society lady Mary Tweed and Arts and
Crafts architect Ralph Nevill. He designed the family home, Clifton House on Guildford's Castle Hill, where their neighbours
were the six unmarried sisters of writer Lewis Carroll.

When Beatrice married Herbert Bamber in 1916, Clifton
House became their home. A daughter, Cecily Diana, was born in
1920, followed by Phyllis Audrey in 1922 and Ralph Nevill on 9
June 1924. All the children were known by their middle names.
They saw little of their father, who was away at sea for long
periods, and their mother was often in London, where she ran an
exclusive dress shop, Asters of Beauchamp Place. The children
were devoted to her nonetheless.

At the age of ten, in September 1934, Nevill was sent to
board at Christ's Hospital School in Horsham, West Sussex.
Former pupils included Samuel Pepys, Isaac Newton and John
Flamsteed. Nevill was a diligent student and nine months after

leaving in December 1940, he applied to join the RAF. Called up for service in September 1941, after passing his exams he was assigned the rank of Temporary Sergeant Pilot, flying with Squadrons 13 and 55, both used for army support.

Operation Torch, the Allied invasion of French North Africa, was launched in November 1942. As the RAF moved inland to carry out day and night raids, aircraft were frequently lost over the precipitous coastline. Nevill was also shot down; one source states that his Mosquito crashed and he spent weeks in hospital with his back encased in plaster, while another claims he was out of action for two years with spinal injuries. His service records show that on 8 June 1943, he was transferred to the Emergency Medical Services Hospital in Lambert's Bay, a small fishing town in the Western Cape province of South Africa. Discharged on 16 August 1943, he returned to England. Months of further training followed, supplemented by occupational therapy, and he became an expert at knitting. In November 1944, he was posted to Jerusalem. After a brief period in Egypt, by July 1945 he was in England again, remaining mostly at Tangmere until being demobbed in September 1947.

Nevill's sisters had married during the war. Audrey's husband Reginald Pargeter was an Allied Mosquito ace and a consultant geologist in peacetime. Their son Anthony was born in Buckinghamshire in August 1945, shortly before they emigrated to Uganda, where Audrey gave birth to Jacqueline in March 1948. Diana had married retired air commodore Ernest Leslie Howard-Williams. Twice her age and divorced, hc held the 1917 Military Cross and was the first person to fly across Africa. The couple began a new life together on a coffee farm in Kenya.

Nevill joined the Royal Agricultural College in Cirencester, sharing rooms and a birthdate with lifelong friend Michael Leyland until Professor Boutflour dispatched him to Essex in 1948. Nevill got on famously with Robert and Pamela, and proved himself gregarious, hard-working and sporty, teaching drinking games to locals and playing frequent practical jokes. He and June began courting after they were paired together for a game of mixed doubles during a tennis tournament. 'She was an attractive, sweet young woman,' her cousin Margaret Grimster recalled. 'She had many offers of marriage from several eligible young men, but

when she met Ralph Nevill Bamber she said there would be
nobody else.'[8]

Nevill and June planned to marry after he graduated in
summer 1949. In January that year, they received shattering
news: Nevill's sister Audrey had died of meningitis at the age of
twenty-six. Her son Anthony was four and daughter Jacqueline
not yet one. Audrey was laid to rest in the European cemetery at
Entebbe, Nigeria.

Nevill and June married on 3 September 1949 at St Peter's
Church in Goldhanger. Michael Leyland was best man and June's
friend Dorothy Barker, whom she had met in India, flew in from
Malaya. The reception was held at Vaulty in a vast marquee on
the lawn.

A fortnight after her sister's wedding, Pamela gave birth to a
daughter, Christine Ann. Nevill was made godfather to his niece,
who was always known by her middle name. The two couples
saw each other almost every day: June, eagerly looking forward
to becoming a mother herself, loved to spend time with Pamela
and her children, while Robert and Nevill had taken up rallying.
'He as the driver and I as his navigator,' Robert recalled. 'He was
not the sort of person to lose his temper easily . . . I would point
him up the wrong track and get temporarily lost, but he never
had a go at me. Even in the evenings, when all the drivers were
loudly having a "pop" at their navigators over a pint of beer,
Nevill never did likewise with me.'[9]

Nevill worked for his father-in-law at Vaulty, a quarter of a
mile from the cottage where he and June lived on Wash Lane.
Soon after their marriage, he was offered a smallholding in
Rhodesia. But Frank Page's watery death determined the course
of their lives; Leslie Speakman approached the Henry Smith
trustees with a glowing testimony of his son-in-law that was
impossible to pass over.

In 1951, Nevill and June Bamber became the new tenants of
White House Farm.

'Everybody makes a point of knowing all about everybody else,' declared resident crime writer Margery Allingham, of Tolleshunt D'Arcy. 'Most people are related, and those who have no kin here have most of them known their neighbours as long as and as well as most cousins, so that the family atmosphere, with all its good and bad qualities, is present all the time.'[1] Allingham's first detective story, written in 1928, concerned the shooting of a farmer at his home White Cottage; she set many of her novels in and around Tolleshunt D'Arcy.

One mile from the village, White House Farm was in an isolated position, surrounded by fields with only the farm workers' cottages, a hundred yards from the house, nearby. But Nevill and June were a popular young couple with a wide circle of family and friends. They were closest to John Wilkin, whose grandfather established the Wilkin's jam company in Tiptree, and his wife Barbara. John had known June all her life, and the two couples became friendly during the tennis fad of the early 1950s, holidaying in Brittany together for years afterwards.

June turned the neglected farmhouse into a welcoming family home, while the garden with its expansive lawns and neat flower beds was her domain and a haven for the birds she loved. In 'Farm House Tea Party', a 1955 feature in *Essex Review*, their home was described as 'in good order and very productive and considerable sums have been spent on the farmhouse, cottages and farm buildings', In addition to a business partnership with his father-in-law, Nevill set up a shooting syndicate. Following an early accident in which he fired a shot that ricocheted off a tree and left Leslie permanently blind in one eye, he became meticulous about firearms safety.

Anthony and Jacqueline Pargeter were regular visitors to White House Farm. Their widowed father's job took him around the world and most of their holidays from boarding school were spent with Nevill and June. Anthony remembered his aunt and uncle as very caring and understanding, while Jacqueline regarded Nevill as a surrogate father. David Boutflour recalls that he and his sister Ann likewise viewed the farm as a second home; it was the heart of family gatherings and a place where they were always welcome.

But six years of marriage without pregnancy had a profound effect on June. Those closest to the couple were under the impression that the difficulty originally lay with Nevill; John Wilkin recalled the strain was such that June suffered a nervous breakdown in 1955. Following treatment at a private psychiatric hospital in London, she and Nevill lived with the Wilkins in Goldhanger for three months before returning to White House Farm.

June's longing for children was undimmed but all hope fled when, in her mid-thirties, an operation to remove a cyst on her ovaries left her unable to bear children. Learning that she was 'sterile', as infertility was commonly called then, provoked a host of painful emotions: shock, grief, anger, guilt, inadequacy and helplessness. In the family-orientated 1950s, when the image of the stay-at-home mother was everywhere, infertility was also viewed as a social stigma.

Nevill and June had to either accept that they would never become parents or adopt. They contacted the Church of England Children's Society, one of the largest adoption agencies in the country. Approval depended upon references, medical checks and formal assessment. Presumably June's recent admission to a psychiatric hospital was disclosed and the society were sufficiently reassured to link them with a child, for in September 1957, the Bambers travelled to the Holy Innocents Sunnyside Nursery in the Wiltshire village of Box. There they were shown a newborn girl with pale eyes and wisps of dark hair.

The baby had been put up for adoption at the insistence of her grandfather, Eric George Jay, acting in what he believed to be everyone's best interests. He was then Senior Chaplain to the Archbishop of Canterbury and had assisted at Queen Elizabeth II's coronation at Westminster Abbey in 1953. Born the son of a hosiery manager, this distinguished clergyman clearly had a streak of non-conformity. Told that he should wear court dress under his cassock, he opted for long socks and football shorts instead.

In late 1956, his unmarried eighteen-year-old daughter Christine was working as a receptionist at Bloomsbury's Bonnington Hotel when she fell pregnant. The press later claimed that the father of her child was a cleric or theology student; the Children's Society informed Sheila that he was a thirty-year-old dry cleaner from Putney. When the relationship with Christine ended, he was said to have gone abroad. Whatever the truth, she kept his identity secret.

Christine's parents were very distressed by the pregnancy and arranged for her to leave London under her mother's maiden name. The decision was punishing for them, too, since the baby would be their first grandchild. 'The reasons for her being given away were not as simple as you might imagine,' the baby's uncle told the *Daily Mirror* on 29 October 1986, when they arrived on his doorstep. 'It is more complex,' he added, although the full meaning of his words has never been made clear.

At the time, he and his sister Susan were oblivious to the reality of Christine's departure and were told that she had been offered another job. Christine wouldn't see them again until after the birth. As 'Mrs Webb', she worked on the reception desk at Sundial, a guesthouse in the quiet village of Coombe Down on the outskirts of Bath. It was rare for girls in her situation to receive advice about the physical and psychological upheavals of pregnancy and childbirth or the separation that would follow. Segregated from everyone she knew, the young mother confronted a cruel irony: the one person who valued her most was the infant she would be forced to relinquish.

Christine gave birth on Thursday, 18 July 1957, at a private address in Bath. She named her daughter Phyllis Webb and was allowed to keep her for two weeks. On 1 August 1957, she handed the tiny girl into the care of the Church of England Children's Society. The grief of parting was felt acutely by most new mothers and many needed sedation. 'She found it very, very hard to give up her child,' explains Tora Tomkinson, who met Christine years later. 'But she loved her father and felt she had to do what was expected of her.'[2]

Phyllis was taken to Sunnyside, a children's home in a grand country house, where she was one of thirty residents under five that summer. The youngest babies were cared for in a ground floor nursery; Phyllis was given a pink cot. Older children were put into three groups – Rosebuds, Daffodils and Bluebells – and had the gardens, paddling pools and pets to enjoy. Every Sunday all the children, including the babies in their prams, visited the local church.

According to the Children's Society, during her two-and-a-half months at Sunnyside, Phyllis thrived and developed into a very healthy baby. The decision to place her with the Bambers was taken largely by her grandfather. In 1986, the *Daily Mirror* quoted Eric Jay saying that he remembered Nevill Bamber from the RAF (Jay had served as a chaplain to the RAF Volunteer Reserve during the war), and was aware that he and June were looking to adopt. The baby's uncle confirmed: 'My parents selected the Bamber family from a small number of suitable households.'[3] On 10 October 1957, Phyllis Webb left the nursery with her new parents for White House Farm.

The adoption was officially sanctioned at Essex County Court in Maldon on 6 February 1958. A few months later, the Jays emigrated to Canada, where Eric was appointed principal of the Montreal Diocesan Theological College and professor of Historical Theology at McGill University.

To prepare David and Ann for the baby's sudden appearance, Pamela told them that their aunt and uncle had become parents to a baby from a person that could no longer look after the child. On her next visit to White House Farm, eleven-year-old Ann peered in at the little girl in a pram on the lawn: 'One of the farm dogs was sitting next to the pram, as if guarding the child, who I was told was going to be a cousin and called Sheila Jean.'[4]

Jasper, the yellow labrador, had immediately appointed himself the baby's chief protector. Sheila claimed that her earliest memories were of his comforting presence when she was left alone in the garden, clutching Cuthbert the teddy bear and screaming for attention. Despite longing for a child and feeling ready to love and nurture her, within months of Sheila's adoption June suffered severe depressions and a second breakdown.

The philosophy accompanying post-war adoptions maintained that raising an adoptive child was no different to rearing a baby of one's own. But in her groundbreaking study *The Primal Wound*, Nancy Verrier argues that babies experience an acute sense of loss upon separation from the birth mother and seldom accept their new parents instinctively. The process is gradual, with pain and confusion on both sides: 'If an adoptive mother, being especially tuned in to her baby, experiences her baby's hesitation in attaching, she may feel it as rejection.'[5] Another doctor explains: 'Bonding difficulties is a hackneyed phrase. However, the adoptive mother misses a whole period of preparation, emotional and physical.'[6] Many are also ashamed and bewildered to find that adoption doesn't heal the torment of infertility, but actually intensifies their grief. 'Auntie June always thought everything she had belonged to somebody else,' recalls a relative. 'She said, "Everything I've had has been somebody else's." Yes, including the children.'[7]

In 1958, June was admitted to Britain's largest private psychiatric clinic, St Andrew's Hospital in Northampton. In those pre-motorway days, it was a three hour drive from Tolleshunt D'Arcy. The hospital records are under restricted access, but Dr Hugh Cameron Ferguson, who joined St Andrew's as a consultant psychiatrist in 1978, is able to shed a little light on her admission. June came under his care in 1982 and he learned that she had been treated there in the 1950s: 'I don't know if her depression following Sheila's adoption took the form of the classical lowering of mood or if it was mixed up with her strong religious beliefs. I suspect it was somewhat religiose, disturbed thoughts as well as disturbed feelings. That's the difference between a clinical depression and a psychotic depression – there's a breaking with reality.'[8]

When June didn't respond to medication or psychoanalysis, she was given a course of electroshock therapy, receiving the treatment on at least six occasions at St Andrew's. Lying on a gurney in a hospital gown, the patient would be injected twice: first with a general anaesthetic, then with a muscle relaxant. A mouth guard stopped her from biting her tongue, and oxygen was administered through a face mask. Two metal plates were applied to the temples where conducting gel had been rubbed onto her skin, delivering a series of high-voltage electrical pulses into the brain to produce an epileptic fit. Electroshock took half an hour, with pulses lasting between five to fifteen seconds. The patient was then turned on her side, ingesting oxygen until the muscle relaxant wore off. A severe headache, sore muscles and nausea habitually followed. Memory loss was another side effect, usually short term, although some patients reported permanent partial loss.

June was said to have made a full recovery as a result, but the procedure could not address underlying issues or prevent remission. During her absence, Nevill had shared the care of Sheila with family members. When his wife returned home, a seventeen-year-old girl was taken on as a full-time nanny. Julia Saye was never aware of any problems in the household and regarded her employers as friends, remaining in touch with them until the end of their lives.

In 1960, June and Nevill applied to adopt a second baby.

They were ideal parents in many ways: thoroughly decent, kind and hard-working, financially secure with a close network of family and friends and a beautiful home. But June had twice required psychiatric care for depression, the second spell triggered by Sheila's adoption. How the Church of England Children's Society reconciled this with their screening process remains confidential. But in spring 1961, Pamela's daughter Ann learned that her aunt and uncle had become parents again: 'I remember seeing the baby at White House Farm and being told he would be another cousin, to be called Jeremy Nevill Bamber.'

He was 'Jeremy' from birth, but Jeremy Paul Marsham, born at St Mary Abbots Hospital in Kensington on 13 January 1961. Fewer facts have emerged about the circumstances of his adoption than of Sheila's; he refused to allow police access to his records during the murder enquiry. But at the time of Jeremy's birth, his father Leslie Brian Marsham was a married sergeant in the Royal Army Medical Corps, stationed at the Royal Artillery Guided Weapons Range on the Hebridean island of St Kilda. Jeremy's mother was not his wife, but twenty-three-year-old Juliet Dorothy Wheeler, a Leicester-born student midwife who lived on Kensington Church Street. 'As far as I am aware, they met at a dance,' Jeremy stated years later.[1]

He was swiftly placed in the care of the Church of England Children's Society 'due to the stigma attached to having an illegitimate child', according to the *Daily Mirror* journalist who traced his father forty-three years later. 'It was traumatic when we had to hand him over,' Leslie Marsham recalled. 'He went to lovely people, who looked after him and gave him the best start in life.' On 16 August 1962, eighteen months after surrendering their son for adoption, and following Leslie's divorce, Jeremy's parents married in Leicester. According to the marriage certificate, his father was no longer Leslie Brian Marsham but Sergeant Leslie Bertie Fitzroy Marsham of 39 Palace Gardens Terrace, while Juliet continued to study midwifery at Leicester's General Hospital. There was no question of reclaiming Jeremy, although the couple remained in touch with the Bambers for some four years. By the end of that period the Marshams were living in Cyprus, where a second son and daughter were born in 1965 and 1967 respectively.

They knew no more about Jeremy and his adoptive family until August 1985.

Sheila's nanny recalled that Jeremy was about six weeks old when the Bambers brought him to White House Farm. The adoption papers were authorized on 27 July 1961 at Maldon County Court. John and Barbara Wilkin were godparents.

'During the earlier years of the children, Sheila was the awkward one, Jeremy was a very pleasant and polite child,' June's friend Agnes Low (née Barrie) remembered.[2] Four years old when she gained a brother, Sheila was sensitive, spirited and open, with a quick temper that she often lost but usually regretted. Friends recall her as an affectionate, spontaneous little girl who loved animals; she was dreamy and imaginative, strongwilled yet easily intimidated. Her Aunt Pamela described her as very loving, and throughout her life Sheila was a tactile person, generous with hugs and habitually touching the arm of the person to whom she was chatting. Her adoptive parents were less demonstrative. Colin Caffell, whom she later married, recalls that their lack of cuddles hurt her. Sheila told one friend that her parents gave her everything she needed except physical affection.

Jeremy was more placid than Sheila, and eager to please. 'He was a polite boy,' his cousin Ann recalls. 'He wanted to be just like his father and would want to eat the same things at breakfast.'[3] Nicknamed 'Jem' by his family, he insists he felt very loved: 'Mum was always home, ready with food and drinks and cuddles when I'd scraped or banged something, and from a young age I'd just tag along with Dad when I fancied.'[4] In contrast, Sheila felt any time with her parents was squeezed into their schedules and that, with June especially, she was a hindrance.

Nevill worked long hours on the farm and from 1961 was a Justice of the Peace at Witham Magistrates' Court. He acted as agent for local Conservative candidates and June accompanied him to party meetings. His status in the village was that of a local squire and, in that tradition, June would go into Tolleshunt D'Arcy almost every day to visit those in need.

Their social life also remained hectic. Richard and Inez Bowen met them after settling in Tolleshunt D'Arcy in 1960. Former air/naval attaché in Caracas, Venezuela, Richard had served in the RAF during the war. 'Nevill and June would often come to our house for drinks [and] after church on Sunday mornings,' Inez stated, remembering how the two men liked to 'reminisce about their experiences' and often played golf.[5] Michael Leyland moved to the area with his wife Patricia and family in 1962, after Nevill successfully bid on his behalf for an Alresford farm. Sunday lunch became a joint fixture for both families, while the two men had a standing date every year to celebrate their shared birthday.

Since living at White House Farm, the Bambers had joined St Nicholas' Church, where June volunteered her services as a flower arranger and enrolled Sheila and Jeremy in Sunday school. At home she taught them prayers, read stories from the Bible and ensured that grace was always said at mealtimes. Julia stayed on as a full-time nanny to both children for two years after Jeremy's adoption, then worked as and when required until he was of school age. Other girls, including a French au pair, were employed on the same casual basis.

Both children attended the local school, St Nicholas Church of England Primary. Sheila was popular with her classmates, but former pupil Bob Cross recalls that Jeremy struggled: 'He was so snooty and spoke so posh on the bus that the local lads used to tease him mercilessly. He was a real wimp and would just burst into tears instead of fighting back. His sister stuck up for him a lot and he hated that.'[6] The relationship between Sheila and Jeremy was punctuated by the odd squabble but mostly benign.

There were several girls of their age within the family circle who were friends with Sheila, including her 'aunt' Betty Howie's daughter Sarah, but no boys, and Jeremy often found himself excluded. He made friends of his own after he and Sheila transferred to Maldon Court, a private prep school in Maldon, eight miles away. They travelled by car with David Hunter, whose father farmed Beckingham Hall in Tolleshunt Major, and Jeremy was soon mixing easily with other farmers' sons. Sheila made lifelong friends at Maldon Court, where she excelled at creative writing and art but made little progress in other subjects. English was Jeremy's weakest subject and he was a poor speller, but maths and science came quite easily to him.

Sheila and Jeremy were each about seven years old when their parents explained they were adopted. 'June told them both that they were not made in Mummy's tummy but out of all the babies in the world they chose them,' Pamela recalled.[7] Sheila felt alienated by the revelation and pressured to demonstrate her gratitude, while Jeremy declares himself unbothered: 'The fact

that I was adopted didn't affect me in the slightest. My mum and
dad are June and Nevill and they will always be so.' He claims
the only adverse consequence was understanding that his cousins
calling him 'a cuckoo' as a child was 'a cruel jibe' at his background.[8]

Until they left school, Sheila and Jeremy saw little of their
cousins David and Ann Boutflour, who were much older. Although
Anthony and Jacqueline Pargeter continued to visit the farm for
several weeks each year, they were closer in age to Ann and
David. Anthony felt that he got on 'extremely well with the
family', but Jacqueline recalled friction: 'Jeremy and Sheila were
jealous of my relationship with my uncle; we had a rapport
between us.'[9] David Boutflour agrees: 'I think Jeremy and Sheila
probably had every reason to have their noses put out of joint a
bit because Nevill and June already had their two children in
some ways – Anthony and Jackie were almost serving that part.
Sometimes Sheila and Jeremy did feel a little bit unloved, particularly when the others came.'[10]

Reginald Pargeter had remarried twice since his wife's death
and had two more sons: Roland, born in 1951, and Clive, born
in 1964. Roland's childhood holidays at the farm were almost as
regular as his half-siblings Anthony and Jacqueline's. He recalls
that the Bambers spoilt Jeremy and Sheila when they were young
and others observed the same. Anne Hunter, whose son David
shared the car to school with Jeremy and Sheila, couldn't remember June 'ever saying no to the children's demands. When our
families were small the children would play together and I recall
frequent tantrums from both Sheila and Jeremy when they would
both simply lie on the floor screaming for attention. Nevill was
at a loss at such times and June could not cope.'[11] David Boutflour admits that his uncle and aunt 'weren't strong disciplinarians.
Very kind, loving people but I don't think they were strong
enough on their children. They did everything they could do
from a financial point of view – sometimes children need more.'

Insecurity was at the root of the couple's reluctance to chastise
Sheila and Jeremy. June once told David that 'when you've
adopted children you have to be very, very careful' and implied
that the adoption agency would 'check up' on them. Dr Ferguson,
June's psychiatrist during the early 1980s, recalls that she was

particularly troubled by an accident in Jeremy's childhood: 'June told me that, having adopted her son, he had banged his head. This would have happened when the boy was aged about two years.'[12] Central to her anxiety about the incident was the fear that he would be removed from her care.

Their Aunt Pamela and grandmother Mabel were more robust, scolding them soundly if they misbehaved. Sheila later told Colin that she felt closer to both these women than to her mother. There were frequent visits to Granny and Grandad Speakman at Vaulty Manor Farm and regular trips to Nevill's widowed mother in Guildford. Sheila was in awe of Granny Bamber, who was kind yet regal, ploughing her finances into Clifton House, her beautiful, decaying home. She much preferred Granny Speakman, who would rock with laughter at the things she said and was generous in slipping June money for gifts. Of all the presents Sheila received over the years, the one she appreciated most was a shih-tzu puppy for her tenth birthday in 1967. She named him Sweepy and was devoted to the little dog. Animals were always her great love; Colin recalls that she was wonderful with them and would invent voices and even languages for her pets.

Within months of Sheila's tenth birthday, she and Jeremy had their first experience of death when their father's remaining sister, Diana, was killed in an accident. As East African Tours consultant for the BOAC airline, Diana had travelled the world giving speeches about life in Kenya. In 1968 she helped organize the annual East African Safari Rally, and was carrying out a final inspection of the track in Mtito Andei on 10 March when the driver of her car lost control in the torrential rain, hitting a stationary lorry. Diana died instantly; she was thirty-eight years old.

Nevill was distraught. No one spoke about his sister after the funeral, and Sheila felt especially shut out by her parents' sorrow. Her bewilderment increased when she was suddenly sent to boarding school two months later.

Why her parents chose to enrol her in the middle of a term remains a mystery. Moira House was a hundred miles south in Eastbourne, Sussex, home to 120 boarders as well as day girls. Former pupils included *Black Narcissus* novelist Rumer Godden and actress Prunella Scales. Sheila was deeply unhappy there. Separated from all that was familiar, including her beloved Sweepy, she was plagued by intense feelings of rejection not only from fellow pupils, but from her parents for sending her away.

Sheila tried to concentrate on her studies but was too miserable to make much progress, although a teacher remembers her taking pleasure in the school's more imaginative pursuits, particularly modern dance. She coped by resorting to mischief and pouring her thoughts into a diary, the latter becoming a lifelong habit.

Art provided another outlet. In one painting, Sheila depicted three girls in long dresses on a spiral staircase and another girl in dark clothes kneeling on the floor below, her face turned away. Years later, she gave the painting to Colin, who examined it again after her death and saw for the first time an abortive picture on the other side of a sinister monochrome face with scarlet lips, crossed out with two broad daubs of red paint. Its disturbing power reminded him of Edvard Munch's 'The Scream'.

Sheila finally succeeded in convincing her parents to remove her from Moira House in December 1970, when she joined Old Hall School in Hethersett, Norfolk as a boarder. Established in 1938, the main school building was a grand Georgian hall set in sixteen acres of woodland and fields. The next four years there would be among the happiest of Sheila's short life.

4

'I wanted to be an astronaut,' Jeremy writes of his childhood dreams. Having watched the first moon landing live on television, 'exploring space was the obvious thing to want to do. There were no street lights around where we lived, so the dark nights meant we could see a million stars in the sky.'[1] Nevill invented stories 'to make the night sky even more magical' and taught him astronomy: 'We'd identify all the major constellations – he'd learned to fly using stars to navigate his Mosquito in North Africa – and he passed all that knowledge on to me.'[2]

In September 1970, nine-year-old Jeremy left stargazing at White House Farm to board at Gresham's in the Norfolk town of Holt. One of the oldest and most illustrious public schools in the country, its alumni include poet W. H. Auden, composer Benjamin Britten, and Nobel prize winner Sir Alan Lloyd Hodgkin. Jeremy was assigned to the junior house of Kenwyn, and Nevill asked a barrister friend whose son was at school nearby for advice on stimulating places to take Jeremy when he and June visited.

There are three apocryphal stories about Jeremy's time at Gresham's. One concerns his attitude to boarding and stems largely from the courtroom testimony of Julie Mugford's mother Mary, who claimed that Jeremy resented his mother 'for sending him away to boarding school. He couldn't understand why she had adopted him only to send him away.' In fact, it was Nevill who made the decision, having enjoyed boarding school himself. June would have preferred the children to be educated locally, although Jeremy may not have been aware of that. He maintains he felt no bitterness, but admits to finding it hard being away from his parents at such a young age, although once the first couple of years were over, he enjoyed school.

A second anecdote concerns the strict pecking order prevalent in boarding schools. Robert Boutflour was under the impression that most of Gresham's pupils hailed from East Anglia's landed gentry, and later told police that as the son of a tenant farmer, his nephew would have ranked on the lowest rung of the school's ladder. In reality, Gresham's offered several scholarships to boys from less affluent homes, but there was still some snobbery among the pupils themselves. Jeremy's confiding in a schoolmate that he was adopted only made matters worse; his peers displayed a sneering superiority, nicknaming him 'the bastard'. But when asked to recall any school nicknames, Jeremy acknowledges only one: 'Gascoigne', which he shared with Sheila, after *University Challenge* presenter Bamber Gascoigne.

Another story was divulged by Brett Collins, later Jeremy's close friend, who told the *Star* on 30 October 1986: 'When Jeremy was eleven, he was sexually molested and that deeply affected him.' Colin Caffell offers some corroboration in his memoir, referring to Jeremy's first years at the school where he was 'emotionally, physically and, according to Jeremy, sexually abused by older boys'.[3] While impossible to verify beyond doubt, the three narratives are often regarded as the genesis of the murders, planting the seed from which Jeremy's resentment towards his parents grew unstoppably.

His contemporaries in Essex – mostly cousins and the children of his parents' friends – saw him only during school holidays for the next few years, but remember a burgeoning arrogance. June's cousin Brenda Wallace and her family visited the farm for a fortnight every summer; her daughter Susan was Sheila's age and thought Jeremy a 'spoiled brat' who could 'sulk for ages' and would march off alone when thwarted.[4] June's wartime friend Dorothy Barker lived nearby with her husband James Carr. He was manager of Osea Road, and found Jeremy thoroughly disagreeable: 'He was growing up to be quite a nasty piece of work. For any time I wanted him to do something, if he did not want to, at his young age he would tell me I was just an employee and he would tell his father how I behaved.'[5]

June often invited the three Carr children to the farm as company for her son but they came to dread being asked. 'Jeremy was a moody, bossy and sometimes cruel child,' Robert Carr recalled. '[He] could be very cruel to animals and he used to take great delight in throwing stones at water hen chicks and hitting farm animals with sticks. He did not have a warm relationship with his parents.'[6] Robert much preferred Sheila, 'a timid but very pleasant-natured girl' who 'always used to get upset whenever [Jeremy] used to be cruel to the animals, and he used to take great delight in carrying on and leaving her in tears'.

Thirteen-year-old Sheila was popular with pupils and teachers at Old Hall School, where everyone knew her as 'Bambs'. Regarded as a good sport with a gift for mimicry, she developed an inseparable friendship with Rosalind Nockold and Jane Hinde, who remember her as bubbly, kind and incapable of carrying a grudge. Rosalind believed Sheila failed to reach her full academic potential because she lacked confidence: 'She needed her friends and was quite demanding of her closest ones. At school she was never able to undertake things on her own.'[7] The two girls lived close enough to each other to visit during the holidays. Rosalind thought Nevill 'a kind, friendly, funny man . . . good at making teenage girls laugh' and while June was 'not on the same wavelength as Sheila', she was always supportive of her. Jeremy just seemed 'very quiet'.

Although Sheila had settled in well at school, her cousin David heard that she caused her parents some concern over truancy outside lessons. Part of a group of girls who sneaked out after hours to catch the bus into Norwich, one evening Sheila found herself alone and decided to hitch back. The driver who offered her a lift pulled into a side road and lunged for her, but she shamed him into retreat, indignantly berating him for being a dirty old man. The encounter didn't deter Sheila from joining her friends on other escapades. 'She was a free spirit,' reflects Tora Tomkinson, her closest friend in adulthood. 'She just wanted to rush around and enjoy her life. She said to me, "I suppose I was a wild child, really," but from what she told me, she didn't sound very wild.'[8]

At home, there was only the occasional hint of the fire that had stalled her would-be attacker. In what was to become a pattern, any displays of anger on Sheila's part were usually sparked by insecurity and a need for reassurance. Jacqueline recalled one Christmas visit when Nevill and June had a blazing row with their daughter because she was upset that Nevill had offered Jacqueline a drink before her. Sheila was also jealous of Jeremy sometimes, complaining to Inez Bowen that he was Nevill's favourite.

Inez's son worked at White House Farm and was friendly

with Sheila, whose blossoming as a young woman caused her mother a great deal of anxiety. 'June was always very protective towards Sheila and would not let her out of her sight unless I was there,' Inez recalled.[9] Jeremy's godfather John Wilkin agreed: 'By the time Sheila was about thirteen to fifteen years old she was obviously going to be an extremely attractive girl. June became very worried by this, if not obsessed with the attention paid to her by men.'[10]

Sheila celebrated her sixteenth birthday on 18 July 1973. Susan Wallace, visiting White House Farm that summer with her parents, found Sheila 'very sure of herself' and keen to try anything once 'for the fun of doing it'. After dark she would climb out of her bedroom window above the kitchen and shin down a ladder to meet friends in Colchester and Maldon. 'She told me this and also I heard it from my mother who had received letters from June,' Susan recalled. During the Wallaces' stay, Sheila smuggled cider into her bedroom one evening and the two girls got tipsy. When June found out, as penance she made them accompany her to the theatre, expecting them to hate it, but the girls enjoyed themselves. Susan thought June 'a very nice, homely person. The worst punishment I ever knew her give was to stop Sheila or Jeremy's pocket money but as soon as they wanted anything, they got it anyway.'

Hoping to curb the opportunity for more mischief, June attempted to fill her daughter's time productively. Sheila had been a bridesmaid at her cousin Ann's wedding to Peter Eaton the previous September; his parents were already part of the family's social circle, owning Frame Farm in Tolleshunt D'Arcy and later Little Renters Farm in Little Totham. As such, Peter had known Nevill and June since he was ten years old and more recently had begun joining Nevill and Ann's brother David on shoots. June asked Ann, who was pregnant in the summer of 1973 with her first child, to give Sheila some household chores and teach her how to cook. When it became obvious that she was never going to turn her daughter entirely into a homebody, David agreed to accompany Sheila to village hops and Young Farmers' dinner dances.

Knowing that he was keeping an eye on Sheila was one less worry for June at a time when life was taking a difficult turn.

Roland Pargeter had moved into the farm some months earlier, following his father Reginald's death, which Jeremy recalls was again never mentioned. Roland was there at June's invitation; hearing that he had developed a cannabis habit while living alone in London, she offered to help him overcome it. Nevill employed him as a labourer, stipulating that no drugs of any sort would be tolerated. When they caught him smoking cannabis, there were no second chances. Roland was asked to leave, but Nevill secured him a job with the Forestry Commission first. It was an action typical of the Bambers' methods of discipline, which almost always included some form of safety net for the miscreant.

June was saddened by what she felt was the failure of her attempt to help her nephew. Soon afterwards, in December 1973, Barbara Wilkin died of a brain tumour, swiftly followed by another close friend who had cancer. 'That kind of left Mum isolated,' Jeremy remembers. 'Her two best friends had died and it was really sad. That's what brought on her depression again.'[11] She internalized her grief as always, feeling the loss of both women deeply. Asked whether his parents' tendency to submerge emotion was dysfunctional, Jeremy responds: 'I don't really see it like that. My mum and dad went through the war, and that's not an excuse but it explains why people's emotions are controlled . . . Dad was not the type to share things.'

June's self-confidence withered as depression took hold. She began to withdraw from social gatherings, apart from church events which gave her comfort. Among her closest friends were the local vicar, Rev. Norman Thorp and his wife Bettine, and Nevill was elected churchwarden at St Nicholas' in early 1974.

Sheila left school that July with no fixed ideas about her future. She and her friends got into trouble for high-spirited 'hell-raising' on her final day, but the headmistress described her afterwards as 'a good, well-mannered, charming pupil'.[12] Sheila's only ambition was to live in London, where she could enjoy a social life away from her mother's watchful eye. Inez Bowen recalled that June resolved her inner turmoil by opening the Bible one night and receiving 'some sort of spiritual guidance' which persuaded her to let Sheila go. June also discussed the matter with Bettine Thorp, who remembered she suffered 'a great deal of concern' about Sheila leaving home but remained 'very loyal indeed' to her.[13]

Those who had known June longer detected a difference in her. Dorothy Carr observed that her friend was 'a very changed person from the old days' and had developed a 'black and white' outlook on life.[14] David Boutflour thought of his aunt as someone who was never able to put her own needs first. He had just begun dating his future wife, Colchester girl Karen Butt. She initially regarded June as the opposite of Pamela, who was 'very outgoing and strong'.[15] But gradually, Karen revised her opinion, sensing that 'underneath it all, Auntie June had a real rod of iron going through her.'

Despite other people's opinions of him, Jeremy had given his parents little cause for concern since starting at Gresham's. His early childhood ambitions had been overtaken by more practical aims. 'I knew from a young age that I'd be a farmer,' he recalls, although his relatives would later dispute it. 'Dad inspired me with the wonder of growing things that made our living and he understood that to engage my interest it had to be on an intellectual basis as well as practical.'

Nevill was keen to involve Jeremy in his work, hoping he would follow in his footsteps. An astute businessman, he and four other farmers had formed North Maldon Growers Ltd in 1962 to sell their produce in bulk and negotiate better contracts. Two years later they became a registered limited company, with premises in Goldhanger where foodstuffs were packaged for distribution to local markets and freezer centres. When Jeremy was twelve, Nevill gave him part of one of White House Farm's fields to grow sweetcorn, which he then picked and sold through North Maldon Growers for a small profit. The company secretary recalled father and son showing him the small crop with great pride.

At the end of summer 1974, as his sister departed for a new life in London, Jeremy entered senior school after sitting the Common Entrance exam. Gresham's was now co-educational, and Jeremy's schoolwork occupied him far less than his new female classmates. Although generally good at maths, he was placed in the third of four sets and dropped French early in the year for technical studies. Leaving junior school meant joining Farfield, where William Thomas was house master. His first impression of Jeremy was of 'someone you did not particularly take notice of, he did not stand out, but he was courteous and enthusiastic'.[16]

Within eighteen months, Thomas recalled, that would change.

Sheila's parents had enrolled her on a two year secretarial 'finishing course' at St Godric's Secretarial College on Arkwright Road, Hampstead. Its students were accommodated at six monitored boarding houses nearby. Sheila was given rooms on Wedderburn Road, a brisk five-minute walk from college. She began her studies on 4 September 1974 with little enthusiasm for the course but thrilled to be living in London.

The girls from St Godric's tended to frequent the same places: the Coffee Cup on Hampstead High Street for coffee and raisin toast, Louis Hungarian Patisserie on Heath Street for poppyseed cake and tea, and on late afternoons and evenings they congregated at a smoky, bohemian pub called The Three Horseshoes, also on Heath Street. It was there that seventeen-year-old Sheila met Colin Caffell. She was chatting with a friend in a corner of the pub when two young, arty-looking men approached. 'The moment I saw Sheila, I wanted her,' Colin recalled.[1] The attraction was mutual and for her there would never really be anyone else again.

Colin was then twenty-one, a soft-spoken, easy-going dreamer, studying for an honours degree in ceramics and three-dimensional design at the Camberwell School of Art. His parents had recently separated after almost thirty years of marriage. Reg Caffell was a television engineer and a genial, sprightly man with a dry humour; Doris was quiet and conscientious, establishing an antiques business with her new partner Bernard Brencher. Colin's sister Diane, six years his senior, had emigrated to Norway after her marriage in 1966 but remained in close contact with her family.

Colin's friend Chris Precious struck up conversation with Sheila and her companion. Two days later, Colin and Sheila met alone for lunch at a nearby cafe. On their second date they became lovers, launching into a passionate relationship. Beguiled by Sheila's beauty and open, trusting nature, Colin was eager to introduce her to his family and friends, including his ex-girlfriends Sandra Elston and Jill Bonney. Sheila and Jill had little in common but Sandra felt drawn to her, sensing that she was vulnerable, and the two girls became friends in their own right. In turn, Sheila took Colin to meet her parents, explaining that her younger brother was at boarding school. He immediately warmed to Nevill and liked June, who deferred to Nevill constantly, always referring to him as 'my husband', never by name.

Sheila abandoned her course at St Godric's in March 1975. A note on her file commented that she had shown no interest. She found work as a trainee hairdresser at the Robert Fielding School of Hairdressing on Regent Street but soon left to pursue a career in modelling. At five foot seven, with huge grey-blue eyes in an elfin face, a cloud of dark hair and the requisite willowy figure, Sheila had the looks but little self-assurance. Colin encouraged her ambitions, but June was apprehensive. Determined to support her daughter nonetheless, she asked Pamela to contact Robert's relative Josie Jacobs, who worked as a fashion model.

Josie invited Sheila and Colin to her home for a chat but was left underwhelmed by her attitude: 'She seemed desperate to leave her parents and be independent and [thought] that being a model would solve all her problems.'[2] Josie dutifully introduced Sheila to her agent but the meeting did not go well.

Undaunted, Sheila asked her parents to fund her portfolio. Some of the shots were taken by Essex press photographer Ronald Crowe, who knew the Eatons: 'One of the poses I asked her to do involved her holding a shotgun and a brace of pheasants. I found that Sheila just did not know how to hold a gun at all. It was obvious to me she had no idea at all about guns.'[3] Taken in the garden at White House Farm, the photograph shows her clad in jumper and jeans, perched on the open boot of a Land Rover, pheasants in one hand, rifle in the other.

June paid for a modelling course at the Lucie Clayton School in South Kensington, whose graduates included Jean Shrimpton and Joanna Lumley. Ann accompanied her aunt to the Coming Out evening. June was openly proud of Sheila but increasingly troubled by the prospect of her earning a living as a model, telling friends of her concern. 'With this worry, June started to show signs of some sort of religious mania,' John Wilkin remembered.[4]

The era's shifting attitudes towards sex and morality heightened June's anxiety. Church attendances were in steep decline and more couples were 'living in sin', while divorces were now possible within two years. Sex was no longer regarded as the prerogative of a committed relationship but as a form of self-expression. The contraceptive pill had been available to single women since 1970 and abortion had been made legal three years earlier. The relaxing of obscenity laws and the availability of European pornography meant that most corner shops and newsagents stocked 'girlie' magazines. Cinema reflected Britain's 'new fascination with sex and self-gratification', from the comedy of the *Confessions of a Window Cleaner* (1974) franchise to art house films such as *Last Tango in Paris* (1972) and *Emmanuelle* (1974). *Straw Dogs* (1971) and *A Clockwork Orange* (1972) combined sex and violence, while *The Devils* (1971) focused on sex and religion. Meanwhile, tight-trousered rock gods straddled the hit parade, football terraces thrummed with aggression, the economy sank, prices soared and many believed that Britain was bracing itself for 'a gathering storm of moral corruption, splintering families and sexual chaos, promoted by an unholy coalition of addled-headed liberals and profit-crazed pornographers'.[5]

In the summer of 1975, shortly after her graduation from Lucie Clayton's, Sheila discovered she was pregnant. She was eighteen, the same age her birth mother had been when she fell pregnant. Colin wanted to marry, but Sheila was more cautious. They discussed their options, including the ethics of a termination. She hated the idea and was worried that it might affect future pregnancies. Nor did she want to consider adoption, explaining her background to Colin. They decided to continue with the pregnancy and marry in the coming year.

To their surprise, Nevill and June reacted more calmly than Colin's parents when they telephoned them with the news. But shock had tempered June's first response; when they arrived at White House Farm a few days later the tension was palpable. Nevill listened as Colin outlined their plans before evenly pointing out some practicalities. June declared that sex before marriage was sinful, adding that she had spoken to Rev. Thorp about the situation and had arranged for Sheila to see the family doctor.

At the surgery, June told her daughter to think carefully and consider how the pregnancy might affect her career. When Sheila returned to Colin, she told him tearfully that her mother had talked a lot of common sense. He could do little but agree, travelling anxiously back to London while June drove Sheila to Chelmsford and Essex Hospital. Family friend Kathleen Whitworth was aware the termination was 'very much against Sheila's wishes' and that June had 'put a great deal of pressure' on her daughter.[6] Colin confirmed that June 'fixed up the abortion. Bambs was upset and very unhappy. It screwed her up [but] we had no money. We lived on my grant from art school, but we were desperately in love.'[7]

When he rang the farm to speak to Sheila, June told him frankly that she hoped their relationship would end. She said nothing when Colin arrived the following day to see Sheila, but when she found them sunbathing nude in a field she flew into a rage. Accusing them of fornicating on her land she gave powerful vent to her anger and disappointment. Shaken by the strength of her fury, Sheila and Colin returned to the house, intending to leave for London. When Sheila went upstairs to pack, June followed.

What passed between mother and daughter at White House Farm that hot summer afternoon in 1975 had consequences no one could have foreseen. Seething with wrath, June branded Sheila 'the Devil's child'.[8] In an instant, her words snagged like hooks in Sheila's mind and in time she would come to 'hang her psychosis on them', in psychiatrist Dr Ferguson's chilling phrase.[9] The suggestion of 'bad blood' tore deeply into Sheila's innermost fears.

'There *was* a time when Bambi was frightened of her mother,' Tora Tomkinson recalls. 'One other thing in particular really scared her. She told me, "Sometimes I would lie on my bed on a hot summer's night and suddenly, my mum would be there, standing in my doorway, staring at me." She felt very frightened by that. There was no explanation but she never forgot it. She said, "I don't know what she thought about me but I always felt she didn't think much." Bambi was genuinely frightened by her mother then. Spooky – that was one of the words she used about her. Spooky.'[10]

Only a few weeks later, in August, Leslie Speakman died at the

age of eighty-two. Her father's death, coupled with Sheila's pregnancy and the ugly confrontation at the farm, left June distraught.
Ann suspected that June found her daughter's abortion too much
to bear given her own history. Adoption after infertility can leave
a legacy of strain, according to an expert in family psychiatry:
'There is always a fear of "bad blood", even if it is only a fear
that the relatives will be looking for it. That can make a parent
over-protective and at the same time over-critical . . . Religion
may be used, or abused, as one way of rigidifying a situation. It
lays down rules.'[11]

June's family and friends were unanimous in citing events
that summer as the catalyst for her increasing reliance on God.
Yet not everyone viewed her involvement with the church nega-
tively; pupils and parents who knew June from Tolleshunt
Sunday school, where she had joined Joan Frost in teaching,
spoke highly of her. But Colin found it almost impossible to forgive June for the catastrophic effect her words would have on
Sheila.

There were other consequences from that ghastly day. Colin
had taken some photographs of Sheila while they were sunbathing; he processed them onto slides and lost the originals.
After Sheila's death, Jeremy informed him that the snapshots were
in his mother's bureau at the farm. When Colin asked how they
had ended up there, Jeremy replied that June had probably taken
the photographs from Sheila's flat in order to manipulate her.

Nevill was a curiously ineffectual figure in the conflict
between mother and daughter. His arbitration could have made
a difference, since both women held him in the highest esteem.
Used to dealing with discord as a magistrate, he was widely
regarded as a man with an endless capacity for compassion and
decency. 'He always tried to do the right thing by everything and
everyone,' Patricia Leyland stated.[12] Yet he very rarely involved
himself in June and Sheila's relationship, since he never understood their battles and didn't want to be seen to be taking sides.
But his determination to be fair meant that clashes and grievances were left unresolved, hissing in the air.

Colin began his final year at art school in September 1975. He
and Sheila shared a room in his student digs overlooking Peck-

ham Rye Park. Their landlady was an eccentric character named Maggie who wrote Gothic horror and dressed flamboyantly; she kept a crystal ball, tarot cards and a life-sized dummy named Alphonse in her front room. London that autumn was a city under siege: the Provisional IRA intensified their campaign, with bomb blasts at the Hilton on Park Lane, and in Piccadilly, Mayfair and Chelsea, killing several and injuring hundreds.

The grim mood over Britain clung on until June 1976, when temperatures began to soar and the sun glittered in cobalt skies day after day. As a member of Gresham's Combined Cadet Force, fifteen-year-old Jeremy attended summer camp in the Peak District, but disliked the discipline. A recurring knee problem dampened his enthusiasm for sports and he developed an interest in technology, building his own gadgets. At school his best subjects remained maths, chemistry and geography, the latter taught by John Walton, who led an annual trip to the Italian Alps. During the visit to Sauze d'Oulx, boys would share cigarettes and knock back alcohol but Jeremy wasn't much of a drinker. He preferred cannabis and experimented with various drugs in his teens.

The heat-wave of 1976 stretched over three months, bringing standpipes to the streets and turning grass to tinder. As England sweltered, the relationship between Sheila and Colin grew turbulent. In his memoir, he recalls how she would ignite tension by finding a weak spot and picking at it; when that failed, she reached for his carefully crafted pottery and dropped it to the floor. On one occasion his reaction left Sheila with a black eye. He felt as if she was testing his love and comparing him to her father, whom no one seemed able to rile.

Sheila discovered she was pregnant again in spring 1977. A second abortion was too terrible to contemplate; her parents offered to buy them a flat if they married before the baby was born, insisting they were doing it for the child. June also tried to persuade them to leave London, but they were happy there and, after graduating from college, Colin had secured a job in advertising. Sheila set her heart on a traditional wedding in Tolleshunt D'Arcy, but June vetoed the idea immediately, declaring, 'Not in *my* church, you don't!'[13] She insisted that her daughter should marry in cream, not white. Sheila liked the idea of emulating her parents' wedding reception in a marquee on the lawn at home, but her suggestion was rejected, and rather than hire a limousine for the day, Nevill would act as chauffeur in his car.

The wedding took place at Chelmsford Registry Office on Saturday, 14 May 1977. Wearing a long cream dress with a Juliet cap and veil over lightly permed hair, Sheila said her vows before a small gathering that included her schoolfriends Jane Hinde and Rosalind Nockold. Colin's own schoolfriend Nicholas Rudge served as best man and his sister Diane flew in from Norway. Among the other guests were Sheila's godfather Basil Tweed and the Boutflours. Ann and Peter Eaton attended the reception at the Marks Tey Motel in Copford with their toddler William and daughter Janie, who was six months old.

Among the most personal wedding gifts was one from Jeremy, who had spent much of his school term making the couple a dining table. 'For all the rebuke he got from her as a child, Jeremy thought the world of his sister,' Colin admitted.[14] Although he later told detectives that Sheila's relationship with Jeremy had always been distant, he also conceded that Jeremy felt brotherly love for Sheila and was very proud of her. John Fielding shared a study room with Jeremy at Gresham's and recalled him showing off about Sheila: 'Of course, we were all jealous. I remember him saying she "doesn't do girly magazines" because she wanted to be a serious model.'[15]

Jeremy states that he and Sheila were closest 'from my being 15 and her 18 or 19, until I was 19 and off to Australia. Those four years were great for both of us and we had lots of good times together. She was so protective of me and really kind and sensitive.'[16] Colin recalls that he and Sheila saw Jeremy more often during this period. He viewed him as a younger brother, and was touched when Jeremy took up his own hobbies of scuba diving and growing cacti.

Returning to school after the wedding, however, Jeremy began to rebel. Surreptitiously smoking cannabis more often, he was also caught sneaking out of the dorm with John Fielding and another friend to watch a band at nearby West Runton Pavilion. Someone betrayed their whereabouts to housemaster William Thomas who 'checked their rooms and found them to be empty'.[17] He cornered Jeremy as he crept in the back door after midnight: 'I questioned Bamber regarding the breaking of School Rules and he refused to admit going to the dance hall.' John Fielding remembers the penalty when Thomas reported them to the headmaster: 'Me and Jeremy got beaten. I remember him suggesting you wear umpteen pairs of underpants. We had the choice: you can either be rusticated – stopped from leaving the grounds for a half-term – or you can get beaten. Jeremy said, "I will take the beating."'

It wasn't the first time Jeremy had snuck out of school to watch live bands with John Fielding. One of the first gigs they attended was Suzi Quatro; in August 1976 they had been among a crowd of thirty pogoing to the Sex Pistols, and in May 1977 they saw The Clash. That month the Sex Pistols released 'God Save The Queen' ahead of the Silver Jubilee. Communities up and down Britain celebrated Elizabeth II's twenty-five year reign with street parties, hog roasts, fetes and cricket matches.

For the special bank holiday on 7 June, Sheila and Colin travelled with his father to Tolleshunt D'Arcy, where Jeremy was home from school. Someone took a photograph of the Bambers that day, standing together in the field. Everyone gamely wears the silly hats Colin helped to make – apart from Sheila, who has decorated her old school straw boater with a red stick-on bow. Jeremy perches on the bonnet of Nevill's blue pickup truck, crouching between Colin and Sheila, whose pregnancy has begun to show. With the setting sun at their backs, they all beam at the camera, merry with the party atmosphere and radiating happiness in a perfect family portrait.

6

'Divine retribution' was Sheila's reaction to the loss of her unborn baby. The foetus died at five-and-a-half months; induced labour culminated in the delivery of a tiny infant whom she insisted was still alive when taken from her. Hospital staff had already asked Colin to leave the room. Afterwards, Sheila told him that the baby's death was due to her earlier termination.

In the wake of their bereavement, June hoped to persuade her daughter and son-in-law to return home by offering to buy them an antique shop in Tollesbury. But Sheila preferred to remain in London and her parents agreed to buy them a flat on a leafy, sloping street in Hampstead. While the sale was going through, Sheila accepted two months' work in Japan and flew to Tokyo alone, sharing a room with another model.

'Going out there was a very adventurous thing to do,' her friend Tora reflects. 'But the assignment in Japan really frightened her.'[1] Sheila shrank from her roommate's confidence and sophistication, and hated the changes the agency made to her own appearance. The hours were punishing and she was obliged to entertain her employers' business associates every evening. Their attempts to coerce her into bed further depleted her self-esteem. Overworked, grieving and isolated on the other side of the world, she poured out her insecurities in letters to Colin, telling him: 'I really think I should go to a psychiatrist when I get back . . . I've never felt so confused and unable to control my brain before . . . it's almost as if I'm schizophrenic or something. I feel so sick of people and stale.'[2] She feared that she had begun to exude an 'evil aura' which caused people to shun her and returned from Japan a shell of her former self.

In her absence Colin had moved into their new home at 12a Carlingford Road, a garden flat in a townhouse near Hampstead Heath. He soon came to feel belittled by the knowledge that it was not their own and bitterly regretted accepting Nevill and June's offer. Sheila became fixated on motherhood, but her joy at discovering she was pregnant again swiftly turned to despair; a botched examination after a cervical stitch led to an infection and enforced termination. Colin was against trying immediately for another baby and the tensions between them escalated.

But Sheila was adept at hiding her feelings. During the reception for her cousin David's wedding that autumn, everyone was convinced that her career mattered most. 'She appeared to have caught the bright lights,' her childhood friend Sarah Howie recalled.[3] Josie Jacobs, who had offered Sheila career advice, was also persuaded: 'She told me she was married and that she had been abroad on a modelling job. She seemed quite happy and full of beans.'[4]

Sheila's family praised her achievements, one of which was a Bacardi advert, although severe sunburn resulted in her being photographed at a distance on a beach. At Witham Magistrates' Court, Nevill's colleagues remembered him bringing in a newspaper featuring Sheila, and, at Gresham's, Jeremy's housemates noticed that she was the only member of his family he ever mentioned. Richard Gale was Jeremy's senior but saw him every week during forestry work: 'Jeremy used to bring newspaper cuttings to school of his sister, he seemed very proud of her.'[5]

Jeremy had completed his O levels in July and entered the Lower Sixth in autumn 1977. He wasn't particularly popular and got in a fight with future rugby international Nick Youngs, who knocked him out. Richard Gale recalled: 'He tended to deliberately wind pupils up. He was small in stature and big in mouth. He did not like criticism and would become angry if he was criticised.'[6] Even Jeremy's friend John Fielding conceded: 'He was a little bit of an oddball. I think he liked to be seen as important. I think the masters saw him as a bit of a disruptive influence.'[7] Housemaster William Thomas thought so, remembering an incident that year when Jeremy was suspected of having procured the key to the chemistry lecture theatre: 'This key was readily available to each House on request. It was thought Jeremy had one copied, where, it is not known. The purpose of Jeremy's possession of a key was, in my opinion, purely prestigious. His suspected possession had no practical use.'[8]

Thomas felt that he had got the measure of Jeremy by then: 'I had come to know him as a boy you could not trust. I ran my House on trust, each boy would be aware how far he could go before I would take action. Bamber was one of those who would go over the limit . . . Whilst at school Bamber had no really close friends and any friendships he struck up would not last very long.'[9] Headmaster Logie Bruce-Lockhart rarely had to severely reprimand Jeremy but felt him to be 'a quiet, prickly sort of boy. I believe some of the boys found him irritating in that he could be a relentless tease. I think he showed a touch of arrogance at a very early age.'[10]

At home, Jeremy could also be a relentless tease, and although he and Sheila generally got on well at this time, he knew how to provoke her, recalling one occasion himself: 'I was winding her up about some nonsense and she opened the bathroom windows and Mum's bath salts – she had a glass thing – she was throwing them in the yard . . .'[11] David Boutflour's wife Karen remembers: 'Sheila and Jeremy used to argue a lot. They were quite violent, really. She used to go to hit him and he would run away and laugh. It would normally be over something that he had said. He used to wind her up a great deal, and Sheila used to be affected by what Jeremy said. I know that Jeremy was quite horrible on some occasions. Sheila was not a violent person normally.'[12]

Colin recalled an incident that especially upset her. David was showing everyone around his new house at Burnt Ash Farm when Jeremy nudged Sheila and told her she'd never have a place like that if she stuck with Colin. Seeing the hurt on Sheila's face, Pamela rounded on her nephew, who turned scarlet and walked out. When Pamela mentioned it to Nevill afterwards, wondering if she had been a bit harsh, he shrugged his shoulders and said that Jeremy would have walked it off. 'He didn't like being criticised at all,' Colin confirmed. 'Often if there was a disagreement in the car, he would get out, storm off, and walk fifteen or twenty miles home.'[13] David remembers a similar episode involving Sheila and Jeremy: 'They had a slanging match out here [Burnt Ash Farm] in the garden once on a christening day. Jeremy literally got to his feet and walked home, *all* the way home – which was thirty miles.'[14]

While studying for his A levels at Gresham's in July 1978, Jeremy decided that eight years of boarding school was enough. His godfather John Wilkin recalled some discussion between Jeremy and his parents about his desire to leave school, but 'he made it known that he did not like it and refused to go back.'[15]

Nevill and June relented when Jeremy agreed to complete his education at a local sixth form.

'When he left I had been his housemaster for five years,' William Thomas reflected. 'I would describe him as someone who was not straightforward. Not very trustworthy. Something of a boaster with regard to his financial potential and basically unstable.' Jeremy's former headmaster has little to say today about his 'somewhat bizarre' character: 'Not particularly distinguished artistically, in acting or sports. He opted for shooting. Nothing unusual about that, it was a hobby which was particularly well taught and often attracted the not very academic or athletically gifted. Anything I said about him would be tainted with "wisdom after the event". I have discussed him, of course, with exact contemporaries in the house where he spent his early teens and whose opinion I respect. The impression was of a bit of an odd man out: arrogant with little cause, not popular.'[16]

Jeremy attended his sister's twenty-first birthday party in Hampstead that July. Most of their family and friends were invited, together with some of Colin's colleagues. During the evening, Sheila noticed that her husband had disappeared with a young woman from his office. Colin returned two hours later, refusing to answer Sheila's frantic questions. When all the guests except her parents and Jeremy had gone, he tried to pretend nothing had happened by 'ignoring all her questions and trying to get to sleep'.[17] In desperation, Sheila smashed her fist through the bedroom window. Colin was horrified but too drunk to drive her to the nearby Royal Free Hospital. It fell to Jeremy to look after his distressed sister, who had gashed the back of her hand and needed stitches; Colin recalls that she would thrust the scars under his nose to make him feel guilty. Sheila's abiding sense of betrayal was heightened by the incident occurring on a special birthday, yet rather than attack her husband, she had turned the anger on herself.

The following month, she joined her father and brother on a three-day shooting trip to Scotland. This was an annual expedition for male and female members of the extended family, although Sheila only attended on this one occasion. June's friend Agnes Low stayed at White House Farm while they were away: 'Nevill didn't like to leave June on her own, mainly because of

her mental condition that wasn't too good at that time.'[18] Nevill
and June took an extended holiday together later that year,
spending six weeks visiting his relations in New Zealand. But in
the aftermath of the murders, it was the expedition to Scotland
which became the focus of discussion, regarding whether or not
Sheila had used a gun during the trip. Jeremy was adamant that
she had, but initially his relatives demurred. More recently,
David Boutflour recalled that Sheila had in fact fired his shotgun.
The party had stopped for coffee and sandwiches on a mountain-
side: 'And she said, "Oh, we girls haven't ever shot a gun, would
you mind if I tried, just tried, to shoot it?" And so I gave her the
12-bore and told her to hold it very tightly into her shoulder.
[She] fired it vertically in the air, virtually.'

Returning from the trip, Jeremy enrolled at the Colchester
Institute to complete his biology and mathematics A levels. For
the first time in his life he experienced true popularity. Biology
lecturer Kenneth Witts thought him 'a pleasant person who got
on well with his fellow students and staff. I don't recall him
being a withdrawn or moody person.'[19] Jeremy had a close circle
of friends and was happy to act as unofficial taxi driver in his
battered Morris. The girls in the group described him as gentle,
kind and fun to be with, always willing to help anyone. He rarely
discussed his home life, except to express pride in Sheila, but told
everyone he was adopted, seeming resentful of it. His friend
Barry Hadden remembered a visit to White House Farm where
Jeremy had 'quite a heated argument with his father about him
wanting a new car. A friend of his, Mark Seabrook, had just been
bought a new Alfa Romeo and Jeremy felt he should also have a
new car.'[20] Although Jeremy insists he and his father were good
mates, he admits that his relationship with his mother deteriorated as he grew more independent.

June had several concerns besides her son. In addition to
making frequent trips every week to check on her own mother,
she was now responsible for the bulk of Beatrice Bamber's care.
'Granny became too elderly and frail to keep running Clifton
House,' Jeremy recalls. 'I remember the house was getting run
down and I think vermin got in, and she and Mum and Dad
decided that she would come and live with us at White House
Farm. We had carers to help us with Granny, and as a family we

would also take it in turns to see her to bed at night.'[21] June's other pressing anxiety was her daughter: at the end of 1978, Sheila discovered that she was pregnant again, with twins.

Snow began to fall heavily across Britain in late December. Blizzards struck during the first few weeks of the new year, but there were no gritting lorries because strikes had crippled the country. Public institutions closed and rubbish rotted in the streets. 'Labour Isn't Working' warned the Conservative Party ahead of the general election, setting their campaign slogan against an image of the dole queue. In May 1979, Margaret Thatcher swept the Tories to a historic victory.

By then, Sheila's marriage to Colin was disintegrating. To add to her unhappiness, there were problems with her pregnancy; complete bed rest and a stitch in her cervix were required to carry the babies to full term. She was admitted to the Royal Free Hospital for the remaining months. 'She wanted to prove she could be a good mother, maybe because her relationship with June was so bad,' Colin recalls. 'When she got pregnant with the twins ... having them was the most important thing in the world for her.'[22] In his memoir, he describes himself as completely broken by the strains in his marriage and longing for the love that he and Sheila had once shared.

To supplement their income, Colin wrote for *Billboard* music magazine. In May he was invited to a reception at the Royal Albert Hall to mark the end of Sky's first UK tour; the band's debut album had been a massive hit in Britain and America. At the party, Colin met bassist Herbie Flowers' eighteen-year-old daughter Jan, a student nurse. There was an instant attraction between them.

Sheila found out about the relationship almost as soon as it had begun. Distraught, she telephoned Sarah Howie from hospital to tell her that Colin was 'seeing another woman', while Ann Eaton heard that he had 'started an affair with a girl in London'.[23] Confined to hospital and needing to focus on her own health, there was little Sheila could do except hope that the affair was an infatuation that would pass.

On the afternoon of 22 June 1979, she gave birth to premature twin boys. There was further anguish when June arrived at the hospital; Colin recalls that rather than making a fuss of Sheila as his own mother did, June stood awkwardly at the door and said with a stiff smile, 'Who's a clever girl then?'[24]

Sheila looked at her mother, pained and deflated, then glanced away.

Despite the uncomfortable moment between mother and daughter at the hospital, when Sheila and the babies returned home June was a constant support, visiting at least once a fortnight. She and Nevill doted on their grandsons, while Jeremy proudly took his friends from college to meet his newborn nephews, Nicholas and Daniel, in Hampstead.

When Colin lost his job shortly after the twins were born, June paid for him to have driving lessons, and once he had passed his test he was able to drive his wife and children to stay at the farm while he searched for work. Sheila's friend Mairead Maguire, whom she had met on the antenatal ward, recalled: 'She said how much she enjoyed going there and getting away from it all. I formed the impression that her parents gave her anything she wanted.'[1] Mairead knew that Sheila's marriage was 'not a good one'. The twins were 'all she lived for'.

By November, Colin had fallen in love with Jan and moved out of the flat on Carlingford Road to live with his father. Sheila remained on good terms with Reg Caffell, but no longer saw her mother-in-law when they had words about something quite trivial shortly after Colin left. The two women were estranged for three years, although Doris saw her grandchildren whenever they were with their father.

Towards the end of the year, Colin and Jan bumped into Jeremy one evening in a London club. They spoke briefly; Jeremy was caught up in his own life, having lost the podgy look of his early teens and slimmed down, with high cheekbones and pale blue eyes below thick, light brown hair. He was suddenly attractive to both sexes, although his only sexual experience to date had been the usual teenage fumblings with girls at school.

'I seemed to mix with all the trendy girls most of the time as I was never a "beer with the lads" kind of bloke,' he reflects. 'I always had lots of gay friends too, though I'd mix easily with the young farmers locally, my friends generally were from a wide circle.'[2] While his relatives dispute that he was ever part of the

Young Farmers scene, his experiments with his appearance raised eyebrows in rural Essex. The flamboyant New Romantic fashions led aunts, uncles and cousins to speculate about his sexuality and label him an attention seeker.

Jeremy was a practical joker like his father – the two of them often compiled complex orders with farm reps only to cancel the lot at the last minute – but one of his pranks spoiled the close-knit college friendships. After collecting his friends Scott and Andrew for a night out in the old van he had acquired, he drove erratically on purpose, ignoring their shouts. 'The vehicle went off the road,' Scott remembered, 'causing some damage to the pickup van. There was a dispute as to who should pay for the damage. He offered free petrol from his grandmother's farm for the equivalent value of the money we owed, or rather the money he said we owed him.'[3] They refused to pay, telling Jeremy he was to blame. 'Our friendship ended there, much to my regret,' Scott reflected. 'Whilst I knew Jeremy he struck me as an extrovert, he was lively and fun to be with.'

Jeremy's studies came to an end at the same time. After failing his A levels he decided not to bother with re-sits, drifting aimlessly for a while. 'Jeremy never seemed to mould to a country life,' Peter Eaton recalled. 'He never used to associate with the young farmers or even socialise in the local pubs. I was around that time visiting White House Farm quite frequently, although Jeremy seemed to prefer to sit and watch television rather than hold a conversation.'[4] Michael Leyland noticed the same rootlessness and boredom when he visited at Christmas: 'Jeremy made it known that he didn't agree with a lot of the things that his parents and their friends approved of, such things as shooting for instance. His general attitude was that it would all come to him in the end, he wouldn't particularly have to work hard to get it.'[5]

His parents hoped that he would take over the tenancy of the farm when Nevill's contract with the owners (the Henry Smith Charity) expired in a few years' time. They were also optimistic that he would manage N. & J. Bamber Ltd, which had replaced Bamber & Speakman in the wake of June's father's death. Nevill's friend John Seabrook thought it unlikely that Jeremy would fulfil his parents' wishes: 'Over the years Jeremy did not take any particular interest in the farm which I feel must have disappointed Nevill to a certain extent, but Nevill was always prepared to give Jeremy a chance in anything he did and indeed gave constructive encouragement.'[6]

For a while at least, Sheila remained her parents' greatest worry. It was clear that she was suffering from undiagnosed post-natal depression as her first Christmas as a single mother approached, but in those days there was little professional help for the 'baby blues'. On 21 December 1979, she made a desperate call to Camden social services, telling them that she was scared she was going to hurt her children. A young female social worker was sent out to assess her and grasped very quickly that the twins were not in danger; their mother had used those words to secure her the help she needed.

The social workers assigned to Sheila were reminded of an exotic bird in a gilded cage. Despite being the most privileged client on their books, she was painfully lonely, with only her babies for interest and company on a day-to-day basis. At six months old, Nicholas and Daniel were peaky with heavy colds, but otherwise fine and related well to their mother. Sheila talked a great deal about how important it was to her to be fertile and about her relationship with June, then going through a particularly difficult spell. Still seething and bewildered over the breakdown of her marriage, she seemed a complex young woman, prone to melodrama but fragile and warm, eager to be around other people. Colin, with his laidback manner and liking for calm, had clearly been unable to cope with her emotional needs.

Camden social services decided the main priority was to provide her with respite from the twins and the chance to find work. But Sheila also admitted to 'temper tantrums' in which she inflicted injuries on herself and deliberately provoked Colin, and sometimes she had 'hallucinations and feelings of paranoia'.[7] She asked to be referred for psychoanalysis.

Colin acknowledged that it was easier for him to leave his marriage having met Jan, and that Sheila struggled afterwards. In February 1980, he and Jan began living together in an apartment on Well Road in Hampstead Village. He made a living from pottery making, using the garage space below a flat that Herbie owned in West Hampstead Mews as a studio. The twins stayed every weekend and occasionally during the week. Jan's parents adored Nicholas and Daniel; her brother treated them as younger siblings and was sympathetic to Sheila, 'a very soft, caring person, but a little distant from reality. I mean that not in a bad way, but rather from the point of view of being unorganised and a little lost.'[8]

Despite their problems, it was June who provided Sheila with most support, still visiting regularly to help with the twins and take care of household bills. On other occasions June would ask Nevill to collect their daughter and grandsons by car. Ann often invited her cousin and the boys to stay at her home, Oak Farm in Tolleshunt Major, finding that she and Sheila got on well together.

But under the weight of so many responsibilities, June's own fortitude began to sag. Travelling back and forth to London, assisting Sheila with the twins, taking care of her mother-in-law at the farm and regularly visiting her own elderly widowed mother, while keeping up with parochial duties, unsurprisingly proved a strain. 'I was aware that aunt June would welcome a rest,' Ann recalls. 'In fact, that situation was causing aunt June to spend more and more time at church and I was of the opinion that she was not getting much support from uncle Nevill.'[9] June's frustrations caused her to snap at her daughter. 'Sheila did at times hate staying at the farm,' Jeremy confirms. 'Her worst times were during her early twenties, when mum wasn't very well herself – she made Sheila feel very guilty for her marriage to Colin and then for it breaking up. I know it drove Sheila mad with anger over how mum made her feel so guilty about it all – and I felt it too, as I was used as the "why can't you be like Jeremy?", as I was a virgin until I was eighteen.'[10]

Undecided about a career and longing to travel, in July 1980 Jeremy departed for a working holiday in Australia and New Zealand.[11] His base for the first couple of weeks was a flat in Sydney, whose occupants happened to include Louise Carr, daughter of Osea Road manager James Carr. She disliked sharing her home with Jeremy: 'He was not interested in normal tourist pursuits or in finding work, his only interests seemed to be in the sunny weather and money.'[12] Jeremy then left for Brisbane, securing several months' employment on a sugar plantation in

Queensland before flying to New Zealand, where he stayed with relatives for a month. 'He lived a good life whilst he was in New Zealand,' his father's cousin Christopher (Chris) Nevill recalled. 'Jeremy was a very lively type of character, he made friends easily. I felt that he was quite extrovert.'[13] Years later, when he began his prison sentence in Wormwood Scrubs, Jeremy's creative writing tutor observed that the only spark of real enthusiasm he ever saw from him was when he spoke long and affectionately of Australia and New Zealand, composing poems filled with memories of the ocean, exotic birds and sunsets.

While Jeremy was abroad, June suffered a nervous collapse and moved in with Pamela and Robert for several weeks. Nevill's secretary at the time remembered that he was frustrated and upset by his wife's absence: 'He used to comment that he couldn't understand why she was away so long, that her place was with him on the farm.'[14] Yet nothing changed after June's return. She carried on as before, striving to care for everyone while neglecting herself, a pattern doomed to failure.

In summer 1980, Camden social services brought a 'day fostering' scheme into effect for Nicholas and Daniel. Far from fostering in the usual sense, it simply involved child-minding on a daily basis with extra support for Sheila. Twenty-three-year-old Judith Jackson, married with two children of her own, cared for the twins every weekday for a few hours. Her home near Parliament Hill Fields was a fifteen minute walk for Sheila and the twins; when Judith later moved to Highgate, social services arranged transport.

The two women became instant friends. Sheila seemed 'scatty and childish' but was 'a loving mother' and open about her problems.[15] She spoke lovingly of her father but described her mother as 'evangelical' and said little about her brother. Judith met him on one occasion when Sheila was ill and he called to take the twins back to White House Farm.

Gradually, Sheila began socializing again and asked Judith for advice on her appearance, wanting to look sophisticated. Her friend Sandra Elston recalls that although Sheila was beautiful, she still lacked confidence 'and was very gullible. I think a lot of people thought she was stupid but this was untrue. She adored her two children and they were very fond of her. She needed to be constantly reassured.'[16]

Sheila didn't go out often but when she did it was usually to Rags, Annabel's and the Purple Pussycat – nightspots that attracted a wealthy crowd. She joked to her cousin Sarah Howie that she hoped to meet a very rich man. Her first experience of dating again was with thirty-seven-year-old actor Don Hawkins, whom she met at a party in Leicester Square. He offered Sheila and her friend a lift home, bored with the party itself, and called the following day to apologize for being irritable. She visited him with the twins for tea and they dated for about four months until he ended the relationship, much to her disappointment.

At another party later that year Sheila met Farhad Emami, who remained involved with her on some level until the end. Known as Freddie to Sheila and her friends, he was born in Iran in 1944 and had travelled to London in his mid-twenties. After completing an English language course, he gained a diploma in catering from Exeter College and married a British-born woman in 1974. They returned briefly to Iran before settling in London with their daughter four years later, when Freddie ran a market stall on Kings Road and worked at the Savoy Hotel. He was employed as a restaurant manager when he and Sheila met at the home of a mutual friend.

Freddie always insisted that their relationship was platonic: 'Sheila needed someone to talk to when a decision needed to be made. From the first time I met her she struck me as being a little slow, unable to grasp simple things and the sort of person who relied on others to make decisions. She would bring her problems to me and we would discuss them. These problems were mainly family or money worries.'[17] But Sheila's family and friends recall a sporadic affair, with Freddie pursuing her. 'He bought her some very nice presents, clothes and things for the home,' Judith Jackson stated. 'Freddie seemed very sweet, a kind and gentle man.'

But Sheila was more interested in resurrecting her career. Judith's brother was an accomplished photographer and worked with Sheila on her new portfolio. In October 1980 she began approaching modelling agencies again and was taken on by Penny Personnel Management Ltd. Director Penny Cotton found

Sheila pleasant and well spoken, if 'a little withdrawn' and 'totally committed to looking after her children'.[18] Her first assignment was advertising Peugeot cars. In early December, she asked her social worker to extend the day care arrangements to give her more time for work. She had three advertising assignments in January 1981 with companies asking specifically for her, which Penny recognized was a sign that she was a good model. It was still not enough to enable Sheila to support herself, so she took a job as a domestic cleaner two days a week in a large property on Hampstead's Downshire Hill. Her employer thought her 'a very pleasant girl, very pretty, an honest and capable worker but I had to direct her in any work or chores that had to be done. She often seemed to be rather dizzy.'[19]

Sheila had also decided to search out her birth mother. Throughout her teenage years, she had fantasized about her, telling friends that she pictured someone young and chic. The possibility of establishing contact had been raised by Nevill and June, following new laws which enabled adoptees to access their original birth certificate once they reached eighteen. 'Our parents informed us that if we wanted to know who our real parents were, then we could contact the adoption agency,' Jeremy stated in 1985, adding that he 'chose not to know'[20] and that his sister's decision upset him because he knew that June would be secretly devastated: 'I recall crying at one point though the actual trigger is beyond my recall, though I know we argued and the whole thing made me angry in contrast to Sheila's happiness.'[21]

Jeremy's assertion that he didn't want to know about his natural parents contradicts his later statements and the recollection of a friend that 'he had read the files on his true parents'.[22] His cousin David declares: 'At different times both of them made an approach to their real parents. I think Jeremy got upset because his real parents didn't want to meet him.'[23] His wife Karen agrees: 'What must have hurt Jeremy terribly was finding his own parents and finding that after they'd had him and given him away, they got married and had other children.' David adds: 'I think I would find that a bit gutting too.'

Jeremy's birth father appeared on newsreels across the world in September 1984, one year before the Bamber murders. As a senior staff member at Buckingham Palace, Major Leslie

Marsham was seen attaching the formal proclamation of Prince Harry's birth to the Palace gates, chatting with royalists and the press. Jeremy has never mentioned whether he was aware of the connection at the time, but Karen Boutflour observes: 'I think, psychologically, rather than blame his own parents for giving him up for adoption, Jeremy blamed June and Nevill for adopting him.'

Jeremy arrived home from New Zealand on 15 June 1981, having lived abroad for almost a year. In the wake of the murders four years later, his relatives discussed the circumstances of his return with Essex Police, when their suspicions about his activities abroad may have been heightened by the shootings.

Robert Boutflour declared that, while in Australia, Jeremy had been 'associating with a man who had just come out of prison'.[1] David heard that he left the country 'in a hurry', having 'obtained some money' from Chris Nevill's sister.[2] Both Robert and Chris informed detectives that Jeremy's father had paid for his stay in New Zealand, but funds ran out during his journey home via the Middle East. He had then requested money from his parents, who sent him an air ticket instead. Other rumours included that he had spent ten days 'in Hong Kong or Singapore without a cent in his pocket', sharing a flat with two BOAC stewards before finally flying home.[3]

Jeremy dismisses the stories: 'The truth was that I always knew the date of my return from Australia prior to leaving the UK – I had a one year visa! The offer my mum made was I'd pay for my plane ticket to Australia, but as security in case it went wrong I'd always have a ticket home as she'd pay for that. As it happened I worked a lot while I was there and earned good money, and I purchased my ticket from selling my car in Adelaide and a couple of hundred bucks – and once home mum paid me back the cost of the return ticket. I think in total I was in Australia [and New Zealand] about 350 days – so there was nothing sinister, and no debt to mum and dad, and no leaving "in a hurry", it was simply the end of my year long visa.'[4]

Before he returned, a new secretary was taken on at the farm to replace the former one. Thirty-seven-year-old Barbara Wilson lived in Tolleshunt D'Arcy with her husband Keith – incapacitated after a recent accident – and their children. 'The Bambers were always very kind to me,' she declares. 'I looked on them as parent figures and took notice of any advice they gave me. Mr Bamber was a proper gentleman, always so even-tempered. Mrs

Bamber was very quiet but once you got her talking you could have a really good conversation. She was a sweet sort of lady.'[5] Barbara's unswerving loyalty to her employers was matched by Jean Bouttell, whose husband George had worked for Leslie Speakman after the war. In the early 1960s, Jean undertook seasonal work at the farm and became housekeeper in 1975, working three days a week.

Barbara was curious to meet Jeremy: 'The first time I really had any conversation with him, I thought he was so nice. *He* thought he was the bees' knees himself, although to be fair, he was a very pleasant-looking chap. Very jolly, really a nice guy to chat to, and he was like that most of the time. Until latterly. But in the early days he could charm the birds off the trees. He got on well with his parents then, and they bent over backwards trying to encourage him to take an interest in the farm.'

Living at home again, Jeremy joined a local committee chaired by his father to organize the village celebrations for the wedding of Prince Charles and Lady Diana Spencer. Virtually the entire population of Tolleshunt D'Arcy gathered at the recreation ground for a barbeque and fete, with Jeremy cooking and dishing out food. But family friends also remember friction within weeks of his homecoming.

His months in New Zealand had fired his passion for diving and he was eager to accept an offer to go into partnership with a scuba diving company. When Nevill refused to lend him the necessary finances, Jeremy enrolled in a diving school and took a job at the Little Chef near Witham. His parents were disappointed that he didn't want to work full time at the farm and equally bemused by the company he brought home. Agnes Low was present on one occasion: 'Jeremy's friend was most odd, he wore a very long coat and a feather through one ear. Jeremy introduced his friend, then spoke in a very effeminate manner about going for a bath and to wash his hair. I had never seen Jeremy act or speak in that manner before.'[6]

The innocuous encounter caused a further stir among his relatives, illustrating the widening gulf between how Jeremy wished to live his life and his family's conservative expectations of him. Sharply aware of it, Jeremy kept his first serious relationship secret for months, knowing his mother especially would be unlikely to accept his choice: a married mother-of-three, thirteen years his senior.

Sheila asked Penny Cotton to remove her name from the agency's books in August 1981, after four months without a modelling assignment. Penny was disappointed, feeling that Sheila could have worked more if she hadn't been a single mother of twins who always put her children first. Yet Sheila was convinced that the problem was her appearance. She visited her GP to request a breast augmentation and underwent surgery at Hammersmith Hospital.

Camden social services held a case conference about Sheila and the twins that August after a health worker expressed concern. Daniel had scalds on his cheek, knee and stomach, as well as an ear infection, and the health worker felt that Sheila was slow to seek medical attention unless prompted by someone. Social services found that the scalds were unquestionably accidental and that Sheila had in fact taken her son to hospital about the ear infection. Although she had a tendency to be forgetful and disorganized, her GP declared that she had no psychiatric history and her only medication had been night sedation. Colin and Jan also had a meeting with a social worker to discuss whether he ought to apply for full custody because 'Sheila was finding the pressures of motherhood difficult'.[7] They decided to continue as before, but he admitted noticing 'a slow change in her, she began to be less lively than she had been'.

Sheila ended her affair with Freddie Emami that summer and briefly rekindled her romance with Don Hawkins. She continued to visit wine bars and discotheques with friends in the West End, but nothing serious ever developed with the men she met. Although she responded to a few adverts in the 'Lonely Hearts' column of *Time Out* and even joined Dateline, the possibility of falling for someone was remote; she admitted to those closest to her that she was still in love with her husband.

'I fell in love with Sue,' Jeremy recalls. 'Mum was not impressed, though dad liked her.'

'Sue' was Suzette Ford, a Jersey-born woman in her early thirties. Married since 1969 to Geoff Ford, with whom she had two sons and a daughter, by 1981 she and her husband were growing apart. Sue worked most evenings as a barmaid in Colchester's Andromeda nightclub, where Jeremy was a fairly regular visitor. On a night off, Sue was sitting alone in the Frog & Beans wine bar in North Hill, Colchester when Jeremy walked in: 'He came over and started chatting. We went on to another nightclub for a few drinks and then he drove me home.'[8] Within days, they were seeing each other as often as commitments allowed.

'He seemed so sensitive, but was also a bit of a clown as well,' Sue recalled. 'After being married for thirteen years and having three children I found it marvellously refreshing to be with someone who didn't seem to have a care in the world. But I was almost old enough to be his mother.' Jeremy's prime concern was to hide the relationship from his parents: 'They were still very strict with him and he had to be home by a certain time or there would be trouble. I found it quite funny. He was making love to this much older woman every night and then going home because his parents didn't like him staying out late.'

Most of the early stages of the affair were played out at the Frog & Beans, which became the hub of Jeremy's social life. It was a place where friendships became blurred by one-night stands and romantic entanglements, including other extra-marital affairs. Jeremy's group of friends dated each other, often in secret while other relationships were still ongoing, and there were frequent alcohol-fuelled eruptions, yet the circle remained close-knit.

Central to the group were Michael Deckers and Malcolm Waters, who jointly owned the bar and allowed Jeremy to have drinks on the house in return for potatoes from the farm. Both in their early thirties, they seem to have viewed Jeremy as a slightly troubled younger brother, helping him out when necessary but vocal about his faults. Michael thought him immature, particularly in his complaints about his parents. Malcolm told the *Star* in 1986 that Jeremy was 'a Walter Mitty type. He dreams up situations and then convinces himself it's true. At certain periods he was very much a loner.'[9] He sensed that Jeremy was 'easily led and susceptible to others' and 'always looking for affection, especially from girls'.[10]

Malcolm's girlfriend was nineteen-year-old Elizabeth Rimington. Working at the Frog & Beans, she saw a lot of Jeremy and

Sue: 'They used to sit in the corner all night, drinking black coffee and gazing into each other's eyes. When Suzette was out with Jeremy, her unsuspecting husband used to babysit with the children.'[11] Another regular who became friendly with them was twenty-four-year-old salesman Mark Chard, who was initially wary of Jeremy because he created 'quite a sensation by wearing make up'.[12] Matthew McDonald remembered his first encounter with Jeremy for the same reason: 'He looked very bizarre because his face was covered in lady's make-up and [he wore] very bright red, skin-tight jeans.'[13]

Matthew, a thirty-seven-year-old self-employed plumber, would play an unwitting role in events to come. He had several criminal convictions, mostly for burglary, but renounced his lawless ways after marrying a young nurse in 1979. Meeting Jeremy at the Frog & Beans on Bonfire Night 1981, his primary interest was Sue's companion, Christine Bacon. The two women had known each other for years, becoming close friends through their children when they were neighbours. Christine had recently separated from her husband and began an affair with Matthew, who bonded with Jeremy over a taste for cannabis.

When Sue's husband moved out of the family home Jeremy moved in, presenting her with his childhood teddy bear as a gift. She described him in 1985 as 'very good' with her children, who were twelve, four and three years old at the time of the affair: 'They loved him. They still talk of him now, although they haven't seen him for quite a while. He'd play with them a lot. He used to love playing Lego with them.'[14]

Jeremy told his parents that he was staying with a friend in Colchester, but the truth caused uproar when it emerged. Sue believed the problem lay entirely with June, recalling that Jeremy got on well with his father, whom he referred to as 'Matey', and was proud of his work as a magistrate. But Nevill objected to the affair almost as strongly as his wife. Confronting his son with uncharacteristic severity, he warned Jeremy that if he didn't end the relationship, he could expect to be disinherited.

'That's typical of them, so bloody narrow-minded,' Jeremy fumed to Liz Rimington, adding that he had reluctantly promised to obey his father.[15]

Nevill and June were going through a difficult period themselves. June found Beatrice Bamber's habits, including only emerging from her bedroom at White House Farm for an hour or so during the evening for a sherry, increasingly stressful. Aware that his wife was struggling again, Nevill reluctantly placed his mother in an old people's home and took June on holiday to the Channel Islands, hoping to stave off a full breakdown.

Unbeknown to his parents, Jeremy had proposed to Sue, asking her to marry him when her divorce was granted. 'I was thrilled at that because I was so in love with him,' Sue recalled, 'but in my heart I thought it would never happen.' Jeremy's parents were deeply troubled when they found out; David Boutflour recalls that it caused June a great deal of heartache, while Bettine Thorp remembered that her friend refused to have Jeremy in the house until the relationship was finished.

The pendulum of June's anxiety swung from Jeremy to Sheila and back again. Unwisely, Sheila had mentioned to her mother that she had been on a handful of dates and, with that in mind, June called on her friend Henry Frost to discuss her daughter's flat: 'She felt that she was condoning Sheila's immoral behaviour by the fact that she owned the premises which Sheila was using in this way.'[16] He advised June 'to give the premises to Sheila as I knew that she could well afford to do so. I cannot recall if she was in tears when she discussed this matter with me but I have frequently seen her in tears when she discussed similar matters with my wife Joan.'

June disregarded his advice, but spoke to Pamela and Robert about the unofficial allowance she gave Sheila each month, fearing that her daughter was spending it on nights out rather than on food and bills. She told Agnes Low that she preferred to buy clothes for her grandsons rather than hand over the money, but didn't like to think of 'poor little Sheila' being unhappy either.[17]

Once more June began to flounder under the weight of her worries. When Beatrice Bamber passed away on the day before Christmas Eve, June's mental health deteriorated further, exacerbated by guilt. Nevill was given three months' leave of absence from his magisterial duties at the end of December to look after his wife. He explained to his colleagues that June had been 'very ill with a nervous breakdown' and it was 'going to take some time to get her back into running order again'.[18]

Recovering in the new year, June made a huge effort to overcome her troubles, inviting Sue to a family meal for Jeremy's twenty-first birthday. Together with John Wilkin and his second wife Daphne, they dined at Le Talbooth, a riverside restaurant in Dedham. Sue remembered Jeremy introducing her as his girl-friend: 'I could see it was a big step for him to do that. He also told them I was only thirty, although he did say I had been married and had three children. They were both very nice to me. Jeremy seemed fond of them both, although I know things were a bit strained with his mother.' But Daphne Wilkin recalled: 'During this evening, June Bamber told me how unhappy she was about his relationship and that she hoped they would not get married. She feared that the girl may have been after Jeremy's expectations.'[19]

In fact, the relationship was already in difficulties. While she and Jeremy were out in the car, Sue confessed that she had spent a night with Matthew McDonald, although they were both so drunk that no sex was involved. Jeremy was enraged; he couldn't vent his fury on Matthew, who was working abroad, but tried to push Sue from the car after the revelation and drove off at speed. Christine wasn't happy that her lover had intended to sleep with her best friend, but had no interest in listening to Jeremy's outbursts when he visited.

The couple parted for a month, dating other people from the Frog & Beans crowd. Jeremy began a relationship with a girl named Jane, whom he continued to see after reconciling with Sue. Jane found him very affectionate, even-tempered and generous without being extravagant. He told her that he had no intention of becoming a farmer and hoped to set up his own diving school in Australia one day. Jane ended the relationship when he suddenly started moving his belongings into her flat.

Jeremy and Sue were together again by the time Matthew arrived home from Libya. When a rumour began circulating that he had been involved in something more adventurous than the overseas building industry, Matthew did nothing to dispel the stories; Michael Deckers heard him boasting in the Frog & Beans about being a mercenary. Three years later Matthew admitted ruefully: 'There seemed to be some glamour in it . . . I've never been anywhere, I've never done anything in my life. I've never been the subject of anybody's admiration.'[20] Matthew and Christine's affair continued but the friendship between the two couples was spoiled. A year would pass before their paths crossed again, when the adage 'be careful what you wish for' came nightmarishly true for the older man.

With Freddie's help, Sheila succeeded in tracing her birth mother in spring 1982. The previous March she had contacted the Church of England Children's Society, who sent her a letter containing details of her birth family background. The information was to prove invaluable to her search.

Since emigrating to Canada in 1957, the Jays had led busy, fulfilling lives. In Montreal, Sheila's grandfather Eric Jay held a number of distinguished titles before retiring as Canon Emeritus in 1976. In 1958 he had written a study of New Testament Greek that was hailed as an instant classic; his son Peter emerged as a gifted Greek scholar at Lancing College in Sussex before winning a place at Oxford. While there he launched a poetry magazine, *New Measure*, which became the springboard for his publishing company, Anvil Press, established in 1968.

Sheila's birth mother Christine had married in 1967. Her husband Oscar Sykora, nine years her senior, left Czechoslovakia with his parents in 1948 when Communists took control of the country. In June 1959 he achieved the unprecedented feat of obtaining two doctor's degrees from two Montreal universities on the same day and was invited to dine with the Queen in Ottawa. By the time of his marriage to Christine, he was at the peak of his career as a leading dentist, historian and author. The couple settled in Nova Scotia and had three children.

Christine's husband was aware that she had given up a baby for adoption in England, but their children didn't know about Sheila, who made contact by telephoning her grandparents' apartment in Montreal. It was the middle of the night in Canada when Eric answered and Sheila explained who she was, asking for her birth mother's address. He suggested that she should write to Christine via them and they would pass on her letter. 'And so Christine's correspondence began with Sheila,' recalled Peter Jay, who first learned about his niece from his mother in 1978.[1]

'The biggest times of stress for Sheila were in the finding of and meeting with her natural mother, and in discovering why she

had been adopted,' social worker Barbara Babic stated.[2] Sheila's
first contact with Christine coincided with her divorce from
Colin in May 1982; for the next fifteen months, the couple's only
communication would be regarding their children. Sheila's GP
referred her to the community psychiatric nurse that month for
group therapy to help regulate her moods, although her social
worker saw no evidence of mental instability. But Sheila was suffering from depression and had begun to resent social services'
involvement in their lives. A pre-arranged case conference was
positive nonetheless, recording that she 'showed great affection
towards her children' and that no further measures were needed.[3]

Day care for Nicholas and Daniel had been transferred from
Judith Jackson to Patricia Lester in Camden. The boys were now
two-and-a-half years old. Nicholas, the slightly younger of the
two, was smaller than his brother, full of laughter and always
keen that people should be able to tell him apart from Daniel.
Most could, since he had a small scar on his left cheek from trip-
ping over a glass coffee table. Daniel was lively but more serious,
with a soft heart and sensitive to everyone's feelings. He loved
children younger than himself and had a doll that he liked to
cuddle and call his baby. Patricia remembered the boys as bois-
terous and needing a lot of attention, but extremely well brought
up.

June's own depression lingered. To ease the pressure, Pamela
engaged a live-in companion for their mother at Vaulty Manor,
but June continued to take on more responsibilities. She prepared
food for Meals on Wheels, helped run a pensioners' club, organized village functions, held fundraising activities for children's
charities, shared the cost of sponsoring a child in Rwanda with
friends, and joined the local prayer and Bible reading group who
met on Tuesday evenings.

The growing intensity of her religious beliefs prompted
varied responses from those closest to her. Janet Ashcroft served
on the parochial church council with the Bambers and remembered June was 'very dedicated to the church and very religious.
She got to the stage of banning a raffle, saying it was gambling.
She didn't like drinking and I can remember one occasion, we
were in the car when she stopped and said we should pray for a

safe journey.'[4] Barbara Wilson described her as 'a woman who believed in God and was not afraid to let people know it if circumstances dictated.' But she added, 'To my knowledge she never pushed religion towards anyone.'[5]

Today, Jeremy states that although his mother felt her beliefs 'with passion, and it did irritate me sometimes if mum was trying to persuade me to come to church or be more involved with Christianity, it did not define mum as a person, not by a country mile.'[6] Her great loves were nature and conservation. She refused to allow any hedge cutting while birds were raising their young and could identify most birds by song. 'Mum was gifted in flower-arranging too, and art,' Jeremy recalls. 'Like me, mum loved Barbara Hepworth – my love of sculpture came from her.'

He believes June's interest in religion sprang from her intellect and circumstances: 'Much of mum's enjoyment of the church came from companionship and the intellectual study of the bible. Mum was really intelligent but part of her mental illness was being so unfulfilled intellectually. The bible studies really helped her find meaning and purpose in her life.' In that sense, there was no link between his mother and sister's mental health problems: 'My Mum didn't suffer from schizophrenia, she suffered from depression. That was from not being able to have children . . . that hurt her. She found that very, very difficult. And I think she wanted more than just being a housewife and a mother. She was a very intelligent woman and I think she found that cleaning and providing meals, and just flower arranging for the local church, not fulfilling enough. Religion's a great filler of empty space. And of want and desire.'

By the end of May 1982, June's depression was so acute that she was admitted again to St Andrew's Hospital in Northampton. A BBC film about mental health care in 1981 compared the hospital to 'a stately home . . . There's almost an atmosphere of luxury about it.'[7] Patient numbers averaged about 400; long-term residents had included James Joyce's daughter Lucia, who died at St Andrew's in 1982 after many years of confinement.

June's consultant psychiatrist, Dr Hugh Cameron Ferguson, was then in his early fifties and had worked at the hospital for four years: 'I found her very intelligent, self-contained and likeable. She had a kind of gravitas. Her husband was very

level-headed and obviously devoted to her. He told me that it
was a nasty depression she had, that she was deeply religious and
how worried he was about her.'[8] Letters, phone calls and visits
were encouraged at St Andrew's. 'In those days it had a very well
appointed short stay admission unit,' Dr Ferguson declares.
'Standards were very high. It was a precursor to the "Priory"
type of place.'

Robert Boutflour visited his sister-in-law and found her agitated: 'She was convinced that the staff were listening to us and
in order to pacify her I took her into my car in the car park
and we talked there. June was convinced that she was going to
die at the hospital and insisted that she wrote her will out.'[9] June
had already drawn up a will legally a few years before but on
20 May 1982 she wrote to Robert:

> In case – I am not <u>well.</u>
>   I hereby authorise my sister Pam Boutflour to take care
> of any money or properties I have and I validate the money
> (the sum of £10,000) which is a mortgage to my daughter
> Sheila – this is to be given to her.
>   I also release to my husband anything held in the Farm.
>   signed by June Bamber.[10]

Dr Ferguson diagnosed paranoid psychosis, which distorted 'her
already strong religious beliefs' until she saw 'everything in terms
of good and evil'.[11] He explains:

> A psychotic depression is where a person has more than the
> usual depression and depletion of energy, concentration and
> memory, feelings of worthlessness and despair, and the sense
> of loss and futility that goes with clinical depression. It's not
> just that a person is unhappy because upsetting things are
> happening to them. It goes beyond that – reality itself is
> altered. The content is likely to come from what is there
> anyway, which in June's case was her religiosity. She didn't
> have a healthy focus on religion. That's why I gave her ECT.

Electric shock therapy had formed part of June's treatment
during her earlier admission to St Andrew's in 1958, although
her psychiatrist was unaware of that at the time. 'But it was
probably for the same reasons that I used it,' he states. 'To me,

the only criteria for administering ECT is a psychotic depression. I have never given ECT to someone who was clinically depressed because it doesn't work and it's not without side effects. But psychotic depression responds very well to ECT. It can be very effective in those cases. June had a good response to it. The reality testing was normal. Her mood improved.' June had around six sessions of electroshock and was encouraged to talk through her emotions at length. She said little about her family, however. 'She may well have discussed her unease about Sheila, but I don't remember any details,' Dr Ferguson reflects. 'She did mention her son but there was nothing to suggest there were any deep-seated problems there. But then again, I didn't enquire.'

While his wife was in hospital, Nevill accepted the Wilkins' invitation to dinner, confiding that he was deeply worried. 'He told us that June was convinced that she had a brain tumour,' Daphne recalled. 'She did at the time suffer headaches but I don't think there was medical evidence to support this belief of hers.'[12] Nevill rarely spoke about his private troubles, but family friend Anne Hunter also remembered him divulging, 'June is not the girl I married 30 years ago,' and that he felt the vicar had 'more influence' over his wife than he did.[13]

To Nevill's relief, June's depression was brought under control within a month. 'She responded well to treatment,' Dr Ferguson confirms. 'She maintained her improvement and settled back into her life. She was on medication and continued with that, supervised by her GP.' June's friends and family were pleasantly surprised when she returned. Farm secretary Barbara Wilson thought she seemed 'a lot better. She was much brighter. We didn't see so much of her to start with, but gradually she improved and we saw more of her. She would ask me down for coffee at the kitchen table and she started having various charitable functions again.'[14]

The £10,000 to which June had referred in her hospital letter was a loan to Sheila, secured by a mortgage on the apartment she and the twins moved into at the end of July 1982. The flat on Carlingford Road held too many unhappy memories; Jeremy recalls that his sister 'believed her insecurity and depression stemmed from the house'.[15] Her new home at 2 Morshead

Mansions was on a quiet street in Maida Vale and was a spacious, three-bedroom flat with a separate dining room. Sheila turned the smaller bedroom into a colourful playroom and decorated the walls of the living room with antique Chinese plates borrowed from home. 'She appeared very happy, as did the children,' Freddie remembered. 'In fact, the only person who was not happy was Colin, who had told her he was worried in case she could not afford to run the flat.'[16]

Reg Caffell kept a fatherly eye on Sheila, helping with practicalities such as fixing the central heating and collecting shopping. Sheila occasionally asked him to meet the twins from nursery while she went job hunting, having handed in her notice as a cleaner in Hampstead before the move. She was determined to make a fresh start.

Jeremy flew out to New Zealand on 2 August 1982.[17] While his previous trip had been the subject of much discussion afterwards among his relatives and friends of the family, his second visit provoked a barrage of suspicion from the moment he left.

Robert Boutflour later informed Essex Police that Nevill had expressed concern about his son's unexpected departure in the middle of the harvest but Jacqueline Pargeter recalled otherwise. She told detectives that her uncle was aware of Jeremy's plans to travel and had loaned him several thousand pounds for a course in deep-sea diving, with the cash subsequently disappearing. Jeremy informed his father that he had given the money to a friend, who had failed to repay it. Robert also heard that Jeremy had demanded further funds from his mother, who sent around £1,500 to cover the cost of his course but refused to send more.

When questioned by Essex Police in 1985, Jeremy refuted the claims, declaring that his father had told him that 'he wouldn't mind when or if ever the money came back . . . it was forgotten about'.[18] Their enquiries revealed that Jeremy had signed up for a course in deep-sea diving in New Zealand but retracted his application due to insufficient funds. At the time, a rumour spread among family and friends that he had failed the medical: David Boutflour heard Jeremy had been forced to abandon 'diving for pearls' because of a fractured skull due to either falling or being dropped as a child.[19] June's friend Agnes Low echoed that Jeremy blamed his mother for dropping him on his head when he was a baby.

Jeremy was still living with Sue Ford when he left for New Zealand. As far as she knew, he had gone to visit a friend named Geoff Reeves, whom he'd met during his flight home the previous year. According to Sue, Jeremy telephoned from a stopover point two days after his departure; he was deeply unhappy, wanting to return home and marry her. But he didn't return, calling her again from Auckland. 'Something had gone wrong between himself and Jeff [sic],' she remembered. 'He had moved out of Jeff's flat and moved upstairs with a man called Brett Collins.'[20]

Eight years older than Jeremy, Auckland-born Brett was a restless extrovert with a taste for clubbing, expensive cars and antiques. Reasonably wealthy, he had shares in a Brisbane restaurant while his brother owned an executive cars dealership. Brett later told detectives that he had allowed Jeremy the rent-free use of the flat below his own for three months: 'At that time he had almost $2,000 and that didn't seem a vast amount to give away.'[21] It was a curious statement which enquiries were unable to resolve; although Brett insisted that Jeremy hadn't given him the money intended for his diving course, Sue heard otherwise from Jeremy himself.

Detectives also questioned Brett about the precise nature of his relationship with Jeremy. He replied that it was 'non-sexual' and that although he himself was bisexual, 'I have never entered into any form of homosexuality with him.'[22] Jeremy told Sue that 'he had spent one night in bed with Brett and nothing had happened and that he could handle the situation.'

Eventually, Jeremy left for Queensland with Brett, working as a cocktail barman. Brett taught him how to body surf and they indulged their love of cannabis together. It emerged in 1985 that Brett had convictions for drug offences and Essex Police also received information about Jeremy dealing while in New Zealand. Both men emphatically denied the allegations.

There were other stories: Julie Mugford later told police that Jeremy had disguised himself to rob a jewellers, stealing the two Cartier watches he brought home from his travels. Detectives were unable to determine how he had obtained the watches and

Jeremy refused to give a straight answer when questioned. Julie mentioned further thefts: 'Jeremy used to take diamonds from people's rings by conning them, although I do not know how, and replacing the diamond with a glass stone. He would then sell the stones for cash.'[23] Brett admitted that Jeremy had 'four or five small rose-cut diamonds' when they first met but was unable to say how he had acquired them.[24] Jeremy acknowledged that he had 'some diamonds' in New Zealand but refused to be drawn on their origin.

Then there was fraud. Julie informed police that Jeremy had arranged for a friend to cash his traveller's cheques, then reported it as theft, but 'the bank were suspicious and Jeremy had to stand on an ID parade'. The news filtered home, with slight embellishments and some confusion about Jeremy asking his father for funds to replace 'a stolen wallet'.[25] Barbara Wilson recalls: 'We had to send money to him. I don't know what happened but he did get into trouble. We sent quite a lot of money.'

Essex Police confirmed that detectives in New Zealand suspected him of a scam, but he had fled the country before they caught up with him. Jeremy's cousin Jacqueline recalled him arriving home much earlier than expected; Nevill told her that 'something' had occurred in New Zealand, but didn't explain further. David Boutflour heard from someone that Jeremy 'was implicated in an armed robbery and killing' but police investigations uncovered no evidence of either.[26]

While Jeremy was away, Sue Ford had sold her house. She was staying at a Colchester hotel when he suddenly turned up, handing her a kangaroo skin purse and telling her to open it. Inside were the two Cartier watches. As Sue chose the watch she liked best, Jeremy told her he had bought them 'at Orly Airport'.

Jeremy's second trip to the other side of the world seems to have marked a turning point in his behaviour. Clearly, something went wrong even before he reached New Zealand, where he retracted his application for the diving course, apparently 'loaning' the substantial funds his father had given him to his new friend Brett Collins. He acquired the Cartier watches in dubious circumstances and put in a false claim for stolen traveller's cheques, leaving the country before the police could catch up with him.

Whatever occurred had unnerved him. He returned home craving security and willing to work harder than he ever had before. When things settled down, he changed again, shrugging off some of the responsibility he had accepted and behaving erratically in relationships. His second stay in New Zealand revealed a devious streak in his character that might have surprised even Jeremy himself.

Sheila was in very good spirits after the move to Maida Vale, according to her neighbour Christine Finlay, an unmarried secretary in her late forties. Meeting her natural uncle, Peter Jay, that summer, she began socializing more, placing an advert in the local newsagents' window for a babysitter. It was answered by Lea Wood, in her early twenties, who would arrive after the twins had been put to bed, allowing Sheila to spend an occasional evening at her favourite wine bar in Holland Park. 'She was one of those people who was never on time,' Lea recalled, 'and always asked me how she looked before she left.'[1]

Sheila and the twins came briefly under the care of Westminster social services following the move. Her new social worker observed that Sheila ('a heavy smoker of cigars') was very focused on becoming a successful model.[2] A favourable evaluation of her care of the twins led to Westminster social services closing their file on the family in December 1982. That same month, Nicholas and Daniel began attending Carlton Hill nursery in St John's Wood, where they were regarded as quiet, but always content and very well looked after.

Sheila took the boys to White House Farm for Christmas. Her father's cousin Chris Nevill had arrived from New Zealand and got on very well with Sheila and the twins. He was less impressed with Jeremy, feeling that he was 'condescending to put in an appearance' and 'seemed to treat his mother in particular like dirt'.[3] Others disagreed, believing that Jeremy was making an effort to settle down. His relationship with Sue began to falter; although she initially found Jeremy 'more intense' and sensed that 'something had happened' to him during his travels, he started to go out alone more and 'things started to cool off'.[4]

Christine Bacon described his relationship with Sue as always 'very stormy. They were both quite hot-tempered people. I know that Jeremy showed some aggression towards both Suzette and her children.'[5] Sue disputed the claims: 'Jeremy has never been violent towards me and he has never hit me. He has been angry with me on occasions but we usually provoked each other.' She insisted that their relationship might have endured but for out-side negativity, and cited the failure of their 'desperate' wish to have a child together as another factor: 'I got pregnant three times but miscarried each time in the third month. He was extremely upset about that and I suspect that had something to do with our eventual break up.'[6]

Jeremy began putting in long hours at the farm. When Barbara Wilson arrived for work one morning, Nevill appeared especially cheerful, telling her, 'Jeremy worked very late last night. I actually think he's turned a corner, Barbara.'

'Oh that's nice to know,' she replied.

Nevill gave a broad smile: 'Yes, he really has pulled out all the stops.'

Privately, Barbara had reservations: 'Jeremy always had an ulterior motive in everything he did. I think he was trying to make Mr Bamber think well of him so that he would offer him a higher wage or a new car – that sort of thing.'[7]

Nonetheless, Jeremy and his father did become closer. They were regulars at Cues Snooker Club in Colchester, where Jeremy was already a member. Owner Paul Osborne regarded him as 'a very polite and quiet person. I enjoyed his company and he was not at all offensive. From what I saw of him in his father's company, I would say that they appeared to have a good relationship.'[8] Graham Johnson, secretary of North Maldon Growers, was surprised when Nevill informed him that Jeremy would act as crop sampler for the company that year; it entailed rising about 5am to walk through the fields, pulling up ten of the biggest plants in each field and removing the largest bean, then measuring the seed and reporting back. The process took around four hours to complete.

In recognition of his efforts, June asked her fellow directors at Osea Road to permit Jeremy a more active role at the caravan site. In March 1983, they agreed that he should sit in on their meetings. By then the site had expanded considerably, with over 500 static caravans dotted about the fields of the Blackwater Estuary, close to the water's edge. Many had been privately bought; the owners paid an annual rent to Osea Road for use of the land. Mabel Speakman had transferred all her interest in the company to June and Pamela, who owned 42 per cent each.

The remaining 16 per cent was divided equally between Jeremy and Ann. Having worked at Osea Road in some capacity since her teenage years, Ann was made a director in 1977 and helped manage the park. She recalled that Jeremy 'was pressing' to be made a director himself: 'He kept saying, "Go on, Ann, you go so I can be made a director" and I said to my father Jeremy keeps going on and on about it.'[9]

Robert believed that Jeremy's interest in Osea Road was purely pecuniary: 'He fully understood the value of money in life. At the caravan site meetings he was always on his best behaviour and at the AGMs he would have had the books and knew how much his mother and my wife Pam received from the site's profits. As a result he was aware that my wife gave Ann and her husband half of her profits. At one of the AGM's I recall Jeremy asking June why she didn't give him more and I recall she replied something like, "Not until you learn to live properly."'[10]

One conversation with Jeremy about Osea Road made Ann uneasy. Discussing an argument with Nevill over the cost of a new perimeter fence, Jeremy told her, 'Never mind Ann. It'll be yours and mine in two years' time.'[11] When Ann asked him to explain, he replied, 'Just you wait and see.' She was also concerned about Jeremy's intimation 'that he would have a larger share than me and I had always thought that when we did take it over it would be on an equal footing'.

Nevill and June seemed encouraged by his new work ethic nonetheless. It was one less worry at a time when Sheila's behaviour was proving increasingly troubled. The catalyst was an accident involving Nicholas in May 1983, following a turbulent visit to White House Farm. Sheila had returned with her sons by train and took a taxi home. At some point during the journey, probably as the taxi came to a stop, Nicholas tumbled out, sustaining a minor head wound. He was examined at Paddington Green Children's Hospital, where the practice was to call in a social worker for all children's injuries. Susan Elliott-Brown found Sheila with Daniel at Nicholas's bedside. She 'seemed a little depressed' and 'and welcomed the opportunity to have a chat'.[12] The matter had been reported to Paddington Green police station, with 'no suggestion of non-accidental injury', and Sheila 'related well with her children on the ward'.

Afterwards, Sheila told a friend that during her visit to the farm prior to the accident, her mother's 'desire to impose religion' on the twins had led to a furious argument.[13] The boys were 'frightened' and Sheila had insisted they leave. In the taxi from the train station, she had been in a ferment and wasn't concentrating on the children, 'only on her mother's religious rantings'.[14] She blamed herself for Nicholas's accident, which Freddie described as 'the final straw' to the breakdown that she had been 'building up to . . . for some time'.

When Sheila visited the farm again, Barbara Wilson noticed how much 'quieter and withdrawn' she had become, seeming to 'change personalities'.[15] Privately, Sheila had begun to dwell on thoughts of God and the devil and felt 'caught up in a coven of evil' with her mother.[16] Returning to London, she began hearing voices telling her that she was someone else – always a figure of unassailable virtuousness: Joan of Arc or, on one occasion when she kept her father on the telephone all night, the Virgin Mary.

She sought help from her GP, Dr Myrto Angeloglou, who made an appointment for her at the Royal Free Hospital psychiatric out-patients clinic. Nevill and June insisted that she should be referred to Dr Ferguson instead, and on 2 August Sheila visited him at his consulting rooms in Devonshire Place. He recalls that she was 'very agitated and psychotic', plagued by 'disturbed, delusional thoughts and over-valued ideas that she accepted as truth'.[17] She had been in a state of 'acute psychosis' for at least a fortnight, and 'depressed and unconfident' for the previous eighteen months, with 'an increasing sensitivity about other people'.[18] He conferred with her parents before admitting her to hospital: 'They were quite clear that she had not committed any acts of violence, but they were of course extremely worried about her.'[19]

On 4 August 1983, a little over a year since June had been discharged as a patient, Sheila entered St Andrew's. She was accommodated in Isham House, overlooking the golf course; it was 'a modern block, acting as the admissions area and forming one of two acute units dealing with such disorders as depression, alcoholism and eating problems'.[20] The individual rooms were functional, in plain beech with neat divans and wall-mounted televisions, and private bathrooms. A week's stay with treatment cost around £300 a week.

During the consultations that followed, Dr Ferguson observed that Sheila's problems had begun two or three years earlier, when she became 'more liable to misinterpreting the world around her, to draw the wrong conclusions, to feel threatened in some way, particularly with the concept of good and evil.'[21] Two weeks prior to admission, Sheila had grown 'more acutely disturbed', feeling that she was 'evil, and at risk of being affected by evil in some way' until eventually 'her control over these ideas was overwhelmed.' The delusions appeared to stem from her relationship with June and her standards of good and evil; she saw June as 'a threat' and shunned the farm on occasion.[22] Even when Sheila felt relatively better, she remained 'uneasy' about her mother's 'very censorious' views.[23]

Today, Dr Ferguson is at pains to point out that although Sheila found her mother's beliefs difficult to handle, June was not culpable for her illness: 'I think Sheila's delusional thoughts would have been shaped by her mother's religiosity but that wouldn't have happened if she hadn't been schizophrenic.' During her first admission, Sheila was diagnosed with a schizo-affective disorder because although the feelings she expressed were 'clear symptoms of paranoid schizophrenia', there appeared to be less mood disturbance with her ideas. Dr Ferguson later stated that the first diagnosis was mistaken, declaring himself firmly convinced that she suffered from paranoid schizophrenia.

He identified the root of Sheila's obsession with good and evil as the 'devil's child incident', which had lingered painfully in her mind. As a result, she believed herself to be inherently evil with an ability to 'create evil in others'.[24] She was 'particularly caught up with the idea that the devil had taken her over, giving her the power to project the devil's evil not only onto other people, but particularly her twin sons'. She feared being able 'to create in her two sons a source of ability to have sex with her or to do violence with her'. She then began 'to perceive in them other malign, adult intelligence' which they projected onto her until she was 'at risk of having to have sex with them or to join with them in some violence'. It was an extension of her troubled thinking of the past two years, in which she had felt 'particularly uneasy in the acts of masturbation and had other eerie feelings that she was sharing this with her baby sons'. In the fortnight prior to her hospital admission, Sheila's delusions became more vivid and real; she thought her sons would 'seduce' her and saw 'evil in both of them'. She especially feared that Nicholas was becoming 'a woman hater' and 'potential murderer'.

Colin later found it almost impossible to believe that Sheila had such thoughts, even while ill, and concluded that the medical professionals to whom she had spoken might be 'overreacting' to 'completely innocuous situations'.[25] Four-year-old Nicholas and Daniel were lively children, but with a gentleness that everyone recognized, including Sheila herself. Her otherwise normal, healthy thoughts about her sons had become entangled with her anxieties about June's puritanical ideas regarding sexuality and the threat of 'bad blood'.

Sheila's delusions also sprang from an era in which religious horror and the idea of 'Devil's spawn' dominated literature and cinema: *Rosemary's Baby* (1968), *The Exorcist* (1973), *The Omen* (1976) and *Carrie* (1976) are the best-known examples of a prolific genre. June was an admirer of evangelical preacher Billy Graham, who railed publicly against such films. The early 1980s phenomenon of 'Satanic Panic' saw parents being urged to be vigilant for signs that their children were drawn to devil worship. Bizarre indictors ranged from playing Dungeons & Dragons to listening to Judas Priest. The concept entered mainstream adult psychotherapy, with children forcibly removed from loving homes to protect them from imagined satanic abuse. *Michelle Remembers* (1980), written by a psychiatrist and his former patient about her alleged escape from a satanic cult, became a worldwide best-seller.

But such hysteria is noticeably absent from a letter Sheila wrote to Colin shortly after her hospital admission, in which she expresses sorrowful, tender concern for her children: 'I've been worried that the boys will have problems in their future life with girlfriends etc. I look so horrible sometimes that they must think I don't want them to have a good time, which is just what I do want them to do . . . I never would have thought I could become so insular a person, I love the boys as much as I ever did but something is stopping me from feeling free to be myself.'[26]

Dr Ferguson observed that Sheila had 'a very wide area of

disturbed thinking going beyond the twins. In fact, she felt that people could read her thoughts and be shocked by them.' [27] She sensed that she was being 'persecuted or watched, or in some way being threatened', but there were never any instances in which she was violent; instead, she was bewildered. Although Sheila was not 'actively suicidal', she talked to Dr Ferguson of the need for 'exorcism' or 'brain cleansing' and if there was no hope of that, then she 'would want to die'.

Sheila's relationship with Nevill was deemed crucial to her recovery. Dr Ferguson referred to him in his notes as her mentor, providing 'a very secure, caring and strong support'. Today he reflects: 'I used the word "mentor" in relation to her father but it wasn't the appropriate word, really. He was a strength and shield. Sheila really loved him and had the best of feelings that one has towards another human being. He was everything he could have been to her – kind, fatherly, protective.'[28] In contrast, even when Sheila was no longer delusional, 'she still had problems with her mother's fairly fixed and rigid ideas. She had a worry of her disapproval.' There appeared to be no problems in Sheila's relationship with Jeremy. Her treatment at St Andrew's was based on anti-psychotic medicines, together with therapy, 'unburdening herself, thinking out loud, of being taken seriously and surrounded by people who cared'. Dr Ferguson strongly refutes Jeremy's claim that Sheila was given 'major' electric shock therapy: 'I wouldn't have given ECT to her. She wasn't a candidate for ECT, ever.'

Towards the end of her stay, Sheila was overjoyed when Colin brought the twins to visit. Staying with their father, they showed no ill effects from the disruption, which included being temporarily removed from their nursery. Among Sheila's other visitors were her parents and brother, and she was reconciled with Colin's mother, but had no desire to see anyone else.

As part of her recovery, Sheila was prescribed Stelazine, which blocks dopamine receptors in the brain; psychotic conditions, particularly schizophrenia, are thought to be caused by dopamine over-activity. In an explanatory letter to her GP, Dr Ferguson summarized Sheila's initial sense of the world being 'a frightening place', that she believed she had 'evil in her mind', that her adoptive mother 'also had evil in her mind, and that both would need this evil to be cleansed'.[29] He described her 'morbid thoughts' upon admission and how she had expressed 'a measure of doing violence to her children ... that she was capable of murdering them or communicating some ability for them to become evil or murderers at a later date.'

Sheila was discharged on 10 September 1983. Dr Ferguson was confident that she had responded well to treatment and had rebuilt a normal relationship with her sons. Today he reflects that Sheila had made 'a partial recovery' upon leaving St Andrew's: 'She was not deluded or hallucinating. She was discharged to go home with her parents for a few weeks before returning to London. She needed a place of safety, which I think the farm was, albeit not somewhere that she could have lived permanently. Sheila knew her parents cared about her. And when she was well, she was truly lovely. She had a kind of naivety, a sweetness of spirit. Deep down she was somewhat immature, although of course she was very young anyway.'[30]

Nevill and June did not discuss their daughter's illness with anyone. Jacqueline Pargeter later told detectives: 'My uncle and aunt were very private people and would therefore keep private family business within the confines of the close family.' Jeremy admits that neither he nor his parents understood Sheila's illness: 'What it was or how it actually manifested itself – we never discussed it as a family and so were all ignorant of the "hows and wherefores" of schizophrenia. We should have done some research and learnt all we could – but I guess we just thought that you pay specialists for that.'[31] His reaction was to dismiss Sheila as 'going bonkers': 'That was the term that we had as a family. "Go bonkers." I saw it as a bit of a joke – "pull yourself together" – and I share guilt. I feel guilty for lots of things. I feel guilty for not being a better brother.' [32]

Matthew McDonald called at White House Farm in autumn 1983 with a small bag of hemp seeds, which he exchanged with Jeremy for some marijuana. He called twice again, once on a similar errand. Oblivious to their son's continuing penchant for mild drugs, Nevill and June offered Jeremy a permanent position at the farm, together with a home of his own.

That meant redundancy for David Foakes, who had worked there for twenty-five years; he and his wife Jill lived next door to his brother Len and family in the cottages on Pages Lane. David accepted the change and was able to keep his home, but his mother was less fortunate. Kate Foakes lived at Bourtree Cottage, a semi-detached house with a large garden on Head Street in Goldhanger, owned by Nevill. 'Jeremy wanted that house badly,' Barbara Wilson recalls. 'It wasn't quite "just kick the old biddy out", but it was along those lines.'[1] Nevill gave Kate Foakes six months' notice and found her alternative accommodation in the village.

Jeremy moved out of White House Farm before then, renting a room in Michael Deckers' house in Lexden. Michael's girlfriend Liz Rimington and his business partner Malcolm Waters also shared the property. The two men had sold the Frog & Beans and were running Sloppy Joe's, an American-style pizzeria on Colchester High Street, with Liz as manager. Jeremy worked behind the bar most evenings after finishing his shift on the farm. Temporary staff were employed as Christmas approached, including former Frog & Beans waitress Karen Napier. She and Liz had been friendly with the other new waitress for years; her name was Julie Mugford.

Dr Ferguson arranged to see Sheila as an out-patient after she returned to London, but recommended further treatment on the NHS. The Bambers disregarded his advice, preferring Sheila to visit him at Devonshire Place. Nicholas and Daniel began attending nursery again in October, after moving back in with their mother who found afternoon work in a clothes shop on the King's Road. When Sheila lost her job through poor time-keeping, she contacted Freddie for financial help. 'She appeared well in herself, although you could see she had not completely recovered,' he recalled.[2]

One of the most positive developments in Sheila's life was her friendship with Tora and David Tomkinson, whose daughter Chloe attended nursery with the twins. Ten years her senior, the Tomkinsons lived a short walk from Morshead Mansions. Sheila began chatting to Tora at nursery and introduced herself as Bambi, the name she had started using instead of 'Bambs'. Tora remembers: 'The first time I met Bambi, I just thought: "Wow!" She was so lovely – a very warm, open person. She had huge, beautiful eyes. I thought she and Colin were still together when I saw them with the twins. He was devoted to his sons and would pop in to make sure the boys and Bambi were okay. I know he loved Bambi too – and she was definitely still in love with him. But he was a bit more grounded than she was, perhaps. She got on well with Colin's parents, who were very good to her.'[3]

Tora found she had much in common with Sheila: 'She lacked confidence and so did I. We both had wonderful adoptive fathers and hard-to-please mothers. We talked endlessly about these things. Bambi's mother was very critical of her, even to me. She would say, "Oh, Sheila just doesn't know how to cope." It wasn't true, but the criticism wore Bambi down. Whenever June was at Bambi's flat, she would marshal the twins about, telling them what to do and what not to do. I said at one point, "Look, it doesn't matter about the cups," or whatever it was she was fussing over. She seemed to regard herself as a country lady and was frightened to lose control, I suppose. She was very dogmatic.' Tora never saw Sheila stand her ground against June except on one occasion: 'Her mum rang about something to do with the boys and I heard Bambi say firmly, "That's *not* what I want to do." I was amazed. Afterwards I asked, "Can you say what happened?" because I was so taken aback. Bambi just said, "Mum's always telling me what to do but they're *my* children."'

Sheila much preferred visits from her father, 'but he couldn't come more often because he was tied to the farm. She loved him very much and felt sorry for him because he was gregarious but had been forced to forgo most of his social life because June didn't like to go out to dinners and dances. Jeremy didn't really get on with their mother either. She didn't approve of his life-style. Bambi told me that he could never do right and he resented not being more involved in running the farm. She was quite in awe of him. He was very handsome and a bit arrogant. I only met him once, in passing, at Bambi's flat. He had very piercing eyes. Bambi told me that he had a nasty temper. She said, "I try to keep on the good side of him. He frightens me. I don't know what it is. But it's there."'

Tora's husband David describes the twins as 'always full of energy. They loved to dress up and play in the garden here and very often we'd all go swimming at the leisure centre. Sheila would jump into the pool and splash about happily with them. We used to go for day trips to Brighton and places like that. She used to give terrific children's parties as well – they were really the *best* parties.'[4] Tora agrees: 'Bambi loved children and was a very caring mum. Dan and Nick had really taken to our daugh-ter Chloe and sometimes they came here for a sleepover. Our son Tim was only a baby then. Whenever the little guys stayed, before leaving Bambi would say to them, "Are you going to stay here all night? *Really?*" I'd tell her, "Leave them be, they're fine." Then she would ring up not long afterwards and say, "Hi, it's me, Bambi, are the guys alright? Are they asleep yet?" The next day she would bring all the children presents. The boys always used to say, "Isn't our mummy beautiful?" They were so proud of her and they meant the world to her.'

Tora believes Sheila's problems stemmed from having 'very little confidence even though she was so beautiful – her photos don't do her justice at all. One evening she turned up looking wonderful and wearing incredibly high heels but said doubtfully, "Do I look alright?" I said, "Alright? You look *stunning*. I'll help you down the stairs in those heels." We tottered down the stairs and outside. All the cars started going, "Beep, beep!" It was as if Sophia Loren had suddenly emerged. But Sheila asked, "Oh dear – what's wrong?" I said to her, laughing, because she really *didn't* know, "It's because you look so beautiful."'

The only man Tora ever saw Sheila with apart from Colin was Freddie: 'He seemed okay. He used to get a bit fed up with her when she was being scatty, but he was good for Bambi in respect of her mother, telling her to ignore any criticisms. But I still always hoped she would find someone who truly appreciated her. Someone who would give her confidence without intruding, someone to love her and let her enjoy her time with her children. She just needed time to breathe.'

On Boxing Day 1983, with a nudge from Liz Rimington, Jeremy invited Julie to dinner at the house in Lexden. Afterwards he took her home; Julie's mother and stepfather lived in the same Colchester suburb. Mary Mugford's first impression of her daughter's new boyfriend was that he was 'odd. I told Julie I thought he was a homosexual but she said, "Oh no, mummy."'[5]

Born on 26 August 1964 in Middlesex, Julie was ten when her divorced mother married Brian Mugford and settled in Cheshire. Six years later the family moved to Essex. Julie joined Colchester County High School for Girls' sixth form where acting head Betty Nicholls remembers her as 'a quiet, average student. She was in the first netball squad and did a lot of work coaching juniors in the game. She worked at a local primary school one afternoon a week, getting work experience leading her towards her training. She always seemed to know she wanted to be a teacher.'[6]

Julie was studying for an honours degree in education at Goldsmiths, University of London when she began working at Sloppy Joe's in the holidays. Her second date with Jeremy was a trip to Tollesbury's windswept marina, followed by tea at White House Farm. They spent the rest of her Christmas holiday together. Julie's best friend Susan Battersby, who had the room next to hers at Deptford's Hall of Residence, met Jeremy on the first day of the new term: 'He took Julie and myself out for a meal. He was quite charming.'[7] In a 1986 interview with the *News of the World*, Julie recalled that Jeremy inundated her with 'flowers, candlelit dinners, and then the honeymoon suite in a posh hotel . . . Jeremy completely swept me off my feet . . . As long as he was happy, I was happy. I gave everything to him, including myself. He knew I was under his spell.'[8]

At the beginning of 1984, Jan Flowers ended her five-year relationship with Colin. She retained a close friendship with him and saw the twins often; on one occasion Sheila invited her in for tea and they chatted amiably. Colin admits that it was his turn to feel devastated. To lift his spirits, he and the twins stayed with his sister and family in Norway. He then moved into a rented room on West Hampstead's Ulysses Road, where his housemates remember Sheila from her visits as a very reserved, exceptionally heavy smoker, who rolled her own cigarettes and sometimes smoked cigars.

Colin's mother began looking after the twins once a week while Sheila attended evening classes in art. 'Bambi brought me some of her pictures,' Tora recalls. 'They were *very* good – quite abstract, forests and people. Then she said, "I'm going to show them to my mother," and I thought, "Oh God . . ." Her mother didn't like them and that was the end of that. Bambi said unhappily, "I'm not good at anything."'

Although Ann Eaton described her cousin as impractical, someone who could neither drive nor cook, Sheila's friends remember otherwise. 'She was a brilliant cook,' Tora affirms. 'Freddie always used to say, "You could not want for a better meal" when she cooked for him. She was intelligent and creative, but nobody seemed to treat her with the respect she deserved. That's what dulled her confidence. She once told me that she wanted to decorate her flat but she was so nervous. I tried to help her get everything she needed in a way that left her to make the decisions. She painted the whole place herself and it was fantastic. I remember Nick and Dan exclaiming, "Oh Mum, we love it" and she was really happy.'

Sheila's dream of becoming a successful model was fading; she flitted from job to job and was unemployed at the start of 1984. Jeremy recalled that she started 'to go downhill again. Family discussions had taken place regarding what could be done to help Sheila.' Most of these involved her returning to live in Essex but Jeremy stated that 'Sheila was adamant she wanted to remain independent and stayed in London. She was getting more and more depressed.'[9]

Jeremy saw little of his sister. He appeared to be a devoted boyfriend to Julie, but Liz Rimington suspected that he was unfaithful to her with Sue, who confirms: 'After we parted we carried on having a physical relationship even though he was

also seeing Julie.'[10] While Julie was at university, Jeremy socialized with the old Frog & Beans crowd, including Charles
Marsden, who recalled him having a lot of girlfriends and one-
night stands.

At the end of February 1984, Jeremy bought a Vauxhall
Astra for almost £6,350 on the N. & J. Bamber account. He sold
his old Mini to a labourer helping builder Dennis Wager renovate White House Farm's scullery. Everyone used the back door
as the main point of entry to the house and Nevill had decided
to modernize the whole area. He got rid of the old fireplace and
bread oven, installed a stairway to the first floor office where
Barbara worked, and had a new office built for himself.

Dennis Wager was also hired to construct a new shop at
Osea Road after the old one was destroyed by fire; it was the
second case of suspected arson at the site. Jeremy was given the
responsibility of planning the layout, advertising the lease, and
estimating costs. Wager disliked working with him: 'He appeared
full of his own importance. He was also always trying to impress
upon people that he was one of the governors.'[11]

In Goldhanger, Jeremy's imminent arrival at Bourtree Cottage
caused further discontent, with locals blaming him for Nevill
'getting rid' of Kate Foakes. When an opportunity arose to ingra-
tiate himself a little with the villagers, Jeremy readily accepted. It
involved playing the part of 'The Thing' in the Tiptree and District Choral Society's performance of *Horrortorio* at the village
hall in April 1984. His only acting experience to date was at
Gresham's, where as a junior he had a non-speaking part as a
Roman soldier, and a minor role in Sheridan's *The School for
Scandal* in winter 1976. In *Horrortorio*, he had to wear a gro-
tesque mask, cape and double-thumbed hairy hand, then enter
the hall behind the audience, wailing and moaning, grasping
people's shoulders. His parents and Charles Marsden were there,
and he impressed regular members of the society with his spooky
performance. 'He did scare people,' recalled the actress playing
Dracula's daughter. 'There were shrieks and jumps from the
audience.'[12]

Jeremy moved into Bourtree Cottage a few days later. He
spent £3,000 of his savings and took out a £1,000 bank loan to
replace the old kitchen units and buy new furniture and electrical

goods, including a sunbed and television with Teletext. Julie
helped choose the carpets and colour schemes, and did most of
the decorating during her Easter holidays while Jeremy was at
the farm. June appeared one afternoon with Sheila to see the
work being done.

'The atmosphere was very tense,' Julie recalled. 'I believe Mrs
Bamber didn't expect me to be there, as she didn't approve.'[13]
June confronted her about staying overnight at the cottage,
accusing Julie of being 'a harlot'. She then offered to buy her a
flat in London or Colchester before declaring that she didn't
understand how Julie's mother 'could allow it to go on'.[14] Afterwards, June confided in Joan Frost that she was deeply upset at
the thought of people assuming she condoned the relationship
and was relieved when Julie returned to university.

Jeremy's chief companion at the cottage was a lively little
mongrel called Brambles. 'He cared about the dog a lot more
than his family or girlfriends,' one of his friends recalled. 'When
it was run over [some months after Jeremy's move to Bourtree
Cottage] he was really and truly devastated.'[15] He also began to
grow cannabis quite openly, putting seedlings on his windowsill
and cultivating a small crop in the back garden. It grew unhin-
dered, while among the extended family rumours of drug use
revolved not around Jeremy, but Sheila.

12

In May 1984, Nicholas and Daniel joined Robinsfield Infant School in St John's Wood where Sheila became friendly with a group of glamorous single mothers, mostly in their late twenties. Tora recalls that Sheila's new friends were 'rather sophisticated. I used to walk about in maternity wear, but those women looked like they had come straight out of Bond Street.'[1] Among the group were Kirstie, an American model whose daughter attended Robinsfield; Sonja, a model from Denmark with a son at the school; Jilly, a model whose daughter knew the twins from nursery; Helen, who had been a model in the 1960s; and Caroline, in the midst of a divorce and whose children were at Robinsfield.

On fine afternoons the women would head for the park opposite Sheila's flat to chat, while the children played in the paddling pool. Despite their good looks, they all had difficult personal lives and struggled to find work, but Sheila was the most insecure. 'She used to ask my advice about every little thing,' Jilly recalled. 'She needed to be reminded to make an effort with her clothes and make-up. She had shoulder-length dark hair that used to get straggly and every so often I would have to tell her, "Bambi, your hair is in rat's tails, get it cut," and she would.'[2] The women babysat for each other, consulted a clairvoyant, and held parties for the children. They then began socializing in the evenings with wealthy visiting businessmen whom Caroline described as 'creeps who were practically all pushing drugs'.[3]

Like many of her contemporaries growing up in the seventies, Sheila had experimented with cannabis. Her occasional use of it in the last years of her life was consistently linked to Freddie. Independent witnesses claim that he supplied both Sheila and Jeremy with cannabis. Tora also believes that 'Freddie took Bambi into a situation where drugs were' and Colin heard from a friend that Sheila had 'boasted of Freddie being a drugs dealer', specifying cocaine.[4] When he asked his ex-wife about the stories she insisted they weren't true. During the 1985 murder enquiry,

Essex Police investigated Freddie and exonerated him of supplying drugs, finding no evidence to substantiate the claims.

In early 1984, Sheila's inability to keep appointments was a
more pressing concern for her Dr Ferguson: 'She was erratic in
attendance. It was difficult to keep a steady and regular contact
with her.'[5] He wrote to her GP on 8 May, explaining that he
had seen Sheila 'on two separate occasions recently because of
some risk of relapse', which was linked to her 'over-sensitivity
about people disliking her' and 'her mother being disapproving'.
Although the concepts of good and evil were 'still very difficult
for her to handle', she had developed a fixation about 'whether or
not she was a good mother, in the sense that she could produce
children'. Sheila 'made a great deal' of the stitch put in her cervix
to enable her to carry the twins to full term, viewing the issue 'as
a kind of female impotence'. She was also having 'particularly
difficult visits with her mother' and had been 'very upset' after
one 'very stormy visit'.

Dr Ferguson saw Sheila on six occasions that year and recommended the closer monitoring available on the NHS, but
again she and her family rejected the suggestion. He was aware
that she was inconsistent in taking the Stelazine and tried to convince her to talk to Dr Angeloglou, her GP, about it. He also
warned her against recreational drugs, pointing out that somebody with her condition was at greater risk than the average
person, exhorting her to abstain from all drugs which might
affect her mind.

In addition to the odd dalliance with Sue Ford, Jeremy was
unfaithful to Julie in the first half of 1984 with two other
women. The first was Liz Rimington, whose relationship with
Malcolm Waters had come to an end. After spending the night
with Jeremy, Liz felt 'terribly guilty', telling Essex Police in 1985
that they were never 'romantically involved' and Julie knew
nothing about it.[6]

Jeremy's second liaison was with another friend of Julie's. He
and Charles Marsden had spent an evening drinking with the girl
at the Chequers. Returning to Bourtree Cottage after the pub
closed, Charles went to bed while Jeremy and the girl stayed

downstairs drinking. She told detectives in 1985 that she had suddenly found herself in Jeremy's bedroom with him 'on top of me having intercourse'.[7] Charles Marsden lay next to them; he recalled waking up to find the couple having sex but both he and the girl confirmed he had taken no part in what was going on.

The following day, the girl wondered whether she had been drugged. Feeling 'shocked, angry and abused', after hearing that Jeremy had told Julie about the episode, she called at the cottage while Jeremy was working. Julie recalled the girl describing a threesome and, when she confronted Jeremy, he told her that the girl was neurotic. Leaving Julie sobbing in the garden, he returned later and charged at the locked door, splintering it. Julie decided to believe him and broke off her friendship with the girl as he asked.

Malcolm Deckers described Julie as 'too clingy' for Jeremy; their relationship seemed to 'deteriorate' that summer and he was 'surprised that they stayed together so long'.[8] Stories of Jeremy's sexual activities abounded during the 1985 investigation, although they had no bearing on the murders. Detectives heard that he was bisexual, homosexual, took part in cocaine-fuelled orgies, threesomes and 'weird sex'.[9] Julie stated that she had a 'normal sexual relationship' with Jeremy but believed he was bisexual, 'although to my knowledge he has not practiced it since knowing me'.[10] Jeremy denied the stories, declaring twenty-five years later: 'I was never someone who had loads of girlfriends or loads of one-night stands. I went out with Sue for quite some time and I went out [with] Julie quite some time. And those were really the only two long-term girlfriends that I had . . .'[11]

Sheila accompanied her mother to a Billy Graham convention in June 1984. Jeremy recalls attending a 'dire' church hall screening of one of Graham's earlier campaigns with his mother and sister.[12] For the live event at Ipswich's Portman Road football stadium, where Graham was appearing as part of his 'Mission England' tour, June publicized the convention locally and organized coach travel. One of the other attendees recalled that Sheila 'spoke to no one and I got the impression she did not want to be there'.[13]

Inviting Sheila over to lunch one day that summer, Ann found her cousin keen to talk about London, the boys and Colin. Ann remembers Sheila as very protective towards the twins, recalling an occasion when 'one of the boys was putting marmalade on some toast in my lounge at Oak Farm without asking and was making a real mess of it on my settee. I didn't like that and was in the process of telling him off, when Sheila interrupted and told me not to make such a fuss about it.'[14] She felt that Sheila 'took charge' when it came to the children: 'I do not think she would let anybody take over. She would interfere, like saying, "No, let Daniel have that" or "Nicholas have that" and "what's wrong, darling?" "Darling", she used to say.'[15]

During her visit, Sheila asked Ann to take a photograph of her to send to Christine in Canada: 'She expressly wanted me to take it in the garden at Oak Farm, I assume so that aunt June would not find out because I'm sure she would have been hurt by such a move and Sheila was, I think, trying to protect aunt June from such emotional pain.'[16] Jeremy states otherwise: 'Sheila was cruel to mum about not understanding what it was like to be a real mother, and what it meant. Although mum (June) said nothing to Sheila about being upset about her contacting Christine, it broke mum's heart. I knew it would when Sheila was telling me what she planned. I have no idea what dad thought about Sheila contacting Christine, we never talked about it.'[17] Sheila didn't invite her family to the dinner party she gave with her uncle, Peter Jay, as guest of honour. Nor did they meet her natural grandparents, who were in England that summer. Margaret Jay was left 'distressed' by Sheila's 'endless questions' about Christine.[18]

Julie felt that she was able to communicate with Sheila 'more readily than Jeremy could. I think this was because I would give her the benefit of the doubt if she said something odd and carry on talking, whereas Jeremy would tend to freeze and be stuck for words.'[19] She later told detectives that Jeremy 'didn't like Sheila, who he thought was crazy. He told me that she had mental problems and had done some horrible things to him in the past. He would not tell me what she had exactly done to him.'[20] Asked by the same detectives about the 'horrible things', Jeremy responded: 'Only one that I can remember, when travelling to see some family friends we had an argument in the car, she hit me a couple of times, but I wouldn't call it horrible.'[21]

Sheila told her friends that Julie was good for Jeremy. Sandra Elston remembered: 'She said that he'd got a lot better since he'd got a nice girlfriend – Julie. By a lot better I understood her to mean in himself, and not the relationship between herself and him. I always got the impression from Sheila that she and Jeremy weren't particularly close.'[22] Julie left for a working holiday in France in July but, when it didn't turn out as expected, Jeremy bought her an early ticket home. She spent the rest of the summer at Bourtree Cottage, seeing Sheila and the twins whenever they visited, calling at the caravan site with them and going for walks along the sea wall.

Mary Mugford's initial misgivings about Jeremy had mellowed: 'I got on well with him and he was accepted by my family. He would converse openly about his background and family. He would refer to me as "Mummy" and he would often refer to himself as my favourite son-in-law even though he wasn't married to Julie. I would point out to him that he wasn't married to my daughter but he would then indicate that marriage was intended.'[23] Jeremy once told her that he and June weren't talking after a row: 'Over a period of weeks I would often ask Jeremy if he was still not speaking to his mother and how could he not speak to her, to which he would reply, "It's easy, I just don't," and shrugged his shoulders.' Jeremy admitted to Essex Police that there were 'heated arguments' between himself and June, caused by 'a lack of understanding for each other's views, and due in part to mother's strong character and to some extent my immaturity', but that 'things were more loving' in the last few months before her death.[24]

In August, Jeremy and Julie bumped into Liz Rimington in Colchester. She had purposely stayed away from the couple after her night with Jeremy, but soon began socializing with them again. She recalled Jeremy talking to her about his plans to rob an expensive house in Goldhanger but 'nothing ever came of it'.[25] She also related another incident involving a young student nicknamed 'Moose' who was working at the farm. Liz called at Bourtree Cottage while he was visiting: 'I was sitting on the bonnet of Jeremy's GTE car with Jeremy sitting at the driver's seat and Moose in the passenger seat. Suddenly Jeremy started driving the car very fast along Head Street with me still on the bonnet. He drove for about 500 yards. He then stopped and I got off, shaken and quite upset.' Moose was equally alarmed, spluttering that Jeremy had reached 60mph and could have killed her. Laughing at them both, Jeremy roared off to White House Farm.

By then, Jeremy had quite literally developed a small cottage industry for the cultivation and selling of cannabis. As a teenager, he had grown cannabis for his own use at White House Farm until his father found out and put a stop to it, but at Bourtree Cottage, the hemp seeds Matthew McDonald had given him produced a crop of twenty-five plants. They flourished at the foot of the long garden, ready to harvest and sell to a contact in London.

Susan Battersby had already made it clear that she was against Jeremy bringing cannabis to the house in Lewisham she and Julie began sharing that September. To her dismay, when Jeremy's contact in London fell through, Julie agreed to try selling it at university. After she had sold about £100 worth of cannabis, taking a £30 cut for herself, Susan persuaded her to stop, fearing that Jeremy was involving her friend 'with his way of life so that she would be unable to tell anyone about what he was doing'.[26] Jeremy was infuriated that Julie had agreed, and whenever there was a knock at the door he would rag Susan that the Drugs Squad had come for her.

Eventually, he set up another deal with a man in Scotland, telling Julie that he'd picked up 'Hamish McTavish' as a hitch-hiker heading back from London. Jeremy would send him small, carefully wrapped packages through the post in return for recorded deliveries of cash. These were sent to Bourtree Cottage under the name of the previous tenant's grandson, who knew nothing about it. The arrangement came to light when the postman delivered one of the recorded deliveries direct to Kate Foakes so that she could pass it on to her grandson Kevin. He then called at the cottage and spoke to Julie, who was there alone, telling her that he would report Jeremy if he ever found him using his name again.[27]

Julie recalled that Jeremy made about £800 that year through small-scale drug deals. She had tried cannabis prior to meeting him and occasionally they smoked it together. Throughout their relationship, Jeremy 'always' had cannabis in his possession: 'He dislikes being without it and becomes very moody. When smoking cannabis he is a different person.' Susan observed that Jeremy would smoke 'all the time', whether 'socially or even driving his car'. Her opinion of him had plunged but she conceded that he and Julie 'always appeared to be happy together'.

Julie recalled that she and Jeremy only ever had one serious argument. It started as a row in a supermarket over which soap to buy: 'I ended up agreeing with his choice and threw him the bar of soap which he wanted. It accidentally hit him on the nose and he retaliated by pushing my nose with the palm of his hand. This really annoyed me and after throwing some items from the shopping trolley on the floor, I left the store leaving Jeremy behind.'[28] Jeremy remembered it as 'quite a tiff', in which 'I got hit on the nose and she did as well, though not hard'.[29] He added that Julie had talked about being 'extremely scared of being hit and that if I ever hit her she would leave me'. He secretly met Sue Ford again in the autumn, after she told him she was moving back to Jersey with her husband and children. After a lengthy goodbye at Bourtree Cottage, without Jeremy's knowledge Sue sold the Cartier watch to a mutual friend for £150.

In October, Julie invited Jeremy to the twenty-first birthday party of her friend Karen Napier, then a medical student at Cambridge University. He got on well with Karen's boyfriend Andrew Bishop, who was also studying medicine at Cambridge. They regularly made up a foursome afterwards, and Jeremy confided in Andrew that he thought it 'worthwhile to be obedient' to his parents in order to claim his inheritance, although he didn't enjoy the 'restrictions' it imposed on his lifestyle.[30]

That same month, despite Susan's belief that Jeremy was a bad influence on Julie, the two girls decided 'as a sort of dare' to report Susan's cheque book as stolen, then 'go shopping and not pay for it'.[31] Julie later insisted that she got the idea from another friend and had convinced Susan to go along with it. They caught a train into central London one Saturday morning and reported Susan's handbag and cheque book stolen at a police station near Oxford Street. They then headed for the department stores, spending £634 (£1,780 in today's money) on clothing for themselves, and jeans and a coffee percolator for Jeremy.

That evening Julie presented him with his gifts: 'I told him how and where we had got the goods. All he said was that we had been naughty. This was said in a jovial manner and not as an admonishment. He said we had taken a risk in view of his alleged theft of traveller's cheques whilst in Australia or New Zealand.' She and Susan felt so guilty that they donated some clothes to the Salvation Army and threw the rest away. Although Jeremy had no prior knowledge of their plan, both girls blamed him. Julie recalled that she hadn't liked him teasing her about being a 'goody two shoes', and Susan disliked how he often told her she was 'too straight-laced'.[32]

A few weeks later, on the morning of Monday, 12 November, Jeremy was driving along Maldon Road when a car ploughed into him, wrecking his Vauxhall Astra. He escaped with minor injuries and was treated in hospital for shock, while Underwoods Garage in Tiptree provided a replacement silver Vauxhall Astra in a straight exchange on the insurance claim. Two constables called at White House Farm; PC Robin Saxby chatted and took down the accident details. He and Jeremy would meet again within a year, in very different circumstances.

The Bambers were Conservative stalwarts. Nevill and June had campaigned locally on behalf of the party since the 1960s and Jeremy followed their lead in voting Tory, although Sheila had no interest in politics. Britain's economy began to recover following Margaret Thatcher's second election victory in 1983; salaries rose among young professionals, high earners received tax cuts and credit boomed.

Suddenly it was socially acceptable to flaunt one's wealth with champagne lunches, Sony Walkmans, brick-sized mobile phones, flash cars and loft apartments. Privatization reigned, conspicuous consumption was embraced, and commercial branding saw 'models mutate into supermodels, supermarkets into superstores, cinemas into multiplexes. Building societies became banks and humble record shops developed delusions of grandeur, turning themselves into megastores.'[1] Pop videos celebrated affluence, with Princess Diana's favourite band Duran Duran lounging in designer suits on a yacht in the Caribbean for 'Rio' and Madonna dripping diamonds in 'Material Girl'. The zeitgeist was Harry Enfield's boorish cockney plasterer 'Loadsamoney', appearing on Channel 4's *Saturday Live* waving a thick pile of cash while crowing: 'Shut your mouth and look at my wad!'

Jeremy was in the privileged position of knowing that permanent work and inherited wealth awaited him. N. & J. Bamber Ltd managed approximately 750 acres of arable land in total, with its own herd of cattle and a large amount of agricultural machinery. Profits had risen considerably due to crop diversity, including cultivation of plants for pharmaceutical companies. Nevill owned 79 per cent of the issued share capital, Jeremy 20 per cent and June 1 per cent. In November 1984, Nevill added to their portfolio by purchasing 48.5 acres of Little Renters Farm.

It proved a contentious decision. After Bill Eaton's death, the farm had passed to his widow and sons, Peter and John, who split their inheritance equally and worked their own acres. Discovering that John was planning to sell his share to property developers, Ann and Peter asked Nevill to buy the land on their

behalf and they would reimburse him later. After he had paid
£2,000 per acre for the land, a regular at the Chequers pub in
Goldhanger claimed to have witnessed Nevill arguing with John
Eaton about the sale, but Essex Police were unable to verify the
allegation. Although only Nevill and the Eatons were said to
have been aware of the purchase and their arrangement with
Nevill, the Bambers' solicitor Basil Cock stated that the land was
bought with a bank loan and £25,000 of cash belonging to June.
Peter Eaton remembered Jeremy mentioning the land was almost
paid for during a visit to Oak Farm, and glimpsed father and son
walking around the farm on at least three occasions.

The Bambers had other assets to their name: Nevill's 20 per
cent share in North Maldon Growers, Bourtree Cottage in Goldhanger, Sheila's flat in Maida Vale and Clifton House in Guildford.
Valuables from the latter were stored at White House Farm,
where Nevill invited Jacqueline, Anthony, Sheila and Jeremy to
choose a few items from their grandmother's estate. Jacqueline
told other family members that Jeremy had viewed everything
beforehand and consulted antique dealers. At the same time,
Anthony's wife Regine recalled Jeremy expressing irritation that
his parents had helped finance Jacqueline's recent wedding and
that he had dismissed Bourtree Cottage as much too small, adding
that he would prefer to live at Vaulty.

Nevill had inherited Clifton House alone but gave his niece
and nephew a 25 per cent share each. Abandoning an early plan
to convert the property into retirement flats, he decided to sell
five apartments individually. Each would be sold on a 99 year
lease with the stables converted into another flat for the family's
exclusive use. Modifications cost around £100,000, most of
which Nevill borrowed from his bank. He loaned Anthony and
Jacqueline another £25,000 each to fund their share of the work.
Jeremy told police that he was never 'exactly au fait with the
family position in Guildford', but Julie's mother remembered him
discussing it 'on a number of occasions', and he and Julie visited
Clifton House to view the work being done.[2]

Osea Road was June's most valuable business asset. In addition to her 42 per cent share of the company, she owned a field
within the site which was to be left to Sheila and managed by
James Carr. Ann was uncomfortable with the 'buttering up' she

herself had from Jeremy that year, suspecting it related to his ambitions within the company: 'He kept wanting me to go and use his sunray lamp in his cottage and I made a joke, he had not got a key on the other side of the door. He was very pleasant with me. I had got on well with him on decisions in the camp and anything I suggested, he said, "Good idea."'[3] When she thanked him for the birthday card he sent her that September – the first in years – he replied, 'Oh well, I am your favourite cousin after all.'[4]

While everyone agreed that Jeremy showed an interest in Osea Road, opinions remained divided on his attitude to farming. Robert Boutflour recalled how Nevill had difficulty persuading Jeremy to work evenings and weekends. On one occasion, after 'tipping a load of potatoes into a ditch', Jeremy jumped into his car and drove off, 'leaving others to clear up the muddle'.[5] Hearing that Nevill had been reduced to tears by his behaviour, Robert demanded, 'Why don't you throw the bugger out?'

'June wouldn't let me,' Nevill replied.[6]

But Pamela felt that her nephew was settling down at the farm and labourer Len Foakes recalled him working almost full time on the land. Michael Deckers noticed during his conversations with Jeremy that he had become more tolerant of his parents' views and ceased 'belittling' his father, who was 'paving the way' for him to take over fully in about five years' time.[7] His observation appears to be borne out by Nevill asking the trustees to include his son's name on the tenancy that year. They declined on the grounds that he was too young and inexperienced.

Nevill then invited Jeremy to join him at meetings of North Maldon Growers. Thomas Howie noted that he contributed 'very valid points' to their discussions, appeared to take 'a very keen interest in the farm' and that 'Nevill and Jeremy seemed to enjoy each other's company'.[8] Colin Caffell informed detectives that father and son were very close: 'They shared the same work and some of the same interests. Their humour was similar and they both liked to play practical jokes on the farm reps who called from time to time.'[9]

Others felt that any progress on Jeremy's part was conducted with one eye on his inheritance. Julie Mugford declared that her boyfriend still 'resented his parents ruling his life and trying to control him as well. I, in fact, told him I couldn't understand why, if he hated them so much, he just didn't clear out. He told me he had too much to lose. He didn't actually say what he had to lose but I assumed that he would lose the farm and caravan site which he knew he would get one day. Jeremy became very frustrated as he resented the fact that his parents would not give him things which he had worked for and had earned.'[10] Christine Bacon agreed that Jeremy 'used to blame his parents for everything that happened and that they were constantly restricting him by limiting and controlling his finances. I once asked him if he was that unhappy why didn't he leave and he told me that he wasn't prepared to forfeit the money which would eventually be left to him one day.'[11]

Julie also stated that Jeremy resented working hard for an income while his sister received money from their parents while 'do[ing] nothing for it'.[12] Jacqueline confirmed that he was jealous of Sheila because June had bought her the flat in Maida Vale and often paid her bills, while Agnes Low told detectives that Jeremy had grown 'even more jealous' after looking at the Osea Road accounts and discovering that June was spending 'lots of this money' on Sheila and the twins.[13]

Jeremy insisted that such views were mistaken, that his parents 'did not rule or control my life', nor did they keep him short of money. He lived rent-free, with a company car and free petrol, insurance, private medical cover, free telephone usage and bottled gas to heat his cottage. He summarized his earnings in 1985 for the benefit of detectives: '£6,000 farm income with £1,000 bonus. I earned £1,750 from the caravan site, plus a car – a £7,000 car.' Among other perks were days off work 'over and above my month's holiday'. He estimated that his yearly income and privileges amounted to £18–20,000, which 'is not short of money'. Twenty-five years later, he described himself as someone who 'didn't go on flash holidays, didn't have flash clothes – or wear designer things – didn't have any desire or want for those. The farm provided me with a nice new car. I had a house paid for by the company. I had everything there that I wanted.'[14]

Radcliffe's Gunmakers stood opposite Sloppy Joe's on Colchester High Street. Owner Robert Radcliffe was familiar with Nevill, but recalled that he tended to use London-based gunsmiths for buying and repairing firearms. However, on 30 November 1984, Nevill arrived at the store with Jeremy and purchased the gun that would become the murder weapon.

David Boutflour had suggested Radcliffe's after Nevill called him to discuss buying a rifle. The .22 Anschütz came with a 10-shot magazine, plus telescopic sight, Parker Hale sound moderator, and 500 rounds of ammunition. In 1985, Essex Police stated that it was 'safe to assume that these were purchased for Jeremy at his request'.[15] Jeremy declared that the Anschütz belonged to his father: 'He paid for it, he was licensed to use it, but he had my opinions on which one to buy through advice from my cousin Anthony, to both of us. But I did have access to use it.' Three months before the purchase, a constable visited Nevill regarding his firearms renewal and noted: 'Mr Bamber was meticulous in the safekeeping of these weapons, which were all stored in a padlocked cupboard within the house.'[16]

Jeremy had never held nor applied for a Firearms Certificate. Relatives and friends later confirmed that prior to his father buying the Anschütz, which was widely used by farmers for shooting rabbits and birds, he had little interest in guns and abhorred blood sports, although he attended the annual shoots in Scotland. To the police, Jeremy declared that he disliked shooting 'pheasants, partridges, foxes, but realize[d] that pigeons and rabbits and hares have to be controlled'.

Several people had seen him handle a gun, including his cousin Anthony, who confirmed that Jeremy was 'a reasonable shot and proficient with guns'.[17] The two of them had had 'a shooting competition' behind one of the barns at the farm that summer, using Anthony's gun to shoot at a brick until it was obliterated.[18] David Boutflour remembers Jeremy acquiring an air rifle in his teens and learning to shoot with Anthony's old .410 shotgun. In his memoir, Colin mentions Jeremy using a small-bore shotgun on a Boxing Day shoot many years before when he and Sheila acted as beaters. Both David and Anthony kept guns at White House Farm. David was licensed to use a rifle on Nevill's property, while Anthony kept his shotguns at the farm because virtually all of his shooting was done there.

Christine Bacon was surprised when Jeremy arrived at her

home with two ducks he had shot himself. It was December 1984, a few weeks after she had given birth to a son by Matthew McDonald. Jeremy told her that he had used the new Anschütz, scattering maize on the water to attract the birds. She gave them to her neighbour, who noticed there were no bullets in the bodies, indicating they had been shot at close range, 'a particularly cruel way to shoot ducks and not sporting'.[19]

Jeremy sometimes called on Christine to hear news of Sue; the two women were still in regular contact. Christine recalled that during one visit, 'he suggested that he stay the night. He said he was looking for an older woman to have an affair with. He never forced his intentions upon me and he did leave when I asked him to. As a result of this our friendship broke up.'

Dr Ferguson saw Sheila at his consulting rooms one week before Christmas. He found her settled and about to start work in a shop, but felt there were causes for concern. In addition to her continuing fixation with future pregnancies, she had 'disturbances' in her thinking and heard voices, although he wasn't convinced that she was hallucinating as she had 'very good insight' into the voices.[20] Tentatively, he recommended a course of Anafranil. Used to treat conditions such as depression and obsessional states, it could increase melancholia and suicidal thoughts in the short term, but most patients found it beneficial. Uneasy about her being able to cope with Anafranil, he asked for a very small trial dose to be given. Sheila was prescribed one 10mg capsule each night, which she would begin taking early in the new year.

Colin joined his ex-wife and sons at White House Farm for Christmas. Julie stayed at Bourtree Cottage with Jeremy and, to her astonishment, he proposed: 'After I told him I thought he was joking and he said he wasn't, I said I would marry him. We decided we would go to a registry office after Christmas, not tell anyone and get married.'[21] Invited to spend Boxing Day at White House Farm with Jeremy, Julie felt as if the Bambers were making a firm effort to accept her. But there was an unexpected outcome. 'His parents had told him that it was about time he got married,' Julie recalled. 'He said that because they wanted him to get married he wouldn't, because he didn't feel it was his decision.' No more was said about it and Jeremy was curiously evasive about the subject when quizzed by Essex Police. On an early incarnation of his official website he said of the proposal to Julie: 'I'm sure that I did no such thing and I would surely recall if I had.'[22]

Colin's visit had raised Sheila's hopes of a reconciliation and she found separating again painful. Tora recalls that she changed afterwards: 'She became more vacant and didn't appear to be aware of what was going on around her.'[23] Freddie agreed: 'She became extremely depressed and withdrew into herself. She would not discuss all her problems, although whenever she visited her father, she would return even more depressed because of her mother. Apparently the mother would preach to her about her boyfriends and how it was wrong that she should make love with them and that Sheila should always remember God. She gradually deteriorated.'[24]

On New Year's Eve, Sheila salvaged her optimism to join a group of friends, including David Tomkinson, at Rags nightclub in Mayfair. Above the music, she shouted to David that the club was boring, but otherwise she was on sparkling form as the countdown to 1985 began.

2: GROWTH

1 January 1985 to 6 August 1985

Only a few days into January 1985, Sheila visited her doctor feeling lonely and depressed. Her prescription for Anafranil was increased from one tablet per evening to three, but when the twins were in bed she was unable to sleep and would ring her father, talking into the early hours.

Money was an ever-present worry. Sheila and her friend Kirstie applied for work at School Dinners, a notorious restaurant off Baker Street whose menu offered school dinner staples served by waitresses in uniform, stockings and suspenders. Sheila wore her old straw boater to the interview and was offered a job, but resigned within a week, hating it.

Shortly afterwards, an Australian photographer asked her to pose for a 'tasteful' nude shoot, which he would sell to *Mayfair* or *Penthouse*. Realizing that Sheila was 'absolutely desperate', a friend allowed them to use her garden, hanging sheets around the perimeter to shield them from view.[1] The photographer brought a paddling pool and gave it to the woman's daughter afterwards. Sheila was stricken when she saw the results of the session, which were far more explicit than she had imagined, and pleaded with the photographer for the original slides. Hiding the boxes away, she wept inconsolably to friends about it.

The nude session destroyed Sheila's fragile morale. Some of her newer friends retreated, describing her as stifling, but Tora and her husband remained loyal. Dr Ferguson recalled that Sheila admitted using cocaine fairly frequently around this time. He suspected that she 'kept bad company', although he didn't explore that with her, 'just the fact that she had used cocaine and cannabis'.[2] Freebasing was popular at parties for the young and rich during the 1980s and Sheila admitted that she smoked the cocaine 'in a social context'.

As her depression deepened, she visited the farm more often. Whenever Barbara encountered her she was 'always dressed in black clothing. She was very quiet, sitting most of the time smoking cigarettes. She appeared very frail and slow.'[3] On one occasion Sheila told her that the world was 'a dreadful place', the devil was after her and she kept seeing 'images of Hitler'. At other times she thought terrible, unspecified things were happening and people were chasing her.

On Saturday, 2 March 1985, matters came to a head. It was Sheila's weekend with the twins. She had invited Chloe Tomkinson to stay the night; David dropped his daughter off at midday. Freddie was already there and later described Sheila as 'jumpy, uptight and panicky', although she was fine when David left.[4] After lunch the children went to play in the bedroom and Sheila telephoned Tora to apologize about June, who had called round two days earlier with a religious book. Freddie stated that Sheila became hysterical when the line suddenly went dead, 'mumbling about the phone being bugged. She became like someone possessed, ranting and raving. She was striking herself and beating the wall with her fists.' He tried to pacify her, 'but she did not seem to hear me'. She talked about the devil and God, whom she said was sitting opposite her and loved her, 'unlike what her mother said'.

Sheila then tried to call Dr Ferguson but mistakenly rang her ex-mother-in-law instead. 'I told her that she was talking to me,' Doris recalled, 'and she went into a torrent of words, saying she was hearing voices from God.'[5] A worried Doris called round and found Sheila 'very hyperactive', talking about voices from God and the devil, how she had to 'put the world to rights' because it was 'all wrong', and that when she watched television, the figures came out of the screen and entered her body.

Doris called for a doctor and Sheila sat down quietly, looking sad and forlorn. Catching her former mother-in-law's eye, she gave a very quick, bright smile that vanished immediately. Doris asked Freddie if he had called Sheila's parents and he replied that they were not to be brought into it. Nevertheless, Doris attempted to ring them while Sheila paced the room, but Freddie put his hand over the receiver, telling her, 'I'd rather you didn't.' When he left to answer the doorbell, Doris telephoned her ex-husband and asked him to visit. She then went through to check on the children and found them all laughing because Daniel had put on Chloe's clothes and cut his fringe.

Dr Steven Iliffe arrived and introduced himself to Sheila.

During the 'long but difficult discussion' that followed, she told him about the voices.[6] He recalled that she seemed 'extremely tense and agitated' and 'intensely suspicious of my motives for talking to her'. Her speech was 'coherent and lucid, but answers to questions were often monosyllabic, and she volunteered very little information. There were silences during which she seemed to be trying to think of answers to my suggestions and questions, and for long periods of the consultation she stared at me without blinking and without any change in facial expression. Although I could find no conclusive signs of a schizophrenic disorder, my impression at the time was that she was on the edge of a psychotic state, possibly of a paranoid character.' Sheila refused an injection to calm her, shouting: 'You're trying to poison me!'

Doris explained to the doctor that Sheila had previously received treatment at St Andrew's Hospital and her parents would probably have her admitted there. Colin recalled hearing from his mother afterwards that the doctor believed Sheila was a danger to herself and others, and it was a wonder no harm had been done, yet in his statement Dr Iliffe declared nothing of that nature. Sheila and the children were 'well supported' and the twins seemed 'relatively unperturbed' by their mother's behaviour. He observed with some surprise that Sheila herself was 'elegant' and the flat 'comfortable and orderly'. Freddie, however, recalled feeling 'extremely scared for everyone's safety' and worried that Sheila might 'use violence towards someone'. Fearing 'something nasty might happen', he telephoned David Tomkinson to collect Chloe because Sheila was 'in a really bad state'. David arrived and agreed that Sheila 'did appear very bad' and was noticeably 'depressed and withdrawn'.[7]

Reg Caffell called round shortly after the Tomkinsons left and saw that Sheila 'was under some stress. She thought she was the devil.'[8] He took his grandchildren to the leisure centre while Dr Iliffe wrote out a prescription. Before departing, Dr Iliffe told Freddie to contact the duty doctor if necessary and advised a visit to Dr Angeloglou on Monday. Freddie collected the prescription from the chemist, leaving Doris with Sheila, who 'sat on the settee, smoothing out her skirt' and telling the older woman 'very definitely' that she should leave. Doris waited until Freddie returned, then drove home.

Freddie remained at Sheila's flat until the following morning. He stated that during the night she was 'like a person possessed, rambling about the devil and God. I went next door to her neighbour, who came through. Sheila sat down and combed or brushed her hair. She had a blank expression on her face and was staring into space. Every now and again she would suddenly become violent again, ranting and raving, then stopping as quickly as it started, when she combed her hair.' Eventually, Freddie telephoned Nevill who said he would call round in the morning: 'I asked if he could make it sooner but he could not.'

Sheila's mental state did not improve. Dr Michael Finnegan called to see her first thing the following morning and found her unable to hold a rational conversation. She refused sedation and he left feeling that 'a formal admission to the nearest mental institution' was imperative.[9] According to Freddie, Sheila thought all visitors to the flat were 'trying to hurt or kill her' and he was astonished when she 'became a different person' upon her father's arrival, speaking to him 'in a calm and collected manner'.

Dr Ferguson later clarified that seeing Nevill would have relieved Sheila's anxiety: 'The kind of disordered thinking she has is a very frightening experience, I am sure. Her father's presence would have allayed that panic.'[10] But June confided in a friend that she had had 'a terrible time with Sheila' on the journey to hospital, despite her daughter being under heavy sedation from the medication Dr Iliffe had prescribed.[11] Nevill telephoned ahead to ask the hospital to re-admit Sheila urgently. Staff found her 'psychotic', 'virtually incoherent', 'very agitated,' 'very disturbed,' 'highly suspicious' and 'bewildered' when she arrived.[12] She refused to speak to the duty doctor at times and was resistive and uncooperative, although not aggressive, when he attempted to examine her physically. For the second time in two years, Sheila was admitted to Isham House.

Dr Ferguson could not pinpoint any particular external event which had caused Sheila's second breakdown. He regarded it as a naturally occurring relapse which had been exacerbated by the occasional use of cocaine and cannabis. She was much more acutely disturbed in terms of her ability to think and speak coherently than on her previous admission, more uncooperative and agitated, and had relapsed into an acute psychotic state. Her behaviour was 'more disconnected than before – she laughed inappropriately and was restless. She said she had some religious feelings – she had found God and felt relaxed.'[13] She believed herself to be in touch with God and told Dr Ferguson she wanted to be by Jesus's side, declaring that Freddie was the devil and posed a risk to her. Although she expressed a wish to go to heaven she did not appear suicidal.

Dr Ferguson noted that 'whilst in 1983 she expressed fears of harming or doing violence to her children, those fears did not seem to recur.'[14] He found it difficult to imagine Sheila hurting her children or father but 'could conceive of her harming her mother or herself', although only if faced with 'what she regarded as real, pressing fears'.

Today he reflects: 'It never crossed my mind that she would act out any aggression towards her children. It was all to do with mental aberration rather than physical manifestations of anger or acting out that anger.'[15] And despite the complexities of Sheila's relationship with June, at no time did she ever talk about using violence towards her mother. He was satisfied that Sheila's parents were both supportive of her: 'I am sure her mother would have helped in any way that she could because she really cared. I don't think she was anything other than a very worried, very caring mother. She was a very worthwhile figure in her daughter's life.'

Sheila was formally diagnosed with schizophrenia upon her second admission to St Andrew's. The term does not refer to multiple personality disorder but to a 'split mind' and a 'loosening of the associations between the different functions of the mind so that thoughts become disconnected and coordination weaker'.[16] Research into the causes of the condition shows that it is 'fundamentally a biological problem that is no different in principle from other such problems, like cancer or heart disease or diabetes. We know that schizophrenia is not caused by possession by evil spirits, or by a weak personality or a bad mother.'[17] There is some evidence to support the idea that schizophrenia is a neurodevelopmental condition presenting as early as gestation, but symptoms do not usually appear until early adulthood.

The correlation between schizophrenia and violence is small but significant. Around 2 per cent of the population without mental health problems will commit a serious violent act; for schizophrenia sufferers that figure stands at 8 per cent, a lower number than for those with depression or a personality disorder. Violence occurs when patients actively experience threat or control override, believing that people are trying to harm them, or that they are dominated by a force outside their control. Most patients who hear voices commanding them to be violent are able to resist.

The best known description of the illness belongs to Scottish psychiatrist R. D. Laing. He declared that 'schizophrenia cannot be understood without understanding despair' and that 'the experience and behaviour that gets labelled schizophrenic is a special strategy that a person invents in order to live in an unliveable situation.'[18]

Colin spoke to Dr Ferguson about Sheila's diagnosis soon after her admission to St Andrews. The psychiatrist told him that she would always have the illness and that relapses would become more frequent and intense. Colin was stunned. Dr Ferguson assured him that Sheila was not a danger to the children or to herself but required constant medication to manage her condition. They also discussed Freddie's influence on Sheila and agreed that the friendship was troubling.

Colin then visited Sheila, who told him about her conversations with God. He decided that Nicholas and Daniel should remain living with him for the time being; their teacher had already contacted him to express 'serious concern for their progress and welfare'.[19] Their marks had fallen far behind the rest of their class, their behaviour was 'erratic and moody', and they 'lacked self-motivation'. The twins also told Doris that they sometimes arrived late for school because they had to dress themselves, fetch their own breakfast and then attempt to wake Sheila. Colin made an appointment with the headmistress, who admitted to being greatly relieved that they would be living with him for the foreseeable future. Over the coming weeks, the boys settled again and became 'leaders in their classroom'.

Colin – who had a new partner, nineteen-year-old Heather Amos – never doubted Sheila's love for their sons. He was satisfied that any problems were a result of her illness. His greatest worry was June's habit of taking 'every opportunity to preach to the children' about God; the boys were 'disturbed' by her behaviour and 'the things that she wanted them to do'.[20] He had 'always been unhappy' about Nicholas and Daniel's visits to White House Farm but 'had never really been in a position to stop it'. His attempts to speak calmly to June about it had little effect.

One incident proved instrumental in his decision to restrict her access to the children. While Sheila was in hospital, June asked if the twins might stay at the farm, but when Colin put the idea to them they burst into tears. He told June that she and Nevill could see the boys instead when they called to check on Sheila's flat. Jan Flowers brought the twins to Morshead Mansions that day and June took the boys into their bedroom. When they emerged a few minutes later, she reminded them not to forget what she had told them. After their grandparents had gone, the twins became upset as they described how Granny had made them kneel by their beds to pray. Colin fumed when told about it. In his eyes June was 'a religious monster' who terrified his sons and kicked up a fuss about visits only to leave them with babysitters while she attended church.[21]

Three weeks into Sheila's treatment, Dr Ferguson observed that her 'psychotic symptoms' had receded briefly on medication, but when it was reduced she again 'flared up into paranoid interpretations of the nursing staff', whom she believed were conspiring with the devil to 'take away her godliness'.[22] At other times she insisted that she was being watched by everyone around her. Dr Ferguson wrote to her GP about the need for better psychiatric support at home, recommending local NHS resources. The Bambers were still reluctant to follow his advice, despite the expense of private long-term medical care: Sheila's second stay at St Andrew's cost £3,120 (approximately £8,750 today).

Sheila had telephoned the Tomkinsons shortly after her admission. 'She told us she would be in touch when she was properly better,' Tora recalls. 'I respected her wishes and left her to recuperate. But Bambi's real problem was the perpetual draining of her character from certain quarters. Then the minute they began medicating her, she just collapsed, physically and emotionally. She was very weepy and used to say to me, "I want to be alright for the boys, but I can hardly get anything together." I'd offer to help, but she'd say, "No, it'll be fine. I just wish I wasn't so tired." She came back to us eventually, but after that . . . she just looked terrible.'[23]

'Jeremy must have a very friendly bank manager,' Nevill remarked during Agnes Low's visit to White House Farm in March 1985. 'He seems to be able to get bank loans without any trouble.'[1] The subject arose when Nevill came under pressure from his bank to lease out the flats at Clifton House in Guildford to realize some cash. Jeremy had just left the room after mentioning that he had bought a microwave oven and other items for Bourtree Cottage. 'Neither Nevill nor June could understand where Jeremy got the money from,' Agnes recalled.

Another conversation about finance occurred at Julie's student digs in Caterham Road, Lewisham. Housemate James Richards recalled: [Jeremy] told me that his parents kept him short of money and that his mother was a religious freak. He then went on to say how he hated his parents and I remember quite distinctly that he said, "I hate my fucking parents."'[2] When James responded, 'Oh, come off it, Jeremy, we all say that, but we don't really mean it,' Jeremy replied fervently, 'I fucking do.' Jeremy later refuted the remarks: 'I never hated my mum, she frustrated me at times, she made me angry at times, she annoyed me at times, but I never hated her.'[3]

Michael Deckers remembered hearing about arguments between Jeremy and June over Osea Road that spring: 'He wanted to modernise the set up, build a shop, and properly organise the layout of the site but he was up against his mother and the other directors, apart from his cousin Ann, who he said was on his side.'[4] The cousins conducted interviews for the shop lease amid talk of Julie running it, eventually settling on Stuart Sinclair, in his thirties and from Preston.

The interviews had taken place in the manager's office close to the sea wall. James Carr worked there most weekends but a serious illness kept him at home during March. Ann and her father ran the office for the first two weekends and Jeremy and Nevill took over for the remainder. On the last Monday in March, builder Michael Horsnell arrived early at the site for work and noticed the small office window was broken. Peering inside, he saw the drawer from the cash register on the floor, papers scattered about, the safe cupboard open and a length of pipe near the broken window.

The police were called. Ann arrived quickly after being informed about the break in and was puzzled to see the leaflets she had left on the windowsill were undisturbed and there were no footprints on the ground outside. £970 was missing from the safe and £10 from the till and petty cash box. The culprit had gained entry using a key Jeremy had left in the letter cage inside the front door. Ann discussed the matter with James Carr, who responded archly that it was strange the office should have been burgled that particular weekend. He had no doubt that Jeremy was guilty, but felt unable to accuse him without upsetting the Bambers. Talking to Nevill in general terms about it, he learned that Jeremy had persuaded his father to put the money in the safe instead of banking it, and that Nevill had left the key on its hook in the office. James passed the information to Robert Boutflour, who already suspected his nephew. At a directors' meeting three weeks later, Jeremy mentioned that the office was still insecure and he had been able to retrieve the key from the letter cage. Noting that Jeremy was 'a good actor', James Carr removed the cage.[5]

Six months later, during the investigation into his family's murders, Jeremy admitted stealing the money. Julie had acted as his lookout and gave a full account of the matter, recalling how the two of them had driven out to Mill Beach Hotel after supper that evening. They parked the car and walked along the seafront to the shop. 'He held my hand and we walked to the office,' Julie recalled. 'When we got there Jeremy told me to wait out of sight which I did. I saw him put his hand through the letter box to find the key which he knew would be there. He could not get the key so asked if I could reach it. I couldn't reach it and so he tried again and succeeded in getting it.'[6] He told her to keep watch while he went inside. After fifteen minutes, he reappeared, having ransacked the office to make it look like a random break-in. He put the key back through the letter box and smashed the window. 'Then he grabbed hold of my hand and we started to run back the way we came,' Julie stated. Jeremy went into the toilet at the hotel and pushed the money down his trousers, then played pool with Julie before heading back to the cottage. 'We put all the money on the floor and looked at it,' Julie remembered. 'I said that I had never seen that much money before. He put all the money in his little Chinese trick box.'

Jeremy's stated reasons for committing the burglary vary. In September 1985, he asserted that it was to prove a point about security, but stopped short of conceding it could have been done without pocketing the money. Twenty-five years later, his rationale was more convoluted, declaring that he had been annoyed by Ann receiving a higher income from Osea Road: 'I said: "That's not fair. You know, if we're going to do this, we do it equitably. If she has ten thousand pounds, I have ten thousand pounds. If she has five, then I have five . . . My mum said "No, it doesn't matter." And I said "No, it does matter. It really does matter."'[7]

In 1985, he indicated with reasonable accuracy that the amount stolen was 'under £900'.[8] In 2010, he thought there was £1,800 in the office safe and the shareholders 'owed' him £1,400 – 'the differential' between his and Ann's income. He claimed he had intended to tell his family that security was useless and point out the unfairness of the financial situation. His later story is untenable, particularly the contention that he left £400 in the safe which was then mysteriously stolen by someone else on the same night.

According to Barbara Wilson, Nevill Bamber was aware that his son was guilty and it troubled him deeply: 'He told me himself that Jeremy was responsible for the holiday camp break in. But he never reported him, probably because he hoped it was just a lapse on Jeremy's part.'[9]

Jeremy proclaimed himself 'ashamed' twenty-five years later: 'I shouldn't have done what I did in the way that I did it.' He had cause to regret it at his trial in 1986, since the crown prosecution used the burglary as a gauge of his ethics: 'They tried to say that my actions there mirrored the fact that I was prepared to do a crime out of greed and disrespect for the family.'[10]

Sheila chafed against confinement at St Andrew's. She made numerous telephone calls, often ringing her mother four times a day. She also telephoned the flat in West Hampstead Mews, where her calls were answered by temporary resident and American musician Susan Harvey. Each time, Sheila sounded 'really depressed', asking for someone to get her out of hospital because the doctors were 'filling her up with drugs and she was just sitting about, thinking she would go insane'.[11] Susan telephoned the hospital to enquire after Sheila and was told that she wasn't being detained against her will and could leave whenever she wished. Susan passed the message on to Sheila, who said she wasn't capable of catching the right train home due to her medication. Ex-boyfriend Don Hawkins also received 'very disturbing' calls from her: 'Sheila appeared to have lost touch with reality. She would say "God was in touch."'[12]

On 25 March, Sheila sent a letter to Oak Farm:

Dear Ann and Peter,

I expect by now you have got wind of the fact that I am here.

I didn't want everyone to know because I thought as usual they would get the wrong end of the stick. I am not in here because I am worrying about my body, so let's get this one perfectly clear. I could never look you straight in the face if you thought that, because it is all so futile. In fact, I couldn't possibly be in here for that, because to begin with there is nothing specially terribly wrong with my body. In fact when I had the twins when I was in hospital they decided there was nothing wrong with my cervix and that I quite possibly had a sensitive womb which is why I started off early. So in future with God's blessing I won't have any troubles. I am sorry for saying this but it is important.

The reason I am here is because of general stress and I haven't been taking care of myself. I didn't want to come in but Dad said I should. I asked God into my life so I could understand Mum's moods more and became completely high on his love, so much so that I wanted to join CND thinking I had a calling from God to sort the world's problems out myself. Then I got a thing about the CIA following me. I finally thought a friend was the Devil, so I went through a tough time of unreality. But I am getting over it now and everything will be OK.

I'm missing the boys.

With love, Sheila.[13]

On the back of the envelope she wrote: 'PS, I have found God in a very simple way. PPS. Please don't tell anyone else in the family I have come here.'

Ann didn't mention the letter to her husband or her aunt and uncle: 'I was very busy at the time. I put it away.'[14] She hadn't known that Sheila was in hospital until she received the letter. Regarding the reference to June's moods, Ann stated: 'Auntie June was not a moody person. She was religious and maybe that got on top of Sheila sometimes.'

Dr Ferguson remembered that thoughts of her birth mother were 'very much to the fore' in Sheila's mind.[15] Calling her Uncle Peter to explain that she was receiving treatment for visions and a Madonna complex, Sheila's main concern was a meeting she had planned with Christine. Dr Ferguson recalls that she 'almost insisted on discharging herself because of that'. She was anxious not only to be well, but to be seen to be well enough to leave hospital so as to avoid having to meet her mother while a patient. At one stage a three-day Mental Health Order was issued to ensure that Sheila remained on the premises, but on 29 March, she was officially discharged.

Dr Ferguson was not 'entirely comfortable' about her departure: 'She put herself under such pressure to see her real mother. She had a sort of pleased anticipation about it. So I would say that she was better, but not as well as she could have been.' Even when she left hospital 'she was prone at times to look quite distracted, vague, somewhat distanced, somewhat withdrawn', but a complete recovery was not a realistic prospect.[16] He 'never felt she was safe in terms of well-being or risk of relapse. She wasn't psychotic but I asked her GP to tie her in to the local psychiatric support service. I didn't feel that seeing me was adequate and she didn't always arrive for her appointments anyway.'

Prior to leaving St Andrew's, Sheila was given a 200mg injection of haloperidol, used to treat a number of conditions including schizophrenia and in veterinary practice, most commonly for birds prone to plucking out their feathers. Sheila was prescribed a monthly injection by her GP to lessen the risk of relapse. She was then released into her parents' care and returned to White House Farm.

The following day, June's cousin, Margaret Grimster, and her teenage children, David and Helen, arrived for a visit. After lunch, everyone except Sheila and thirteen-year-old Helen set off for a walk. Helen joined Sheila for a chat in the sitting room: 'Sheila asked me if I liked school. She said she had been bullied at school and that she hadn't enjoyed her school days.'[17] As she spoke, Sheila rolled a joint and offered it to Helen, who declined. She asked Helen if she had ever thought of killing herself and said that she had contemplated suicide several times. To the younger girl's alarm, she then described herself as 'a white witch' who had to 'get rid of the evil in the world'. Helen recalled that Sheila 'kept going on about this' and about June telling her she 'had lost her soul' and 'should be more religious'. Sheila mentioned being 'on better terms' with Colin, then discussed the medication she had been given. She asked Helen if she had ever tried drugs and told her that everybody should try taking drugs. The conversation lasted about an hour. 'It frightened me,' Helen remembered, 'and I thought she was very strange.'

Sheila's other relatives were unaware that she was recuperating at the farm. David Boutflour admits having had 'very little practical experience' of Sheila's illness because her parents were 'particularly secretive' about it.[18] Jeremy's only memory of Sheila's post-hospital stay at the farm was that she kept apologizing all the time. But Mary Mugford recalled that over Easter he described his sister behaving 'like a frightened rabbit' because June would allow 'no opinions' in the house except her own.[19] Julie stated that Jeremy rowed with his mother during Easter and 'wouldn't speak to her again unless she wrote him out a cheque. He didn't say what the argument was about.'[20] Her mother understood that it was due to June considering changing her will 'in favour of the twins'.[21] Julie told detectives that Jeremy had secretly looked at the wills years before, believing that his mother intended to leave her money to the church but 'she hadn't'.[22]

Barbara Wilson was privy to most legal matters at White House Farm. She was unable to remember whether June had intended to make Nicholas and Daniel the main beneficiaries in her will 'but it could well have been the case. Perhaps that's what sparked everything off.' Jeremy admitted glancing at drafts of his parents' wills out of curiosity. His father had bequeathed his estate to June, but in the event of her death 'it was divided up between my sister and me with an opportunity for me to buy my sister's share of the farm.'[23] June's will stipulated that Sheila was to have her mother's freehold ownership of the caravan site and Jeremy would have shares in it. Asked if he could recall whether the twins were mentioned in the wills, Jeremy replied: 'I don't remember. I think they are but I'm not sure, but certainly not in name.'[24]

The actual wills, drawn up in 1979, largely bear out his assertions. June stipulated that any loan to Sheila and Colin was to be written off and that her share of Osea Road would go to Sheila on the understanding that the company would manage it for her. The rest would pass to Jeremy when he reached the age of twenty-five. In his will, Nevill bequeathed Bourtree Cottage and other personal effects to June. Apart from some small financial gifts, the bulk of his estate was to go to Jeremy, on one condition: 'If my son, Jeremy Nevill Bamber, is, in the opinion of my trustees, farming with me at the date of my death, or the date of the death of my wife, whichever is the later, and/or they are reasonably satisfied that he intends to carry on farming thereafter, then subject to a legacy of £10,000 to my daughter Sheila Jean Caffell, the remainder of my residuary estate shall go to my said son.'[25]

Essex Police drew attention to the clause in their report to the Director of Public Prosecutions, noting that it 'could go a long way to explaining Jeremy's sudden and recent surge of interest in farming'.[26] When the proviso was discussed in court, Jeremy declared: 'I didn't know it existed until I read it just now,' and agreed that it effectively tied him to the farm in order to inherit.[27] However, the police report observed, 'the deaths of Sheila and the twins does tend to negate that part of the will' and as sole survivor Jeremy was almost certain to acquire everything. His parents' combined wealth was estimated at £436,000, around £1,225,000 in today's money.

Sheila returned to London in mid-April. She rang Susan Harvey to thank her for her kindness and the two women met up: 'She was afraid to be on her own. Even having the twins there did not seem to allay her fears. She was in need of adult company.'[1] On his visits with the twins, Colin found that Sheila couldn't hold her concentration. Freddie likewise observed that she 'seemed to do things at a much slower pace' and was 'very slow and deliberate in her speech and difficult to converse with'.[2] When he talked about the episode at her flat in March she couldn't remember anything about it.

In a 2013 letter, Jeremy disputes accounts of Sheila's extreme listlessness, which would obviously have some bearing on her ability to carry out the murders: 'Ann Eaton and Robert Bout-flour promoted the nonsense about Sheila's slowness and lack of coordination – but no one else ever saw that, and I certainly never experienced Sheila acting in such a way.'[3] In fact, there are many such descriptions. Tora saw her friend every week that summer and remembers: 'She was extremely tired and so weak. Normally she was a lively person but she really couldn't function and was very aware of not wanting to be around the children in such a state. One day she asked, "Tora, can you help me?" I said, "In any way I can, Bambi, I will." She told me, "I must get away from this doctor. He's giving me medicine and I hate it. I'm not feeling right at all." She wasn't being listened to – decisions were made without her consideration. The change in Bambi was just huge.'[4]

Dr Ferguson acknowledged that over-sedation was a possible side-effect of haloperidol and in extreme cases led to involuntary movements and drug-induced parkinsonism. In April, Sheila called him to complain that the injections were 'flattening' her.[5] She visited her GP, who prescribed procyclidene twice daily to counter problems with muscles and joints movement. Despite her lethargy, she was also given a supply of Noctec, a nocturnal sedative. On 2 May she received another injection of haloperidol, together with a prescription for Triludan, an anti-histamine that was withdrawn from production seven years later following adverse reports about its effects on the heart.

Dr Ferguson had no further contact with Sheila but wrote to her GP tentatively recommending that she should continue with the haloperidol, although he was unsure whether she would be able to tolerate the side-effects. He also recommended that Sheila's long-term case management should include visits from a community psychiatric nurse. Dr Angeloglou arranged for Sheila to be seen at St Mary's Hospital, but the appointment was scheduled weeks in advance and fell after her death.

Among the friends who remained loyal to Sheila were George Gros and his partner Jane Robinson, who lived in Maida Vale with their four-year-old daughter. Jane was struck by Sheila's loneliness and suggested taking in a lodger, which would also help with her financial difficulties, but Nevill and June baulked at the idea. Instead, Sheila joined a church in Kilburn for company and began talking more about God to family and friends.

Barbara Wilson remembers seeing her in the kitchen at the farm: 'She was wearing a pink jumper, which was unusual as she always wore black, she got up off her stool and came and spoke to me. She said she was feeling happier having put her trust in God and was feeling better herself, and God would sort it out. Although she was still slow in her movements, she did seem to have a bit of her old self back again.'[6] Colin was concerned that Sheila 'seemed to have found religion similar to her mother' but conceded that it brought mother and daughter closer.[7]

While Sheila's relationship with June improved, in May her birth mother flew into London from Canada. Christine had arranged to meet Sheila four days before the end of her visit and they got on so well that they were never apart. They met at Tora's home for the first time. 'It was *incredible*,' she recalls. 'Bambi's mother was so like her. She was very beautiful, strikingly similar to her daughter in how she dressed and carried herself. She was vibrant and very chic, but so warm, just like Bambi. She expressed her feelings openly and smiled *all* the time. It was like looking into a mirror – except that Christine was more confident. The most wonderful thing was that Bambi's mother understood her. It was the best thing that could have happened to her, especially when she found out that Christine had never wanted to give her up. I remember looking at them both and thinking: in twenty-five years' time, that will be Bambi.'

Sheila introduced Christine to Colin: 'I will never forget the look of sheer joy on Bambs' face when I first saw them together. She was beaming from ear to ear.'[8] Christine was delighted to meet her two grandsons, lavishing hugs and kisses on Daniel and Nicholas. Colin took a photograph of them all sprawled out on the floor at Sheila's flat. She invited her friends round too, but June and Nevill never met Christine. Nor did Jeremy, who recalls that his sister 'didn't bring me in on the plans. We did speak about how it went after she'd met Christine – but in bland terms.'[9] The emotional wrench for Sheila when Christine departed was considerable, but tempered by the joy of their time together and the certainty of further meetings. Knowing that her birth mother would be part of her future meant the world to Sheila. It was, as Colin phrased it, 'the catalyst in her recovery that gave her hope'.[10]

After returning to college for summer term, Liz Rimington received an unexpected visit from Julie, who was 'upset. She told me that her and Jeremy had been arguing and that he said he didn't love her anymore and called her all sorts of names. He said that he had just been using her. I tried to help her and advise her as best I could. Eventually they patched things up.'[11]

Julie cancelled the holiday she and Liz had planned after Jeremy said he was taking her to the Bahamas as a twenty-first birthday present. But Jeremy was far from dedicated to their relationship. He had telephoned Sue in Jersey, asking if she still loved him, and pursued a Colchester barmaid named Anne, seven years his senior. Anne agreed to a couple of dates, during which Jeremy showed her his family's farmland and Osea Road, telling her that he was very wealthy and intended to buy a Porsche someday. She decided she didn't want to see him again, although he and Charles Marsden were regulars at the bar where she worked.

Robert Boutflour recalled that in May, Jeremy 'blew his top' at an Osea Road directors' meeting when Pamela proposed that Ann should receive a bonus for setting up a temporary shop on site.[12] 'There was a lot of jealousy on Jeremy's part,' Robert stated, 'he went very red in the face and angrily spluttered out his objections.' The permanent shop opened the following day. Ann and Jeremy were keen to install fruit machines in the basement, but June disapproved. She had been appointed churchwarden in Tolleshunt D'Arcy over Easter, following the investiture of a new vicar. Colin recalled that Nevill had been churchwarden for many years, but 'due to June's activities' and disliking the previous vicar's influence over her, he had resigned in 1982.[13]

June was in good spirits when she visited Sheila early the following month, pleased that her daughter had found work. Sheila was employed two mornings a week as a cleaner at Butterflies lingerie store, where she was eager to chat to staff about her children and show photographs of them. But June departed feeling very worried about her daughter, whose mood remained low and lethargic.

She was pleased by Jeremy's progress however, telling Joan Frost that he had a more active and voluntary part in the family business and seemed to be enjoying his role. She regretted some of her past anger over his choices and only wanted him to be happy and have a belief in God. Nevill also seemed content with his son: when his business adviser George Nicholls called at White House Farm on 17 June, Nevill declared himself 'very pleased with the way Jeremy is shaping up on the farm'.[14]

But within a matter of days, there was a seismic shift in the atmosphere at White House Farm. Although the cause is impossible to ascertain, Nevill and June's equilibrium had always depended to a great extent on what was going on in the lives of their children. And everything changed around the time that Jeremy's friend, New Zealander Brett Collins, flew in from Hawaii to stay in Goldhanger.

When Jeremy and Julie met up with Brett in London a few hours after his arrival, their first port of call was Stringfellows, where Jeremy went unsuccessfully in search of cocaine. Eventually the three of them returned to Goldhanger where, over the course of the next few weeks, Brett caused a stir, walking freely about the cottage and garden in his underpants, hanging his laundry on the communal fence to dry, and sunbathing with the radio blaring out. Julie told her friend Karen that Jeremy's behaviour deteriorated around Brett, with the two men drinking and taking drugs and being openly affectionate with each other.

Jeremy was still cultivating cannabis at the cottage and had managed to plant eighty seedlings at the farm without his parents' knowledge.

Nevill had begun thinking ahead to his retirement, aware that his son's ideas for the future of the farm were different to his own. He often told his secretary, 'File that, Barbara, but I don't know why, Jeremy will throw it all away when he takes over.'[15] She remembers Jeremy joking about installing a computer and making her redundant. He discussed the idea with his father, but Nevill was attached to more traditional methods. 'I would describe him as a sentimental man,' Barbara states. 'He kept his momentoes [sic] in his desk and in the office, such as theatre programmes, birthday cards, letters and even bills from Jeremy's school.'[16] One of his prized possessions was a golf bag that had belonged to his father; Barbara describes it as 'quite tatty, but it meant a lot to him. A mouse popped out of that bag one day and gave me an awful scare. I jumped on the chair and Mr Bamber was beside himself with laughter.'[17]

Reminded of their disparate attitudes years later, Jeremy reflects that he was 'no different from any other young man in being interested in engineering, computers and technology. The world was changing rapidly [and] we would certainly have developed our business using computing.'[18] In late June, Nevill grumbled about Jeremy's desire to have 'all the latest gadgets in his house' to a friend who thought him 'quite low and not his normal optimistic self'.[19] Barbara noticed that Nevill's ebullience seemed to have deserted him: 'It was as if he had the weight of the world on his shoulders. He sat hunched over, exhausted with worry. It wasn't like him. He was a very tall man who usually held himself extremely upright. There was an odd sort of stiffness to Mr Bamber's back if Jeremy came upstairs. He was more brusque too. Occasionally it erupted into something more – not a row, because Mr Bamber was not the type of man to row. Instead, he would speak sharply to Jeremy and leave the room, indicating that he should go with him. Then I'd hear raised voices.'

One morning in late June, Nevill asked Barbara if she would object to him having a cigarette in the office; he usually waited until the end of the day, when he would retire with a generous gin and tonic. Exhaling slowly, he mused how ungrateful children could be before mentioning that a new hiding place was needed for the safe key. Then he picked up his mother's prayer book and asked, 'Barbara, if anything ever happens to me, will you promise to look after the farm?'

'Of course,' Barbara replied, startled. She looked at him a moment, then asked: 'How are you, Mr Bamber? Are you sure you're not ill?'

'What makes you think that?' Nevill said.

'Well, because you seem so unhappy and always look as if you're carrying some sort of dreadful burden.' She paused. '*Are* you ill?'

Nevill slowly shook his head. 'No, Barbara, but we're all going to die at some stage, aren't we? Though I wouldn't be surprised if it happens to me while I'm out shooting.'

Recounting the conversation today, Barbara grows visibly upset: 'I don't know if he had a premonition or if there had been an actual threat. But it was such a strange thing for him to come out with so close to his death. People do say, don't they, that if you're going to die, you start planning for it? We'd started sorting out the office that last summer. Mr Bamber began getting his own personal things in order as well. For instance, there was a hymn he wanted sung and a passage to be read out at his funeral. He and Mrs Bamber planned on being buried, not cremated. Whatever was happening spurred him on. And Mrs Bamber was not a well woman in the summer of 1985. She withdrew from everything. About a month before her death, she came up to the office a couple of times, crying. Once she asked me how I managed with my children. She said how difficult things were and that there didn't seem to be a way of solving their problems. Sheila was in a dark place most of the time and Jeremy walked around with a perpetual smirk.'

June began copying out passages from the Bible to place about the house. 'People thought of Mrs Bamber as a Bible-basher, but she wasn't,' Barbara states firmly. 'She felt that answers to her problems could be found there and if she prayed, then solutions would come. A lot of it was just to give herself hope – she was always jumbled up with worry. Mr Bamber was very concerned about her and often asked me to stay on when he had to leave for magistrate duties. "It's just so that June has company," he would say, but I knew he wanted someone with her in case she got upset.'

The monthly Osea Road directors' meeting on 20 June focused on site security. Jeremy was responsible for the installation of an electronic surveillance system; in the meantime, Ann hired a local security company. Jeremy was unimpressed: 'They used to just sit in her caravan and drink tea and smoke cigarettes and watch the portable TV.'[20] Robert Boutflour agreed: 'You could hear them chatting all night around the site. Nevill raised this point at a site meeting. He said you could hear them as far as 150 yards away [and] commented that if they were like the police at Witham, they were no more good than Dad's Army.'[21] Robert later told detectives that he had spoken to his nephew about tackling any intruders and warned him about committing a crime that would prey on his conscience: 'Jeremy then made an extraordinary statement, "Oh no Uncle Bobby, that wouldn't worry me, I could easily kill my parents." This remark shocked me and I said, "Don't be so stupid." I then walked off.'[22]

A police officer acting on a tip-off about Jeremy's cannabis plants called at Bourtree Cottage on 23 June. The place was empty, but he spotted the crop and made a note to return. An irate neighbour told Jeremy about the visit and he promptly destroyed the plants. Julie remembered him being extremely angry when he found his other crop at the farm had been eaten by rats. He left later that month for a short break in Amsterdam with Brett, whose brother lived there. The Colchester barmaid whom Jeremy had pursued earlier was visiting friends on the Netherlands' Texel Island; Anne had mentioned her trip to him but was shocked when he suddenly appeared, having booked into the same hotel. After a couple of days, Jeremy accepted that she wasn't interested and returned home, followed by Brett.

Sheila visited the farm again in late June without the twins, who had just celebrated their sixth birthday. Colin threw a large party for them at his new apartment in Kilburn, introducing his ex-wife to his girlfriend Heather. Sheila broke down in Colin's mother's arms afterwards: 'She was very upset and miserable about her life and she wanted her children to live with her again.

She stayed with me for a few hours and was obviously unhappy and distressed.'[23]

At Osea Road, Sheila met Sarah Howie with her husband and children. Sarah was taken aback by her cool greeting: 'Normally she would embrace me, give me a kiss and be much warmer. I asked how she was getting on and she replied that she was alright . . . She didn't seem "all there" and seemed vague, she appeared to be in a slight trance, and didn't seem to be interested.'[24] Ann Eaton also spoke to her cousin at Osea Road and was struck by how tired Sheila appeared: 'She always wanted to look pretty and young, but I thought when she smiled you could see crows' feet, like I have.'[25]

Sheila remained at the farmhouse while her mother attended the vicarage garden party and the village fete where she judged a children's fancy dress competition. Barbara remembers an unsettling encounter at some point during her visit: 'We had coffee at the kitchen table, just the three of us. Sheila was at the head, opposite the door, where she usually sat, I was on her left and her mother was on her right. For a while she just sat there, looking very weak. Mrs Bamber and I were chatting and suddenly Sheila said: "All people are bad and deserve to be killed." She just came out with it. But she wasn't herself anyway. Her eyes would look right past you. I only saw her once more after that. I was indoors, watching her cross the yard. The geese were about – perishing things, they used to cackle and chase people. But on this particular occasion I saw Sheila walking across the yard, her body and legs very stiff, staring straight ahead. She moved through the geese as if they weren't there.'

Ethel Taylor attended Bible classes in Tolleshunt Major with June, who often gave her a lift to meetings. Around the time of Sheila's penultimate visit to the farm, Ethel recalls that June seemed troubled: 'About a month before she died, she said to me, "Pray for Sheila." She didn't say why.'[26]

Torrential rain and thunderstorms at the end of June brought down power lines in the area. White House Farm was struck by lightning, cutting off the electricity supply and wreaking havoc with the telephones. Soon after Sheila returned to London at the beginning of July, Jeremy drove out to Oak Farm one evening and told Ann that he wanted to buy a five shot automatic 12 bore. When she asked him why, he replied: 'I rather fancied myself as the country squire and thought I might go shooting.'[1] Peter explained that it wasn't the done thing and suggested he try one of his father's guns before buying one himself. Jeremy later told detectives that his interest was due to the landlord of the Chequers inviting him to go pigeon shooting. Trevor Jones confirmed it, adding that Jeremy had declined his offer, saying he couldn't hit a barn door.

On Friday, 5 July, Jeremy and Ann attended a caravan exhibition in St Osyth. Before they left, Jeremy told her that he would introduce himself 'as a director, not as a director's son'.[2] At the show, Ann listened to him chatting about Osea Road to a salesman, 'implying that he had a lot to do with the working of the caravan site'.

Afterwards, she remarked, 'That man believed everything you told him.'

'If you say something convincingly enough you can convince anybody of anything,' Jeremy replied. 'And Osea Road will belong to you and me in two years' time.'

Ann stared at him, baffled. 'What do you mean?'

'Never mind,' Jeremy said, 'you just wait and see.'

She shook her head: 'But my mother isn't ready to go out yet, so what do you mean?'

After a moment, he told her: 'We're going to take an early settlement to get out of White House Farm, then buy Vaulty and renovate it using money from the sale of the land at Little Renters Farm. It was mother who bought that and the payments are almost complete.'[3]

She later learned that the land had been registered in Jeremy's name, but his revelations that day already left her distraught. She and Peter had assumed that Nevill was holding the land until they could afford it, and her dream was to manage Osea Road while living at Vaulty. She had even spoken about it to Nevill, who replied that he would never be able to afford Vaulty himself.

Ann telephoned her father with the news as soon as Jeremy dropped her at Oak Farm. Regarding her cousin's words as 'a threat' she was so filled with rage that she tore down all the wallpaper in the toilet.

Jeremy, having set the cat among the pigeons, departed with Brett for Andrew Bishop's stag night in London; Julie was to be a bridesmaid at his wedding to Karen Napier. Andrew recalled strolling through Covent Garden in the early hours with Jeremy, who spoke about his sister's illness being caused 'by her home circumstances'.[4] Either then or possibly on another occasion – Andrew could not be certain – he was startled when Jeremy suddenly asked, 'Do you think I'm mentally ill too?' Andrew replied firmly that he did not, and the conversation ended there.

Sheila was due her monthly haloperidol injection on 11 July. Seen by assistant GP Dr Ann Wilkinson, she told her that she felt fine and would 'know when things were going wrong again', but due to 'sleepiness' and other effects from haloperidol, she asked to be given half her normal dosage.[5] Dr Wilkinson asked when she was next due to see a consultant, but Sheila couldn't remember. The GP then administered 100mg of haloperidol instead of the usual 200mg. Dr Angeloglou had previously recommended that it should be reduced to 150mg. Following a discussion with Dr Wilkinson she noted the halved dosage and observed that Sheila's tiredness might have been due to not taking her procyclidine.

The reduced injection on 11 July was Sheila's last. Asked at trial about the effect of halving the dosage, Dr Ferguson responded: 'I do not think it is a question of pure arithmetic, I am afraid. People's responses to drugs are so idiosyncratic, but 100 milligrams would be regarded as a small dose.'[6] Thirty years later, he considers the question of whether the dosage might have 'worn off' by the night of the murders: 'The defence asked whether that might have caused her to become aggressive, cutting the dose, and I said no, I didn't think that was the case. But I gather there were friends who were worried about her agitated state. I think Sheila was finding haloperidol very difficult. People don't like those major tranquillizing drugs because they often make them feel so confused and lethargic. It was slow release and I accepted Dr Angeloglou's suggestion that it should be cut. You would have thought that Sheila would still have had the benefit of it as well as the effects.'[7]

On the Sunday after her injection, Sheila was stood up by a date at a wine bar near her flat but bumped into an old friend, John Morgan. He and another man invited her for a drink in Hampstead. During the drive, John noticed that Sheila's eyes were glazed and she was very quiet. He asked if she was on drugs. Sheila replied that she used to smoke marijuana but hadn't had any for months because of her medication. During the evening, John's friend Michael mentioned that he was opening a new shop in Kilburn and Sheila asked if he could find work for her. Later, they all returned to her flat and talked until the early hours. 'Bambi came out of herself,' Michael remembered. 'She told me that her parents owned a farm. She said she liked her parents and that they had helped her with her flat, and been very good to her with regard to helping her with her two children and her life.'[8] Both men noticed that she spoke of her sons with great affection but seemed depressed and lonely.

The following morning, Sheila began a new job as a baby-sitter after advertising her services in the local newsagents. The woman whose son she looked after twice a week thought her lonely and rather strange. Sheila had also arranged to babysit for her friends Jane and George, but didn't appear. When George telephoned her, 'she said she'd forgot and she came straight round. When she arrived she had a glazed look and I asked her if she was ok and happy to be with the kids. She said she was fine and I left her to babysit.'[9]

As 80,000 people crowded into Wembley Stadium for Live Aid on 13 July 1985, Jeremy and Julie attended Karen and Andrew's wedding. Earlier that day, June had bought herself a second-hand bicycle from a shop in Maldon. When Barbara was next at work, June showed her the bike, explaining that it was for the church charity ride in August and to help her get back to nature. Jeremy appeared as they were examining it and June mentioned that it had a squeak.

'By this time she had wheeled the bicycle out of the garage into the yard where Jeremy stood,' Barbara stated. 'He replied, "I don't expect that there is anything wrong with that,"' before riding it around the yard 'as if it were a motorcycle, he himself making the noises of an engine. He was screeching about, turning tight corners and then riding towards us at speed, screeching to a halt inches from his mother to tease her. She called out to him to be careful.'[10] Barbara swallowed her anger; he was an inveterate practical joker, but Barbara rarely found his pranks – such as a wriggling bag of rats smuggled into her car – amusing.

It was Nevill with whom Jeremy had a blazing row at the Osea Road directors' meeting on 18 July. The 'sudden flash of temper' took Ann Eaton 'completely by surprise. I can't remember what it was about but my mother and father were there. I was surprised that uncle Nevill didn't hit Jeremy, it was that heated. But I must say this was the only time that I saw them shouting at each other.'[11] Her parents returned with June and Nevill to White House Farm afterwards. The men went off to inspect the borage field while the two sisters strolled about the garden before sitting down for coffee. 'We had a really lovely time,' Pamela recalled. 'We did not discuss family matters and I cannot really say what we did talk about.'[12] Their husbands joined them in the kitchen until Robert asked to see the new den off the scullery.

Nevill took him through, stopping to pick up a rifle and some ammunition from the settle. Robert recalled that his brother-in-law made a remark that shocked him. He was unable to remember the exact words but 'it was something like, "don't want to make it easy for the next gun to jump into my shoes."'[13] He later regretted 'not pursuing Nevill's line of conversation about the rifle and the remark, which I thought then and still do, concerned Jeremy.' Instead he was distracted by a newly framed caricature of Herbert Bamber that stood propped on the fireplace; Nevill put the gun in the cupboard and told him the story behind the picture. They remained there for some time before returning to their wives. 'I know it was quite late when we left,'

Pamela recalled, 'and I made the remark that we ought to do it more often.'

But when they said goodbye, it was for the last time.

Sheila turned twenty-eight on 18 July 1985. A few days prior to her birthday, June contacted solicitor Basil Cock to discuss an annual allowance for her daughter. 'She felt that the time had come for Sheila to manage and be responsible for her own financial affairs,' Basil Cock recalled.[14] They agreed a figure of £3,000, payable each quarter as £750. He suggested that June should make the first payment herself and he would draw up a deed of covenant, ready for the second quarter. The unsigned deed was found among June's belongings after her death.

Two days later, Sheila called on her friend Agnes Mennie to discuss a documentary she had watched the previous evening. ITV's *The Making of a Model* told the story of Kim Vaughan, who had become disillusioned following her experiences in the industry. Sheila told Agnes that it was a lot harder to be a model than the programme showed, then talked in a light-hearted manner about her breakdown. Their mutual friend Jane Robinson was pleased to see Sheila regaining some confidence; plans for work and evening classes had lifted her spirits and she was looking forward to a week's holiday at her parents' farm with the children. Originally, Sheila had planned to take the twins to France with the Tomkinsons during the first week in August, but cancelled in favour of the farm. Colin was apprehensive, ignoring a nagging fear about the visit because Sheila had assured him the whole family would be there.

Peter Jay recalled that his sister had a chatty letter and photos from Sheila in July. He hadn't seen his niece since the previous month, but she rang him a week or two before the trip to Essex and left a message on his answerphone: 'Sounding perfectly bright and breezy, she said she was just ringing for a chat, and would ring again soon.'[15]

But Sheila's upbeat mood quickly began to falter. Colin noticed long periods where she was again distant and vague. He recalled that she 'made it quite clear that she wanted me back. She also wanted the boys back.'[16] Although he stated after her death that there was a lot of hope for a reconciliation, at the time he was still in a relationship with Heather. In early August he invited Sheila to his housewarming party and told her to ask Jeremy and Julie along too; Brett had flown to Greece for three weeks on 19 July. But Sheila seemed reluctant to speak to her brother and handed the phone to him when Jeremy answered.

Colin discussed his worries about his ex-wife over dinner with Sandra Elston. He was concerned about her medical care and knew that Sheila was 'terrified of losing the visits to her children' because 'her mother had said that she was unfit to look after them due to her illness.'[17]

Their conversation tallies with Jeremy's account of his family's last discussion at the supper table, just hours before the murders. He told detectives that it was precisely those points – Sheila's treatment and the welfare of the twins – which he heard his parents raise with his sister. Only Jeremy knows the truth of whether the discussion took place or not, but his parents certainly gave some thought to the future care of their grandsons. Yet apparently the ideas they put forward were confused and contradictory.

Jeremy claims that his sister's final visit to the farm with her children was orchestrated by his parents with a view to offering Sheila 'options for her long-term care. I think mum found the weekly visits to Sheila in London were becoming more tiring . . . One of the things discussed was that Sheila and the boys could live in my house in Goldhanger. I'd move into the house on Gardener's Farm, ie., once we owned it and did it up.'[18] It seems unlikely, albeit not impossible, that Jeremy himself would have been pleased with this suggestion, given that he had only recently acquired Bourtree Cottage and had spent a considerable amount of money and effort renovating it to his tastes, including installing a new kitchen. However, he also recalls that in tandem with this solution, his parents proposed that Sheila should work at Osea Road. They had already discussed the job with her; Tora remembers Sheila mentioning it and how pleased she was by the prospect of earning £40 per week.

Jeremy later told Essex Police that his parents also asked Sheila to consider whether she might 'have the children fostered locally where my parents could still take an active part in being grandparents'.[19] Unless Nevill and June were referring to the sort of daily childcare that had certainly been in place when the twins were babies, rather than traditional fostering, no one to whom the police spoke felt the idea to be viable. Inez Bowen declared that it would be 'out of character for June to allow anyone from outside the family to look after the twins'.[20] Dr Ferguson agreed: 'In my view June Bamber would not have entertained fostering out Sheila's children. She was a devoted grandmother.'[21] Colin's mother was even more convinced, remembering a telephone conversation with June around three months before the murders. June spoke then of her fear that, because of Sheila's illness, 'the boys might be put into foster homes. She was obviously against this idea.'[22]

Jeremy raised a further alternative, telling Julie and Liz on separate occasions that his parents had been thinking of adopting their grandsons. Speaking to a policeman at the farm after the shootings, he referred to the family talking about having the twins adopted two years earlier, but that nothing had seemed to come of it. Nothing came of police enquiries into the matter either. Yet there is corroboration from Barbara Wilson who was too frightened to speak out during the investigation, but today insists that the Bambers were indeed hoping to gain custody of Nicholas and Daniel: 'That's what Mr Bamber told me. I think he was more worried about the boys than anything. He was eager to get things organized for them, because Sheila wasn't well and she wasn't getting any better. There was a possibility that she would have to go into hospital again and might lose regular access to the children. Perhaps he and Mrs Bamber feared that in time they might no longer see the twins. They were definitely making formal arrangements. I know they discussed sending the children to boarding school. They felt they could provide a safe, stable life for them and a stimulating environment at the farm.'[23]

But none of the options were viable without Colin's permission, since he and Sheila shared custody of their sons and the boys lived with him. Curiously, Jeremy states: 'I don't think Mum and Dad knew that Colin took an active role in their care. I don't think Sheila would have told them because they never thought much of Colin and his lifestyle and wouldn't have been keen on him looking after their grandchildren.'[24] Although

Barbara believes the Bambers consulted both Sheila and Colin, the twins' father knew nothing of any alternative plans for his sons' care and would never have given his consent. Besides enjoying being a full-time parent, Colin's feelings about June Bamber were unequivocal; he found it hard enough to allow the twins to visit the farm for short periods.

Sheila's friend Tora shared his views, explaining that although June loved her grandsons, there were difficulties:

> Bambi's mother came here quite often. I got an uneasy feeling around her sometimes with the children. For instance, Nick and Dan usually had a bath together. They were only six, but that wasn't right at all in her eyes. Nudity was sinful to her. Bambi said that her mother didn't like to see them after their bath, running around naked, and Dan himself once said to me, 'Granny told me that I have a dirty body.' He was really upset. Dan and Nick were always so bright but sometimes they seemed muted around Sheila's mother. She got fixated on the oddest things – even trying to make out that the boys would grow up gay. Because of something she had said, Bambi asked me, 'Dan always chooses dolls, should I worry about it?' And I said, 'No, not at all. Let him get on with it.' Then she said, 'But you know, he's tried on my clothes.' I said, 'Well, that's normal as well. Boys do like dressing up and that's just what's there. Let them be what they want to be.'[25]

Nicholas and Daniel were intensely creative children, who put great energy into everything. Only weeks before the last visit, Daniel drew a series of deeply unsettling pictures of White House Farm. He entrusted them to Colin's mother, telling her that they had to be kept in order and that she should make them into a book. 'It's very important,' he implored, 'you must promise.'[26] Doris put the drawings away and forgot about them until months after the murders. Colin includes them in his memoir, *In Search of the Rainbow's End*, where they are reproduced in black and white, but Daniel filled them with colour.

All art is open to interpretation, but as Colin himself observed, children's drawings do not lie. Hence the development of art therapy for children who have been traumatized; pictures express what words cannot. Daniel's sketches were the means by which he tried to communicate his anxiety about White House Farm. The house itself dominates the sequence, occurring in every other image. The sun is another recurring motif.

The story Daniel tells through his drawings is one of dream-like horror. Smoke billows from the farmhouse chimney in the first picture, the sun seems to bleed, and the number '9' appears repeatedly on the side of the page beneath a small object floating in the sky, which features in four of the drawings. The sun smiles before vanishing in the second picture as a headless figure without hands walks upwards. In the third, the sun cries as an injured animal flees the house. The fourth shows people seemingly parachuting away from a figure brandishing guns below a disembodied head with red gushing from its neck; in one corner is what appears to be a hand grenade. In the fifth drawing, the chimney continues to belch smoke but the house itself has been blotted out. The sixth picture shows a dragon carrying a baby in its mouth beside a second, smaller dragon.

The last two drawings feature a frightening female figure. Colin states: 'Daniel identified the monster as Granny [June].'[27] The penultimate picture depicts her in bed, teeth bared and eyes narrowed. Her hands are jagged saws, the lower half of her face is covered by a mask, and red spurts violently from her head and chest. Next to her is a clock with the hands set at eleven and one. The final image shows the figure explicitly naked but for an Easter bonnet and red shoes. Her hair is a mass of tight curls, her eyes dark holes. She holds four creatures on leashes, two of which are insects. Colin surmises that the red shoes were inspired by one of Daniel's favourite films, *The Wizard of Oz*; the ruby slippers are all that can be seen of the Wicked Witch after she is crushed by the storm-tossed house.

18

'I think Nevill had a secret that he knew he couldn't tell the rest of the world,' David Boutflour muses, reflecting on his uncle's state of mind that summer.[1] Yet Nevill did confide in someone: Barbara Wilson. Friday, 26 July was her last day at the farm for a fortnight; she was due to return on 7 August. Before she left, Nevill finally unburdened himself. 'I must have caught him at a vulnerable time,' she recalls. 'I promised him I would never tell another soul what he told me that day and I haven't. He was starting to sort it out himself, but he needed to share it with someone. I think he was hoping that I would go to the police about it. But I had no proof . . .'[2]

That same Friday, the Pargeters arrived with their two young daughters to spend the weekend at the farm. Anthony left his wife and children chatting to June while he went in search of his rifle. He kept it at the farm minus the bolt as a safety precaution. It was usually stored in its case on a bench in the ground floor shower room, together with his two shotguns. But the rifle wasn't there and June directed him to the cupboard in the den, where he found it in its case, along with a 12 bore shotgun and the .22 Anschütz, both propped upright.

He hadn't seen the Anschütz before and took it out. It was in 'pristine condition', fitted with the Parker Hale silencer and a scope.[3] The scope interested him; he had bought one for his own rifle to fit that afternoon. He couldn't recall a magazine in the Anschütz, but noticed two boxes of fifty rounds on the desk nearby. Anthony replaced the Anschütz and had just begun fitting the scope on his rifle when Nevill and Jeremy appeared.

'Have you seen the new rifle?' Jeremy asked.

Anthony told him that he had and remarked on the quality of the weapon. Jeremy then invited him to inspect the borage crop, but Anthony told them he wanted to finish fitting the sight and Nevill and Jeremy left with the Anschütz.

Later, Anthony found a spot behind the barns to zero the sight in on his rifle, firing at a block of wood: 'Jeremy came around to where I was to find out how I was getting on. I told him my thoughts on the gun's performance. I said to him, "You try it and see what you think", he then fired a magazine containing approximately ten bullets into the wood from a distance of twenty-five yards.' Jeremy returned to the house while Anthony loped off to shoot a few rabbits around the farm.

The following morning, the Pargeter girls called their mother out to the yard to try June's new bicycle. Regine thought June seemed distracted, and said so to Nevill that evening after his wife had gone to bed: 'He simply said that Sheila had previously been in a nursing home but I had no idea what her problems were.'[4] Regine suspected that Jeremy was more likely to be the source of June's troubles, having 'showed himself to be a particularly callous and heartless sort of person on several occasions when I saw him.' There was an incident that weekend: 'My husband asked why Uncle Nevill didn't bring his labrador into the kitchen or into the house more often. Uncle Nevill said that the labrador and Auntie June's dog did not get on too well when Jeremy said, "Why don't you shoot the pest?"' Jeremy detested Crispy, his mother's spirited shih tzu, and much preferred Bruce the labrador, who was a yard dog.

In contrast to his wife, Anthony regarded Jeremy as 'a likeable young man' whose attitude towards his parents was pleasant 'but not overly effusive'.[5] Nevill discussed his recent acquisition of the land at Little Renters Farm with his nephew, explaining that his aim was 'to give Jeremy an opportunity to try farming on his own'. When Anthony remarked that he doubted Jeremy's long-term commitment to farming, Nevill declared, 'No doubt I'll be around for a few years yet, and I'll be able to follow him along the line.'

Before the Pargeters left on Sunday, Regine approached June to tell her that she knew about Sheila's recent illness. June replied vaguely, 'You know, we would like to have the boys and Sheila living with us but she can't drive.' Then she mentioned how much she was looking forward to Sheila and the boys visiting the following weekend and Regine realized the subject was closed.

The Pargeters departed that afternoon; Anthony took his rifle with him.

*

In London, Sheila's weekend had gone badly. The haircut she could ill afford didn't suit her and Don Hawkins failed to turn up for their date on Saturday night. She telephoned Reg Caffell after returning home that evening and asked to see him. They drove to Jack Straw's Castle on Hampstead Heath and stayed for a meal, leaving the pub at half-past nine. It was the last time he ever saw her: 'She was slow that night but I think this was because of the drug that she had been prescribed to calm her down. She was talkative but not her usual bubbling self.'[6]

On Monday morning, Sheila called at Massey's employment agency on Baker Street, recommended by her friend Agnes Mennie. Sheila's cleaning job at Butterflies hung in the balance; the proprietor liked her but found her standard of work poor and recalled that towards the end of July 'her general appearance was untidy and she smelt quite badly of body odour. Normally her clothing was quite unkempt and on one occasion I noticed she had a lot of holes in her tights. She smoked her own rolled cigarettes and seemed addicted to tobacco. Her general demeanour was very lethargic and she spoke very slowly.'[7] The woman at the agency found it odd such a 'pretty and well-spoken' girl wanted work as a domestic but was disconcerted by her 'strange habit of staring . . . her eyes appeared to be blank.'[8]

Sheila spent the afternoon at Jane and George's home, close to her own. Jane's friend Caroline Heath, a nurse from Nottingham, was present and heard that Sheila had asked to visit because she was feeling fed up and lonely. Sheila joined them in the sunshine on the veranda. 'She looked a mess,' Caroline remembered. 'Her make up looked as though it had just been put on anyhow, her hair looked greasy. She looked very pale and she constantly wore a pair of very dark sunglasses as though she was trying to hide. Throughout the afternoon she appeared to be fidgety and on edge and at times would stare blankly into space. She drank a couple of glasses of wine and smoked about 20 cigarettes.'[9] When Caroline mentioned her work as a nurse, Sheila opened up about her last breakdown, 'brought about because of her divorce and a number of things'. Caroline thought her 'very frightened and paranoid' and 'always on the defensive'.

Later Sheila called on Tora, who remembers: 'She said, "Tora, would you and Chloe come with me this weekend to my mum and dad's?" And I don't know why – because I'd always wanted to go – I said, "I don't know if I can." I had no reason to say that. She said, "Well, think about it. I'll give you a ring." But I just couldn't say yes. It was weird.' Tora was upset by the deterioration in her: 'I noticed an acrid smell coming from her, like clothes that don't get washed often. Bambi *always* smelled very nice, but there was this sort of pungent smell. She looked worn out. Her hair was limp, she wasn't cleaning it. When it was time for her to go, she was unable to get up. I said to her, "Are you alright, Bambi?" She said, "Oh, I am *so* tired." I really wondered what was going to happen to her. She looked as if she needed to sleep for a hundred years.'[10]

By the following day, Sheila had undergone a transformation. Jane and George had invited her to their barbeque that evening with Colin and the twins. Caroline Heath was also there: 'Bambi looked much better. She had had her hair done, her make up was straight, she was dressed nicely and she looked pretty. She was far more talkative than the previous day . . . [but] underneath all was not well with Bambi. She seemed to be trying to make a good show of it, but at times she seemed to have a vacant look about her.'

None of Sheila's close friends ever saw her again. Agnes Mennie remembered that on that last evening she seemed 'like a totally new person. It was as though when I met her she was wilting and she suddenly came back to life and was blooming.'[11]

On Friday evening, Sheila bumped into Freddie at Rags. She was with a group of casual friends and saw him again at a neighbour's party later. 'We had a pleasant evening,' Freddie recalled. 'She told me she was going to another party on the Saturday night with her ex-husband and that she was going to her parents' farm on the Sunday with the twins.'[12] He agreed to keep an eye on her flat while she was away.

In Goldhanger the following morning, Julie presented Jeremy with a bottle of hair dye, having been nagging him to darken his hair to complement hers. She regretted it afterwards, but Jeremy seemed happy with his new colour and left for the farm, where Sheila's godfather Basil Tweed was visiting with his wife Doris. June had already told Agnes Low that she wasn't looking forward to her daughter's visit after all, 'considering Sheila's condition', and that afternoon she said something similar to the Tweeds.[13]

Jeremy's appearance unsettled Colin at the housewarming party that evening before he even set foot in the flat: 'His silhouetted figure at my front door sent a cold shudder through me before I switched on the hall light and recognised him.'[14] Sheila had been at the flat all afternoon, helping with preparations. She withdrew as other guests arrived, speaking only to people whom she knew, and shared a joint with her brother. Herbie Flowers appeared unexpectedly after a trip to Australia and made small talk with her for a while.

Colin's girlfriend Heather arrived at 10.30pm. Jeremy spent most of the evening in the kitchen, where her flatmate Judith thought him 'a pleasant young man. He was entertaining, doing magic tricks.'[15] She noticed Sheila enter the kitchen and sit down awkwardly: 'Her movements were rigid and when her son jumped up on her lap, she didn't react in any way.' Sheila and Jeremy didn't chat, but he asked her a few times if she was okay. Colin recalled that she 'just sat there looking detached. She continuously kept staring out of the window.'[16] Sheila told Julie that her make-up looked nice, but stared at her repeatedly afterwards, making her feel uncomfortable.

Jeremy and Julie drove Sheila home around midnight. Daniel had gone to bed by the time they returned; Nicholas was tired but eager for Julie to tell him a bedtime story. Afterwards, she and Jeremy sat with Colin discussing Sheila's illness. He talked about alternative therapies and explained that he had mentioned his ideas to Nevill and June, but they couldn't afford to spend more on her care. Jeremy told him that was nonsense – their parents were 'loaded'.[17]

He then launched into an extraordinary tirade: 'My parents have dealt you a rough deal all along, Colin. Bludgeoning you into marrying Sheila. I know my sister is a difficult and selfish person. She's incapable of looking after Nicholas and Daniel. You've been forced to be a single parent in effect, with the twins a millstone around your neck . . .' Astonished and angry at his outburst, Colin interjected forcefully that Nicholas and Daniel were no such thing; he loved caring for them. Jeremy backed down immediately. Soon afterwards, he and Julie left for Gold-hanger.

The following Sunday afternoon, Colin took Sheila and the twins to White House Farm. On Monday morning, around ten o'clock, Douglas Pike called at the farm to collect the faulty cordless telephone from the kitchen; it had been a replacement for the original one, damaged during the lightning strikes. Sheila greeted him at the back door. He noticed Nicholas and Daniel: 'I was very impressed, as a grandfather, by the way that the two boys were behaving. They were standing at the end of the kitchen table making paper flags and colouring them in with pencils.'[18] Pike left thinking what a happy family they seemed.

Housekeeper Jean Bouttell shared a coffee with June and Sheila later that morning. Sheila seemed her normal self, if a little quiet. Mother and daughter then went into Tollesbury together, leaving the twins with Jean. After lunch, Sheila and her parents sat in the kitchen with the boys, reading *The Little Red Hen*. It was the last time Jean saw the family; she left work at half-past three and wasn't due at the farm the following day.

June then drove out to Vaulty with Sheila and the twins to visit her mother. Sheila watched the boys romping about the garden while June went upstairs, where Mabel's housekeeper recalled: 'We got her mother out of bed and sat her on a chair in the bedroom. While we were changing the bedclothes her mother was moaning because she wanted to get back into bed. Suddenly June was looking at me and muttering, "For heavens' sake, mother. I've got problems you know nothing about."'[19] It was out of character for June, who was always 'very sweet' towards her mother, but that day she 'looked and sounded very strained and tired'.

Stuart Sinclair noticed nothing amiss when the four of them arrived at Osea Road's shop later that afternoon. Nor did Barbara Wilson's son Philip, who saw Sheila afterwards at the farm, 'walking down Pages Lane away from the main road. The twins were with her. I was on the tractor at that time and I just waved to her. Sheila and the twins waved back. Sheila smiled and appeared quite happy.'[20] In the evening, Regine Pargeter tele-phoned June to enquire about them all: 'She said that they were fine and the boys were upstairs having a bath. That was the last time I spoke to her.'

After Sheila had put the boys to bed she rang her cousin Yvonne, who recalled: 'She sounded quite happy and we had a ten minute chat about jobs, boyfriends and the church. We arranged for her to come over to see me for a day with the twins on 7 August 1985 at 10.30am.'[21] But there would be no meeting; by then, everyone within White House Farm would be dead.

It is, mercifully, rare for children to kill their families. But studies show that such murders tend to be within the middle classes. Anthropologist Elliott Leyton explains: 'It is the family that regulates the social rise or fall of its members, and this task structures much of the thought and behaviour of an aspiring family. In such a milieu, children can become the vehicles for the social expectations of the parents: sometimes, that is all they are. In the insecure aspiring family, a corollary to this is often an atmosphere of diminished affection and inattentiveness to the child's true needs and abilities. The children may thus be ordered to curtail their social lives, surround themselves with the appropriate friends and possessions, obtain the "correct" occupations, and otherwise submerge their identities merely to fulfil their parents' ambitions.'[22]

The Bambers were part of 'the conservative backbone of rural society', highly regarded community leaders with 'long-term inter-generational commitment to their locality'.[23] When they adopted Sheila and Jeremy, they did so in the expectation that their children would become part of an established family network of shared business interests – much as Ann and David Boutflour grew up absorbing their parents' way of life, with jobs and marriages that reflected their upbringing. Robert Boutflour later declared that it was 'a sadness for Nevill and June that their children Sheila and Jeremy, both of whom were adopted, despite being brought up in the beautiful Essex countryside near Tolleshunt D'Arcy were not, like other farmers' children, interested in farming life'.[24]

In the wake of the trial, Sue Ryan, writing in *Today* on 29 October 1986, waded into the nature versus nurture debate with 'Bad Upbringing or Bad Blood': 'When an adopted child turns out well the parents are given the credit. When he turns out badly there is much nodding of heads, "Well, of course, he was adopted."' Almost twenty-five years later, David's wife Karen Boutflour inadvertently echoed the observation: 'When I first met David I can remember thinking, oh it seems slightly odd that it was made known to me that Sheila and Jeremy were adopted. Because they should just be part of the family, but I think it was partly to explain their sort of wayward behaviour.'[25]

Sheila told her husband and friends that she always felt like an outsider, while Jeremy declares that as far as other relations were concerned: 'I wasn't "blood." I was only adopted.'[26] But 'nurture' played a part in that too; where their cousins were schooled locally, Sheila and Jeremy were sent to board, weakening their ties with the area, its people and routines. 'They weren't brought up here as such,' Barbara Wilson states. 'They only came back for holidays and hadn't really got close friends in the village, kids their own age to bond with properly. Whereas if you live here, you become part of the fabric of the place.'

When the siblings reached their teens, their parents' closely guarded respectability bred anxiety in Sheila and resentment in Jeremy. Emotions were submerged and June's religious beliefs made it difficult for her to accept that her much-loved son and daughter had a more relaxed attitude to sex and relationships. June's preoccupation with the church led to fraught interactions with her children and occasionally alienated her peaceable husband, who tried with grace and good humour to keep everyone on an even keel. To what extent Sheila's breakdowns may have acted, as one psychiatrist suggests, as 'a screen for the divides within the family', can only be surmised.[27]

Jeremy's reaction to his mother's attempts at moral guidance was more prosaic than his sister's. He admitted there were rows as he became more independent, while June's closest confidante, Agnes Low, described him as 'spiteful towards his mother. He would make very cruel remarks to her and "run her down" in all sorts of ways.' Seasonal workers at the farm recalled that Jeremy could be equally rude to his father, but Nevill would not react. The overwhelming impression of Jeremy during those last years of family life is of an outgoing, somewhat immature young man who wanted the trappings of wealth without necessarily having to work hard, although there were undoubtedly periods where he did impress his parents and others with the efforts that he put in. But mostly, 'he was flash', as his friend Charles recalls. 'He was impressed by people who spend a lot and the things that money can buy, such as expensive cars.'[28]

Nevill and June had always provided the best for their children, but as Sheila and Jeremy moved into adulthood, this continued support came with obligation. Money was the means by which the Bambers strove to shape their children's lives, telling Jeremy that he couldn't expect his inheritance if he didn't break off an unsuitable relationship and knuckle down to work, and offering to buy a flat for Sheila when she fell pregnant if she and the father-to-be married before the birth. By succumbing to such inducements, both Sheila and Jeremy found themselves trapped in the net of their parents' good intentions.

The outcome for all of them, including Sheila's two young children, was calamitous.

The sun rose at half-past five over White House Farm on Tuesday 6 August.

In Goldhanger, Jeremy woke alone at seven o'clock and pulled on a white T-shirt, grey tracksuit bottoms and dirty white plimsolls. By half-past seven his silver Vauxhall Astra was parked in the farm's kitchen yard. At eight o'clock he and Nevill left the house to allocate jobs to the workers. An hour later Jeremy briefly returned to the house where Sheila and June were having breakfast with the twins. Tasked with harvesting rape all day, Jeremy was 'quite happy' driving the new tractor, collecting the combined rape seed and carting it to the barn where it was dressed, dried and stored.[1]

Nevill took a call that morning from his friend and fellow farmer Laurie Lawrence about some business. Laurie thought Nevill seemed somewhat subdued as he indicated that he had 'problems that were causing him more concern than losing an amount of money on a grain deal'.[2] June attended the half-past ten service at the village church, where she read the lesson. Len Foakes saw Sheila and one of the boys walking along Pages Lane with Crispy at half-past twelve: 'I slowed down the van that I was driving. The window was down and Sheila said to me, "Hello Len" and smiled. She seemed very happy then.'[3]

Throughout the day, there would be conflicting accounts of Sheila's mood and general appearance. At some points she seemed fine, yet others recall odd behaviour. The dichotomy may have been due to the effects of her medication, which influenced both her state of mind and her ability to function physically. What does emerge is an unsettling picture of her final day.

Painting the exterior walls at Vaulty that afternoon, Michael Horsnell noticed that all wasn't well. At quarter past three he recognized June's silver Renault as it turned in at the drive. He watched June, Sheila and the twins head into the garden: 'Mrs Bamber was playing with the two boys, jumping over small hedges and running up and down the garden. Sheila was with them, but she was like a zombie. She walked very rigidly and the only part of her that moved was from the knees down. She didn't even turn her head from left to right. I did not hear Sheila speak at all. They went into the house.'[4] June sought him out a short while later to discuss repairs: 'I got the definite impression that she was upset about something. She was in a different mood from when she had been playing with the children. It was not anything she said, but just the way she looked and was speaking.' When they left the house, 'Sheila definitely did not look normal' and was again 'walking stiffly, like a zombie from a horror movie'.

At four o'clock, Jeremy stopped the tractor when 'Sheila came down to the rape field with the twins'.[5] Barbara Wilson recalls that in all the time she worked for the Bambers, she rarely saw brother and sister together: 'Occasionally I'd see Jeremy with the twins. He'd bring them up to the office and we'd have peppermints together. Mr Bamber always had extra strong mints and he'd started giving them to the twins, but Mrs Bamber discouraged him so I gave them peppermints instead. After we'd had our peppermints and a little chat, Jeremy would take the twins to see the cows or kick a ball about with them in the garden. But the only time I ever saw Jeremy and Sheila together was when they sat at the table in the kitchen for coffee with everyone else.'[6]

One of the last lines Sheila wrote in her diary that day read: 'I didn't mean to be horrible to Jeremy.'[7] He insisted afterwards that he couldn't remember what they had talked about in the field: 'I had a ten minute chat with her and she returned to the farm.'

Nevill spoke to Alan Fraser-Bell, a South African student from Cirencester Agricultural College, before his tea break at five o'clock, asking him to assist Alf Foakes with the baling in Gold-hanger. Philip Wilson had been assigned the job of carting crops and emptying the trailers. He finished his tea and squinted across the field, watching Jeremy negotiate the turn with the tractor. It was hotter than it had been all day. The light glinted on Jeremy's mirrored sunglasses below the blue baseball cap he'd slung on to keep his hair from his eyes.

Five miles away in Tiptree, Barry Parker glanced up as June and Sheila entered his clothes shop on Church Road. The twins followed their mother, who looked fashionable in tight black pedal pushers and black pumps. The group congregated at the jeans rail. Nicholas and Daniel chose a pair each and went into the changing rooms.

'What do you think?' June asked, turning to Sheila as the boys came out to show them.[8]

'I like them,' Sheila said quietly.

When Parker told them the price, June exclaimed, 'We only want cheap ones for wear on the farm!' But they settled on the more expensive pair; the twins put £5 each towards the cost and June paid the rest. Parker was curious about Sheila, who spoke just twice during their half hour in the shop. She seemed 'vague and distant, she wasn't interested in the children and she struck me as a very strange woman'. As they left, he called out goodbye to see how she would react. He recoiled when Sheila turned and smiled, her red lipstick 'smudged all over her teeth'.

June drove to a nearby bungalow, where elderly widow Elizabeth Smith welcomed them. She had known June all her life and thought a lot of Sheila, 'a nice young woman who always seemed pleasant towards me. She would visit and bring the two boys along.'[9] They chatted for half an hour and all seemed normal.

Sometime after six, Katherine Golding was cycling home to Wycke Cottage and passed June and the twins with Crispy at the garden gate: 'Mrs Bamber said something like, "It's a better evening, isn't it?" I replied, "Yes, and it's about time too." I didn't stop and carried on cycling. She was perfectly polite and the two boys appeared normal and happy.'[10]

Nicholas and Daniel usually went upstairs about half-past seven at the farm for a bath after dinner. That evening they put on matching cotton paisley pyjamas, Daniel in red and Nicholas in blue, before climbing into their candlewick-covered beds in the narrow room next to the bathroom. The surface of the cupboard that stood between their beds was cluttered with toys, drawings and two Mr Men mugs half-filled with orange juice. Laid out at the foot of each bed were clothes for the morning they would not live to see.

Outside, the tractor moved slowly through the field.

*

Daylight was beginning to fade. The sash windows of the farm-house reflected the setting sun and against the evening sky, the surrounding trees stood out like black paper.

At eight o'clock, Philip Wilson began collecting the trailers. After finishing work in Goldhanger, Alan Fraser-Bell decided to leave his car at the farm and drove the tractor back to his cara-van in Osea Road. When Jeremy returned to the farmhouse, between 8pm and 9pm, his parents and Sheila were having supper. His mother usually attended Bible class on Tuesday eve-nings, but never when Sheila and the twins visited.[11] Jeremy made himself a ham sandwich, and stood at the sink to eat it.

As the only living witness, he recalled that the conversation at the supper table revolved around options for the twins' care and Sheila's treatment. His sister 'did not say anything, make any objections or agreements. She just appeared vacant.'[12] He inter-jected to suggest that Sheila should take a holiday to give her some interest, but June and Nevill were thinking more in terms of everyday practicalities. Otherwise, he didn't contribute much: 'I was popping in and out between loads from combining the rape seed. The field being harvested was next to the house and farm buildings.'[13] But while in the kitchen he saw – or remem-bered he had seen – a couple of rabbits outside.

His recollections are ambiguously phrased. In his first witness statement he describes himself 'in a rush, having just seen two rabbits'. In his second he asserts: 'Whilst the discussions were taking place I had to check the barn was running, this I normally did. I left the house for two minutes and returned to the farm-house. I had just seen some rabbits near the potato shed.'[14] In 2002, he recalled that it was 'early in the evening that I had seen the rabbits at the side of the Dutch barn on my return from the field. Once I had tipped the load I decided to grab the rifle and see if I could shoot the rabbits. Mum, Dad and Sheila were sit-ting at the table having supper when I went in to get the rifle.'[15]

He is consistent regarding fetching the Anschütz from the den, minus the sights and silencer, and in his statements about preparing the gun. He picked up 'a box of .22 hollow-nosed low velocity ammunition. The magazine was on the rifle but empty. I left the rifle in the hallway [scullery] by a pair of wellingtons, went into the kitchen with the box of ammunition in my hand

and the empty magazine. At this stage I tipped the box of ammunition out onto the sideboard near the telephone and loaded
between 8 and 10 rounds into the magazine clip.'[16] His parents
and sister were seated directly behind him at the table, but said
nothing to him. Sheila faced away from the dresser and 'would
have had a good view of what I was doing. I had my back to my
parents. I left the kitchen area, picked up the rifle from the hallway, put the magazine on the rifle and cocked [it].' He ran
outside but the rabbits were gone and he returned to the house
five minutes later, having failed to fire a single shot.

Inside the scullery again, he removed the magazine, then
'ejected the round that was in the breech and put it in the magazine' before resting the rifle 'up against the wall near the wellingtons'.[17] He left the magazine on top of an old blanket covering
the settle. His parents and Sheila were 'still in the kitchen. We
didn't speak, I didn't pop my head round the door, as I was in a
hurry to take a trailer to the combine.'

Nevill must have left the kitchen soon after his son. Philip
Wilson saw him 'about 9pm' in the yard near the bullock shed:
'He asked me to go and collect a trailer from Gardener's Farm,
Goldhanger. Mr Bamber appeared tired to me, although he was
calm and polite.'[18] When Jeremy returned to the farmhouse again
shortly afterwards, Nevill was once more in the kitchen with
June and Sheila: 'Everyone appeared happy.'

Keen to get home after a long day, Jeremy didn't notice
whether the rifle, magazine and ammunition were where he had
left them: 'I asked Dad if he would pick up the last trailer full
and he said he would, to save me staying around. I finished up in
the barn, shut the doors and took the trailer back to the field. I
told Len Foakes that Dad would take the trailer back and leave
the shed till morning when I'd process it.'[19] Len confirmed: 'He
said to me, "The old man will come down to collect the last lot."'
There was nothing untoward in his manner: 'Jeremy was quite
alright, not nervous or anything like that.'

Jeremy walked back to the house and said goodnight to
everyone at half-past nine. Dorothy Foakes heard a car 'pull
away from next door at high-speed' just after 9.30 and realized
who was at the wheel: 'The sound I heard was the same sound

Jeremy made when he roared off in his car from work on other occasions.'[20]

Heading for Goldhanger, Jeremy passed the home of electronic engineer Stephen Smith, who lived with his family on Tollesbury Road. His wife was out that evening and he recalled hearing a single gunshot between half-past nine and five past ten. As the details of what he heard have been incorrectly recorded elsewhere, they are included in full here: 'This shot came from a south-westerly direction, which would be in the direction of the village playing field and adjoining farm lands behind my home. The noise of the shot was dull, not crisp, and appeared like a shotgun within 500 yards away.'[21] Smith thought of it immediately the next day, when he heard the news about White House Farm.

Barbara Wilson rang the farm between half-past nine and ten o'clock. She had been working at North Maldon Growers that day and wanted to let Nevill know that her daughter's old bicycle with stabilizers was ready; the Bambers had one child's bike at the farm but needed another to teach the boys how to ride together.

Nevill answered after a couple of rings. 'I asked Mr Bamber if he'd like me to bring Sally's bicycle's over that evening,' Barbara recalls. 'But he said impatiently, "No, no, Barbara. I can pick it up tomorrow when I deliver potatoes to Mrs Bore. No, it's no problem. I'll take it in the truck." Then he said sharply, "And why didn't you come in today?" I was so surprised. I said, "Well – I wasn't due in today, was I, Mr Bamber? I was at North Maldon Growers." He knew but had forgotten. "Oh right," he said, sounding irritated. Then he slammed the phone down. I'd *never* heard him speak like that. I couldn't hear anything in the background, but something was happening at the farm that night. Mr Bamber never spoke to anyone like that – ever. I was upset for the rest of the evening.'

Barbara's son Philip returned the trailer from Goldhanger, leaving White House Farm at quarter to ten. Shortly before ten o'clock, Len saw Nevill on the tractor in the rape field, collecting the last load as agreed with Jeremy. At the house, June answered the telephone when it rang again just after the hour. It was

Pamela, wanting to know if Sheila and the twins had arrived that weekend. June told her that Sheila was just going to bed. 'I then spoke to Sheila,' Pamela recalled, 'and I enquired as to how she was keeping. She told me she was alright and she also said that she had been to visit an elderly lady with June and she had taken the twins.'[22]

Pamela did most of the talking. Sheila didn't chat as she generally did, and after two or three minutes the conversation dried up: 'June came back on the phone. I thought this was strange as [Sheila] didn't even say "goodnight auntie Pam", which she normally would do.'[23] June told her that Sheila had gone to bed, adding that she was 'very worried' about her and wanted Pamela to see her 'and form an opinion about her health'. She had 'no interest in anything, including the twins'. June then explained she had been 'trying to persuade Sheila to take a holiday at a home in Bournemouth'. Pamela invited them all over for lunch on Thursday and, after discussing their mother's care, the sisters said goodnight.

In Wix, Pamela told Robert that the conversation with Sheila had been 'hard-going'.[24] She sounded like 'a zombie' and didn't want to feed the twins or look after herself, which was why June wanted their advice about 'putting Sheila into a nursing home'. Describing the phone call to Colin some days later, Pamela recalled an extra detail: June had wanted Sheila to stay with a 'Christian community in Bournemouth'.[25]

At half-past ten, Len Foakes finished work at the farm. He glanced over at the field and watched Nevill on the tractor for a moment, then trudged off down the lane. He was the last person to see any member of the household that evening.

What happened afterwards, before Jeremy telephoned the police five hours later, can only be surmised. David Boutflour described his Uncle Nevill as 'not a particularly late night person' with a fairly set routine.[26] Each evening he would walk both dogs, Crispy and Bruce, around the front lawn before bed. Afterwards, Bruce would be settled in the barn on the far side of the kitchen yard while Crispy curled up for the night in his basket by the Aga or on a chair next to it. Both dogs were habitually alert to intruders. Crispy was variously described as 'very noisy', 'lively and always nipping at people's ankles' with a 'high-pitched yappy bark' that he used to good effect on callers.[27] Bruce would also bark when anyone approached the house.

After walking the dogs, Nevill had a shower in the down-stairs bathroom every night as a matter of course. It was his normal practice afterwards to pour himself a gin and tonic, then relax in the lounge with a cigarette. Before going upstairs he always checked the doors and windows. That night, the front door had been bolted internally and the back door from the yard was secured with the key inserted in the mortise lock. The door opposite, at the far end of the scullery, was fastened by three substantial bolts. There was one other outside door in the dairy, but it was locked and blocked internally and externally. The window in the dairy was slightly ajar but a metal mesh screwed to the inside of the window kept it secure.

Robert recalled that Nevill 'was the type of person who, when his head hit the pillow, would immediately fall asleep and not much would disturb him after that, whereas June was the opposite, she would hear every sound. I knew that she always had a hell of a job to go to sleep and would read the bible to help her.'[28] June kept her personal Bible, the 1984 NIV paper-back with its light blue cover and gold lettering, on her bedside table. Feeling a chill in the evening of late, she had a single floral eiderdown across the double continental quilt, with her electric blanket on top of the mattress. She and Nevill liked to sleep with their window slightly open and never locked their bedroom door. A nervous sleeper who was afraid of the dark, June often thought she heard noises in the large old house and would wake Nevill to investigate.

What time the adults at the farm went to sleep that night can never be known. Or even if they did.

In Kilburn, Colin felt inexplicably anxious all evening. He drove round to Heather's flat in South Hill Park, where they continued an argument about his relationship with Sheila. 'All these bloody problems with Bambs!' he shouted: 'I sometimes wish she was dead!'[29] Suddenly an overwhelming terror for his sons gripped him, and he broke down, sobbing that he was really frightened for them. Heather suggested ringing the farm to put his mind at rest, but it was almost eleven o'clock; too late to call six-year-old children. Then, as swiftly as it had begun, the tension drained from his body. He returned home and slept soundly until morning.

In his memoir, Colin wrote: 'I have often wondered whether anyone would have answered the telephone that night had I made a call, or whether I had actually picked up, telepathically, the moment of their deaths.'[30]

White House Farm stood silent, cloistered by trees, facing towards the salt marshes and causeway that appear in the ghost story, *The Woman in Black*. The moon rose high behind the house, and a cool breeze drifted across the fields to unsettle the ivy clinging fast to its walls.

In the heart of the home, the Aga was on a low light and the table had been set for breakfast. Sheila's sunglasses lay next to her place setting, closest to the dresser. On the turn on the main staircase, under the oil painting of Beatrice Bamber, stood a plaque bearing a line from Romans 5:1: 'We have peace with God, through our Lord Jesus Christ.'

Downstairs, a hand reached for the rifle.

3: HARVEST

7 August 1985 to 29 September 1985

Four hours after Nevill Bamber was last seen on his tractor, three policemen patrolling a crime-hit industrial estate in Witham decided they were wasting their time there and headed back to the station.

Sergeant Chris Bews and constables Stephen Myall and Robin Saxby were thawing out with mugs of tea when the call came through from Chelmsford Control. 'I got a potted version of the message they'd received,' Bews remembers. 'A chap in his twenties had rung about a call he'd had from his father, who was in a panic because the daughter had gone mad. Chelmsford said, "There might be firearms involved so get out there and have a look. The son will meet you at the house."'[1]

It was 3.35am when they climbed into the area car: Saxby in the back seat, Bews in front and Myall at the wheel. Myall was familiar with the route, a ten mile drive along twisting back roads, and drove fast: 'We reached the Queen's Head, all in darkness. I changed down a gear, passed the Red Lion and changed down again – then a car swung round the bend and crossed the road in front of me. I came up sharply behind it and had to drop a gear again because it was travelling so slowly.'[2] They passed the silver Vauxhall Astra on Tollesbury Road, at the junction with D'Arcy Way, and raced on to moonlit Pages Lane.

Myall pulled in at the passing place, opposite the farm cottages. He switched off the engine and Saxby radioed their time of arrival: 3.48am. Myall and Bews got out. 'We wondered where this fellow who was supposed to be meeting us had got to,' Bews recalls. 'He only lived down the road.' Two minutes later, the headlights of another car flashed at the foot of the lane. Myall thought it was their backup vehicle: 'Then I realized it was the Astra we'd passed earlier. It edged up the lane towards us.' The car drew in behind theirs and the driver climbed out.

Saxby recognized Jeremy from the collision on Maldon Road the previous November. Myall made a mental note of Jeremy's attire (blue blouson jacket, two crew-neck jumpers over a shirt, jeans and trainers) and his composure, which was 'remarkably calm, considering the information that had been relayed to us'.[3]

At Bews' prompting, Jeremy explained: 'About half an hour ago I was at home and father telephoned me. He sounded frightened and said, "Your sister's gone berserk and she's got a gun." Then the phone went dead. I tried phoning him back, but I couldn't get through, so I phoned the police. I phoned Witham first, but couldn't get a reply, so I phoned Chelmsford and told them what had happened. They said to meet you here.'[4]

'What do you mean, "the phone went dead?"' Bews queried. 'Do you mean it was hung up or your father just stopped talking?'

Jeremy shook his head: 'It sounded as though someone had put their finger on it to cut it off.'

'How many people are in the house?'

'My mother and father and my sister and her twin six year olds.'

'Are there any guns in the house?'

'Oh yes,' said Jeremy, 'lots.'

'How many and what sort?'

'A few shotguns and two .22 rifles.'

Bews reflects: 'He asked if we – myself and Steve – would go in, and told us "You can get in at the back." I said, "No, we're not going in, we'll do a reconnoitre." There was no way any of us were going in there unarmed.'

Bews and Myall set off on foot, retracing their steps when Jeremy made no attempt to follow. 'Is it likely your sister's in there with a gun?' Myall asked.[5]

Jeremy nodded.

'Who is she more likely to be annoyed at seeing, you or us?'

'Both of us. I don't get on with her at all. I don't like her and she doesn't like me.'

'I think as it's your family, you ought to come with us.'

'Alright,' Jeremy said, and they headed towards the farmhouse.

Three contemporaneous accounts provide a record of police procedure from the time of Jeremy's initial call to the removal of bodies the following afternoon. Constable Michael West, who answered his call at Chelmsford Police Station, began the 'event log', recording messages passed to the station and requests made by officers there on behalf of those at the scene. At 3.26am, civilian employee Malcolm Bonnett, working in the Information Room at Essex Police Headquarters in Chelmsford, had received PC West's call regarding the information relayed by Jeremy; he and his shift replacement kept the 'radio log', recording messages passed to the Information Room and calls made from there and at the request of officers at the scene. At White House Farm, PC Saxby and later PC William Chaplin maintained the 'scene log', recording each individual who arrived during the police operation.

After receiving Jeremy's call, PC West had tried phoning the farmhouse himself. He received 'an intermittent tone showing the line to be engaged' and contacted the GPO operator.[6] BT switchboard worker Jean Rowe checked the line at 3.42am and found the telephone was off the hook. She checked it again at 3.56am and listened to the open line: 'There wasn't any speech but I could hear a dog barking, the noise was loud so it appeared that the dog was near to the receiver.'[7]

Approaching the kitchen yard, Bews asked Jeremy if Sheila was likely to go berserk with a gun. 'I don't really know,' he replied. 'She's a nutter, she's been having treatment.' He added that she was 'a depressive psychopath' and 'doolally'.[8]

'Why do you think your father called you and not the police?' Bews asked.

'You've got to understand that he's not the sort of person to get organisations involved. He likes to keep it in the family, the family name and all that. All the treatment she's had has been private, he doesn't even like the National Health Service.'

'Why didn't you call 999 instead of going to the trouble of looking up the number of Chelmsford police station?'

'I didn't think it would make any difference to how quickly you got here. I don't know how your system works.'[9]

Bews was baffled by his response but they were already at the gate, thirty yards from the back door. Light spilled from the kitchen window; the curtains were open but there was no sign of movement. Lights also burned behind drawn curtains in two rooms directly above: the bathroom and the twins' bedroom.

'Steve wanted to approach the kitchen,' Bews recalls. 'But we weren't armed and there was no cover, so I decided we'd walk around the perimeter instead. I wasn't happy about Bamber being with us – if our witness got shot, that wouldn't look good for us and it wouldn't have been very nice for him either. But we needed him there.' They made their way to the field at the front, where they could view the house without being seen. Upstairs, a centre light was on and muffled sounds of distress came from June's dog. In the outbuilding to their left, Nevill's labrador unleashed a volley of barks.

'That's really strange, the way those dogs are barking and my father's not coming to see what's happening,' Jeremy told them. 'Usually he's only got to get the smell of a fox in the back garden and he's out there.'[10] Bews decided they ought to return to the area car. Months later, he recounted what happened next: 'As we moved away, I thought we saw something else move, a shadow, something like that. We looked up and after looking for a couple of minutes, I was satisfied that it was perhaps a part in the glass that just shone the light slightly as you looked at it.'[11]

The three men sprinted past the kitchen yard and out into the lane. 'There was nothing more we could do,' Bews shrugs today. 'There's a standard set of rules to follow and I thought we'd either find five dead people inside the house – four murders and a suicide – or four murders and a nutter with a gun.'

He turned to Jeremy: 'You're not going in there.'

Jeremy nodded: 'Alright, but aren't you going in? They might need help.'

'Yes, and if I go in I might need help,' Bews replied, radioing for armed assistance.

Sergeant Douglas Adams and five of his officers were on duty conducting an unarmed surveillance operation when they over-heard talk of a possible firearms incident at Tolleshunt D'Arcy on their radios. Permission for them to obtain their weapons and head to the farm was granted by Chief Superintendent George Harris, Divisional Commander for Chelmsford Police, who had commanded over sixty murder investigations during his twenty-three years in CID.

While they waited in the chill night air of Pages Lane, Bews thought quickly: 'I was a trained firearms officer myself and knew the unit would need as much information as possible. I handed

Bamber a clipboard, paper and pen, and asked him to get on with a floor plan of the house and to list any weapons and ammunition inside.' Jeremy sat in the Astra with the door open, sketching an outline in black pen.

Myall asked him, 'You said your sister was nutty. What did you mean by that?'[12]

'She's a depressive psychopath,' Jeremy repeated. 'She's been having psychiatric treatment, she only came out of hospital about six weeks ago.'

'Is she capable of using a gun?'

'Yes, she used to come target shooting with me and she's used all the guns before.'

At 4.22am, two cars arrived: CA05, containing Constables Robin Norcup and Paul Cracknell, and CA06, containing Constables Alan Batchelor and Robert Lay. Bews briefed the four as Jeremy handed the floor plan to Norcup. A discussion about firearms followed, during which Jeremy stated: 'We always keep a loaded gun lying around in case a fox runs across the garden.'[13] A short while later, Cracknell heard him exclaim, 'Oh God, I hope she hasn't done anything silly.' It was 'one of the few occasions he showed any emotion'.

Bews and Myall returned briefly to the farmhouse, where nothing had changed apart from the dogs ceasing barking. Bews studied Jeremy's floor plan and asked if any of the weapons were likely to be loaded. Jeremy told him about the Anschütz from the night before: 'I thought I heard a rabbit so I loaded the full magazine of ten and went out in the garden but didn't fire it.'[14]

Myall looked at him curiously. 'He was calm, very passive and compliant,' he recalls. 'He seemed totally accepting of the situation. Usually in circumstances like that, you'd put all your efforts into trying to keep the bystander calm, but that wasn't necessary with him.' Years later, Jeremy defended his apparent composure: 'I had no idea about what had or was about to take place in the house and felt with the police there that we could control the situation and resolve matters with a happy ending.'[15]

The firearms team arrived at 4.58am. Officers in flak jackets climbed out of transit vans, accompanied by a police dog unit. Jeremy expressed shock at seeing police officers with guns while Sergeant Adams examined the floor plan. After questioning

Jeremy more closely about guns inside the house, Adams instructed him to lead them to within sight of the kitchen yard, colour-coding the house to aid directions.

Two of the armed officers, constables Laurence Collins and Kenneth Delgado, then made a cursory search of the outbuildings and circled the house to assess a point of entry. There was no sign of any movement. Confirming it was safe to move forward, Collins and Delgado, together with another firearms officer, Constable Adrian Alexander-Smart and Sergeant Adams, converged inside the cattle shed facing the yard. Jeremy remained with them. Collins asked if he knew what sort of thing Sheila liked to talk about and if there was anyone she would prefer to speak to, if they were able to make contact with her.

Jeremy nodded: 'Doctor Ferguson from Harley Street who is treating her, and she does like to be told she is pretty, and she likes to make herself up.'[16]

Adams radioed PC Nigel Dermott to join them in the cattle shed, ordering him to wait with Jeremy while he conferred with Collins and Delgado. Dermott recalled: 'I asked him what sort of state Sheila was in when he last saw her and he said that she was very depressed, that there had been a conversation with the family about fostering the twins to which Sheila made no contribution at all. He told me that Sheila was a paranoid schizophrenic and had been receiving treatment. He said that it made him feel terrible seeing lots of police with guns and that he couldn't help knowing what we were going to find in the house.'[17]

Adams then returned, instructing Dermott to equip PC Mercer with body armour and find a containment position on the 'black' side of the house. As they crossed the geese compound with a police dog, Zeus, padding at their heels, other members of the team were deployed about the place, covering the house from every angle. Constables Matthews and Macintosh had a clear view of the front and were responsible for monitoring radio messages. Other officers were stationed about the farm track and fields, where a pale mist drifted as dawn broke over the estuary.

Collins and Delgado began using a loud hailer to address Sheila.[18] They attempted to make contact with the house for approximately two hours, but the only response was Crispy, yapping frantically inside the property, and Bruce's deeper bark from the outbuilding in the kitchen yard. Adams had Jeremy escorted back to the forward control point, where PC Myall engaged him in conversation, judging him 'calm and controlled' and 'in some instances, quite jovial'.[19] Jeremy mentioned how the Osea Road business would be able to stand him a Porsche sometime that year.

Today, Myall remembers their conversation with a shake of his head: 'Oh yes, the Porsche. He said words to the effect of "if anything happened to the family" he would probably sell the caravan business and buy a Porsche. Very strange, given the situation.' At one point Myall asked whether Sheila was likely to cause herself any harm. Jeremy answered, 'Yes, more than likely, she's tried to commit suicide several times.'[20]

Conversely, when Adams returned briefly to the transit van, Jeremy appeared 'visibly upset', asking, 'What if anything has happened in there, they are all the family I've got?'[21] Myall sought permission for Jeremy to telephone his girlfriend Julie: 'He told me that he had phoned her before he had left home to tell her that something was wrong.'[22]

PC Lay drove Jeremy to the nearest telephone box, next to the village store. The two men only had one coin between them, allowing Jeremy just enough time to tell Julie that a police car was picking her up before the pips went.

In their absence, Sergeant Adams sent for further armed support and asked the GPO to monitor the telephone inside the farmhouse kitchen. At 5.40am, Jean Rowe on the BT switchboard listened to the open line again. As she strained to hear, from inside the room there came faintly but distinctly, 'a very slight moving sound'.

PC Lay left Jeremy at the forward control point and departed for Tiptree to liaise with the incoming firearms units. When Sergeant Adams asked for further clarification on the weapons inside the house, Jeremy responded hesitantly, 'I should say the bolts have been removed and everything is locked away—'

'I'm not interested in what you should say,' Adams interrupted. 'I'm concerned for the safety of my officers and I want to know how the guns have been left.'

Jeremy told him that he had left the loaded Anschütz inside the kitchen door and that his father kept several loaded guns around the house. Adams returned to the cattle shed facing the back door. The telephone line inside the house had been linked up to Essex Police Headquarters for continual monitoring. Officers visited the farm cottages, warning everyone to stay indoors, and a roadblock was set up at the foot of the lane.

Chief Inspector Charles Clark, commander of the Force Support Unit, was directed to the cattle shed upon arrival and studied Jeremy's floor plan. 'At this stage it would be honest of me to say I accepted Jeremy's story and was reacting accordingly,' Sergeant Adams stated afterwards. 'PC Collins voiced concern over the safety of the twins and wanted to enter the house. I refused this. I believe I discussed this with Mr Clark and he was happy with my decision, saying everything appears to be in order. We had discussed that if any entry was going to be effected our best method of achieving that was waiting for reinforcements.'

Adams spoke to Jeremy again at quarter to seven, asking if he had a spare key to the back door. Jeremy replied that the key would be in the lock. They had scarcely finished speaking when two transit vans, escorted by PC Lay, turned in from the main road. The vehicles pulled up at the fork in the track, disgorging Inspector Ivor Montgomery and ten armed officers. As requested by Sergeant Bews, two ambulances followed close behind, 'one for immediate use, one for standby'.[23] Both turned in at the white garden gate, where one of the ambulance staff mistook Jeremy for a detective because he seemed so calm.

Adams briefed Inspector Montgomery 'along the lines of four bodies and a suicide. Fair to say myself and my team were in that frame of mind at this stage.' The newly arrived firearms officers followed Adams and Montgomery to the cattle shed. Adams pointed out his men keeping watch around the property and displayed the floor plan, adding that Sheila was 'capable of using all the weapons, particularly the .22 rifle, as Jeremy Bamber had given her lessons in its use.'[24]

The armed officers were split into two groups: one set to storm the house under Adams's instructions, the other to provide further containment. Montgomery assumed responsibility for the latter, deploying his officers about the grounds to provide maximum cover when the raid team were ready to effect entry.

PC Mercer returned to the forward control point: 'Sat in the

White House Farm.

June and Nevill Bamber at White House Farm in 1957. After eight years of marriage without children, they decided to adopt.

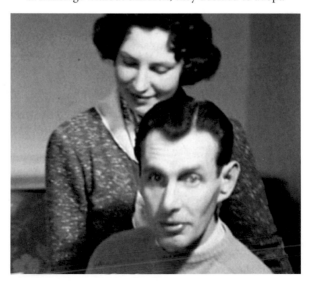

Nevill and June in the kitchen yard of White House Farm with
Bruce and Crispy, their dogs.

Sheila was born on 18 July 1957 and adopted as a baby by the Bambers
through the Church of England Children's Society.

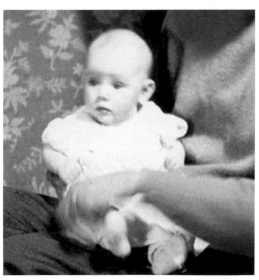

Jeremy was born on 13 January 1961; like Sheila, he was adopted through the Church of England Children's Society.

Sheila and Jeremy at home in the early 1960s. Family and friends remember Jeremy as a placid little boy, eager to please, and Sheila as very affectionate but temperamental.

June with Sheila and Jeremy, and Jasper the dog, on the front lawn of White House Farm in the late 1960s.

Sheila as a young teenager with Jeremy, who was four years her junior.

June with Sheila and Jeremy in the kitchen at White House Farm in April 1974. June loved her children deeply but found their increasing independence difficult.

14 May 1977. Sheila's wedding to Colin Caffell at Chelmsford registry office. From left to right: Jeremy, Nevill, June, best man Nicholas Rudge, Sheila, Colin, Colin's father Reg, and Colin's sister Diane and her daughter.

Silver Jubilee celebrations at Tolleshunt D'Arcy, 7 June 1977. From left to right: Reg Caffell, June, Sheila, Jeremy, Colin and Nevill.

Sheila's dream was to be a successful model. Her portfolio – including this photograph taken at her graduation from Lucie Clayton's – showed promise, but her career stalled shortly before the twins were born and never really recovered despite her attempts to restart it.

Colin with Nicholas and Daniel after his marriage to Sheila ended. They shared custody of the twins and remained on good terms. Colin had a loving relationship with his sons and became their primary carer after Sheila's second breakdown in March 1985.

Sheila with Nicholas and Daniel at White House Farm. She was a devoted mother to her lively young sons and wanted desperately to be well enough to look after them properly again.

Jeremy in the kitchen at White House Farm, c.1981.
Nevill and one of the twins can be seen in the lower right-hand corner,
next to the Aga.

June and Sheila with Nicholas and Daniel (and Crispy) on the
steps of the front porch at White House Farm, c.1981.

police vehicle was Jeremy Bamber. I put police dog Zeus in the van and Mr Bamber said, "That's a nice looking dog." We talked on the subject of dogs and Mr Bamber said how he would like a German shepherd. The conversation went to the incident at the farm and Mr Bamber said, "I feel bad as I was using the rifle last night shooting rabbits. I left it laying against the back door with a full magazine." I said, "Does your sister know how to use it?" He said, "I've taken her out a couple of times and shown her."'[25]

At 7.10am, the sub-divisional commander at Witham, Chief Inspector Terrie Gibbons, arrived and was also directed to the cattle shed. Twenty-three years in the force, with ten years in CID, Gibbons assumed divisional responsibility, approving the decision for the firearms team to force entry. Superintendent George Harris, divisional commander for Chelmsford Police, arrived shortly afterwards. The higher-ranking officers remained in the barn, apart from Inspector Montgomery, who joined two members of the firearms unit near the wall at the rear of the kitchen yard, opposite the back door.

It had been daylight for some time, clouds scudding overhead as the raid team prepared to enter the house at half-past seven. Acting Sergeant Peter Woodcock would force the back door with a sledgehammer while the rest of the group provided cover. Final challenges were issued by loudhailer as the raid team left the barn and inched forward, moving along the outbuildings to the left of the kitchen yard, keeping very close to the wall as they stopped at the back door.

First in line, Collins peered past the door and caught a glimpse through the kitchen window of someone bent forward at an inexplicable angle. He mistakenly radioed that a female body had been sighted. Delgado, directly behind him, could only see the work surface on the right, with the telephone off the hook, its receiver lying next to the cradle.

Collins tried the back door. It was locked with the key inserted on the inside, just as Jeremy had told them. He stood aside while Woodcock swiftly checked the door, confirming it secure. At 7.34am, the police log recorded: '5 knocks on the door heard over phone.'[26] The raid team had tried one last time to see if anyone would answer. But the house stood silent and still.

Woodcock raised the sledgehammer.

Jeremy had been moved from the forward control point to a police vehicle when Collins reported seeing a body. PC Lay kept him talking. He was 'relatively calm but occasionally became upset' and again mentioned acquiring 'a £38000 Porsche – a dream car from my dad'.[1] At one point he appeared near tears, mumbling, 'Oh God, I hope she hasn't done anything stupid.'

On the other side of the farmhouse, Woodcock's repeated sledgehammer blows splintered the back door from its locks.

He stepped inside the scullery. The door at the far end was obviously bolted; the door to his immediate right appeared closed. Collins and Delgado edged past him into the kitchen.

Nevill was hunched over in an almost impossible position next to the Aga, bare from waist to knee, right foot caught in his pyjama bottoms. A toppled chair lay trapped beneath him. The coal scuttle had stopped his fall; his battered head pressed upon it, blood coagulating into a pool at his feet and seeping out from a pair of men's trousers lying on the floor to his right. There were blood smears on a tile above his head, on the kettle on the hob and the Aga at his side. In front of the coal scuttle were four cushions in a neat pile and next to them, a shard of wood. The kitchen table had been pushed into the dresser, sending magazines and Sheila's place setting to the floor, cracking the bowl in two. An earthenware pot had rolled across the room, scattering clumps of brown sugar. The twins' wooden stools and all but one of the chairs had been overturned. Fragments of the lampshade that hung above the table were strewn about the room.[2]

Seeing the disarranged furniture and spots of blood near the cupboards, Collins concluded that 'a violent struggle had taken place' and radioed through that the body he had thought was female was that of a man.[3]

Backing into the kitchen, armed with a shotgun, Constable Michael Hall heard him rectify his mistake. He turned to cover Collins, who pulled open the door to the right of the Aga, revealing the dark, cluttered service stairs. Hall stepped over the pooled blood and spilt sugar to guard the staircase while Collins, Delgado and Woodcock returned to the scullery.

Alexander-Smart stood by the broken back door, letting in Acting Sergeant John Manners, who passed through the kitchen to guard the hallway. Acting Sergeant Raymond Rozga and Constable Paul Webb were called in from the yard; Rozga to cover the stairs at the back of the scullery and Webb to watch the dairy off the kitchen. Manners warned him 'not to tread in all the blood'.[4]

In the den cupboard, Collins found a double barrelled shotgun and boxes of ammunition. Returning to the scullery, he unbolted the door at the far end onto a small, untidy porch. Re-bolting it, he climbed the wooden stairs behind Woodcock and Delgado. A door at the top led into the office where Woodcock discovered 'an old, rusty shotgun in pieces' among the 'papers, books and other general rubbish'.[5] An adjoining storeroom contained old furniture; there was no way through to the bedrooms. Woodcock called Rozga up to maintain cover before he and his colleagues descended the stairs.

In the kitchen, Hall suddenly heard movement overhead. Fearing they were about to be confronted by Sheila, he began calling to her. One of the raid team quickly explained that it was Rozga on the floor above.

Alexander-Smart covered the service stairs while Hall, Woodcock, Collins, Delgado and Manners searched the rest of the ground floor. They unbolted the front door and opened a dining room window to provide an escape route. The cellar door in the hall was stuck fast with congealed paint. As they prepared to head upstairs, Acting Sergeant Timothy Mildenhall entered through the back door, allowing Alexander-Smart to join them. Collins used an extending mirror to assess the area before they went up.

In its reflection was a woman.

They climbed the stairs and found June collapsed against the door of the master bedroom. Between her eyes was a gunshot wound; the lace bib of her blue nightdress was rust-coloured. Her lower limbs were streaked with blood and in the red stream seeping down the carpet divider lay a single cartridge case. Two more cases gleamed beside a jumper in the doorway.

Bloodstained pillows on the antique brass bed bore the impact of two bullets and the eiderdown and sheets were splashed with blood. From under the bed came a whimper; tentatively, Collins moved aside the eiderdown and saw June's little brown and white dog quivering with terror. To protect the crime scene, the traumatized animal was deposited inside the main wardrobe.

It was then that they saw Sheila.

She lay supine on the floor, two bullet wounds to her throat. On her body was the rifle, its barrel against her jaw. Blood had pooled in her mouth and dried on both sides of her face; it bloomed in the armpit of her blue nightdress and upper arm, formed trails on her lower arm and stained her hand where it rested on the gun. Beside her were a pair of blood-spotted blue socks and at her shoulder was June's Bible, its pages fanned on the carpet. A handwritten note on white card had slipped out against her shoulder; a piece of white crocheted material was tucked inside the Bible's back cover. Although the carpet was spattered with blood, Woodcock observed that the soles of her feet were 'spotlessly clean'.[6]

The raid team checked the box room before retracing their steps to the landing, calling Webb upstairs to cover the corridor. Alexander-Smart remained inside the master bedroom and Manners stayed by June's body, surmising that the blood on her limbs was due to being 'dragged by the legs. I was aware of many empty .22 bullet cases on the floor.'[7]

Woodcock made a cursory search of Sheila's room: 'The bed nearest the door appeared undisturbed and there were a collection of cosmetics and a box of Tampax lying on top of the counterpane. The other bed had the bedclothes pulled down and appeared as though someone had been in the bed and then got up.'

Hall covered the upper landing while Woodcock, Collins and Delgado went down into the corridor.

The first door on the left was a cupboard. The door opposite bore a ceramic plate that read 'Jeremy's Room'. It was locked.

They turned to the next room on the left.

Daniel was curled up in the left bed with his thumb in his mouth, facing the wall. The devastating wounds to his skull were scarcely visible through his thick hair. Nicholas lay on his back in the right hand bed, three bullet wounds to his face, the blood heavily congealed. Tucked in beside him was a fur-matted black and white toy dog. On the bed lay a poster of the Care Bears, floating happily in a blue sky with their friend the Cloud Keeper.

The officers stood in the doorway a moment, overcome despite their professionalism. 'The bedclothes on both beds were not unduly disturbed,' Woodcock remembered, 'no more than would be normally expected from a sleeping child.' Spent cartridge cases glinted malevolently in the soft light.

The raid team turned away, searching the rest of the upper floor. Woodcock forced the lock on Jeremy's room and found a jumble of boxes, bags, old suitcases and magazines on every surface, including the narrow bed. Rozga waited in the adjoining first floor office until being stood down, while Mildenhall remained in the small storeroom guarding the hatch to the loft, which was inspected last. Collins also forced the door to the cellar but the stairs began to cave beneath him and he scrambled out.

When the house had been declared safe, Chief Inspector Gibbons called Chris Bews over, telling him: 'They've found everybody dead, including the sister. It looks like she killed them all, she'd got a gun. Let Jeremy know.'[8]

Heavy-hearted, Bews returned to Pages Lane. Jeremy was stood behind a police car, smoking a cigarette. 'I'm afraid it's bad news . . .'

Jeremy looked at him. 'What?'

'There's no hope for any of them,' Bews said. 'They've all been shot.'

'What . . . everybody?'

'Yes.'

There was a flicker in Jeremy's expression.

'Do you want to sit down?' Bews asked.

He said, 'No, I'm alright,' then began to cry.

The cogs of authority started to whirr: scene of crime officers, senior divisional CID officers, the coroner's officer and the police surgeon were all contacted. Chief Inspector Harris rang Assistant Chief Constable Peter Simpson to inform him of developments.

Chief Inspector Clark departed the scene, leaving Harris, Gibbons and Montgomery to view the bodies.

Inspector Montgomery made a mental note of the 'dried blood' leaking from Sheila's mouth and the distribution of blood on her right side, trying to establish how she had shot herself.[9] He was 'unable to come to a solution. I also noticed how clean her feet were, both top and bottom, so much so that it drew one's attention to them.' When Sergeant Adams appeared, they discussed how 'Nevill must have put up a hell of a struggle' and that it appeared the children were killed in their sleep.[10]

Outside, the firearms teams and dog unit prepared to depart, stationing Woodcock and Manners on site to show incoming officers around and make safe any weapons. Sergeant Jeapes noticed Jeremy sitting tearfully inside a police car and asked PC Dermott to fetch him a cup of tea from one of the farm cottages. He recalled Jeremy being in a very distressed state.

As the firearms units travelled back to Chelmsford, a conversation began about something being amiss at the scene. Sergeant Adams remembered one of the team declaring: 'The only people that will ever know the truth are the five in the farm.'

Dr Ian Craig arrived at 8.25am. A police surgeon for thirty years and known to the Bambers, after conferring with Chief Superintendent Harris he realized 'there didn't appear to be any doubt about the murder/suicide aspect.'[11] He then introduced himself to Jeremy, telling him he would be back in a few minutes before departing for the farmhouse with Harris.

PC Saxby sat down beside Jeremy. 'I'm sorry it turned out this way,' he said. 'Are you alright?'[12]

Jeremy turned to him. 'You said everything would be alright.'

'Yes,' Saxby said. 'We obviously hoped that it would.'

'But you said it would be alright.'

'I know. We like to think things will work out.'

Jeremy fell silent.

Inside the farmhouse kitchen, Dr Craig gazed at Nevill's lifeless body. It occurred to him that Nevill must have been 'immobilised first, as I would have expected him to take some action otherwise'. He certified death at 8.40am, then headed upstairs, glancing at the obviously fatal gunshot to June's forehead, then moving across to Sheila's body. He noted the 'quantity of dried blood' from her mouth.[13] Seeing 'only one gunshot wound at that stage', he felt reasonably satisfied that she had taken her own life. He pronounced both women dead at 8.44am and the twins at 8.50am.

Dr Craig's duty that morning was primarily to certify death and inform officers of any specific observations. He was not required to take body temperatures unless specifically asked. Nor was it general practice within Essex Police to estimate times of death based on that method without consulting a pathologist. Dr Craig could only estimate that the deaths at White House Farm had occurred 'some hours' before, within 'a short time' of each other; the twins and their grandparents had died 'due to gunshot wounds inflicted by another person', while in Sheila's case 'the wound had been inflicted by her own hand'.[14]

He and Chief Superintendent Harris returned to Jeremy, whose request to visit the house was refused. To their surprise, he then asked: 'Can't I see my dad?'[15]

Harris explained again that his parents were dead.

Jeremy began to sob: 'I want to see him. Why can't my dad come out to see me?'

The two men attempted to comfort him, aware of another police car rumbling up from the main road. Detective Constable Michael Clark was at the wheel; next to him was the unmistakable figure of Detective Chief Inspector Thomas Jones.

The 1986 internal police review of the Bamber investigation described 'Taff' Jones as 'a proud, strong-minded, hard-working individual' with a 'dynamic approach'. The adjectives were carefully chosen, for Taff Jones was a divisive figure within the constabulary. One officer still exercising caution pronounced him 'a fiery, thundering Welshman. I personally found him difficult to get on with.'[16] But several of Jones's more senior peers feel that he was made a scapegoat for the intense public criticism of the Bamber case. Jones himself was unable to respond to the censure, dying suddenly in May 1986, five months before the case came to trial.

Llandudno-born, Taff Jones joined the police in 1960 at the age of twenty-one and was appointed to the CID three years later. He received ten commendations during his career and was

a very experienced officer, having worked with the Regional
Crime Squad as a detective inspector and as a detective chief
inspector. He also successfully captained the police football team
to the top of their league. At the time of the Bamber enquiry he
had been married twenty-four years and was father to two
daughters and a son.

In Pages Lane, he and DC Clark were met by Sergeant Bews,
with whom Jones had clashed three months earlier during the
investigation into the murder of Patsy Bull, shot by her husband
in Coggeshall. Jones had already been informed that Sheila 'had
gone berserk in possession of a firearm' but was unaware the
entire household was dead until Bews enlightened him.[17]

Chief Inspector Gibbons appeared then, indicating that he
wanted a word. DC Clark, an ex-Army man who had been
stationed in Northern Ireland, moved away slightly. He noticed
Jeremy sitting in a police vehicle, sipping tea and talking to Dr
Craig and Chief Superintendent Harris. When Jeremy asked for
something stronger, Dr Craig fetched a hip flask from his own
car and added a drop of whisky to his cup.

At a nod from DCI Jones, Clark joined the three senior officers heading for the house to view the bodies. PC Chaplin logged
their entry on his clipboard at 9.05am. Clark recalled that in the
master bedroom, DCI Jones looked at Sheila for some time while
discussing the position of the gun, her wounds and the Bible: 'He
concluded that it appeared she had taken her own life.'[18] There
was no mention of calling out a pathologist, ballistics expert or
biologist.

The next group on PC Chaplin's log sheet arrived at 9.16am:
Detective Sergeant Neil Davidson and Detective Constable David
Hammersley, both Scene of Crime, and Detective Inspector
Robert Miller of Braintree CID, accompanied by Detective
Sergeant Stan Jones of Witham CID.[19]

DS Jones was suspicious of Jeremy from the moment he set
eyes on him. A married father in his mid-forties, Jones had joined
the police in 1961 and was regarded by his superiors as 'a very
intelligent, experienced detective' with a 'well developed sense
of humour'.[20] Working on the Bamber enquiry, he never really
faltered in his belief that Jeremy was guilty of massacring his
family.

Davidson recalls being surprised by how many people were at the house and suspected that the scene 'was not being preserved'.[21] DI Miller, having served twenty years on the force – twelve of those in the CID – agreed with him: 'I thought, "What's this all about? It's supposed to be a crime scene." That's the first thing that struck me. It was my patch, but Taff Jones was the on-call officer. I knew him, of course.'[22]

As DS Jones and Miller parked up in Pages Lane, they spotted Jeremy walking towards the field. He had spoken to Dr Craig about the supper table discussion ending in a row about the care of the twins, whom he described as 'ill treated by their mother'.[23] He declared that Sheila should never have been discharged from a 'mental hospital' and that her treatment amounted to 'a lot of tablets and injections'. When Dr Craig asked if the alleged abuse had been reported, Jeremy shook his head, adding that it would have spoiled the good name of the family. He then asked for a walk alone and began retching in the field before disappearing behind a hedge.

He was carrying a small bunch of opium poppies when Dr Craig caught up with him. Explaining that the farm had a special licence to grow them for the pharmaceutical industry, he walked round to the kitchen yard and let the labrador out of the barn. Following him, Dr Craig felt Jeremy was 'grief stricken' and suffering 'emotional shock'. He said as much to Chief Superintendent Harris before departing, but confirmed that Jeremy was fit for interview.

The last Scene of Crime officers arrived. Detective Inspector Ron Cook joined the police in 1958 and became a fingerprint officer in 1964. Seventeen years later he was promoted to Detective Inspector and was one of two deputies working at SOCO in Chelmsford under DCI Charles 'Geordie' Wright. Cook was accompanied by Detective Constable David Bird, who joined the force in 1976, working on murder photography and chemical treatments as part of a crime scene investigation course. The Bamber case was his second as photographer while he was engaged on the lab treatment. Along with Chris Bews and Taff Jones, Bird had recently worked on the Bull murder in Coggeshall. When told at headquarters to collect five post-mortem kits for White House Farm, he assumed it was a wind-up: 'Then I looked at the superintendent's face and saw it was no joke. I went and got the kits.'[24]

DI Cook was briefed by DCI Jones in the kitchen yard: 'He gave me the impression straight away that a woman had shot her family and then shot herself.'[25] At half-past nine he was granted access to the house with DI Miller and DS Jones. Bird, Hammersley and Davidson remained outside. DI Miller was unsettled: 'Because Taff had made up his mind, it had ceased to be a crime scene. Ordinarily, it would have been taped off for the day and only people who needed to go in there would have done. But too many boots had been in already. I'd just been given my instructions: "Right Bob, get in there, get it sorted and the coroner's report done."'

Cook concurs that 'as far as Taff was concerned, it *was* four murders and a suicide. He was very much: "I'll get hold of the coroner's officer to make arrangements for the pathologist, blah-blah . . ." That was routine in normal coroner's cases and he then left us to get the bodies ready for removal to the mortuary. But the two wounds to Sheila's neck caused us concern. I presumed that as the Divisional DCI, Taff had been at the incident for some considerable time. It wasn't until much later that I found out he'd been through the house only fifteen minutes before us.'[26]

DC Michael Clark remained at Pages Lane with Jeremy, puzzling over the state of mind of the last remaining family member. 'I made an effort to converse with him in relation to his family being shot and he didn't appear to want to discuss this,' Clark recalled. 'He showed little signs of any emotion and spoke of getting the harvest in.'[1] Jeremy made only one reference to the murders: 'Sheila ought to be in a nuthouse for what she's done.' Clark looked at him and said nothing but sensed that he 'had not come to terms with the fact that they were all dead'.

A relief officer approached with Crispy in his arms. Jeremy eyed his mother's dog and declared: 'I hate that fucking thing.'[2] Unsettled, Clark quietly had a word with DS Stan Jones.

Turning to Jeremy, Jones said matter-of-factly: 'Your parents, sister and the twin boys are all dead and you must accept it, do you understand?'[3]

'I know,' Jeremy said.

'You have to be strong,' DS Jones went on, 'and brave. The quicker you accept it, the better.'

Jeremy stared at him. 'You're a hard bastard.'

'If I have to bring it home to you in a hard way that your family are all dead, then it's for a reason,' Jones said. 'I'll get DC Clark here to run you home. We need a statement from you.' He suggested the dogs should go with them but Jeremy shook his head: 'I can't take them to my house, it's too small and I've got some very expensive furniture, I don't want them to ruin it. I'll have to get them put down.' When Jones remonstrated with him, he decided to take Crispy home and put Bruce in the barn.

Before leaving, Jeremy called on Len Foakes, who remembered, '[He] said I could carry on working. I was amazed that he did not seem upset in any way about what had happened.'[4]

Discovering that Michael Clark didn't have a vehicle, Jeremy offered to drive and took the Brook House Farm track to evade any press. When Clark mentioned the Astra's reliability, Jeremy replied, 'I was getting a new Porsche, a little present from the caravan site.'[5]

It was 10.10am when they arrived at Bourtree Cottage. As they entered the kitchen, Jeremy stated, 'I'm starving, do you want something to eat?'[6] Clark declined: 'Bamber then fried himself some bacon and made some toast and coffee. Although he looked very tired at this stage he appeared calm. Bamber then sat down with me in his living room with his toast and bacon and said, "I am ready to start when you are."'[7]

Jeremy's behaviour had been inconsistent from the moment Bews informed him that no one inside the farmhouse had survived. He had wept then, and firearms officers preparing to leave the scene recalled seeing his obvious distress. PC Saxby had thought him very childlike in his repeated insistence, 'but you said it would be alright', and both Dr Craig and Chief Superintendent Harris had been taken aback when he kept asking them why his father couldn't come out to speak to him. He had then withdrawn into himself until Dr Craig asked him about the previous evening, after which he was seen retching in the field. His mood between then and leaving the farm had been one of cold detachment. While the police surgeon felt his fluctuating reactions were genuine and appropriate under the circumstances, both DS Jones and Clark questioned what was really going on.

DS Jones was particularly bemused by Jeremy being able to eat at all that morning and referred to it a number of times in interviews with the media after the trial. To this day, Jeremy remains exasperated by the fact, stating in a letter that the whisky he'd been given by Dr Craig had made him throw up and only solid food would shift his lingering nausea: 'I'd stood outside the house, sick with worry and then traumatised and distressed for six hours with nothing but one cup of warm tea to sustain me . . . I microwaved two slices of bacon to have in two slices of toast, that's all I had in my fridge to eat quickly – I ate about two thirds of it as I was talking through things with DC Clark [but] whatever my actions in the hours, days or weeks after losing my entire close family, the argument "Bamber's definitely guilty cos he ate a bacon sandwich and drank coffee – what kind of monster does that when told he's just lost five members

of his family, unless he killed them" – it's so utterly absurd . . .
that's his trump card, his Columbo moment of insight – "I knew
it from the start, that bacon sandwich was all I needed to know
for certain, Bamber killed them all" – that's his best evidence.
That and the bike ride. I know it sounds like I'm being flippant
– but how can you counter such risible nonsense when the police,
and in consequence the prosecution, champion this very "evidence" as proof of my guilt?'[7]

But all that came later. Once the contentious breakfast was over,
Jeremy asked if he might call Julie to check that she was on her
way. No sooner had he replaced the receiver than the telephone
rang.

It was Ann. Betty Howie had called her an hour before,
having heard from Jill Foakes that 'something serious was going
on at the farm'.[8] Jill, along with other residents of Pages Lane
cottages, had heard nothing during the night but was awoken by
police around 5am regarding 'an incident' and saw police vehicles, marksmen and dog handlers outside her window. Betty then
called her son, Thomas, to ask if he knew anything but he had no
idea. At the same time, Vivienne Smith, assistant editor on the
Braintree & Witham Times, received a call at her desk from a
colleague, informing her about the shootings and asking if she
knew the family involved. She did, along with many of their relatives, having only recently moved out of Tolleshunt D'Arcy, where
she had been on the parochial church council with Nevill. After
sitting in silence for a moment, she telephoned Betty Howie's
daughter-in-law Mary, who listened in disbelief before ringing off.
Betty in turn called Ann again, telling her there had been 'a multiple tragedy' at White House Farm.[9]

Frantic, Ann then rang Jill Foakes, who could only confirm
what she had already told Betty. Ann rang the farm and Bourtree
Cottage but there was no reply. She called Witham Police Station
but no one would tell her anything and, in desperation, she rang
her father. Robert panicked, calling the same numbers but getting
nowhere either. He then rang Nevill and June's neighbours but
they only repeated what Jill Foakes had said. David arrived at
Carbonells in the midst of his parents' fraught quest to speak to
someone better informed. After calling Ann, the police and White

House Farm, David set out for Pages Lane himself, his heart 'going up and down like a yo-yo'.[10]

Jeremy confirmed Ann's worst fears, telling her: 'I've got no family left.'[11]

She took a deep lungful of air. 'Yes, you have,' she managed to reply. 'I'm coming over.' In a daze, she packed a few provisions and telephoned her parents before heading out.

'Robert and I were stunned by the news,' Pamela remembered, understating their horror. 'We remained at home, waiting to see if the police would ring . . .'[12]

Coroner's Officer PC Norman Wright was shown around the scene by DI Cook. He drew several tentative conclusions: Nevill's precarious position seemed the result of having 'fallen over the chair after being shot' and June had evidently been 'shot by another person', while Sheila 'appeared to have shot herself, except for the fact that she had been shot twice in the neck and either wound appeared to be fatal'.[13] Inspector Montgomery joined Cook and Wright on the walk through. He speculated that the two wounds in Sheila's throat were due to 'the recoil of the weapon or a body movement after the first shot [which] could have caused the rifle to fire again.'[14]

SOCO got to work. DI Cook had received no 'specific instructions' from DCI Jones, only 'that he wanted the basic examination given the circumstances'.[15] In the absence of a clear directive, Cook told DC Bird to 'photograph each and every room thoroughly', along with the exterior and grounds. His meticulous and detailed photographs not only document the crime scene with pin-sharp accuracy; their musty colours also capture the last vestiges of ordinary life at White House Farm, from the half-played game of Alphabet Teacher lying on the floor in the lounge, to Sheila's cosmetics scattered on the pink quilt of the bed next to hers: Max Factor Powder Crème Puff face powder, Simple cleansing lotion, and a palette of blue and pink eyeshadows.

Inspector Montgomery appeared upstairs at 10.50am after hearing the photography was complete: 'DI Cook pointed out more spent .22 cases, one on the right side of Sheila. I also noticed a trail of blood along the foot of the bed, on the carpet between the two bodies. After several minutes I was still unable to come to a satisfactory conclusion as to how Sheila could have shot herself in the position both she, and the gun, had come to rest, and [with] the head at that angle.'[16]

The two men examined her more closely, noticing a blood-stain on her nightdress under her wrist. In order to see it clearly, Cook moved her hand and asked DC Bird to take shots of it. Crime scene photographs thus show Sheila's hand in two positions and from a slightly different angle. At trial, Cook explained that his aim had been 'to demonstrate the blood marks which were not readily visible under the wrist'. Bird confirmed that he was present and had already taken 'a series of photographs' when Cook moved Sheila's hand 'to show the marks on the nightdress'.[17] Acting Sergeant Woodcock also mentions Cook's action in his witness statement.

The gun itself had not yet been examined. At 11.10am, at the request of DI Cook and in Montgomery's presence, Woodcock removed it from Sheila's body. The wooden stock was blood-stained and damaged, with a piece missing. Woodcock ascertained that the magazine and breech were empty and the rifle was safe. Cook observed that the muzzle to the rifle 'had a thread to it' for a silencer but he gave no thought to looking for one 'because at that point it didn't feature in the scenario'. Blood smearing on the barrel and splashes of blood to the left side of the rifle were consistent with it having been used to attack a person already bleeding. The shard of wood next to the Aga was identified as the missing piece of stock.

DI Cook took possession of the Anschütz. Unlike Woodcock, he was not wearing gloves, which was accepted at trial but became an issue in the press. He explains: 'In that era, the question of whether or not an officer wore gloves was, of course, a personal one usually based in the interests of self-hygiene, although in certain circumstances it was recommended that gloves should be worn.'[18] Since the advent of more sensitive DNA testing techniques, it has been essential that gloves and protective clothing are worn to prevent contamination. Cook states that he and his colleagues didn't use gloves while handling items for general fingerprint examination work: 'Except for those porous type surfaces such as paper, cardboard, etc., or where the surface may be contaminated with body fluids, etc. The examiner usually handled items in such a way that, by using his skill, he avoided leaving his fingerprints on the item.' He lifted the Anschütz using 'the sling fittings on the butt and under the barrel', two very narrow surfaces from which 'there would have been no chance of recovering any identifiable finger marks.'

Cook handed the rifle to exhibits officer DC Hammersley, who confirmed at the trial that he would 'not ordinarily' wear gloves either, for the same reasons given by his superior. The 1986 internal police review further confirmed that Cook's actions were correct.

With the gun removed and stood against the wall awaiting preparation for transportation, DC Hammersley began the routine task of preserving any unseen evidence by placing sterile polythene bags on Sheila's head, hands and feet. He observed that 'both hands were clean and free from debris, with the exception of what appeared to be blood staining on the top surface of the right hand towards the wrist' and that her fingernails were 'intact'.[19]

Inspector Montgomery had examined Sheila's right hand when DI Cook lifted it from the rifle, but made no mention of the stains, describing the hand as 'perfectly clean' and her fingernails 'well manicured and not broken'. He added: 'All her fingertips were clean and free from any blood, dirt or powder, and there appeared to be no trace of any lead dust or coating which is usually present when handling .22 ammunition. I did not examine her left hand.' DC Hammersley noted that her feet were 'clean' and that 'her legs appeared to be very clean and free from bloodstaining.'[20] He sellotaped the protective bags loosely to keep them in place. As Sheila's body was lifted onto a polythene sheet, Woodcock pointed out two empty cartridge cases lying near her head.

Accompanied by Cook and Montgomery, Woodcock then examined the broken, empty shotgun in the downstairs den. Peering into the cupboard, he saw but didn't touch 'a large amount of 12 gauge and .22 ammunition'.[21] Cook recalls that the cupboard was not thoroughly inspected because 'it wasn't a legal or proper place for storing weapons. It was just a cupboard where the family sometimes kept guns. It was full of domestic stuff – a dartboard, a poker and other bits of "tut". The only gun in there was the broken shotgun. What *was* significant was the cardboard box containing mainly 12 bore ammunition and some .22 ammunition. I accept that we didn't examine that thoroughly and agree we should have done.'[22] He considered taking the .22 ammunition as a control sample but decided to use the bullets on the kitchen worktop instead, since that appeared to be the source of the ammunition used in the shootings.

Inspector Montgomery departed, leaving SOCO to collect used cartridge cases and anything else of immediate interest. In all, twenty-five cartridge cases would be recovered from the premises: thirteen from the master bedroom, one from the middle landing, eight from the twins' room and three from the kitchen. Nevill's silver Seiko wristwatch was discovered under the rug in front of the sink, its metal strap detached on one side.

While they worked, Cook received a radio message asking why the bodies hadn't arrived at the mortuary: 'Someone was obviously upset about how long we were taking.' He tried to keep 'an open mind' but found nothing 'out of place to DCI Jones's scenario'. Nonetheless, there were factors that caused him disquiet, not least 'the positioning' of the two wounds to Sheila's throat, because 'the direction of entry was not known. I didn't know if she had been lying down or sitting up, [or] did she slide down, but I was quite happy she had not been shot elsewhere and carried there.'

At 12.50pm, a plain white Toyota van pulled up close to the front door. The undertaker and his assistant carried the bodies out as discreetly as possible, aware that press photographers had their lenses trained on the house. A police officer stood guard in the cool green shade by the garden gate as the family left White House Farm forever.

At Bourtree Cottage, Ann hugged Jeremy tightly. Through the fug of disbelief she noticed a change in his appearance since she had last seen him: his hair was black and his skin, too, seemed darker. They went through to the lounge, where Crispy scrambled onto her knee. DC Clark felt that Jeremy showed the first signs of being emotionally upset when Ann pressed him to explain what had happened.

He told her, 'Sheila has killed them all.'[1]

At quarter past eleven they were joined by DS Stan Jones and ten minutes later Julie arrived. The first police officer who spoke to her that morning in Lewisham had been surprised when, in response to his question of whether she understood there had been a serious incident involving her boyfriend's family, she replied calmly, 'Yes. Sheila, his sister, had been behaving strangely the weekend before.'[2] Constable Jonathan Turner was tasked with driving her to Tolleshunt D'Arcy: 'She seemed very confident and appeared intelligent. She didn't seem at all anxious and in fact, was very relaxed. She showed no signs of concern or anxiety.'[3] Her only reference to the shootings was the unprompted comment: 'I hope I don't have to see any bodies.'

As Julie embraced Jeremy, DS Jones suggested they might like a moment alone. They went through to the dining room, shutting the door. Opening it again, Jones heard 'what I thought was a short cough or a chuckle. I opened the door wider and saw them break away from each other.'[4]

Jeremy crossed to the sofa and sat down. Ann perched on one side of him and Julie on the other as he began giving a statement to Mick Clark. During short periods of sobbing he would reach for their hands, but Ann was so distraught herself that she found it impossible to sit still, making endless hot drinks instead and telephoning her cousin Anthony and her devastated parents again to confirm the news.

David arrived at quarter to twelve, ten minutes after Stan Jones left for White House Farm. Already shaking with emotion, he still knew nothing for certain until Ann told him: 'You've got to be strong for Jeremy, he's lost all his family.'[5] He broke down, holding Jeremy and unable to speak.

Ann's husband Peter appeared briefly at midday. Desperate to be of use, he offered to help with the harvest and noticed Jeremy was smoking a lot, something he had never seen him do.

At half-past twelve, David and Julie walked up to the Chequers to order lunch. They returned with laden trays just as Robert and Pamela arrived, both looking gaunt with strain. After hugging Jeremy, Pamela busied herself agitatedly about the place, beginning to feel the shock of it all. Her husband sat down in the lounge, interrupting DC Clark to ask his nephew what precisely had happened. Ann could barely look at her father: 'I thought he was going to have a heart attack, I was so worried, mum kept talking and talking. Dad was so emotional and went very red in the face.'[6] Crispy kept clambering onto everyone's laps and Jeremy remarked: 'If only dogs could talk.'[7]

Three miles away in Tolleshunt D'Arcy, Barbara Wilson hadn't known what to do when her son Philip returned from the farm saying there were police everywhere: 'I rang the house but it was engaged all the time. In the end, I decided to go to work at North Maldon Growers. There was already a lot of talk in the village and Graham, our manager, said he'd heard that Mr Bamber had been killed. I had to do the post and remember walking to the Post Office in a daze. A group of people were in there, listening to the Essex Radio report that a family of five had been killed at D'Arcy. I nearly collapsed. I made it back to the office, crying my eyes out, then went home.'[8]

In the midst of the turmoil, one person seemed forgotten: the twins' father. Two policewomen managed to reach Colin around midday, calling at his flat in Kilburn. When they told him on the doorstep that his ex-wife was dead, he immediately assumed Sheila had committed suicide. It was only when the officers stepped inside the flat that he learned his sons had been murdered. Screaming out, he felt a suffocating blanket of unfathomable grief descend.

The police contacted Heather but had orders to transport Colin to Essex and would not allow him time to call his parents. In the car, Colin felt himself growing hot and delirious with confusion, then snapping back to a warped new reality. It was

Constable Jonathan Turner's second journey of the day to Gold-hanger. He recalled a 'great deal of difference' in Colin and Heather's emotional state and that of 'calm, confident' Julie.

At White House Farm, Sergeant Stephen Golding and WPC Allison Bourne conducted a final security check. Golding found an unsecured window in the downstairs shower room and another in the kitchen. The window in the shower room was closed but the catch was open. 'I noticed that the window only had net curtaining on the lower half and that it was covering some toiletries,' Golding recalled. 'I secured the window by closing the catch, therefore neither part of the window could be moved.'[9] The narrow window that opened horizontally above the kitchen sink was noticeably ajar: 'To my knowledge no other police officer had opened the fanlight or indeed had reason to place the catch on the bathroom window in the insecure position.' Sergeant Golding fastened the kitchen window as well, but omitted to inform a senior officer of his actions.

DCI Jones made no mention of either window in his witness statement, declaring that he had entered 'every room in the house' at about 9.15am for a security check.[10] The only window he found unlocked was the one in the dairy, covered by wire mesh with dirt and cobwebs on the gauze and sill. Considering the issue several weeks later, Acting Chief Superintendent Mike Ainsley concluded that the kitchen window must have been opened after Jones's inspection of the house: 'I have been unable to discover the person responsible but there was comment made of the smell in the kitchen and the flies gathering. There is no reason to believe that the bathroom window was opened.'[11]

DS Stan Jones arrived at the house to liaise with officers fitting an ultrasonic detector in the scullery and another on the main staircase. There was some difficulty with the signal, necessitating an extension aerial in the upstairs office. A new back door was fitted at the same time by Dennis Wager, who never left the scullery but could not help noticing the large pool of blood on the kitchen floor.

Sixteen miles away at Chelmsford and Essex Hospital, the first post-mortems were underway. All four Scene of Crime officers were present, together with DI Miller, Coroner's Officer Norman Wright, two pathology students and both morticians.

Home Office pathologist Peter Vanezis had begun his career in 1974 and had been senior lecturer at the London Hospital Medical College since 1979. His secretary had called that morning regarding a 'murder-suicide situation' in Essex. Vanezis spoke to a junior officer at Witham who confirmed that a woman had shot her family before killing herself and that he wasn't needed until 3pm at the mortuary. 'That was unusual,' Vanezis reflects. 'Normally I'd go to the scene but they appeared to be confident of their view.'[12]

He requested the presence of a ballistics expert at the mortuary: 'You never know what you're going to find and we didn't see a large number of firearm cases at the time, so a ballistics expert was essential. We don't always take gunshot residues at post-mortem and I could have deferred to him on that issue, as well as the range of fire, the calibre of the bullet, etc.' DI Cook telephoned the Forensic Science Laboratory in Huntingdon but was told that a ballistics expert couldn't be spared. Vanezis was 'not happy that they couldn't get one out to us. I can't understand why it didn't happen, but quite frankly they were already far down the road of murder-suicide.' Ballistics expert Malcolm Fletcher, who would later work on the case, counters: 'I was in the room when this call was received and the question was put to my colleague Geoff Brunt: "We've got four murders and a suicide, do you want to come?" We were certainly busy at that time but he would have organised someone to go if there had been some encouragement. As it was, he agreed a list of items to be submitted to cover the bases.'[13] Bird's photographs at the crime scene and the mortuary would also prove of immense importance to the ballistics scientists at a later stage.

Nevill's body was the first to be examined, after X-rays had been taken. Rigor mortis was well established; heavily congealed blood obscured the injuries to his head and face and caked his right hand, lower left leg and foot. After routine washing, his head was shaved to locate the damage to his skull. There were eight gunshot wounds in all: two to the top right of his head, two to his right temple, one to his lower lip from the left, one under the left of his chin into his mouth, one to his left shoulder, fracturing the bone and one to his left upper arm. The four wounds to his head had fractured his skull and were almost certainly inflicted when he had ceased to resist his killer, possibly after his head had come to rest in the coal scuttle. Those bullets penetrating his midbrain structure had caused immediate unconsciousness and an inability to perform any purposeful function.

The bullet wound to Nevill's lower lip had penetrated his left jaw into his backbone, producing severe fractures in his jawbone, shattering his teeth, disrupting neck tissue, the structures of his larynx and the main gland beneath his neck. Later forensic evidence would indicate that he sustained those injuries in the bedroom. With that in mind today, Vanezis states unequivocally: 'Someone shot in the jaw would not be able to talk. The idea of him making the call to Jeremy after that doesn't work at all.' The pain and nature of the injury would have left him only able to attempt to try and cough the blood out.

Nevill had suffered other injuries besides gunshot wounds. The severe bruising to his eyes and a laceration to the right side of his nose were due to a blow from a fist or blunt object. Bruising on his forehead and the right side of his face and ear, together with lateral marks to his left cheek, were the result of contact with a blunt object or surface. Lacerations to the top of his head were caused by something with an edge to it, inducing a lot of mostly veinous bleeding. Two deep score lines on the left side of his head had been produced by pressing against the coal scuttle. A laceration to his right shoulder was thought to have been caused by the impact of the rifle stock and there was an unexplained graze on the right side of his chest. His right hand had bled from loss of skin while gouges and bruises on his right forearm later led to speculation that fingernails had been dug into his skin, but Vanezis states firmly: 'They're not nail marks at all. Absolutely not – it's much more like pistol-whipping.'

Three burn marks were plainly visible at the base of his neck. The lower two were almost circular, the uppermost approximately oval. There were no corresponding marks on his pyjama top and a tear in the material was not thought to be associated with them. The police came to believe the burns were caused by a heated poker. Vanezis was reluctant to agree and would only confirm that the marks had been inflicted on the night of Nevill's death by a hot object most likely applied to bare flesh. He was doubtful that the marks were caused by the muzzle of the rifle because they were 'so well defined . . . one would not expect to see the degree of mark left.'[14]

Tests conducted in an attempt to replicate the marks were inconclusive; ballistics expert Malcolm Fletcher comments: 'None of the tests, either by me or the defence, were able to reproduce this effect. Initially we fired the rifle a load of times and grabbed the end of the barrel and sound moderator with our hands. It would warm up, but there's a lot of steel there and it just wasn't hot enough. Without actually pushing the gun into his back . . . you would certainly get the possibility of a black ring, which I've seen many times. But they certainly weren't from the gun. Only multiple direction shots could hope to produce any burns. Then, of course, there would be attendant bullet holes.'

With hindsight, Vanezis disagrees: 'I've thought about this a lot, with the benefit of another twenty-eight years' experience. If you put something hot against fairly thick clothing, you're more likely to burn the skin than the clothing because of the properties of the skin. If you pushed a rifle against someone's back, that would fit in very nicely with the gun having already been fired and the muzzle still being hot when touching the back.' He discounts the poker: 'No, I think it's the gun pressed against his skin. I don't think you can read too much into the slight difference in the shape of the marks either. They're all fairly circular, skin is not totally flat, and the way you hold something is not always the same. My guess is that those marks are the effect of the muzzle of the rifle being prodded against Nevill's pyjama top whilst he was still alive. The temperature is such that the clothing doesn't burn. You don't need a lot of heat for that. Don't forget that we're seeing those marks after death, which dries the skin and makes it darker.'

With Nevill's post-mortem complete, Vanezis turned to Sheila. After removing the polythene bags from her head and hands, DC Hammersley swabbed each hand separately, noting that 'each swab was clean to the eye'.[15] He placed them in sealed containers for inspection at the laboratory in Huntingdon. There was no debris attached to the feet bags, nor to Sheila's legs. DS Davidson took possession of her turquoise nightdress and stud earrings, pendant necklace, wristwatch and two rings. Her body was then washed and her head shaved, as was the case with all the victims.

Hypostasis was clearly present. The mottled pattern showed that the position in which Sheila was found was the position in which she died. The pathologist inspected her hands first. 'Her fingernails were an issue,' Ron Cook recalls. 'We queried whether her long nails would have hindered her in loading the gun. It may have made it much more difficult.'[16] Vanezis believed that depended upon her familiarity with the weapon; if she was used to it then she could have loaded it without damaging her nails. He was then unaware that Sheila had no firearms experience. She was right-handed; Bird's mortuary photographs show nicotine stains on her fingers and some bloodstaining to the hand before washing. Vanezis recorded in his initial notes: 'Bloodstained palm print on nightdress matches bloodstains appear to have been transferred from r. hand . . . Both hands not contaminated apart from bloodstains.'[17] But in court he declared that Sheila's hands were 'completely free of blood and if she'd pressed against the nightdress I would have still seen some traces of blood on her palms.'[18] He explained that blood on her nightdress 'appeared to have been transferred from her wrist' although 'the palms of her hand were certainly not contaminated with blood, but there was spotting of blood associated and close to the wrist.'

Asked to address the discrepancy today, Vanezis muses: 'I'm not sure whether I said that after the blood had been washed from her hands.' Regarding his courtroom statement about the stain on her nightdress, he reflects: 'The smear in the blood on her neck wounds is obviously from putting her hand up to it. Her fingers could then have made the marks on her nightdress because there are three streaks forming the stain – two together and one slightly apart. The marks could be from her wrist, but the thickness of them definitely resembles fingers and she certainly has some blood on the side of her hand. There's also a line through the streaks where the material has folded, giving a slightly distorted pattern.' The blood trails evident on Sheila's lower right arm, together with substantial bloodstaining on the right side of the nightdress in the armpit area and below, rein-forced the probability that she had raised her hand to her neck.

The lower wound on the right side of Sheila's throat showed bruising and residue marks and was the first to have been inflicted. At the trial, Vanezis explained the trajectory of the bullet as 'slightly upwards and backwards, causing severe soft tissue haemorrhage on the right side of the neck, principally from the right external jugular vein' with the bullet finishing to the side of the main part of the spine, causing fractures. Despite the shock and pain, Sheila would have been able to register what was happening. 'It was basically a flesh wound,' Vanezis explains, 'and there's no reason why she shouldn't have been conscious. Stunned obviously, but conscious.' The wound had bled immedi-ately but was venous rather than arterial and 'that bit less fast', although 'quite a big build up' of blood had formed on the inside of her neck.[19]

The upper wound, just beneath Sheila's chin, was smaller with firearm residue and slight bruising. The bullet had gone upwards through the hard palate of her mouth and skull to embed itself in the upper part of the brain. Sheila's X-rays showed the bullet as a white opacity at the top of her skull, with further white fragments that had broken off the bullet as it struck bone. In court, Vanezis described the effect of the second injury as 'severe incapacitation' with death occurring 'almost instantaneously'. He was unable to specify how much time had elapsed between the shots: 'All I can say is there was enough time for there to be a fairly large build up of blood in the neck area.' Asked whether it was possible for Sheila to have stood and walked around after the first wound was inflicted, he replied that it was unlikely because the wound would have discharged 'a lot of blood' and the dispersal of blood on her nightdress was clearly indicative it was not the case.

Today he is firmer still: 'She hadn't got up at all.'[20]

Both injuries were 'very loose' contact wounds, lacking the associated grazing and distribution of residue within the skin from full contact wounds. Regarding Sheila's position when the wounds were inflicted, Vanezis declared in court that having taken into account the pattern of bloodstaining, 'both injuries were produced while she was slightly on her right side and partially sitting up.' She was shot from close range upwards and after the second bullet was fired, had instantly 'gone back', since the injury was 'virtually immediately fatal'. Bleeding from her wounds had ceased at that point because her circulation had stopped.

Vanezis's examination revealed that Sheila had been menstruating. When consulted, Dr Ferguson declared that as far as he was aware 'she did not appear to have any marked disturbances in mood' during her periods. But Sheila's friend Christine Finlay recalled: 'Bambi told me she suffered from pre-menstrual tension. It's to my knowledge that she ordered various items from health food shops for this complaint. She would tell me when she was suffering with this but it was not obvious to me.'[21]

A tiny graze just above Sheila's left hipbone was unrelated to the murders and scarcely warranted the plaster previously applied to it. Her stomach contained 'partially digested food'.[22] Vanezis made no reference to the stomach contents of the other victims, leading to speculation that Sheila might have eaten later than her family. 'I'm sure they all had some food in their stomachs – I noted it for her and took it as read with the others.'

He did not attempt to estimate a time of death: 'That's hard enough at the best of times. If the police ask us then we do look into it, but usually you get a better idea from other sources. If you're dealing with a time of death some time in a range of five or six hours, then generally you're better off getting the information from when the victim was last seen alive through to when their body was discovered.' There was nothing at all to indicate that Sheila had died some significant time after her parents and sons.

Examination complete, the pathologist admitted to being a little concerned about the fact that Sheila, an apparent suicide, had two gunshot wounds to her throat. Coroner's Officer Norman Wright recalled that Vanezis did not seem to like the theory that Sheila had killed her family before turning the gun on herself. 'I wasn't comfortable with it,' Vanezis confirms today. 'Which is another reason why I wanted the ballistics expert there as well.' At the time, he conceded that 'bearing in mind the low velocity of the weapon, whilst unusual, suicide with two shots does occur' and that he had experienced four or five such cases.[23]

The officers present then debated Sheila's ability to over-power her father. Nevill was six foot four and a robust farmer of sixty-one years; his daughter weighed eight stone six, stood five foot seven tall, and was plainly affected to some extent by the haloperidol injections. More relevant yet was the order in which Nevill had received his wounds. Presupposing that he had been largely incapacitated before grappling with his attacker, it would have been 'quite possible' for Sheila to cause him further harm 'without sustaining any injury herself'.[24] DI Cook acknowledged that Nevill had 'put up some resistance' but it 'must have been limited' because of his initial wounds and broken arm.[25]

Vanezis submits that in such a scenario, the length of the rifle must also be taken into account: 'If Sheila had the gun in her hands, she would be able to wave it around and hit him with it – and Nevill would have to be careful how he grabbed it, because if it had already been fired, then it would have been hot. Plus, I'm never surprised by the strength women have when they're filled with anger.' But at the time of the post-mortems, there was no information available about the exact location of the cartridges found at the scene and, without it, Vanezis was unable to make a more accurate analysis. He accepted there was nothing glaringly apparent to contradict the murder-suicide theory: 'Although I could not from my examination confirm murder or suicide, from what I had been told, suicide was a high probability.'[26] DI Cook recalled that 'the two wounds to the neck caused [the patholo-gist] no concern because the first wound would have caused temporary unconsciousness and it was quite feasible she could have come round and killed herself with the second shot.'[27]

Proceedings were brought to an end at 6.20pm. The remain-ing post-mortems would be carried out the following day.

Hunched on the sofa at Bourtree Cottage, Colin reacted angrily to Jeremy's revelation that cross words had been exchanged the previous evening when his parents told Sheila they wanted custody of the twins. Colin responded that June's 'religious mania' had forced him to restrict their visits and that Sheila knew as well as he did that her mother was a 'religious monster'.[1]

His words upset Ann, who spoke up on June's behalf. But Colin was in turmoil, certain that Sheila would rather kill than be parted from her children. Dimly, he heard Jeremy say 'he sounded very distressed, as if he had already been shot' and realized he was referring to Nevill's panicked call. Heather remembered the comment, but the Boutflours couldn't be certain. Nor did they recall, as Colin did, hearing Jeremy declare that he felt 'partly responsible' for his family's deaths because he hadn't put the gun away.

When Heather began to cry, Ann led her through to the kitchen, returning to find David gone. She caught up with him outside, where he was speaking to their mother's elderly aunt, Connie Lugg, who lived in a bungalow near the village hall. The old lady knew nothing about the shootings, telling them how pleased June had been with her new bicycle on a recent visit.

Ann and David arrived back at the cottage just as their parents were leaving. Pamela told Jeremy there were some possessions of June's which had sentimental value for her. 'It's my responsibility, I will sort it out,' he replied.[2]

David left with his parents while Ann stayed behind 'trying to catch everything Jeremy said'.[3] She scribbled notes for her own reference on odd pieces of paper, fast becoming 'bloody suspicious' of her cousin as she listened to him talking to the police about the conversation at the supper table and his handling of the gun that evening. Later she recalled: 'I told people to be strong for Jeremy's sake, but also for my own sake, because if I saw too many people I would cry for the people I loved, and once I started crying I would not be able to stop.'

Detective Sergeant Jones had returned from White House

Farm and took a statement from Colin in the dining room. They were interrupted by an anguished telephone call from Reg Caffell and again by Jeremy, who put his head round the door to ask how they were getting on, informing them that he had covered everything 'apart from the fact that Sheila had taken drugs'.[4]

Later, Jones asked Jeremy if he would like any heavily blood-stained items in the house destroyed. He agreed, but stipulated that anything valuable was to be salvaged, giving written permission for the disposal of soiled items such as carpets and bedding.

Ann left for home around seven o'clock, worn out but with her mind racing. Soon afterwards, a car arrived for Colin and Heather, who returned brokenly to London.

Stan Jones and Mick Clark were left with Julie and Jeremy, whom Jones treated as bereaved despite his suspicions and instinctive dislike: 'It was a PR job. Chat, laugh, joke, trying to lighten things up. In fact, Jeremy was already cheerful enough.'[5] An hour later the two detectives set out for Witham. 'Bamber appeared to be very calm and jovial,' DC Clark stated, 'and made a joke about us drinking and driving.'[6]

The two men arrived slightly late for a debriefing at Witham led by DI Miller. Officers who had attended White House Farm were given the opportunity to speak about it. Coroner's Officer Norman Wright recalled either Miller or DS Jones pointing out that Jeremy stood to gain financially from the deaths. Another officer remembered hearing Jeremy say that he had definitely taken shots at the rabbits by the barn, yet he had told DC Clark that no shots were fired. Clark and Jones were instructed to interview Jeremy again the following day.

Years later, Colin stated that he would never have accepted the explanation he was given about the killings had he known that the murder weapon was a semi-automatic rifle, not a shotgun: 'Bambs wouldn't have had the first idea how to use one, let alone reload it.'[7]

The same thought had already struck those who were aware of the fact. In the kitchen at Oak Farm, Ann and Peter Eaton sat with her father Robert, methodically working their way through everything that didn't make sense to them. Pamela was too distressed to speak and took care of her grandchildren, holding them close.

Shock lent a strange energy to the discussion around the Oak Farm kitchen table. All three agreed that Sheila was incapable of using the Anschütz and disliked hunting, yet Jeremy had told police she had been out rabbit shooting several times with Anthony and Nevill.

'Had she?' Ann wanted to know, but neither her husband nor her father could remember such an occasion. Nor could they explain why Nevill hadn't put the rifle away safely, while Jeremy's assertion that the silencer and telescopic sight had been removed to fit the gun in the den cupboard didn't ring true either.

As they went over the alleged last conversation between Sheila and her parents, Ann found it impossible to believe that her aunt and uncle would be so heartless as to suggest their daughter was an incapable mother, or that Jeremy hadn't engaged in the debate: 'To me, it would have been just like him to get involved.'

She found his account of other events that night, such as loading the gun on the kitchen worktop and leaving it in the scullery, difficult to accept. Equally, she declared, the telephone call he claimed to have received from his father made no sense to her: 'I would have picked up a kitchen chair or gone after Sheila like a lion tamer. That's the sort of thing I would have expected uncle Nevill to do.'

She recalled asking Jeremy to account for not dialling 999. His explanation – 'because I didn't think it was that important' – baffled her. 'Can you believe that!' she wondered. It also seemed completely illogical that he had telephoned Julie immediately after speaking to Chelmsford Police.[8]

She remembered asking Jeremy why he hadn't driven immediately to the farm. He had replied that he was frightened it was a trick to lure him there so that Sheila could shoot him too. She was mystified that he had arrived after the police, given that he was such a fast driver, and by his declaration to the officers during the siege that there was an 'armoury of guns' inside the house and Sheila was capable of using them all.

At the cottage, she had heard DC Clark asking Jeremy how he got on with his father. When he replied 'like a normal son', she had felt compelled to speak out: 'DS Jones went to the kitchen and I followed him in . . . I took him by the arm and I said, "He didn't get on well with his father, you know – he didn't."' But she was reluctant to say more: 'I didn't want Jeremy to hear me. I didn't want to be killed next.'

It grew late. They brought the discussion around the table to a close, exhausted but not knowing how they would sleep. Robert was 'even more convinced that Jeremy had done it'.[9] Pamela was reticent, but intuitively felt that Sheila 'would not harm the twins, she was devoted to them. Although she was not well and was suffering from depression, she would never have harmed her children.'[10]

At home with his wife Karen, David Boutflour was less certain, although they too had spent the evening going over everything: 'I did not conclude Jerry had done it. There was a grey area. I didn't think he had the gumption to do it. I was not convinced, but others were.'[11]

'Five Killed in House of Horror' declared the local *Evening Gazette* that day, announcing that June – rather than Sheila – was believed to be the killer. Two *Daily Mail* reporters approached Freddie as he checked on Sheila's flat and he almost collapsed as they broke the news.

Afterwards, he called Tora in a terrible state. 'Tora – the whole family,' he blurted. 'Have you seen the news?'[12]

Tora didn't understand. 'No, what are you talking about?'

'They're all dead, they're all dead . . .' He kept repeating the phrase. She finally got him to explain and remembers: 'I couldn't believe it. The following day the press named Bambi as the instigator. I thought back to the last time I'd seen her. She could hardly get up from my sofa without help, let alone go berserk with a rifle.'

Those who knew Sheila spurned the idea that she had killed her family. Mairead Maguire spoke for friends, relatives, social workers, babysitters, former employers and ex-boyfriends when she vowed: 'No matter what state she was in, she would not harm her children.'[13] Don Hawkins declared that his former girlfriend 'didn't have the manual dexterity to handle a gun. I remember that she had trouble opening a can of beans with the tin opener.'[14] It crossed his mind that Sheila might have returned to the troubled state of mind she was in when she had rung him from hospital, but felt she was incapable of violence nonetheless. Sandra Elston remembered that June had thought her daughter 'unfit' to care for the twins because of her illness and wondered if Sheila had killed them 'thinking that she was protecting them in some way', but found it too 'difficult to believe'.[15]

Social worker Barbara Babic recalled that Sheila had a temper 'but *only* in relationships with men'.[16] Colin confirmed that during his marriage there were 'times when we could have killed each other; violence was just below the surface', but he was adamant that Sheila was far more likely to smash an inanimate object or harm herself.[17] Only one person who knew Sheila well seemed ready to believe that she was capable of committing the murders: Jeremy.

According to police officers attending the siege at White House Farm, the terms Jeremy used to describe his sister included 'a nutter', 'doolally', 'a depressive psychopath', a 'paranoid schizophrenic' who was 'certifiable' and 'should be locked up'. The portrait of Sheila that emerges from his first witness statement is based upon that preliminary sketch.

He began by telling DC Clark that Sheila was 'very introvert' and had been 'expelled from both of the boarding schools she attended'.[18] This information quickly found its way to the media, some of whom continue to repeat it today. But Sheila was never expelled; Nevill and June removed her from Moira House following a campaign of sustained bullying by her peers, after which she attended Hethersett Old Hall, graduating on the same day as the rest of her classmates.

Jeremy's statement includes a brief account of his sister's relationship with Colin and how, in the two years following her divorce, 'Sheila had problems with debts and the pressure of bringing up the twins. As a result of this she occasionally hit the children quite aggressively and forcibly. This was never, ever reported.' Nor was it – the only person who has ever gone on record with such allegations was Jeremy, in his statements to police and at trial. Sue Ford discussed the purported abuse with detectives but was merely reiterating what she had heard from a single source: 'Jeremy often told me that Sheila was cruel to the children and she had given one of them a black eye' and 'he said she used to punch them directly in the face'.[19]

Later in court, Jeremy described a car journey with his family: 'We were travelling to see some friends when one of the twins interrupted Dad and Sheila turned round and punched him full in the face.' Colin saw his sons on a weekly basis until they moved in with him in March 1985. He responds: 'Apart from the fact that Jeremy is the only living person to have witnessed this alleged attack, it is extremely unlikely to have happened. The main reason being that, as two very empowered and talkative little boys, I have never known either of the twins to remain quiet about any "injustice" for very long. One of them would have told me about it very quickly. Also, with them living in my custody, I would have seen any bruises because they both bruised very easily. Finally, I find it highly unlikely that Jeremy would have been going anywhere with the whole family in his father's car, because for most of that final year I had not allowed the family any significant time alone with my sons.'[20]

In his first statement, Jeremy declared that prior to his sister's 1983 admission to hospital, Nicholas 'fell from a speeding taxi in London. Sheila jumped out after him, sustaining no injury to herself, although the twin received hospital treatment for a week. I can't say how this happened but it was very distressing to Sheila.' He referred to the incident again in September 1985 when detectives asked if she had ever attempted suicide: 'There is an occasion when we were all frightened that she had, and I drove to London. But it was ok, she had only lost one of the boys out of a speeding taxi.'[21]

The inference that Nicholas's fall was a deliberate act on Sheila's part appears explicitly in Sue Ford's witness statement: 'She had thrown one of [the twins] out of a taxi in London once. Jeremy said it was a pity Sheila had the children.'[22] While it is a matter of record that Nicholas sustained a head injury after tumbling from a taxi, nowhere is it mentioned that the vehicle had been 'speeding', nor that Sheila had 'thrown' her son. The social worker who spoke to Sheila at the hospital where Nicholas was examined found her glad to talk and clarified that there was no suggestion of non-accidental injury.

*

On his official website in 2002, Jeremy denied his own earlier claims: 'I said that it was *suspected* that when she said that the kids' bruises were caused when they had fallen over, that we believed that Sheila *might* be responsible for causing these injuries.'[23]

There is no mention in any documentation of suspicious bruising. In 1981 a health visitor expressed concern about an ear infection and three scalds suffered by Daniel, but the case conference found that Sheila had correctly sought help for both and there was no evidence to suggest the scalds were deliberate. Social services' involvement with the family was only in terms of 'preventative' work; they regarded Sheila as 'a disorganised person who loved her boys'.[24] Her GP commented on the twins: 'Neither boy has ever had anything wrong with him except for colds, standard immunisations and other childlike things. Neither boy has ever broken any bones nor, under my care, did they contract the normal viral infections that young children are prone to.'[25]

Jeremy outlined Sheila's psychiatric care in his initial statement, but his account of her receiving 'major' ECT and 'massive' drug therapy has been disproved by Dr Ferguson. He referred to his sister taking 'hard drugs' but declined to have it included in his statement because 'I don't want to blacken her character any further', although it was damaging enough to mention it to the police.[26] He described his own relationship with Sheila as 'amicable', admitting that he only saw her 'about once a month. We got on alright together and I could understand the problems she was going through.' Yet according to the first police officers who arrived at White House Farm on the night of the murders, Jeremy said bluntly that he didn't get on with his sister: 'I don't like her and she doesn't like me.'[27]

The newspapers announced Sheila's guilt as a given on their front pages the following morning: 'Berserk Mother Blasts Family: Slaughter at Farmhouse', 'Mother Slaughters Family', 'Suicide Girl Kills Twins and Parents', 'Model Murders Four of Her Family: Drugs Probe After Massacre by Mother of Twins'. In the midst of his own grief, Colin felt compelled to issue a statement in Sheila's defence, declaring: 'No mother on earth could have loved her children more. Nothing was more precious to her than Nicholas and Daniel.'[28]

After reading the papers that morning, Jeremy and Julie set out for the farm, where Jeremy spoke to the workers and let Bruce out of the barn. Constable David Ware, stationed in the kitchen yard, spoke to Jeremy about the shootings while Julie returned to the car.

'She must have been pretty desperate to kill her own children,' he ventured.[29]

'I can't understand what must have been going through her mind,' Jeremy answered.

'Did she have much to do with the children?'

'Actually the family talked about having them adopted, about two years ago.'

The conversation then turned to the farm. Jeremy said he wasn't going 'to carry it on' and that everything would be sorted out by solicitors. He didn't want riches: 'I'm not that sort of person, give me a little two bedroomed house, a car to run around in and a bit of spending money in my pocket.'

After a chat about post and the dog's welfare Jeremy departed, leaving Ware to reflect: 'He spoke quietly, calmly, rationally, and I got the overall impression that he either hadn't accepted what had happened, or that he didn't care.'

In the Chelmsford and Essex Hospital mortuary, where all those present the previous day had assembled again, Dr Vanezis established that June had been shot seven times.

Her wounds were above her right ear, to the right of her neck, the upper right of her chest, the lower right of her chest, her right forearm, the outer aspect of her right knee and between the eyes. The bullet to her forehead was recovered with further fragments from the left side of her skull, where another bullet was also found, having caused extensive damage to her brain and almost immediate incapacitation and unconsciousness. A bruise under her left breast was due to the ricochet of a bullet, while the severe bruising to her left eye was caused either by a blow or the impact of a gunshot.

Apart from the forehead injury, which was the last, Vanezis was unable to assess the order in which June had received her wounds. He suspected that the shots to her right arm and leg were fired as she tried to ward off her killer, while the copious blood smears on her lower limbs occurred as she lay on the floor: 'If you're on the ground you can get smearing by just moving your legs, even if there is only a very little bit of blood on them. There was no surrounding blood on the carpet to indicate she had been dragged.'[1] The blood spots on the carpet and splashes of blood on the bedding – from which two bullets had been recovered – would eventually be identified as belonging to June. Shot initially in bed, she had struggled to a sitting position, then staggered around the bed before turning for the door, where the killer had fired straight at her, causing the fatal forehead wound. Her shoulder had struck the door as she slumped to the floor.

With June's post-mortem complete, Vanezis turned to the twins. Nicholas had three gunshot wounds: one on his left cheekbone, one to the left of the bridge of his nose, and a third to the outer aspect of his right eyebrow. Daniel was found to have five gunshot wounds to the back of his head, four in extremely close proximity towards the base of his skull and the fifth just above his left ear, forming a precise crescent. Vanezis believed that the shots had been fired in quick succession and 'there had not been much movement after the first bullet.'[2]

The pathologist then discussed the number of shots: twenty-five in all, from a magazine with a capacity of ten. Random shots had been fired together with 'accurate, calculated shots to cause death' by a person with 'a good knowledge of how to fire that weapon'.[3] The injuries to Nicholas and Daniel were lethally precise, but since Vanezis had been told that Sheila was perfectly capable of using the Anschütz, he saw no reason for concern.

Jeremy and Julie returned to Bourtree Cottage shortly before a vet arrived to put Crispy to sleep. 'I know that Jeremy had asked a number of his family if they would like the dog but none wanted it,' Julie recalled.[4] Jeremy told the vet that the dog had been very attached to his mother and had turned a bit nasty since the killings.

DS Jones and DC Clark appeared just after midday, followed by Ann Eaton and Anthony Pargeter, who was convinced that the silencer and telescopic sight had been attached to the Anschütz when he saw it in July. Anthony had already spoken to DCI Jones about the matter and arrangements were made for him to be interviewed at Bourtree Cottage. Clark's first task was to take a statement from Jeremy regarding the Anschütz. Clarifying that he had loaded the rifle that night minus its silencer and telescopic sight, Jeremy confirmed that he hadn't fired any shots, adding: 'To my knowledge Sheila had never fired the rifle before, although she has walked with me on occasions when I have been out shooting.'[5]

A little later, Ann asked Jeremy, 'Are the stories about Sheila taking drugs true?'[6]

He looked at her. 'I shouldn't tell you this, but she was on the hard stuff and that's what she was being treated for.'

'I never noticed any needle marks on her arm,' Ann said.

'There are much more sophisticated ways of doing it these days,' he replied. 'Anyway, they will soon be able to tell if she was on drugs when they cut into the fatty tissues of the body and have it analysed.' He added that he had an appointment that afternoon with a solicitor and accountant.

Jones and Clark retired to the Chequers for lunch, viewing

Jeremy's impending absence as a useful opportunity to speak to Julie alone. Jones was keen to discuss the timing of Jeremy's calls and pleased to find he had already left by the time they returned. Clark took a statement from Anthony, who made no reference to having seen the rifle with the sight and silencer attached on his last visit to the farm. Other than asserting that money was very important to Jeremy and his commitment to farming was dubious, Anthony voiced no qualms about him.

Jones then questioned Julie about the phone call she had received from Jeremy in the middle of the night. Ann sat nearby, listening. Jeremy had said that his call to Julie was made after he rang Chelmsford Police, but two issues troubled Jones: firstly, why Jeremy had telephoned her at all and, secondly, the order of the calls. To help with the latter, Julie rang Caterham Road and spoke to her friend Helen, who was staying there temporarily. Helen believed that Jeremy had telephoned about 3am. Yet afterwards Ann recalled Julie's friend giving a later time of 3.15am and also remembered DS Jones 'saying something about 3.30am'.[7] The latter was included in Julie's first witness statement.

Asked if Jeremy had told her what was happening when he rang, Julie replied that he had not. Dissatisfied with her reply and convinced that something else was going on below the surface, Jones rang DI Miller at the mortuary.

'We're not happy with this bloke,' he told Miller quietly. 'His demeanour, his answers to our questions – this ain't a bloke grieving. This is an oddball, a guy who's not all he seems.'[8]

Miller listened, then said, 'Right, hold everything down there. I'll give Taff a ring and get him to meet us at the farm.' He put a call through to DCI Jones's office, asking, 'Any chance of meeting you down at the farm in about half-hour? We're not happy with this fella.'

'What do you mean, you're not happy?' the DCI demanded.

'We think he knows a lot more than he's letting on.'

Miller recalls that he didn't get the chance to say anything else: 'Taff went into one and put the phone down on me.'

DS Jones left for White House Farm while DC Clark set out for the Chelmsford and Essex Hospital with Julie and Ann, leaving Anthony at the cottage. Much to everyone's surprise, Julie had volunteered to identify the bodies after Colin and Jeremy had refused. In a 1986 post-trial interview with the *News of the World*, Julie declared that her offer was 'not only to save [Jeremy] but to convince myself that this really had happened. I don't think I really believed it until I saw those five dead bodies.'

Ann agreed to accompany Julie but remained in the car while she and DC Clark went through to the viewing room. Coroner's Officer Norman Wright guided Julie from table to table: 'She was very deliberate and pointed to each body and took care to note the slight old scar in the case of the twin boys. She did not appear to be unduly distressed and was not hasty about the identifications.'[9]

Waiting outside, Ann grew anxious: 'They were in there for what appeared to me as an awful long time and I had started to pace up and down when they came out.'[10] She noticed that Julie 'was not crying or emotional and asked me if I had any objection to her smoking. I told her that I hadn't. Julie told me during the return journey that the identification of the bodies was not as difficult as she had thought it would be.' In the notes Ann was still jotting down to help her memory, she recorded: 'All looked peaceful, except uncle Nevill. His face . . .'[11]

Two officers visited St Andrew's Hospital in Northampton that day, where they took a statement from Dr Ferguson. 'The police were clearly making assumptions and my responses were based on what I was told,' he recalls. 'I had to accept that Sheila had killed them all and herself as well. I could envisage her being so angry towards her mother perhaps, but not her children or father. Even then, I don't believe she hated her mother – it was more anxiety that she felt towards June.'[12] His first statement concluded: 'It is suggested that Sheila killed her family and committed suicide. In hindsight I believe that Sheila would have relapsed into a state of acute psychosis, probably having a firmly held belief or delusion involving concepts of good and evil, and certainly paranoid, possibly involving her mother. Sheila is likely to have been in a disturbed psychotic state at the time of the tragedy, although in my experience with her there has never been any issue of threats or violence towards her family.'[13]

Attending the 4.30pm meeting at White House Farm were DCI Jones, DS Jones, DI Miller, DI Cook, DC Bird, DC Hammersley, DS Davidson, Dr Vanezis and two of his students. Miller recalls that when Taff arrived, he was 'purple with rage'.

The DCI pointed to the pathologist. 'What's he doing here?'

'I want him on the scene,' Miller responded.

'It's all tied up,' Taff insisted.

'No it's not,' said Miller. 'We're not happy—'

Jones thundered, 'You *are* going to be happy and that's it,' before stalking off.

After Dr Vanezis was shown where the bodies had been found, everyone gathered in the dining room for what he tactfully described as a candid discussion. DCI Jones was also present.

DI Cook remembered some talk about Sheila not being able to load the weapon but Taff Jones reasoned that she had lived on a farm and therefore would know all about guns. Cook was familiar with Jones but had never worked with him: 'He was very dogmatic in his approach, one of those who would say, "I've made a decision" or "I've a gut feeling". He was in charge.'[14]

Stan Jones, however, was determined to have his say. He listed his concerns: Jeremy's behaviour since the deaths of his family; his call to Julie on the night of the shootings; the Boutflours' certainty that Sheila was incapable of murder and could never have used the rifle; Sheila's remarkable cleanliness despite apparently killing four people; and Jeremy's appointment with a solicitor and accountant, which seemed premature for a man in mourning. Taff batted aside each issue, pointing out that the relatives had had little contact with Sheila in recent years, and asserted that Jones was projecting his own expectations of grief onto Jeremy. As for forensics – the ballistics experts were better placed to address those matters.

DC Clark had arrived late after the mortuary visit, but voiced his support for DS Jones. The pathology students looked on in surprise as voices boomed across the dining table. 'It was a *very* candid discussion,' Vanezis remembers with a rueful laugh. 'Stan Jones was extremely unhappy. It came through to all of us that there were areas we needed to reconsider.' Vanezis interjected with a few observations of his own, not least that Jeremy would have to have a 'warped state of mind' and be callously ingenious to engineer events as they were presented: 'This was almost too incredible to believe. Additionally, in order to stage manage Sheila she would probably need to be under the influence of drugs.'[15]

Today, he reflects: 'I was aware that if Jeremy was the guilty party, it must have taken a lot of planning. There were aspects of the case that were, frankly, the sort of thing you see on TV all the time but not in real life. Most murders are done not by criminal intellectuals but by people who don't think things through, which is why they get caught. But then you have odd ones who go to the extreme to cover their tracks. That's why I wouldn't compile my report until further tests had been done. I wanted to see if Sheila was under the influence of any drugs at the time of her death.'

The meeting in the dining room came to an ignominious end. DCI Jones rounded on his namesake in the kitchen yard. 'Stan got a hell of a telling off,' Bird recalls. 'One *hell* of a rollicking.'[16] Ridiculing Stan for allowing himself to be unduly influenced by the family, DCI Jones yelled, 'you're wrong on this one, boy' before storming off across the yard.

When everyone else had departed, the Scene of Crime officers began searching the premises, primarily for cartridge cases. They collected one bullet and three bullet cases from the twins' room, a bullet case from underneath the kitchen table, two pillows from June's side of the bed, and cut away two sections of carpet from the master bedroom. 'It would be fair to say that this search was perhaps more detailed than the first,' Cook conceded, 'mainly because we knew what we were looking for and were now more "au fait" with the case.'[17] There was no full fingerprint search, which would have taken three officers more than two weeks to complete. Cook explains: 'It was a typical, working, rambling farmhouse. The untidiness is there to be seen in the photographs. The decision not to do a fingerprint search was made by the senior investigating officer, not the Scene of Crime department. But what would we have been trying to prove? Were we trying to support Jeremy's contention that his sister was guilty or were we trying to disprove it? Whose fingerprints would we have been looking for and where? Both suspects were in and out of the house on a constant basis and were present on the day of the shootings.

'The only useful fingerprints would have been those in blood.'

Jeremy arrived early at Basil Cock's Colchester office, indicating to the family's solicitor that he would keep the farm running. They discussed the funeral, and Basil found his behaviour in keeping with his bereavement. Afterwards, Jeremy visited Charles Marsden and drove out to a village pub, where they spent an hour and a half talking. Charles was surprised that Jeremy showed no emotion or anger towards his sister.

Early that evening, Jeremy headed back to Goldhanger where DC Clark was completing a formal statement from Julie. Ann and Anthony were present as she went over the telephone calls she had received from Jeremy on the night of the murders. The police had been unaware that he had first called her at 9.50pm. Julie recounted: 'I spoke to him for between 17-20 minutes. He told me he had had supper with his parents during the conversation that evening and that he had a "pleasant as could be expected day due to harvesting."'[18]

She next heard from him a few hours later, when he sounded 'disjointed and worried', telling her, 'there's something wrong at home' and that he didn't know what to do. 'I told him to go to bed,' Julie recalled. 'I was half asleep and didn't ask him what was wrong.' His final call was at 5.40am from a public call box: '[He] said "Sheila has gone wild" or something like that. He said, "I can't say much, I've only got one 10p", then he said, "don't go to work, the police car is picking you up," the pips went and he hung up.'

DC Clark left shortly after Jeremy arrived home. Ann observed that her cousin seemed 'very pleased and was smiling' as he 'started to quote huge figures of what various properties and assets were worth'. He planned to retain his mother's interests in Osea Road and informed his cousins that they were to be minor beneficiaries in the wills. 'Jeremy showed no distress about the previous day's events or any remorse,' Ann stated. When he spoke about the funerals, she was shocked to hear that he wanted his sister and parents cremated 'because they were not whole'. Colin had already decided that Nicholas and Daniel should be buried in London.[19]

While they talked, Jeremy made and received several telephone calls. One was from Sue Ford, who asked him how he was coping; Liz Rimington rang after seeing the news on television that evening, and Susan Battersby called to speak to Julie, telling her that Jeremy had phoned on the night of the murders at 3.12am. She originally said that the call came through at 3.15am, but then remembered looking at her clock radio display, which had showed 3.12am.

After a second day spent closely observing Jeremy, Ann departed for home with Anthony at her side, both resolved to make the police aware of their concerns.

With detectives at Witham leading the investigation, Freddie Emami was driven to the police station there for an interview. He acknowledged that Sheila had had 'a very quick and violent temper which she would lose over the simplest of things' but had never seen her use physical violence towards anyone.[20] He ended his statement: 'Had it just been her [adoptive] mother who had been killed I could accept it, as she disliked her intensely, but to think she has killed her father and children is difficult to comprehend.'

'Bambi's Fella is Quizzed by Cops' read the *Sun*'s front page on Friday, 9 August, while the *Daily Mail* named Freddie the 'Gambling Man'. Both papers featured dramatic stories from Sheila's female neighbour at Morshead Mansions. Tora felt the tales were exaggerated. 'I saw Sheila literally every day and I know what I witnessed.'[1]

Sheila's fingerprints and those of her parents were taken at the mortuary by DS Davidson. Her hand swabs, blood samples, stomach contents, liver and urine samples, together with June's blood and urine samples, and Nevill and the twins' blood samples, were submitted to the Forensic Science Laboratory in Huntingdon that morning. The laboratory served ten police forces in eastern England with almost seventy expert staff. The submission form for Sheila's hand swabs was marked 'not accepted at Lab'.[2] The swabs were taken in order to detect firearm residue, but since Sheila had obviously been in the room when the rifle was fired, and her right hand was found to be in contact with the trigger area, it felt that nothing of evidential value could be gleaned from them. A further reason appears in a message from a police liaison officer at the laboratory to DCI Charles Wright, one of the SOCO officers in charge of the inquiry: 'Advised that item 17 not accepted at Lab due to contamination risk as it came into Laboratory with firearms (not connected with this case).'[3] Sheila's hand swabs were returned to police that same day.

At White House Farm, Cook and Hammersley discovered a spent cartridge case under the wardrobe on June's side of the bed and took scrapings from two bloodspots on the landing between the master bedroom and Sheila's room. Hammersley seized the bloodstained Bible that had lain next to Sheila's body and cut away a section of the wallpaper in the corridor between kitchen and hall which bore a smear of blood about five feet from the floor. The two men, together with another constable drafted in to assist, then began a task that was not normally in their remit.

Cook explains: 'Stan Jones had asked on behalf of the family if we could clean the place up a bit when we finished our initial examination. We started by removing the bloodstained mattresses from the twins' bedroom. I asked one of the farm workers if there was somewhere we could dispose of them and he said, "We have a pit where we burn lots of farm waste." The mattresses were dropped out of the window onto a trailer. Some carpet pieces left over from where we cut away the bloodstained sections ended up in there as well. The farm worker told us he would burn it the following day, but he left it for a while. The press got to hear about it and turned it into a tale of "destroyed evidence". But we'd already removed those items essential to the investigation.'[4] The 1986 internal review of the case confirmed that 'the necessary control samples had been taken and the items destroyed would have been of no further evidential value,' but acknowledged that 'had the matter been treated as five murders from the outset, these items would not have been destroyed at that stage.'

The three officers also generally tidied up the kitchen. After scrubbing the bloodstained floor, the assistant constable emptied the murky water into the kitchen sink 'where it splashed the window and surrounding area, which were not wiped down afterwards'.[5] By 1pm, the officers were ready to leave.

DC Bird reflects: 'As far as Scenes of Crime was concerned, we went to the scene, we did our job and were gone. Today they nail it down for weeks, don't they? But we were in and out of there in two or three days. It was a different world back then.'[6]

'9.45am. Witham on murder', reads the entry in Taff Jones' pocket book. 'Interview with DS Jones, relatives, close friends of Bambers – Ann Eaton, who stated that neither Jeremy nor Sheila knew very much about firearms and did not think Sheila was capable of carrying out the crimes. Certain facts explained to them which made them reasonably happy that stories they had heard and read were near the truth.'[7]

Arriving by prior appointment, Anthony, David and Ann had prepared a list of questions. Ann made notes as DCI Jones confirmed that the telescopic sight hadn't been fixed to the rifle on the night of the shootings, during which twenty-five rounds had been fired. Immediately grasping that the magazine must have been reloaded at least twice in that case, Ann declared in an outraged voice that there was no possibility Sheila was responsible.

Taff Jones rose to his feet. 'I don't have to put up with this,' he bellowed. 'And stop writing!'[8] Ann sat speechless, taken aback by the force of his anger. Her brother recalls that DCI Jones had made his mind up: 'He said, "It's murder and suicide." He wouldn't go back on that, he wanted to throw us out.'[9] Ann began trying to press their point about Sheila's inability to fire such a weapon, until Anthony shushed her and asked DCI Jones to continue. More calmly, Anthony and David then tried to explain how much louder the Anschütz would have sounded in the house if fired minus its silencer, and discussed whether the rifle would fit in the den cupboard with silencer and sight attached.

DS Jones asked if they were willing to accept that Sheila had committed suicide. David replied that he wanted proof that she had handled the cartridges; Anthony stated that they didn't like to accuse anyone unnecessarily but felt alternatives should be considered. When DS Jones asked Ann how she would feel if her accusations against Jeremy turned out to be wrong, she said nothing, privately thinking that she could live with it because she was convinced that he was guilty.

DCI Jones was not impressed by their arguments. He dubbed Ann an interfering Miss Marple and used his free afternoon to simmer down on the golf course. But Ann went over and over things, refusing offers of a brandy to settle her, and wouldn't watch television or read a book for months to come. She had trouble sleeping, imagining Jeremy 'climbing through a window to get me, with a gun'.[10]

Her husband Peter was not as convinced initially, calling at Bourtree Cottage that morning with a firm offer of assistance on the farm. Chris Nevill (Nevill's cousin) arrived at the cottage while Peter was there; he had travelled from New Zealand expecting to stay with Nevill and June but had seen the headlines during his journey and was in a state of shock. The three of them were joined by David, who called in after the meeting at Witham. Jeremy told them that the Henry Smith trustees who owned the farm had given him notice to quit, since their contract was with his father. Aware that the tenancy was in fact likely to be offered to Jeremy should he want it, Peter thought it doubtful that the trustees had issued such an ultimatum: 'They wouldn't do that to him, not over an accident [the murders]. I told him that he had to keep hold of the farm to fall back on.'[11]

David recalled that Jeremy then made a comment about having received two small cuts on his hand while working on the farm but he couldn't see the marks when Jeremy held out his palm. After Ann and Anthony arrived, something explosive passed between the group, although precise details have never emerged. Later, Ann would only say that they 'must have accused Jeremy' since he 'showed the first sign of real emotion' as they brought their simmering suspicions about him into the open. Whatever was said, he was in such a state that a doctor was called and prescribed him Valium. Still wound up and wanting to find out if Jeremy could be prodded into any sort of admission, Ann remarked that Sheila deserved only black flowers on her coffin, implying that she was guilty of the murders. Jeremy said nothing, but did not forget her comment.

After lunch, Jeremy and Julie collected Bruce the labrador and left him with the vet in Maldon, who had found him a new home on another farm. Jeremy then headed to Basil Cock's office for a meeting with Peter Eaton, who accepted an offer to manage White House Farm. Later he returned with Julie to Bourtree Cottage, where Ann was keeping Chris Nevill company; David and Anthony had gone. She agreed to find a security team to watch the farm over the weekend while Jeremy and Julie stayed with Colin. When Jeremy mentioned that Sotheby's were going to value and store all the furniture from the farm, she asked him if he intended to live there in the future, 'but he said he would not go into the house now or ever again. I asked him why he couldn't and his answer was that he kept seeing their faces.'[12]

At half-past seven, DCI Jones and Stan Jones turned up, startling Ann, who immediately thought they had come to arrest Jeremy. Instead, they needed some to act as key holder to the farm and since Jeremy had made his feelings clear, Ann took responsibility. DCI Jones announced that they wanted to speak to Jeremy alone and arranged to contact Ann that later that evening about the keys. Before leaving, she asked about June's engagement ring; her mother wanted it as a keepsake. Jeremy's

response was definite: the ring would be cremated with his
mother and nothing should be removed from the farmhouse
either: it was his shrine. Nettled, Ann told him that he ought to
settle down and marry Julie and stay at White House Farm forever. Jeremy replied that he much preferred Vaulty and Julie
agreed, adding that she had seen his grandmother's beautiful
home from a bus.

Unbeknown to Jeremy, DCI Jones was there to prove to Stan
Jones that his suspicions were wrong. As the three men went
through to the dining room, Jeremy explained that he had taken
Valium, 'so if I appear to be drifting away, you'll understand it's
the effect of the tablets.'[13] DCI Jones replied that he simply
wanted to clarify a few matters and began by asking Jeremy if he
remembered telling an officer that he had fired a couple of shots
at the rabbits on the night of the murders.

Jeremy answered, 'No, I didn't. When I went outside they had
gone.'

Asked about the state of the gun when he left it, he replied: 'I
took the magazine out and left it on the settle. I also took one
[bullet] out of the breech, which I put back in the magazine and
left the gun up against the wall.' He stated that the silencer
and telescopic sight were definitely not on the rifle at the time.
When DCI Jones reminded him that they had been attached
two weekends before, he declared that his father must have removed them. Jones asked if there was already ammunition in the
magazine when he loaded the gun.

'I don't think so,' Jeremy answered.

'You took a new box with fifty rounds in it,' Jones said.
'There were thirty rounds left on the work surface in the kitchen
and we know that twenty-five shots were fired. Can you explain
where the extra five rounds have come from?'

'No,' said Jeremy. After a brief discussion about family relationships, he asked: 'Can you chaps tell in which order they were
killed?'

Stan Jones stared at him. 'Why do you ask that?'

'Because I saw my accountant yesterday and he told me that
it affects the will,' Jeremy replied. 'It's important. Can't you tell?'

'I doubt it,' Stan said.

As the two detectives drove back to Witham, DCI Jones

asked Stan if he felt any easier. Keen to avoid further argument, Stan fibbed that he did but had found the query about the order of deaths strange. DCI Jones told him it was quite common for people to ask about such things.

While Jeremy packed for London, Julie telephoned Liz Rimington in 'a very distressed state'.[14] Liz recalled: 'She just asked me to talk to her about anything. I asked her what was happening and she told me that there were police everywhere and somebody had been talking about drugs.' Liz assumed she was referring to Jeremy's cannabis. She invited Julie to stay but her friend answered tearfully that she 'didn't know if it was possible'.

The couple arrived in Kilburn shortly before 10pm. In the days that had passed since the murders, Colin's shock and grief had given way to an almost preternatural calm as family and friends gathered round in a house that seemed to radiate with his sons' bright, affectionate personalities. He immediately sensed that his guests were in a very dark mood. Heather went upstairs with her father and his partner to give them some privacy, but Colin's ex-girlfriend Jan Flowers remained.

Conversation soon turned to the last night at the farm and Jeremy repeated that he felt his father had been wounded before ringing him. He described his relatives as 'a load of fucking magpies', nattering about his mother's jewellery and the farm.[15] He talked about the meeting with Basil Cock and explained that he was the sole heir to the estate, including Sheila's property, provided she hadn't left a will. Colin thought it unlikely and asked if he might bury Sheila's ashes with their sons. Jeremy agreed, passing on Ann's 'black flowers' remark. The comment hurt Colin deeply and led to a wedge of mistrust between him and Sheila's relatives for a long time.

Just before midnight, Heather and her family joined them and the mood began to lift. They looked through old photographs and Jeremy talked about opening a bistro in the future or buying a smallholding in Dorset.

Seventy miles away in Essex, Ann spent the evening waiting for a call from the police. It came just as the light was fading. With Peter at her side, she set out for White House Farm, where they

found the two Joneses parked in the kitchen yard. Before they
went in, Stan asked them to let them know if they noticed anything out of place. Ann shivered as the detective unlocked the
back door: 'It was getting late and I was a bit scared to go in.'

The replacement door swung open into the scullery. There
was just enough twilight to see by as they entered the kitchen.
In an oblique reference to the violence Nevill had suffered, one
of the detectives commented that there had been 'quite a lot of
activity' in the room.[16] Ann observed that the coal scuttle was
missing and saw the broken lampshade above the table. 'We continued along the passage on the ground floor and turned right
into the lounge,' she remembered. 'The police told me that nothing had happened in this room.' She noticed the children's game
on the rug, the fallen drinks mats next to it and a child's toy gun
on the occasional table next to the settee. Then she noticed something else, next to the gun: part of a tampon. The end with the
cord was missing 'as if the remainder had been used.' She was
baffled as to why it was in the lounge. Following her husband
and the detectives into the dining room, she saw the twins' cray-
ons and drawings abandoned on the round mahogany table.

They returned to the hall and climbed the main staircase.
One of the detectives mentioned there had been some blood on
the carpet. Ann gazed into the master bedroom. The blankets
had been stripped from the bed and great swathes of carpet had
been cut away, leaving the floorboards exposed. She asked
whether the Bible had 'actually been on Sheila's chest', or if there
had been any blood or sugar on her feet 'from the struggle in the
kitchen', but neither officer committed himself to an answer.
They crossed the landing to Sheila's room: two pairs of her shoes
stood next to the bed by the smaller wardrobe and there was a
large black suitcase in the room. Ann assumed that Sheila had
slept in the bed closest to the fireplace, given the toiletries scattered on the bed nearest the door. She noticed the opened box of
Tampax; the tampon in the lounge must have come from there.

The group retraced their steps to the lower landing, walking
along the narrow corridor to the twins' room. 'All of us entered
the room,' Ann remembered. 'I noticed that the mattresses and
pillows were missing from the bed. I asked the officers about this
and my husband and I were told that they had been burned. A

large patch of wallpaper and part of the foam backing beneath had been steadily torn away around the bed on the left, where Daniel had slept.'[17]

Ann observed nothing amiss in the other upstairs rooms, but saw a thin belt with loose triangular type objects on both ends draped over the banister near Sheila's room, which struck her as a little odd. Downstairs, they entered those rooms they had missed before, including the shower room where the shower head hung loose. Ann asked about the broken shotgun lying against the wall in the den and was told that it was found there. Peter picked it up, commenting on the cleanliness of the barrels.

They had gone into every room and to her surprise Ann felt 'alright, fairly comfortable. I must have been asking questions virtually all the time but can't now recall anything of what was said.'[18] DS Jones showed her how the new alarm they had fitted worked before handing over the keys. It was dark as they stepped outside. The detectives departed in their car, gravel spitting under the wheels as the vehicle turned for Pages Lane.

Ann stood looking up at the house. She had left a couple of lights on; they shone dully behind the curtains, as if there was still life inside. After a moment, she climbed into the car beside her husband and they set out for home.

Early on Saturday morning, Ann returned alone to White House Farm. In what became a routine for months to come, she let herself in and switched off the alarm and lights. Then she swept the floor, tipping the spilled sugar into the waste bin containing the broken lampshade and crockery. Under her breath she muttered, 'Give us a clue, Uncle Nevill, tell us what happened.'[1]

Two buckets stood on the floor beside the sink, one containing two pairs of badly bloodstained women's knickers, the other a pair of boy's tracksuit bottoms and socks; it had been June's habit to soak exceptionally dirty clothes prior to washing them. Deeply upset and trying to cling to some semblance of normality, Ann set about rinsing the clothing in the sink. As she worked, she noticed smudge marks on the inside of the window and diluted blood marks on the sill. She left the clothing to soak in clean water and wiped down the window, wondering about the marks.

David appeared at 11am and Ann took him through the house, trying to remember everything the police had told her. Their father joined them that afternoon, together with Basil Cock, and again Ann led them through the rooms. Robert was mystified by the tampon in the lounge, knowing that June would not have allowed that sort of thing to be left lying about, especially in the sitting room. It was one issue in the case which would never be resolved.

Later in court, David recalled that they then 'went round the house with the intent of putting anything of specific value into safekeeping'. According to Basil Cock, 'this was arranged by Ann Eaton who stated that Jeremy had asked that we do so,' but she maintained that they were to 'remove cash, papers, etc., from the house under Basil Cock's instructions for safe keeping.'[2]

They began by looking for money. Robert was convinced that Nevill would have cash about the house, but they found none. Ann searched for June's everyday handbag and purse. Although she found several, again none contained cash. The four of them then removed various valuables from sight, storing silver and copperware in a chest in the lounge, and consigned paintings to the cupboard in the upstairs corridor. They discovered Beatrice Bamber's jewellery in a wardrobe in Sheila's room, while June's jewellery, including a locket Pamela wanted, was in her dressing table drawer. Basil located Nevill's firearms certificate and the receipt for the Anschütz in a kitchen dresser drawer, together with the house contents insurance policy, and a blue envelope in June's handwriting with instructions that it was to remain sealed until after her death. The envelope had been opened; Basil scanned the single page inside and replaced it, removing the drawer to examine at his leisure.

Jeremy had warned Ann that they were in for a surprise when they unlocked the safe in the upstairs office. Robert located the key on an overhead fluorescent light, but the only unexpected item was an envelope containing cannabis resin confiscated from Roland Pargeter years before. Basil took out the sealed wills belonging to Nevill and June, then telephoned Barbara Wilson to ask her assistance on legal matters.

'They had to come out and get me,' Barbara recalls. 'I drove straight there but I couldn't walk across that yard. Normally I'd drive up to the door, but I parked outside the gate instead and David Boutflour took me in. Ann said, "It's quite alright, Barbara. There's nothing to see, everything is fine." But it was awful, so upsetting.'[3]

Surprised to discover guns left on the premises, David decided to remove them. In the downstairs shower room he found two dismantled 12 bore shotguns belonging to Anthony Pargeter, and on the service stairs in the kitchen were a BSA Meteor .22 airgun and a Webley & Scott .410 shotgun, the latter leaning against the wall with the barrel pointing upwards. None of the weapons were loaded. Then he headed for the den.

In the thirty years that have passed since that day, those present have fully accounted for the discovery of the single most contentious item of evidence in the case. Their versions differ only in very minor instances that have no further bearing on the investigation, with David's 17 September 1985 witness statement providing the most straightforward narrative. In it, he describes peering into the understairs cupboard, whose door was secured only by a nylon ball catch. To the left was a rusty poker with an angled end, 'like a golf club', a cardboard box containing boxes of 12 bore ammunition, and a dart board. To the right against the back wall, inside another cardboard box with a cellophane top, was an electric spray gun and pipe. On top of that was yet another box containing a Parker & Hale type gun silencer about seven inches in length and about one inch in diameter standing upright. A white carrier bag contained a quantity of .22 low velocity ammunition, neatly packed in clear plastic boxes. Partly on top of the bag was a telescopic sight in its original packaging. There were a few loose 12 bore cartridges in the bottom of the box. David checked the cupboard again and saw a brown gun case containing a Webley & Scott 12 bore shotgun that he recognized as belonging to Nevill.

David removed everything from the cupboard except the dart board, poker, spray gun and the empty box which had contained the plastic bag, silencer and telescopic sight. Robert had a clear view of the silencer but made no attempt to touch it as David carried everything through to the kitchen.

Examining the silencer more closely, David observed that the knurled end bore 'deposits of what appeared to be red paint. I also saw a spot the size of a match head, coloured red on the leading face of that knurled end, there was also a fresh silver coloured scratch mark about 1" long about halfway along its length.'[4] He counted the .22 ammunition inside the plastic bag; there were 'about five full boxes of 50 rounds and one similar box half full'. Realizing the potential significance of his discovery, particularly the silencer, he resolved to investigate further.

Robert then checked all the windows for signs of entry or exit and identified six which he believed could be used without detection. In the kitchen, Ann emptied the water from the buckets, pushing the tracksuit bottoms, socks and bloodstained knickers into the waste bin by the dishwasher. David loaded the guns and items from the den cupboard into the boot of Ann's Sierra, placing June's dressing table drawer and Beatrice Bamber's jewellery on the back seat, then drove to Oak Farm in his own car. Basil departed with kitchen dresser drawer, followed by Barbara Wilson in her car.

Ann and her father travelled to Vaulty, where he and Pamela were spending the night. She handed June's dressing table drawer to her mother, who placed it discreetly in the spare bedroom with a cover draped across it. Mabel Speakman knew nothing as yet about the murders; Pamela feared the shock might kill her.

Jeremy spent most of the day asleep on the makeshift bed in Colin's sitting room. Getting up, he was introduced to Colin's ex-girlfriend Jill, who found him 'a strong presence. At one point I commented to him about his being strong, but he said he wasn't strong, just hardened. I felt that he was not as devastated about the deaths as I expected but he was in control. I felt that he had very strong undercurrents to his personality.'[5]

Colin's mother arrived while Jeremy was freshening up. She later told her son that Jeremy had run giggling into the room with his hair in soapy spikes, then rushed out again upon seeing her. That evening the two couples, together with Colin's ex-girlfriends Sandra and Jill, walked to Raffles restaurant in Kilburn High Road. Colin recalled that Jeremy paid for the meal with a thick wad of banknotes. The atmosphere was surprisingly positive, although Jeremy declared that 'nobody could understand' the grief he and Colin shared.[6]

Afterwards, despite having taken Valium with alcohol, Jeremy drove the group to a church hall in Hampstead, where Herbie Flowers was performing in aid of Ethiopia. Jeremy made no attempt to chat to anyone and seemed sapped when they arrived back at Maygrove Road. No one was surprised when he and Julie immediately retired for the night.

At Oak Farm, Peter Eaton and David Boutflour scrutinized the silencer at the kitchen table. David noted that it was 'sticky' to touch, either because it had been heavily oiled or 'had some matter on it'.[7] The scratch was bright and appeared recent. He tried unsuccessfully to remove the tightly fastened knurl end in order to look inside the chamber. It was then that he realized the red-brown substance on the end was almost certainly blood, 'thick enough to peel off with a razor blade' had they wished.[8]

'I went to take it from him,' Ann remembered. 'David told me sharply not to touch it, so I never did touch it, but I did see what appeared to be dried blood around the exit hole of the silencer and flecks of what appeared to be red paint.'[9] She described it in court as looking like 'a blob of jam'.

Her husband questioned how the silencer had come to be in such a bad condition, since it took quite a lot of force to mark gun metal. David telephoned Anthony Pargeter, who listened to him describing the scratch mark, paint and 'what looked like a drop of blood', then told him to 'wrap it up'.[10] David put the silencer into a bag, which together with the sight and ammunition were placed inside a wardrobe at Oak Farm. The guns were hidden in a blanket box and the jewellery deposited in the attic.

Ann sat down with her husband and brother to discuss 'the implications of how this silencer could be in the gun cupboard with blood and paint on it. Obviously if it was being alleged that somebody had had a brainstorm and shot dead four people [she] would surely not have stopped to remove the silencer, put it back in the gun cupboard, go back upstairs and shoot herself dead.'[11] The inference was glaringly obvious: if the blood on the silencer related to the shootings, then Sheila was almost certainly not the killer.

It was a fact that had already occurred to Robert Boutflour, who lay awake at Vaulty, convinced 'beyond all shadow of doubt that Sheila had not committed the murder and then shot herself'.[12] His thoughts turned to Jeremy. He spent the entire night trying to reconstruct events from all he had heard, read and seen. In a 'diary' he compiled in the immediate aftermath of the murders, Robert concluded that Jeremy had 'sold his soul to the Devil' and that 'a consuming greed and envy and possibly the immediate need for cash' had driven his nephew to kill.[13] He decided to share his thoughts with the police as soon as possible.

At 10am the following Sunday morning, Ann returned to White House Farm with Jean Bouttell, who gave the place a thorough clean, finally clearing the breakfast table and emptying the dishwasher. She handed Ann the spare key to the original back door, explaining that it had been kept in the coal shed, which left Ann puzzling over why Jeremy hadn't told the police about it.

Knowing that her mother intended to visit, Ann asked Jean and Chris Nevill – who had spent the night in his campervan in the yard – to help her cover the exposed floorboards in the master bedroom. They struggled with the heavy brass bed but managed to lay an unused carpet Nevill had originally bought for the den. When Pamela arrived with David and Karen, Ann took her through the house, then decided to change the sheets on Sheila's bed. In the twins' room, Karen became very upset at the sight of the barren bed frames but helped tidy up, storing toys, clothes and Sheila's belongings in the wardrobe. They looked again in vain for June's everyday handbag and purse.

Despite their efforts to ensure that nothing was overlooked, no one had yet contacted the police about the silencer. In court, David asserted that 'we rang the police immediately', but that the silencer wasn't collected 'until some two or three days later'. In 1991 he revised his position: 'Police informed but not straight away. The silencer was left with Ann and I presumed she would phone the police.'[14] Ann stated in evidence that she had made the call on Saturday night and today remains certain that she telephoned the police promptly.

While his relatives scoured White House Farm, Jeremy and Julie left Kilburn for Caterham Road. Julie's housemates Susan, Doug and Joanna were watching television in the lounge when they arrived. The conversation was stilted until Doug and Julie left for the off-licence. Jeremy then began talking about his 'money-grabbing' relatives, whom he said were worried he was about to become the major shareholder of Osea Road.[15] 'He did not appear to be too upset about the deaths,' Susan recalled. 'He appeared to be more upset about other people's attitude about the money situation.'

Jeremy and Julie departed for Goldhanger early on Monday morning. After a quick freshen up at home, Jeremy drove to the farm, where he met Peter acting in his new role as manager. Jeremy declared that the White House Farm trustees had offered him £80,000 to quit and he intended to accept. Peter didn't believe him: 'I told him that they just didn't pay money out like that. Jeremy said that I wasn't to use a new tractor that was there as it was going back. He thought he could get £20,000 for it. He also said the combine harvester was going back.'[16]

Barbara was due to return to work that day but couldn't face it alone, and asked Jean to accompany her. Ann arrived shortly afterwards with her eight-year-old daughter Janie. She took both women through the house in an effort to reassure them. 'I didn't want to be shown round,' Barbara recalls. 'But Ann insisted. It

was so strange and quiet. Ann would say, "This is where . . ."
But I didn't want to know. She kept saying that I would feel
better if I went into every room. Well, I didn't.'

Robert appeared after visiting Maldon Police Station, where
a sergeant had arranged for him and Pamela to be seen that
afternoon at Witham. Jeremy had returned home by then, but
Ann invited him over to the farm for coffee. Remembering his
comment about seeing his family's faces everywhere, she was
surprised when he agreed. She took Janie upstairs to the twins'
room, where they pushed the beds together and remade them as
a double bed, 'just in case he had not done it – we made it more
bearable.'[17]

Jeremy and Julie were there within ten minutes. Julie sat in
Sheila's old spot at the kitchen table while Jeremy eased himself
into his father's chair. 'He was not in any way emotional,' Ann
recalled. 'He then said that he didn't know where anything was.
This meant to me that he hadn't asked or in any way established
where the bodies had been found.'[18] She offered to take him
through the house to explain. Jeremy agreed but turned back in
the corridor for Julie, who shook her head and began to cry, but
got to her feet when he asked again.

Ann showed them into the lounge and dining room. Jeremy
queried the empty spaces on the walls and she told him the most
valuable items had been put away. They climbed the stairs;
Robert waited for them in the master bedroom but Jeremy
remained mutely at the door. Ann walked across to Sheila's room
and glanced back at Jeremy, who had turned to follow her and
seemed 'absolutely petrified. He froze and stood still, eyes staring
and black looking. He didn't go into the room, he didn't want to.
He stayed on the landing. I said "nothing happened in here" and
pulled him by the arm and took him in.' His reaction was not
lost on Robert either. Ann was disturbed, thinking 'something
went on in that room, but what?'

They went down the short flight of stairs to the twins' bedroom and Ann watched as Jeremy 'started stooping, hunched up
and crept towards this room, slowly'. Julie went in and eventually he joined her. Ann and her father left them there, bemused
by Jeremy's reactions. Robert felt he 'showed no curiosity, only
what appeared to be fear, by that I mean frightened by what he

might find and he never asked questions. I know that Pam and I were grief-stricken and Pam went in with a broken heart but with Jeremy it was very different.'[19]

Jeremy regained his composure in the kitchen, remarking on the number of belongings that appeared to be missing, and ran back upstairs to look for his father's wallet. Unable to find it, he telephoned Witham to report it lost, explaining that it contained his father's credit cards and four or five hundred pounds. Ending the call, he asked how the kitchen light fitting had come to be broken before going through to the lounge. Ann followed him: 'Jeremy picked up the video cassette recorder from its position under the colour television. I asked him what he was doing and he said that it was his. He carried this out to his car. He then returned to the kitchen and went to a shelf above the telephone. He checked among some letters on the shelf and removed one and walked to the rubbish bin where he tore the letter open. He then threw this in the rubbish bin. I asked Jeremy what he was doing. He said that it was somebody who had been using White House Farm as an address.'[20]

Seated at the kitchen table, Robert had begun to breathe heavily, evidently worked up. Ann massaged his shoulders while Jeremy sat back in his father's chair, crooking one leg over the other. Incensed by his relaxed pose, Robert got to his feet, recalling afterwards that 'it was at that point that I loathed the boy and couldn't bear being anywhere near him.'[21] He drove home, still fuming. Ann gave Jeremy a key to the new back door and kept the other for herself before she departed.

Jeremy later described his own anger at finding items missing or hidden, despite having impressed upon his relatives that nothing was to be touched. One of the many documents disseminated by his current campaign team asserts that it was his relatives' actions that led to him arranging for Sotheby's to value the house contents, but Basil Cock stated in 1985 that he had realized on the previous Saturday (10 August) that the Bambers were under insured. He had then suggested to Jeremy that cover should be increased from £17,000 to £50,000. Because Jeremy thought the figure still too low, as well as increasing the cover to £150,000, Basil 'also contacted Sothebys to ask them to inspect the contents to determine anything of high value'.[22]

That afternoon, Pamela gave a witness statement to Stan Jones at Witham. Robert sat listening impatiently: 'I was determined to tell him I thought it was Jeremy who had killed his family, I wanted to point the finger at him, but Detective Sergeant Jones was more concerned with speaking with my wife.'

Eventually Robert began: 'I don't like to interfere, but the story the press have is wrong' before listing his suspicions about Jeremy's behaviour both before and after the murders, and his certainty that Sheila was innocent. To his disappointment, Jones was not as sympathetic as he had been before, having made no headway in discussing his own reservations with DCI Jones. Robert swallowed his anger as Stan suggested that he was 'in collusion' with his son and daughter. He reiterated his concerns nonetheless, detailing how he believed Jeremy might have carried out the murders.

'Detective Inspector Miller came into the room and I repeated my theory to him,' Robert remembered. 'He said something like, "We have done all the tests bar one and they all point to Sheila." I recall that I also mentioned the security of the windows with Inspector Miller. He said to me that they had "sophisticated equipment" to ascertain if anyone got in or out of the house.'

Exasperated, Robert told them that Jeremy had remarked only a few weeks earlier that he was capable of shooting his parents.

Jones shrugged: 'He could have said that in the heat of the moment.'

'I don't think so,' Robert replied sharply.

Jones said nothing for a moment, then asked, 'What would convince you that Sheila did it?'

'I'd like to see her fingerprints on every bullet,' Robert replied, unwittingly echoing his son's words. He then demanded: 'Can you explain how they were all shot without the silencer on the gun?'

Jones frowned: 'What silencer?'

Robert, grasping the chance to impress the implications of finding the silencer, explained its discovery. When he left with Pamela afterwards, he felt relieved and somewhat vindicated to have seen the dawning realization on Jones's face. DS Jones put a call through to DI Cook, who planned to visit the laboratory in Huntingdon the following day. Cook arranged to collect the silencer from Jones beforehand.

Tests conducted at the laboratory 'across the board, for all drugs' on Sheila's blood and urine samples had returned negative results.[23] A 'slight positive for the presence of cannabis type compounds' was found in her urine sample, indicating that Sheila had used the drug several days before her death, consistent with her smoking at Colin's party.[24] The Huntingdon toxicologist stated that it was highly unlikely there had been any interaction between the cannabis and the haloperidol detected in her liver and blood. Dr Ferguson confirmed at the trial: 'The impact on someone of Sheila's problems of having some cannabis a few days before would be minimal, considering she had been using it for some time anyway.' The blood and urine tests on all the other victims showed no drugs or alcohol present.

The pathologist had already suggested that, for Sheila's death to be murder, she would probably have required sedation. Acknowledging the toxicology results demonstrated that wasn't the case, today Vanezis also points out that the haloperidol would have helped maintain Sheila's equilibrium without numbing her to the point where she could be manipulated against her will: 'Sheila was taking her medication, so her mental state was controlled. If she wasn't, that might support Jeremy's story of her "going mad". But she was medicated and that showed up in the tests, which is why I wanted to defer my report until those results were in. But before then, I was told about the silencer being found by the relatives. So we went back and did a further review.'

At 5.30pm, Jeremy and Julie met Liz Rimington in Colchester to go bowling. Jeremy telephoned Charles Marsden, asking him to make up a foursome. While he was away, Julie turned to Liz with a troubled expression: 'Lizzie, Jeremy is so cold, he just doesn't care about anything. Believe me, if the devil has a human form on this earth then his name is Jeremy. He's the devil incarnate.'[25] Liz ventured that Jeremy might be in shock. 'If only you knew,' Julie said quietly as he returned.

Liz recalled that Jeremy 'became very chatty and was laughing and joking' when Charles joined them. Finding the bowling

alley fully booked they headed to Fifi's for a meal. The atmosphere grew strained as Jeremy's mood dipped and he left to be
alone for a while. He returned to pay for the meal with another
large wad of cash. Charles went home, but Liz stayed the night
in Jeremy's spare room.

DS Jones called at Oak Farm that evening. Peter showed him
the silencer; Ann and her mother were at the vicarage, discussing
the funeral. Jones was not wearing gloves, but later surmised that
he had a handkerchief over his hand while inspecting the silencer.
He saw 'a substance which looked like blood' on one end, paint
on the knurl, and a grey hair 'about three quarters of an inch
long' attached to the scratch, which he pointed out to Peter.[26]
How the family had missed the hair during their examination
remains a puzzle. Jones had no suitable packaging with him and
used the inner cardboard tube of a kitchen towel roll taped at
both ends.

Ann arrived home shortly after Jones had taken possession of
the silencer. The detective was still chatting to her husband, but
her attention was diverted by a huge bouquet of flowers and a
card that read: 'Thank you for all your loving – Jeremy.' A
moment later the local police telephoned, informing her that the
alarm had gone off at White House Farm and she was needed
there. Nothing appeared amiss and she was soon home again.
Stan Jones stayed for some time, drinking whisky with Peter. He
returned to Witham with the silencer but minus the sight and
ammunition; Ann stated in court that the police 'did not ask for
them to start with'.

Jones made no note of the silencer in Witham's miscellaneous
property register, assuming that it would 'go into the Scenes of
Crime system and [be] recorded in that fashion'.[27] DI Cook
regarded the omission as useful 'because it totally minimised the
handling of the silencer by others, which would have occurred in
the registering of it in property books.'[28] Jones placed the packaged silencer in his desk drawer where it remained until 8am the
following morning, Tuesday, 13 August, when he handed it to DI
Miller, who was in charge that week while DCI Jones attended a
course.

Miller recalls: 'I saw a grey hair attached to it and something
red, possibly paint.'[29]

DI Cook arrived at Witham Police Station at 9.15am to collect the silencer. He found one end of the cardboard tube 'not
sealed properly' and squeezed it 'so that I could just about make
out the end of the silencer, which had a very small speck of what
could have been blood on it. I also saw a hair.'[30] He secured the
open end with a yellow sticker on which he wrote his initials, but
at some stage during transportation in his car, the hair became
detached from the silencer and was lost. Cook presented the
silencer, Anschütz, magazine, two carpet samples and Sheila's
nightdress for examination, omitting to mention the grey hair on
the submission form. 'When I got to the laboratory I forgot all
about the hair,' he admitted. 'It was not until several months
later, when I was asked to make a further statement concerning
the loss of the hair, that I recalled it.' In an unpublished letter he
questions its evidential worth, stating that it 'could have been
picked up by the silencer from anywhere within the farmhouse,
the cardboard box in which it was found, or even from the house
of the relatives.'[31]

Cook instructed biologist Glynis Howard to examine the
silencer for blood, watching as she opened the cardboard tube
and placed the silencer on clean blotting paper. Howard described
it as in fair condition and observed four apparent bloodstains on
its surface. She took samples from two of the four stains before
replacing the silencer in its cardboard tube and resealing it, then
made a preliminary examination of the Anschütz and took
samples from five areas of staining. The rifle and silencer were
returned to DI Cook while the carpet samples and Sheila's nightdress were retained for more detailed examination.

Cook then discussed the case at the laboratory. Malcolm
Fletcher, a forensic scientist since 1964 and ballistics expert since
1974, recalls: 'The difficulty was that we hadn't seen the crime
scene first-hand. The police had already decided that it was four
murders and a suicide and didn't want us there, whereas normally we'd get to a crime scene as soon as possible. Fortunately,
there was evidence enough from the photographs and by the
time we had our meeting with Ron Cook, queries were coming
in from other investigators that indicated doubts about the initial
interpretation. I think that's probably what instigated our meeting on the 13th of August, to give weight to a counter-scenario.

We kept pointing out things that didn't sit right with their original suggestion and they were forced to reconsider.'[32]

He explains further: 'Historically speaking, the police would submit items, provide us with background information and tell us the sort of evidence they were looking for. But quite often we would examine items based on the information we'd been given, then formulate our own tests to bring out evidence which we thought might be helpful. In the Bamber case, the possibility of an alternative explanation for the crime scene meant there was a lot of discussion about what needed to be done, especially with regard to the order of examination. Because testing for blood or fingerprints could mask or destroy other information. Looking for small particulate samples, hairs or spots of blood had to be approached in such a way that the minimum amount of evidence was lost. We discussed which was the most important because that would determine which test was done first. Sometimes there were sacrifices when other things were paramount, but in the Bamber case we gave the police so much information and alternative scenarios that they had to try and recover the case.

'And the truth was certainly growing on us all as we got further along.'

Osea Road manager James Carr was frank with Stan Jones when he interviewed him that Tuesday morning, telling Jones about his dislike of Jeremy, whom he believed was responsible for the March burglary. Carr passed his suspicions on to Robert Boutflour shortly after speaking to Jones, adding that he had also heard a rumour that registered letters from Scotland regularly arrived at Bourtree Cottage containing cash for drugs.

DS Jones headed on to Goldhanger. Julie and Liz had gone into Colchester with Ann to order wreaths; Jeremy was midshower and wearing a towel when he answered the door. Jones had a swift look around the downstairs rooms while Jeremy finished showering. He found nothing incriminating and left after discussing security for the funeral. Jeremy then drove into Colchester, where Brett was due to arrive on the London train, having flown in from Greece after seeing headlines about the murders. Brett told police that his first impression of Jeremy was that he looked 'quite solemn, pale and drawn, like he'd been through hell'.[1]

Later that afternoon, Jeremy drove to the farm with Julie to collect furniture, bric-a-brac and a television. He returned a call from Roland Pargeter – then living in a Somerset commune – who had telephoned out of curiosity after his mother told him Jeremy had some spiritual things to share. In fact, Jeremy's conversation was limited to his parents' plans to take the twins 'into care locally' and his relatives 'grabbing certain property'. But when Ann rang to say the front door of the farmhouse had been found thrown open that morning, strangely without setting off the alarm, he declared: 'I expect it's Dad's spirit trying to get out.'[2] Ann also mentioned a call from her mother's cousin, Betty Howie, who had offended her by suggesting that she should have the wake at Oak Farm because it was the least she could do. 'Jeremy could hear I was upset and he came over straight away,' Ann recalled.[3]

The inquest opened the following morning, Wednesday, 14 August, less than two hours after it was confirmed that the blood on the outside of the silencer was human in origin. Biologist Glynis Howard telephoned DI Cook at 8.50am but afterwards neither of them could recall whether they had spoken or if she had left him a message. Cook was unaware the inquest was scheduled for that morning and DI Miller left for Braintree Magistrates' Court without knowing the blood test result. He gave evidence that Sheila Caffell had killed her family and committed suicide. Essex Deputy Coroner Dr Geoffrey Tompkins granted a two month adjournment, allowing police enquiries to continue, and gave permission for the funerals to be held.

Although the 1986 internal police review declared it doubtful that a second post-mortem would have yielded further evidence, the senior investigating officer on the case from September onwards described the release of the bodies as 'a serious error and a decision which should not have been made at that early time'.[4] In Acting Chief Superintendent Mike Ainsley's view, what might have been 'vital evidence of a ballistic nature could have been taken to the grave by this decision. Whether or not it did will never be known – but thanks to the excellent work of the scenes of crime photographer, vital evidence was recorded on film and was to prove conclusive evidence at the trial.'

When Ann arrived at White House Farm mid-morning she found Jeremy with Basil Cock, John Stancliffe of Sotheby's and his secretary, studying the portrait of Beatrice Bamber on the main staircase. Ann followed as they went from room to room examining silver, porcelain and paintings. Stancliffe was particularly interested in a Meissen clock and an Edward Lear sketch, both of which came from the Bamber home in Guildford.

Brett and Julie arrived in Nevill's Citroen Pallas while Ann was making lunch. Despite being garrulous and friendly, Brett made her feel 'incredibly uncomfortable'; she began to actively dislike him when he commented on the value of the chair he was sitting on. After lunch, John Stancliffe looked at some of Beatrice Bamber's jewellery before visiting Bourtree Cottage with Jeremy. Returning empty-handed, Stancliffe wrote out a receipt for the Edward Lear sketch and departed for London with his secretary.

Ann recalled that Jeremy then asked her, 'Do you want to come and see the goodies?' They went upstairs to the master bedroom, where the floor was covered with heirlooms including

the Meissen clock, chinaware, silver service cutlery, antique con-
diment sets and a candelabra. A suitcase filled with old sketches
lay on the bed. Ann reminded him that the clock belonged to
Sheila. 'It's mine now,' Jeremy replied.[5] She asked if he was going
to put it all away. 'No,' he said, 'when I come into this room I
like to see nice things.'

Almost ten years later, she recalled: 'I haven't seen these items
since.'

At 1pm, four police officers including a constable from New
Scotland Yard's Drugs Detection Dogs Unit searched Sheila's flat
in Maida Vale. They found no drugs, but removed a quantity of
documents from the study, among them two of Sheila's diaries.
DC Barlow had already taken possession of three other diaries
belonging to Sheila at White House Farm.[6]

Two hours later, Sergeant Robbie Carr of the Metropolitan
Police arrived at Witham for a pre-arranged meeting with DI
Miller, DI Cook and DS Jones. Robbie was the son of Osea Road
manager James Carr, and discussed his concerns about Jeremy
as someone who had known the Bambers most of his life, but
admitted that much of it was speculation. James Carr wrote to
Robert Boutflour the following day, noting: 'He was told that the
case was not closed and that they would look into every point he
had made.'[7] But he felt duty bound to include his son's impression that the police seemed keener on closing the case than
digging deeper.

Immediately after the meeting with Robbie Carr, the three
officers scrutinized the crime scene photographs. Someone
noticed that the paint on the silencer was a similar colour to the
Aga surround and they decided to visit the farm that evening to
investigate, on the pretext of measuring up for floor plans. Ron
Cook was slightly dubious, feeling that even if the two colours
matched, 'the paint could have been deposited on the silencer at
any time, not necessarily on the night of the killings. However,
circumstantially it had some limited value. Additionally, the
family who had found [the silencer] were stressing that it was of
major importance.'[8]

Jeremy was due at Witham for a short interview at 4.15pm.
Brett Collins arrived with him, but wasn't allowed to sit in.

Jeremy knew DI Miller but hadn't met DI Cook. 'It was quite clear he fancied himself,' Cook recalls, 'and had already decided what he was going to do and not do. It was obvious that all he was interested in was grabbing hold of the family wealth.'[9] Their conversation focused on Sheila. When Jones asked Jeremy if he had argued with his sister recently, Jeremy replied that he hadn't. He gave his consent for them to meet Ann at the farmhouse that evening, adding, 'I don't want anything stolen though.'[10]

Jones frowned: 'Don't start saying these sort of things to me, Jeremy. I don't like it.'

Jeremy smiled, 'I was only joking.'

At 6.15pm, Miller, Cook and Jones met Ann in the kitchen yard of White House Farm. Jones told her that if anyone asked what they had been doing there, she was to say 'measuring up' or 'I haven't seen anything'. They gave the property a cursory search, starting in the garage before heading upstairs. DI Cook took possession of two pairs of shoes – black plimsolls and flip-flops – from Sheila's room. In the lounge they examined the sash window next to Nevill's armchair, then went through to the kitchen, where they asked Ann about the letter Jeremy had thrown into the waste bin a couple of days earlier. Unable to find it, she presumed it was among the rubbish she had taken to Oak Farm.

After inspecting the telephone on the work surface they turned their attention to the mantelpiece. Six years later, Cook stated that Ann had indicated where she believed the silencer had struck the Aga surround and remains certain today: 'Ann Eaton drew our attention to the marks.'[11] Jones argued otherwise: 'She never showed us where the marks were on the mantle, we found them because it was there that we really wanted to look. The marks were very obvious on the underside of the mantle, you couldn't miss them and I was now convinced the paint had got onto the silencer during the struggle with Mr Bamber.'[12] He observed two deep gouge marks in the paintwork. Ann couldn't remember being given an explanation for their interest in the Aga surround: 'It was not until I mentioned it to my husband later that it clicked, red paint on the silencer, red paint on the mantle.'

DI Cook obtained a sample of paint, marking the chipped

area with a yellow sticker for future reference. No photographs were taken of the marks that day or indeed for some weeks afterwards. The officers then returned to Witham, but later that evening Miller and Jones called at Oak Farm, sharing a bottle of whisky with Peter as they listened to Ann's concerns, seeming 'interested at last'. She urged them to look again at the farmhouse windows and told them about Jeremy removing his father's video recorder. She also rifled through the rubbish sack containing the stained clothing, broken crockery and shards of lampshade for the letter Jeremy had thrown away, but it wasn't there.

Thursday's newspapers focused on the inquest and impending funerals. The *Daily Mirror* announced that the twins 'killed by their demented mother will be buried apart from her. Their father has refused to let them share the same resting place.' The *Sun* ran a similar story: 'Funeral Snub for Mum in Massacre'. Others followed suit, oblivious to the arrangements Colin had made for Sheila's ashes to be laid to rest with their sons at their funeral on Monday, 19 August. Although Jeremy had offered to meet all funeral expenses, he deferred reimbursement until after probate, several months away.

At half-past nine on Thursday, 15 August, DI Cook collected the Anschütz, silencer, magazine, cartridges and two shotguns from the Scenes of Crime store on the third floor of Chelmsford Police Headquarters and drove to the Home Office Central Research Establishment at Sandridge. He explains: 'One of the fingerprint development techniques being researched then was cyanoacrylate – superglue fuming – which was ideal for untreated metals such as guns. Sandridge was an experimental research establishment where authorized personnel were allowed to use the equipment, but it took time. You had to book a slot, then take items away to be photographed because Sandridge didn't have those facilities, and take them back to complete the process. It wasn't a matter of just rolling up at the door. The other issue was that we didn't know then whether superglue treatment affected blood groupings. Fortunately, that turned out fine.'[13]

Laser equipment was used first to enhance any fingerprints: the Anschütz and one of the shotguns showed visible marks. Oddly, no fingerprints were revealed on the remaining items, including the silencer, despite its handling by the relatives; all were then subjected to cyanoacrylate vapours (superglue), again without result. Because the Anschütz and shotgun required photographing before the next stage of treatment, Cook returned all the items to Chelmsford.

Making her routine visit to White House Farm on Thursday morning, Ann found the letter Jeremy had thrown away in the scullery bin. It was only a circular but she set it aside and searched the grounds fruitlessly for June's bike, certain that the one in the garage didn't match the description Barbara Wilson had given her.

Jeremy and Julie spent most of the day shopping in Colchester for funeral clothes with Liz and Brett. Later in court, Liz recalled that Brett urged his friend: 'Buy yourself something really slick. You're inheriting all this money. Play the part.' The girls left them in the Subway boutique, where Jeremy selected a black Hugo Boss suit for £190. He and Brett were just departing when Julie and Liz returned. The shop was quiet, and staff vividly recalled the visit, not least because the girls pretended that Julie and Jeremy were siblings whose parents had died in an accident. Julie tried on a revealing black skirt and top but told one of the assistants that it was too expensive. Jeremy eventually bought her a £32.99 dress from Miss Selfridge.

DI Miller's meeting with Chief Superintendent George Harris had left him 'in the doghouse' due to his refusal to conform with the accepted theory that Sheila was the killer.[14] He was glad to be going on annual leave at the end of the week, but spoke to DCI Jones in Chelmsford that afternoon, reiterating his reasons for suspecting Jeremy. Jones remained firm in his belief that Sheila was the killer and Miller had to concede that the relatives clearly had no love for Jeremy, knew very little about Sheila's life and were 'very much interested parties in relation to the estate'.[15] Afterwards, Miller briefed DC Mick Barlow, standing in for him during his absence, which also coincided with Stan Jones's annual leave: 'Keep an open mind and do a bit of digging because some things are not right. If anything comes up contact DCI Jones.'[16]

At 5pm, Barbara Wilson called on Jeremy to discuss the farm workers' pay, due the following day. Each man was to receive his wages plus whatever was owed from the previous week, while any overtime would be paid the following week. Jeremy took £140 in cash for himself, having learned from Barbara that his father was owed a month's salary from his nominal fee. When she pointed out that Mabel Speakman hadn't received her nominal wage either, he dismissed it as a quirk that could be shelved. Leaving Bourtree Cottage, Barbara noticed June's bicycle propped against the rear wall.

Jeremy then drove out to the farm with Julie, Liz and Brett to collect drinks for the wake. According to Liz, 'Jeremy spent the entire time there searching for money, because he said he thought that his father had hidden some away.'[17] Over dinner he talked about buying an expensive car and a jet ski, along with a bar or restaurant, and told Julie that he would 'reimburse her for loss of earnings' while staying at Bourtree Cottage.

June's friend Agnes Low telephoned Jeremy at home later that night: 'He told me he was alright, he was taking some "herbal tranquillisers." He was very polite and said he would come and see me after the following Monday, when the twins were to be buried. I heard lots of voices in the background and laughter and music.'[18] Julie recalled that throughout the evening, 'Jeremy and Brett were constantly joking about the money Jeremy was to get as a result of the deaths.'[19] When conversation turned to Friday's funeral, Brett told Jeremy that he should make himself look more grief-stricken by powdering his face and rubbing black beneath his eyes. Julie admitted: 'Both Jeremy and Brett laughed over this and in fact, we all laughed, and I said it was dreadful the way they were acting.'

Julie retired to bed first, followed by Brett soon afterwards. Alone with Jeremy, Liz was surprised when he began talking about his family, appearing to 'delight in the fact' that his father had weakened with age in the months before his death. He mused that he might have married Julie and stayed in Goldhanger forever, but 'with all this happening' his life would be very different.

Liz broached the subject of the murders: 'I asked him what was the matter with Sheila and he said something about the adoption of the children.'[20]

After a pause, he told her, 'But I'm the only person who will really know what happened that night. The family all thought she was just going back to London but I'm the only one who knew she was going in the nut house.'

Deciding that he was trying to 'make a mystery out of something that wasn't', Liz said goodnight and left him sitting alone in the lounge.

Jeremy woke early on the morning of 16 August, his parents' and sister's funeral. Brett described him as 'in reasonably good spirits. I think that was mainly because we were all there with him.'[1] Liz remembered him taking Valium tablets like they were going out of fashion. He set the video recorder for the funeral on the evening news, joking, 'I hope they get my good side.'[2]

Mourners began arriving early at Bourtree Cottage, including DI Miller and DC Barlow. 'Jeremy came out and gave me a hug,' Karen Boutflour recalled. 'He didn't seem to have any sadness about him.'[3] When the Pargeters arrived it was the first time in years that Roland had seen Jeremy, who appeared to be in control of himself. Jacqueline was perturbed by how Brett seemed to be conducting everything. Colin arrived later than planned in a bright yellow BMW on loan from the garage; his car had broken down. His parents and sister, Diane, were with him, together with Heather and Sheila's Uncle Peter. Devastated Christine remained in Canada, where she and her father said prayers for Sheila.

At two o'clock, three hearses drew into view, followed by a fleet of black limousines. The roads into Tolleshunt D'Arcy teemed with mourners; Tora and David Tomkinson travelled up from London but there was such a huge queue that they arrived too late for the service. Two hundred and thirty people had gathered in the church, where Rev. Robson, taking the service with June's friend Rev. Norman Thorpe, announced that it was a public occasion. To that end, speakers had been set up for those standing outside.

The flower-strewn coffins stood fanned out in front of the altar. A burst of bright roses covered Sheila's coffin, together with two wreaths from Colin, one on behalf of their sons. June's coffin stood in the centre; the service began and ended with her favourite hymns. 'The Lord's My Shepherd' was followed by Rev. Robson's address:

There is here a church that has lost valued leaders: Nevill had been a churchwarden, June had this year become one.

St Paul calls us not to a general faith in God, but to a
specific trust in Jesus Christ. June expressed that trust
openly and backed her words with acts of love. Nevill
expressed trust in Jesus Christ more quietly, in devout and
regular worship. Sheila herself, I am told, knew the Christian gospel. One of the family commented to me on a verse
in the Bible: 'Love does not keep a record of wrongs.' That
is an attitude for us all . . .[4]

At the end of the service Rev. Robson asked those gathered to
pray again 'for God's mercy for Sheila, sadly and tragically
deranged' before the closing hymn 'Lord of All Hopefulness'.[5]
There had been no mention of Nicholas and Daniel. Colin got to
his feet, silently enraged.

Jeremy's knees buckled as he exited the church. Julie and Diane
caught him and Colin reached out to console him. The press
microphones picked up his voluble sobs and DI Miller could
hardly hide his scorn: 'I turned to Micky Barlow and said, "This
bloke's acting." Sure enough, I got a call from Jeremy's teacher at
Gresham's afterwards. He'd seen the footage on the news and
confirmed it.'[6] Jeremy's former housemaster, William Thomas,
informed police: 'It seemed to me that Bamber was acting. My
wife who was also watching the television with me also made
comments about it.'[7]

The detective who would eventually lead the investigation
was at home on leave, also watching the funeral on the news.
'My wife said, "He did it," pointing to Bamber,' Mike Ainsley
recalls. 'I said, "Don't be daft. It's been investigated and they
know that she did it." My wife shook her head, "*He* did it."'[8]

Away from the media glare, Jeremy's behaviour caused
deeper disquiet. 'Jeremy was terribly distraught through the service and could barely walk behind the coffins,' David Boutflour
remembered. 'But when we were a hundred yards down the road,
out of sight of the cameras and other people, Jeremy looked back
at us and gave the biggest grin. It was chilling. Peter, my brother-
in-law, turned to me and said: "He did it, didn't he?"'[9]

Matters worsened on the journey to Colchester crematorium.
In separate accounts Julie and Colin described Jeremy cracking

smutty jokes, while Liz Rimington and Sarah Howie were among those in the car park who heard him tease Julie about looking pregnant. DI Miller, observing from the back of the chapel, noticed that Jeremy was 'very impatient, didn't allow the near relatives as much time as they would have liked viewing the flowers, etc., and seemed rather impatient to get back to his home'.[10]

Miller recalls that Bourtree Cottage was 'packed to the rafters' for the wake: 'Me and Micky Barlow were having a sandwich when Jeremy comes leaping down the stairs, giving it "all that". He opens his jacket and points to the inside pocket where the label is and says, "That's me now – the Boss." I looked at Barlow, shaking my head, and said, "Amazing. That's the sort of bloke we're dealing with."'

Liz Rimington remembered Jeremy 'showing off the label' of his suit and 'having a really good time'.[11] When she expressed surprise that his relatives didn't remonstrate with him, he replied: 'The only reason they're being so bloody pleasant to me is because they're like a pack of vultures, all waiting to see what they're going to get out of it. If they think they're going to get a bloody thing, they're joking.' As the afternoon wore on, he retreated into a corner with Brett and Julie, who approached Anthony Pargeter to ask if she and Jeremy could stay at his home in Ibiza with two friends. Anthony explained that the house belonged to his in-laws, but he would make enquiries.

Most of the guests were gone by six o'clock. Colin asked all those who were attending his sons' funeral on Monday to wear their most colourful clothes. The Eatons, Boutflours and Pargeters left together. Along with Liz and Brett, Julie's friends Karen and Andy Bishop were staying at Bourtree Cottage, having invited Jeremy and Julie to join them for the weekend at Andy's parents' home in Pevensey.

When Andy suggested eating out, Jeremy drove them to Burnham-on-Crouch, where he knew the owner of the Caribbean Cottage restaurant. They ate well and drank heavily. In one account of the evening, Malcolm Waters was said to have joined them, while Jeremy 'was in really high spirits. He was shouting and laughing, being cheeky to the waitresses, touching them up and slapping their bottoms.'[12] In reality, Malcolm and Jeremy no longer socialized and the occasion described had taken place in another restaurant months before.

Julie and Liz remembered Jeremy behaving exuberantly nonetheless. 'I was very upset and not in the mood to go out,' Julie stated. 'The funeral had upset me a lot. Jeremy was happy and the evening was a very boozy affair . . . Brett spent some time standing at the bar, trying to chat up another man. Jeremy joined him and began flirting with both men. They spent a long time talking together. Jeremy spent a lot of time roaring with laughter.'[13] The Bishops made no mention of Jeremy's behaviour and restaurant owner Rodney Brown offered a differing view: 'Jeremy was very quiet, subdued and seemed to be under heavy strain. His friends tried to make him laugh and relax, he seemed when he left a little more relaxed, and said to me, "I'm glad I came now."'[14] Julie and Liz both recalled that Jeremy was annoyed when they arrived home to find the video recorder had missed the news.

At half-past ten on Saturday morning, Jeremy and Julie left in his car to follow the Bishops to the Sussex coast. They lunched at a pub in Sevenoaks, after which Andy and Julie switched vehicles. Jeremy outlined his plans to Andy for either a small farm of his own or a wine bar with Julie. He was upset with his relatives for taking things from the house and annoyed with Brett and Liz, whom he felt were taking advantage of his generosity. Between periods of windsurfing – Jeremy had forgotten his wetsuit and borrowed one from Andy – he talked at length. Away from the girls, he glumly attributed the failure of his relationship with Sue Ford to his mother's objections and the threat of losing his inheritance, but declared himself pleased by the 'tug of love' between Julie and Brett for his affection. Over the weekend, he and Julie argued about the matter; she told him that he didn't need her anymore with Brett there, but he insisted that he did. On Sunday evening they returned to London with the Bishops.

Colin had asked everyone to meet at his flat at midday on Monday, 19 August. That morning he headed alone to St James' church in West Hampstead with two sunflowers Nicholas and Daniel had grown, adding them to the bouquets covering the small white coffin in which both boys lay together. The casket holding Sheila's ashes close by, wreathed in flowers. Sitting beside the coffin, Colin read from the twins' favourite story, *The Magic Faraway Tree*, while rain pattered against the stained glass windows.

The shower had turned to a deluge by the time the mourners began descending the steps at Maygrove Road. One of Colin's friends realized he had locked his keys inside his vehicle; Jeremy, calm and collected, helped him out. Regine Pargeter found him more abrasive. As she attempted to climb into the car he and Julie shared, Jeremy told her, 'You're not coming in here,' and thrust a hand towards another vehicle: 'Go with that lot.'[15]

More than seventy mourners packed into the large, welcoming interior of the red brick church. Rev. Patrick Rös, a priest from Dutch Guyana who had known Nicholas and Daniel well, opened the service: 'Everyone is deeply moved by the tragic events which brought us here. The little ones were well-loved.'[16] Although he had never met Sheila or her parents he spoke kindly of them all and picked up his guitar for one song. The last hymn, 'Morning Has Broken', resonated about the church as the congregation got to their feet.

The burial at Highgate Cemetery was for family and close friends only. Rev. Rös blessed the coffin as it was lowered into the earth; Sheila's ashes were placed at the head with a single red flower from the blooms on the boys' coffin. Cuthbert the teddy bear, passed from Sheila to her sons, lay with them.

Afterwards, Herbie Flowers' wife Ann felt such hostility from Jeremy that she changed cars on the journey back from the cemetery to avoid him. The atmosphere at Maygrove Road was deeply subdued, a stark contrast to the bright clothes everyone wore. Julie asked Anthony again about the house in Ibiza and he assured her he would look into it.

Returning to Goldhanger that evening, the couple dined again at the Caribbean Cottage, where owner Rodney Brown observed that Jeremy was quiet: 'We did not speak about the tragedies. I said to him, "I think you are handling it very well." He replied to that, "I don't think the shock has set in yet, I'm a bit worried about when it does." On this occasion Julie appeared under much more strain and cried a lot. We just spoke about light subjects until they left.'

On Tuesday, 20 August, Jeremy met Basil Cock, who mentioned a letter he had received from the Pargeters regarding items from their grandmother's unsettled estate; they were concerned that possessions left to them but kept at the farm might be sold without their knowledge. After Jeremy reiterated that he had no wish to remain at White House Farm, Peter Eaton was officially appointed farm manager. Together with his wife and father-in-law, he consulted the trustees to ask whether Jeremy had been given notice to quit and was told that no such notice had been issued. Ann and her father then headed to Witham, where DC Barlow listened to their concerns, including their discovery that one of the farmhouse windows could be closed from the outside to give the impression it had been secured internally.

Jeremy had gone into Maldon to book tickets for a trip to Amsterdam with Brett and Julie. The travel agent was disconcerted when she recognized the name, since all three appeared to be in such high spirits. Although Brett later described the short break as an escape from the press, Julie informed detectives that the sole purpose was 'to purchase some cannabis'.

They travelled 'deluxe' on the Sea Ferry to Hoek van Holland, disembarking early on Wednesday morning. Jeremy had booked a triple-bedded room at Hotel De L'Europe, a five star hotel overlooking the River Amstel. After checking in, they visited a nearby 'smoking' cafe and sat at the bar to order drinks and peruse the soft drugs menu. Jeremy and Brett consulted the staff before purchasing several grams of cannabis. Back at the hotel, they packed the cannabis into straws which were then inserted inside toothpaste tubes. Julie recalled: 'Because Jeremy could not fit all the straws into the toothpaste tube he placed some into a bottle of cocoa butter lotion I had with me. He also carried some loose in his bag.'

When the time came to catch the bus to the ferry port on Thursday, Jeremy couldn't find their return tickets and bought new first-class travel and cabin tickets. 'Throughout the boat crossing Brett and Jeremy were smoking cannabis,' Julie recalled, admitting, 'I also smoked some.'

*

In their absence, Ann had visited Bourtree Cottage to have a look around and telephoned DC Barlow to let him know that June's bicycle was in Jeremy's garden. He visited White House Farm on Thursday morning to examine the windows, paying particular attention to the kitchen window whose metal catch was 'slightly stiff and when fully opened, stuck in the open position. This enabled the window to be closed from the outside of the premises and by tapping the frame in the area of the catch, I found that the catch dropped into the locked position, giving the appearance that the window had been locked from inside.'[17] He was able to remove items from the sill, climb out over the sink, and replace everything before locking the window from outside. After noting that June's maroon and white bicycle was indeed at Bourtree Cottage, he telephoned DCI Jones to arrange a meeting.

On Friday, 23 August, arriving back from Amsterdam, Jeremy drove to White House Farm with Brett, leaving Julie in Goldhanger. He gave Barbara instructions to clear out the first floor office and sat in his father's chair with his feet on the desk, which Barbara found disrespectful and upsetting. Uncomfortable with the task he had given her, she tried to avoid looking at the letters, cards and other keepsakes as she dropped them into the bins brought up by Jean, who had also been told to clear the kitchen of clutter. As she picked up a stack of magazines wedged beside the electric baby oven, Jean noticed a fawn coloured telephone in the middle of the pile with the cord wrapped around it. She assumed it was a spare.

There were normally four telephones at White House Farm. Two were kept in the kitchen on the worktop next to the drinks cupboard. One was a cream-coloured Envoy Cordless telephone with a recall facility; Nevill had often taken it into the den where there was no phone connection but at the end of each day it was replaced on its stand in the kitchen. June had disliked the Envoy and thus a fawn-coloured Statesman digital handset was also kept in the kitchen, its cord extending to a socket in the drinks cupboard. Upstairs were two further telephones. A blue digital Sceptre 100 with a ten number memory and recall facility was kept permanently on Nevill's desk in the office, while an ivory rotary dial telephone sat on his bedside table in the master bedroom, plugged into the socket by the bed. Barbara remembers that the bedroom telephone was sometimes 'taken down to the kitchen when the push button phone went wrong'.[18]

On the night of the shootings, there were three telephones in the farmhouse; the cordless Envoy had been removed by Douglas Pike on 5 August, after it developed a fault, and no replacement had been left. The telephone discovered on the kitchen worktop on 7 August was from the master bedroom. No one realized that the fawn Statesman was missing until Jean found it sequestered among the magazines. The blue Sceptre 100 remained in its usual spot in the upstairs office.[19]

Barbara recognized the Statesman immediately when Jean brought it to her, explaining to the housekeeper that it wasn't a spare. She tested it in the office; it worked perfectly, as did the other telephones. Not knowing what to do with the Statesman, she placed it on a nearby shelf. Jean went through to the master bedroom and saw the gap on Nevill's table for the rotary dial telephone. Later that morning she bumped into Jeremy in the hall and mentioned the telephone she had found. He told her that it *was* a spare, adding: 'The kitchen telephone went wrong so we brought the bedroom phone down to replace it.'[20] Jean thought his comment a bit odd but forgot about it until the police asked her sometime after the shootings where the kitchen telephone had gone.

Senior investigating officer Mike Ainsley came to believe that Jeremy had deliberately hidden the Statesman in preparation for the murders; by replacing it on the worktop with the bedroom telephone, he left his parents unable to call for help upstairs. His theory also provided one explanation for June Bamber's attempt to reach the other side of the bed. Already suffering multiple wounds, she would have realized too late that the telephone was missing. Moments later, her attacker had returned to kill her.

Julie spent much of Saturday recovering from a severe asthma attack. Jeremy collected emergency medication for her and obtained a further supply of Valium for himself. At 9am, he telephoned Ann, who asked about the items bequeathed to the Pargeters. He replied that if they wanted to put in a claim, they should do it before probate because he would keep whatever he wished and sell the rest.[1]

DC Barlow and DCI Taff Jones met at Witham that morning to discuss the case. The day before, DI Cook had called at Sandridge, where the Anschütz was subjected to cyanoacrylate testing; photography had been delayed due to difficulties in obtaining the correct lighting. The superglue treatment failed to enhance the marks on the barrel, but brought out a single fingerprint on the wooden butt. At Witham, Barlow told Jones that he was dissatisfied with the prevailing murder-suicide theory but had nothing substantial to disprove it.

On Saturday evening, Jeremy and Julie called at her parents' home in Colchester. 'He offered me his mother's small car which had been bought that Christmas,' Mary Mugford recalled at the trial. 'A list had been drawn up and he was going to keep no mementoes, which I thought very strange. He said he wanted to sell everything and that it was a pity I had just bought a car.' Jeremy had also placed an advert in the *Maldon and Burnham Standard* asking £900 for Nevill's blue Citroen.

The next morning he drove to London for the Notting Hill Carnival with Julie and Brett. They met Liz and headed to Sheila's flat, hitting a kerb on the way and damaging the Astra's offside tyres and wheels. Liz remembered Jeremy fruitlessly hunting about the flat, saying he was looking for drugs. At Liz's place after the carnival, Julie was unnerved when Brett 'laid his head on Jeremy's lap, whereupon Jeremy started stroking his hair'.[2] Unhappy about their close friendship and increasingly insecure about her own relationship with Jeremy, she felt as if everything was beginning to unravel.

The following day, Bank Holiday Monday, 26 August, was

Julie's twenty-first birthday. Mary Mugford had organized a family dinner at a restaurant near Colchester. Brett joined them and midway through the meal proposed a toast, not just for Julie's birthday, but to 'the engaged couple'.[3] His misjudged prank nonplussed everyone, while Jeremy's embarrassment, anger and stuttered refutation spoke volumes.

At White House Farm that morning, Ann and her father had conducted an experiment to test her theory about the kitchen window. She found that by opening the casement window and setting the catch, she could close it from the outside in such a way that it secured itself, allowing someone to exit the house without detection. Ann put a call through to Witham, unaware that DC Barlow had already tried that particular experiment.[4]

Robert had visited the station the previous day (Sunday) to ask about the progress of the investigation: 'I was told that tests on the silencer would take three weeks. I was getting very concerned because I could not understand why Jeremy had not been detained for questioning and why his house had not been searched by the forensic scientists.'[5] He made enquiries of his own about Brett Collins, urging Chris Nevill and James Carr to find out whatever they could from their New Zealand contacts.

On Tuesday, 27 August, he visited Witham again and was disappointed to be told that nothing of interest had been unearthed about Brett, who accompanied Jeremy to Chelmsford that morning to see Julie onto the London train.

'I had made up my mind to leave the house in Goldhanger,' Julie recalled, 'due to the fact that I could no longer handle the situation.'[6] She wanted her relationship with Jeremy to continue 'but with me living back at my house in London. Prior to leaving Goldhanger, I had arranged for Jeremy and Brett to come to my house on the Thursday.' In Lewisham, she paid the £400 cheque Jeremy had given her in lieu of lost earnings into the bank and returned to Caterham Road, where Susan Battersby was surprised to see her: 'She didn't appear to be her normal self, even allowing for what had happened.'[7]

The two girls decided to eat out that evening. They discussed Jeremy's behaviour as they walked into town, with Julie growing increasingly agitated. Waiting to cross the High Street, she blurted, 'You don't know how evil Jeremy is!' She then ran across the road with Susan in pursuit.

'Jeremy did it, didn't he?' Susan asked, stupefied.

Julie shook her head. 'No, not Jeremy. He didn't do it.'

They went into Pizza Hut and sat down. Susan leaned across the table, repeating the question. There was a moment's silence.

Julie said slowly: 'A mercenary killed all of them . . .'

Suddenly, she began speaking in a rush. Jeremy, she said, had hired his former friend, Matthew McDonald, to murder his family. Jeremy's motive was money; having seen his parents' wills, he resolved to 'get rid of the family' in order to inherit everything.

Before a rapt and horrified Susan, Julie outlined how the murders were committed: 'The whole family were sat at the dinner table in the house. Jeremy had brought up the subject of having Sheila's children adopted. He had done this so that Sheila would become disturbed and cause concern to the rest of the family.' While his parents and sister were still in the kitchen, Jeremy left the table and went outside, ostensibly to shoot rabbits. When he returned, he put the gun against the door and the bullets on the kitchen worktop.

'Why did he put them there?' Susan asked.

'It was common practice,' Julie replied, stating that Jeremy had told Matthew how to get in and out of the house surreptitiously and where to find the gun and ammunition if it had been moved. That night, wearing some kind of mask, Matthew had gained access to the house. Locating the gun and ammunition, he crept upstairs. The twins were shot first, asleep in their beds. Matthew had fought with Nevill, who was 'incredibly strong for an old man'.[8] He had had 'a mental blank and fired seven consecutive shots' into the resisting farmer. June was shot in bed. Sheila was the last to die, 'made to fake suicide by shooting herself under the chin'. She did so 'calmly and without any arguments'.[9] The Bible was a final flourish to imply religious mania.

With everyone dead, Matthew had telephoned Jeremy from the farmhouse to ensure that his number was the last recorded and let him know that 'the job was completed'.[10] He told him about the fight with Nevill, adding that he was leaving the

country for a while and 'it would be best' if Jeremy didn't know
where he was going. He then exited via 'a window which latches
closed from the outside when you bang it, so that the house
would be locked from the inside'.

Immediately after the murders were discovered, Jeremy had
faked emotional upset by thinking of his dog Brambles, killed
by a car. That same evening, when Julie asked Jeremy if he had
killed his family, he replied: 'No, I didn't. I couldn't do it, Matthew
did it.' He had agreed a fee of £2,000, 'which he had to get somehow without the police or other people knowing'. When she
asked why he trusted her not to go to the police, he told her 'they
would most likely laugh in her face.'[11]

Susan had never liked Jeremy. She had long suspected that he
was trying to involve Julie 'with his way of life so that she would
be unable to tell anyone about what he was doing'. She had
never expected to hear that he was behind his family's murders,
but after listening to Julie's story, she thought the same: 'By telling her everything he got involved in, she would feel that she was
involved as well.' Although Julie made her promise not to tell
anyone, Susan was frightened to do so regardless, 'in case Jeremy
found out who had told and came looking for me or Julie. I did
in fact tell my boyfriend Mark.'

Susan begged Julie to contact the police. She refused: 'I said I
couldn't because I loved him, and couldn't bear the thought of
him in prison . . . I told her that I didn't like him as a person but
I still loved him.'[12]

On Wednesday morning Ann arrived at White House Farm to
find Brett upstairs looking at old coins and Jeremy in the den.
Spotting a cigar box in the scullery that she hadn't noticed
before, she reached for it.

'Don't look in there, Ann – it's private,' Jeremy called out.[13]

Apologizing, she handed him her back door key, which he
had mentioned needing for Barbara. A short while later, he and
Brett departed carrying a green suitcase bulging with silverware,
which they delivered to John Stancliffe's office. Everything
Jeremy had decided to sell was to be auctioned under Basil
Cock's name as sole executor. Stancliffe recalled: 'I was given the
impression by Mr Bamber that his reason for wishing to have the

items at Sotheby's was that members of his family were coming to lay some form of claim to the property.'[14]

When Robert Boutflour called at the farm on Thursday morning he met his nephew loading 'family treasures' into his car. Jeremy explained that he was taking everything to Sotheby's and probate was expected in November or December. Twenty-five years later, he was frank about selling family heirlooms: 'I didn't want them. They're just things that belonged to somebody.'[15]

Gritting his teeth, Robert trudged out to the lane behind the house and followed the track to Brook House Farm where it emerged on Maldon Road. He felt certain that Jeremy must have taken such a route on the night of the murders, but there were no imprints of bicycle wheels or noticeable footprints, only muddy tractor trenches. Undaunted, he spent the next three days 'covering all the tracks and footpaths to see if I could find any evidence, also to find the shortest and easiest way without being seen'. He discovered there were three options from Goldhanger: 'One route was a direct route across the fields which was about three miles in distance. Another route also across fields but using footpaths and tracks would be 3½ miles long and a further route was four miles along the sea wall.' He believed Jeremy had walked one of those routes, 'dressed in his ski suit carrying his wetsuit in a plastic bag' and returned using June's new bicycle.[16] He also hit on the idea that Jeremy might have used part of the tampon found in the lounge to wipe the blood off the silencer before disposing of it in the toilet, and rang Witham to ask the startled sergeant on duty whether forensic tests could check for tampon fibres on the silencer. He was advised to speak to DC Barlow the next day.

Ninety-five-year-old Mabel Speakman finally learned the truth about her younger daughter's whereabouts on the afternoon of Thursday, 29 August. Pamela had told her that June and Nevill, together with Sheila and the twins, were on holiday, but Mabel's housekeeper had threatened to quit unless she was told the truth. Pamela asked her mother's doctor and Ann to be present when she broke the news.

Mabel lay resting against her pillows in bed. Robert sat

outside the room to listen, fearing that he would get 'too emotional' otherwise.[17] Suddenly Pamela said: 'Mum – June, Nevill, Sheila and the twins were at White House Farm and they've been shot. They're dead.'[18] Ann was shocked to hear her speak so bluntly but Mabel did not collapse. Instead, she immediately sat upright and declared, 'It's the devil at work.' Then she turned to Dr Ellis, asking, 'When am I going to die, doctor?' before sinking back against her pillows.

According to Ann, neither her mother nor grandmother mentioned Jeremy; it wasn't until December when Mabel finally asked about him.

On Thursday evening, Jeremy and Brett drove to Lewisham for Julie's twenty-first birthday party, arriving late and laden down with alcohol. Most of the guests were fellow students and a few old friends, including Karen and Andy Bishop. Julie recalled that the party was memorable for one reason: 'Jeremy threw my birthday cake at Susan Battersby's head.'[19]

It was the first time Susan and Jeremy had met since Julie's revelations. As a crowd gathered in the kitchen to watch him adding final touches to the birthday cake, Susan grabbed the aerosol of whipped cream 'and jokingly made a gesture to put some cream on his neck.'[20]

Jeremy picked up the cake and shoved it into her face.

'Why did you do that?' she gasped.

'You're such a child, Susan,' he replied contemptuously.

'Sue fled upstairs in floods of tears,' Liz Rimington remembered. 'I went upstairs after her to calm her down.'[21]

Brett wandered in from the lounge to see what the fuss was about and saw the cake on the floor. 'She had been a nuisance,' he stated afterwards, 'she had squirted others in the room and Jeremy was the last, he warned her against it.'[22]

Other guests reacted with shock and laughter, but Liz confronted Jeremy: 'You make me so angry, the things you do are so awful and you are so evil.'

'Why, what have I done?' he said. 'What are you talking about?'

'Well, if you don't know!' Liz replied in disgust.

'What?' he asked, becoming agitated. 'What?'

Brett interjected: 'She means about the cake.'

Jeremy gave a laugh and shrugged, 'Oh, yeah.'

The next morning, Julie told Liz that Jeremy and Brett had stayed the night but left early after she and Jeremy argued. She spent the rest of the day cleaning the house and feeling very low, aware that her relationship with Jeremy was imploding.

Robert was surprised to see Jeremy's silver Astra pull up at Vaulty Manor's private petrol pump at quarter past eight on Friday morning. He noticed Brett in the car and asked if they had been away. Jeremy said nothing about Julie's party, telling his uncle that he had just deposited more items at Sotheby's.

After calling at Bourtree to shower and change – Jeremy put on a smart black suit and YSL sunglasses for a meeting with the bank manager later that day – he and Brett headed to the farm. Brett went upstairs to continue looking through the coin collection while Jeremy sought out Barbara with the key to the back door. 'He gave explicit instructions not to allow any family members inside without him being there,' Barbara recalled, 'and if they telephoned, to get them to go there by appointment. He said that there was unpleasantness within the family and arguments over property in the house.'[23]

At the same time, Jeremy had invited Barbara and Jean to take a keepsake from the farm. 'We didn't want to,' Barbara remembers, 'but he insisted we should choose something. We each picked a tiny silver trinket from the cabinet but told him that we wouldn't have them until probate was settled. We had no intention of taking anything.'[24]

Barbara had already put the farm workers' wages into envelopes, ready to hand out. 'They're earning quite a bit, they must be pleased,' Jeremy said, referring to the rise he had authorized.[25] He told her that he would hand Len and Alf Foakes their wages if she would give Philip, Alan and Jean theirs, and asked if she had paid Len the extra he was owed in back pay, including the rise. Barbara confirmed that she had and he took the envelopes from her. The thick notes inside Len's pay packet made the envelope bulge.

After handing Len his wages, Jeremy asked for a small trailer, explaining that he wanted it for rubbish from the house. He backed it into the yard with the tractor, close to the door. When Jean saw him later that morning he told her to pack the rest of the silverware into a large box, then left for his appointment at Barclays in Maldon. There he was appointed signatory of the N. & J. Bamber Ltd account, handling his parents' various farming interests.

Afterwards he drove to Tiptree to pay for the repairs to his car, which cost £200. The garage owner asked about the shootings. Jeremy briefly ran through the events that led to him meeting the police at the house that night, declaring that he was 'suspicious of the police, inasmuch as he felt information was withheld from him at that time, and subsequently'.[26] Then Jeremy said something even more startling: 'He felt there may have been things kept from him by the police and intimated that there may have been a police involvement in the shootings in the farm or a "shoot out".'

The accusation shocked the garage owner, who kept it to himself. But it wouldn't be the last time Jeremy insinuated that the police had a hand in the murders.

The trailer was still in the yard and piled high with Nevill and June's clothes when Ann and her father called at White House Farm on Friday afternoon. Jean offered them June's collection of commemorative biscuit tins, explaining that Jeremy was at the bank and Brett upstairs. Music was blaring out as Ann walked through the house; chests and cupboards were thrown open and miniature pictures stacked on a table.

Robert sat down to coffee in the kitchen, bristling when Brett appeared with an elaborate seventeenth-century dress coat and announced, 'Very collectible items, these.'[1] Robert asked him about life in New Zealand and plans for the future, but learned nothing worthy of passing on to DC Barlow, whom he met at Witham later that afternoon.

Instead, at the meeting Robert expounded his theories about the tampon, routes between White House Farm and Goldhanger, and clothing Jeremy might have worn to commit murder. He then asked if there was any news on the blood in the silencer. Barlow was unable to tell him, admitting: 'I didn't even know a silencer had been found, as far as I was aware it was just a .22 rifle and that was it.'[2] But the silencer had been re-submitted to the laboratory that day where, together with the Anschütz, spent cartridge cases, bullets and pillows, it would be examined by experts Malcolm Fletcher, John Hayward and Brian Elliott.

Barlow did tell Robert that reports of Sheila suffering from poor muscle coordination had cast doubt on her ability to fire the weapon and that there were timing issues with Jeremy's telephone calls. The detective constable was solicitous and had an open mind about the murders, but felt Robert had 'gone over the top a little bit, and my impression was he was looking too deeply into the matter, trying to find evidence that wasn't there.'[3]

Virginia Greaves had left a message on the answer machine at Bourtree Cottage. She and Jeremy had dated briefly when his relationship with Suzette was on the wane. Now working as a personal assistant in London, she needed new accommodation and was interested in Sheila's flat. Jeremy suggested meeting up and collected her on Friday evening.

Driving back to Goldhanger, he told Virginia that he was 'fed up with relatives going to the house and helping themselves to the property'.[4] At Bourtree Cottage, he telephoned Ann about his mother's biscuit tins, declaring: 'I don't mind you having the things, but I would rather you did it when I'm at the house.'

Brett joined Jeremy and Virginia for dinner at the Caribbean Cottage, where Jeremy 'complained that he was getting no support from the family and that they only seemed interested in what they could get'. Virginia was sympathetic and returned with them to Goldhanger, where she and Jeremy spent the night together.

Julie was expecting him at Caterham Road for three o'clock the following day, Saturday, 31 August. But after driving Virginia home, Jeremy accepted her mother's invitation to lunch. He sat alone in the garden while the two women prepared the meal. Virginia went out to him, concerned that he looked upset, but he assured her that he was fine, telling her how much he cared for her and that he wanted to be around people who cared about him. Hearing that Virginia had arranged to stay with her sister Angela in London, Jeremy offered to drive her there.

They set off from Aldham at three o'clock. 'Do you want me to be sympathetic or not to mention things?' she asked.

'I just want to be around happy people and not be on my own,' he replied.

Calling first at Bourtree Cottage, Jeremy telephoned Julie to tell her he would be late. Brett decided to stay the night at Sheila's flat and the three of them got into Jeremy's car, stopping at Vaulty for petrol. Pamela came out to them. 'We've told Granny what's happened,' she said, 'and she understands that it was Sheila. She seems to have taken it quite well.'

Jeremy's face clouded. Realizing he was angry, Pamela explained that she hadn't been able to put off telling her mother any longer. She then told him that although they had returned some of the items taken from White House Farm, she intended to hold on to June's jewellery because it had been in the family for generations, adding that she would especially like the locket that belonged to her grandmother.

Jeremy said stiffly: 'Remember, Auntie Pammie, it's my family too.'[5]

'Well, you'd look very silly wearing a locket, wouldn't you, Jem?' she replied, lightly.

'Perhaps we could go through them—'

'Come any time,' Pamela said.

He started up the engine. 'I'm interested in the teeth,' he snapped, before accelerating down the driveway.

Pamela stared after the silver Astra, baffled. It wasn't until she looked through other boxes belonging to June that she found two milk teeth, keepsakes from when Jeremy and Sheila were small. But she still had no idea why he wanted them, since their value was purely sentimental.

Tearing down the A12, Jeremy told Brett and Virginia that the shock of hearing the news could have killed his grandmother. Then he said it was stupid to keep things purely out of sentiment when money was needed for legal fees and talked about bringing items to London, either to store or sell. They arrived at Morshead Mansions, where he led Virginia through the apartment. It smelled stale and felt strange but she told him that she wanted it.

Together with Brett, they walked in the sunshine to the shops on nearby Elgin Avenue. Opposite the tube station was Vale Antiques, its dark interior brimming with curios, furniture, jewellery and books. Jeremy enquired about a cheval mirror in the window and was pleased when the owner told him he would be willing to take a look at anything he had to sell.

Leaving Brett in Maida Vale, Jeremy gave Virginia a lift to her sister's before continuing to Caterham Road where Julie greeted him coldly. As they drove to Blazes restaurant in Blackheath, she asked why he had bothered coming to see her. He said that they needed to sort out the holiday because he couldn't get time off, suggesting Liz might go instead. Julie didn't respond until they reached the restaurant. Then she asked, 'Do you still love me?'[6]

'I don't know,' he replied. 'I'm confused. I don't know how I feel.'

Julie later told Essex Police that over the meal she 'tackled him about the killings and asked him how he could have done it,

and how he could be doing this to me. He told me not to feel
guilty as it had nothing to do with me, and there was nothing
I could have done about it, as he would have done it anyway.'

She warned Jeremy that he needed help: 'I was convinced he
was a psychopath. He admitted to having a mental problem and
replied, "How do you think I feel, continuing to hurt people or
being lonely for the rest of my life?" I told him he could be
helped if he wanted to and he then told me that he thought
about going to India with Roland Pargeter and coming back a
reformed person.'[7]

As she grew more distressed 'he asked me to promise not to
kill myself. I told him I couldn't promise anything. I told him
I would like him to feel some of the things I was feeling. It was
quite obvious he was worried what I was going to do and
I promised him that I would not tell anyone of what he had done
even though I had told Susan. I felt sorry for him and I still loved
him.'[8]

They returned to Caterham Road and went straight up to her
room. Jeremy summed up the rest of the evening in a pithy
account seventeen years later: 'I took her home and she asked me
in for one last shag. In her room, she begged me not to dump her.
I recall at one point she was crying. I got up to leave but couldn't
find my keys.'[9]

Julie's version of events was very different. After she had
'begged him to stay', she poured herself a drink and put on a
cassette, then took out a photograph of happier times and
showed him a poem she had written for him: 'He became upset
and started crying. I asked him again, "why did you do it," referring to the killings and why did he have to tell me. He said he
didn't know. I told him that I would really love to hurt him and
told him that I had tried to stab the teddy bear he had given to
me as a present. He was still upset. I tried to mother him as I felt
sorry and assured him that I would never do anything to hurt
him. I asked him what he was going to do with his life.'

In her *News of the World* interview the following year, Julie
recalled that Jeremy sidestepped her question, telling her he was
willing to buy her a bar in London and asked, 'Are you happy
now you've got your pound of flesh?'[10] She reassured him again
that she would 'never hurt him or tell what had happened. He

said he trusted me and that I was his best friend and that I was the only person who had ever made him happy. He said he had entrusted his life into my hands.'

They were interrupted by Doug Dale, who wanted to borrow Julie's game of Trivial Pursuit. He walked in on them lying on the bed, red-eyed, and thought they had been drinking heavily. After he had gone, Julie turned back to Jeremy: 'I asked [him] never to leave me, because I was frightened, and he said he would never leave me as there would always be a place in his heart. We then went to bed.'

But that wasn't the end; Julie gave two accounts of what followed. In a statement she explained briefly: 'We didn't sleep well and at one point I got a pillow and put it over his head. I took it off and he asked me why I did it and I said if he were dead he would always be with me. I had his car keys so he couldn't go. Nothing else much was said after that but eventually I gave him the keys back.'

Her post-trial interview in the *News of the World* recalls the incident in tabloidese: 'We both lay down and tried to sleep. We were still sharing the same bed, even though since the murders I'd been unable to make love to him or respond to him in any way. But sleep that night was impossible. Suddenly I heard his voice in the darkness: "Julie, I really do love you, you know. And I'm so terribly sorry."'

She then put the pillow over his head:

He lay perfectly still. I was sure I'd suffocated him, and I remember thinking how simple it was. Then suddenly the realization of what I'd done hit me like a thunderbolt. Horrified, I pulled the pillow away. He still lay motionless. 'Oh God!' I thought, 'I've killed him!' Later, he told me he was only pretending to be dead . . . I couldn't go on much longer. I was a nervous wreck, smoking sixty cigarettes a day, not really able to speak to anyone without apologizing. I felt I was on the edge of a breakdown and that soon I would have to tell the police everything. That meant I would be responsible for sending the man I loved to prison, perhaps for the rest of his life. Surely death would be better than that.

Jeremy left early the following morning, opting to stay with Michael Deckers in Lexden rather than go home to an empty house while Brett remained in London. Julie described their parting as 'amicable' but rang Liz 'in floods of tears'.[11] The two girls met up and out came the story of Jeremy's visit the previous evening, how he'd said 'he didn't want to see her any more and that he had only been using her for his own ends.'

Liz's reaction was firm: 'You're lucky that you're rid of him.'

Julie welled up again: 'You don't know the half of it . . .'

After some coaxing, she told Liz an almost identical story to the account she had given Susan, but with a precursor. Liz recounted: 'Since Christmas Jeremy had been planning to murder his entire family. Originally he had thought of drugging them and setting the house on fire but because a lot of the contents were valuable he would have lost them.'

Liz, like Susan, did her best to convince Julie to go to the police but she refused. There was nothing to stop Liz or Susan from going to the police either, but both seemed to feel that it was a matter for Julie. Liz invited her friend to stay for the night and did her utmost to persuade her to speak to the police. Liz herself was 'in a state of terror. We locked all the doors because I feared he'd come back and kill us.'[12] They did, however, discuss going on holiday together and made plans to visit Malta the following week.

Jeremy later claimed that Liz had confided in Julie about their fling and that it played a key role in events to come. But according to Liz, she said nothing to Julie about her night with Jeremy, declaring in her initial witness statement: 'I have never mentioned it to anyone and as far as I am aware Julie does not know about it.'

When Barbara and Jean arrived for work on Monday, 2 September a narrow pall of smoke was curling up from the waste pit in the garden, where Philip Wilson had emptied the trailer as instructed. Opening the door, the two women inadvertently set off the new alarm that Jeremy had had fitted.

Barbara puzzled over the alarm, which Jeremy had assured her would be switched off. When he appeared at midday he explained that he had left it on 'to see how the police reacted to it and to make sure it was working correctly'.[13] In turn, Barbara told him that Len Foakes's pay had been £100 short, yet she had checked the sum left in the office safe after making up the wage packets and it was correct. She suspected Jeremy immediately, but did not accuse him. Peter had compensated Len and Barbara made a note to refund him.

Later that day, Peter attended a meeting about the tenancy of White House Farm with Jeremy and George Nicholls at Basil Cock's office. Nicholls had handled the yearly valuation of Nevill's businesses and strongly advised Jeremy to keep his options open regarding the farm; he recommended him to the trustees as a suitable tenant.

There was also the forty-eight-and-a-half acres at Little Renters Farm to consider. Jeremy was thinking of selling the land when he inherited it and duly informed Ann and Peter, who owned the remainder.

Jeremy was about to inherit a number of assets. His paternal grandmother's home, Clifton House in Guildford, had been converted into five flats, two of which were already sold, with another sold subject to contract. The sum would clear Nevill's overdraft of £120,000, borrowed to complete the conversion. The remaining two flats had a ninety-nine year lease and would eventually return to the family. Jeremy would receive a 50 per cent share; the remaining 50 per cent was to be divided equally between Jacqueline and Anthony Pargeter.

June's interest in Osea Road would also pass to her son. Jeremy told Colin that his relatives had made offers to ensure that he didn't have the controlling stock in the company. In addition, he stood to inherit half of his grandmother's estate when she died; Mabel Speakman's will was split between her daughters, and June's share would pass to her sole surviving heir. That included Robert and Pamela's home, Carbonells Farm. When Essex Police asked Ann who owned Carbonells she replied that it belonged to her father, explaining afterwards: 'I said that then because he was paying, I think, a nominal rent to Gran Speakman who actually owned it. Gran was obviously family and to me, therefore, [it was] owned by him.'[14]

Robert Boutflour later informed detectives that Mabel had

decided to change her will after being told of June's death, leaving her entire estate to Pamela. He recalled that Mabel's doctor was satisfied that she was of sound mind and that whenever he visited his mother-in-law 'prior to the amending of the will she kept on saying, "Hurry up, Bobby, hurry up, before I die."'[15] Jeremy has since claimed that undue pressure was put on Mabel and that he was prevented from visiting her, accusations which Robert strenuously denied. Ann concedes that the conversations regarding Mabel's will were conducted partly 'to stop Jeremy benefitting through aunt June' but the family were unanimous that Jeremy showed no interest in calling on his grandmother.

Two days after Mabel was told about the murders, Robert asked her solicitor to call at Vaulty. Six persons were present: Mabel, Robert, Pamela, Dr Ellis and Mr Peek and his secretary. Robert recalled that the meeting 'resulted in a solicitor from this firm and myself being made joint executors to her estate. The new form of the will was that Pam was made the sole beneficiary.' Why Jeremy's name didn't come up at the meeting, and particularly why Mabel apparently failed to ask about him at this point (given that Ann recollected she made no mention of Jeremy until December), is unclear.

Essex Police were fully conversant with the situation regarding the relatives' aversion to Jeremy benefitting financially from his family's deaths. The 1986 internal review affirmed that 'it was known to the Boutflours that had Jeremy inherited the estate he intended to sell what he could, thereby disposing of what had been part of the Speakman family estate. In addition to this, he would also have sold an area of land which [Nevill] Bamber had purchased intending to sell it at a later date to Peter and Ann Eaton when they had sufficient funds.' The review noted that while it was not suggested that this interest had in any way influenced the Boutflours in their statements to the police, it was known to DCI Jones during the initial stages 'and may have been a factor which affected the level of credence he placed upon the information given by the relatives'.

Colin Caffell had flown to Norway with Heather on 23 August to stay with his sister, but soon after the funerals he had pointed out to the family that, as matters stood, they had 'good reason and opportunity to plant evidence against Jeremy, if they chose to'.[16] They were horrified; only Robert recognized that in sowing the seeds of doubt in the minds of the police, 'they had unwittingly put themselves up as suspects, because they too stood to gain by the murders.'[17]

Julie Mugford was in turmoil. Her thoughts revolved endlessly around Jeremy in the hours that passed since they said goodbye at her student digs. Anger and desperation continued to gnaw at her. On Monday, 2 September, she called Karen Bishop, who was so alarmed by her evident unhappiness that she insisted Julie stayed for the week.

Julie had already told Susan and Liz that Jeremy was behind his family's murders; she intimated heavily to Karen that he was guilty, but for some reason stopped just short of saying the actual words, perhaps hoping that one of the three women would take it upon themselves to inform the police. She talked constantly about Jeremy, calling him 'a psychopath' who felt 'no sadness and no emotion' about his lost family; his deeds were 'so terrible' that she couldn't bring herself to speak of them.[1] She was more voluble about his friendship with Brett, whom she felt encouraged his 'obsession with money and materialism'. She declared that Jeremy's behaviour since the shootings had made it impossible for their relationship to continue. Later, Julie said she was amazed that Karen hadn't realized she had been trying to tell her that Jeremy was involved in the shootings.

On Tuesday, Jeremy had a meeting with Basil Cock to discuss the items Anthony and Jacqueline claimed had been left to them by their grandmother and which were in storage at White House Farm. After considering the legal position regarding Sheila's estate, Basil handed Jeremy his mother's letter, with its instruction only to be opened in the event of her death:

My home,
The White House.

My Darlings – Nevill, Sheila & Jem,
    Should anything happen to me and I have to leave you, I write this to tell you of my love for you and to thank you for all you have given me.
    All I ask is that God will love and protect you through

the years ahead, and that some day, God willing, we may meet again.

My love always, my darlings,
   Mums.[2]

A postscript asked that 'some small keepsake' should be found 'for others I love', followed by a list of godchildren, close friends, Pamela, Betty and Bink.

Basil asked Jeremy if he knew when the letter had been written. Jeremy felt it was probably fairly recent, given the inclusion of Jean as their housekeeper. He put the letter away in his pocket.

Robert telephoned Witham on Tuesday evening to enquire about the investigation. He was told to call back the next day, when a forensics report was due. On Wednesday morning he saw Jeremy at White House Farm, loading more possessions into the Sherpa van. He spoke to his nephew about a date for the burial of Nevill and June's ashes and told him that Pamela wanted to speak to him about June's rings, which she had kept 'at Mr Cock's request'.[3]

Together with Ann, Robert then travelled to Witham, with a view to having enquiries re-opened. A mutinous Stan Jones showed them into his office. He had recently contacted one of his superiors, Detective Inspector Connell, to express his unhappiness with the investigation. Although not directly involved with the Bamber case, Connell in turn had called Taff Jones, who flatly refused to discuss the matter with him. Robert realized that Stan was 'very much on his guard' as he told them that forensics had sent back a partial report but were swamped with work and the case wasn't being given priority because the chief suspect had committed suicide.

'Remember the police force is a big machine and I'm only a small cog,' Jones said. 'You'll have to wait until the coroner's inquest. You can say what you want then.'[4]

Ann told him that Jeremy was stripping White House Farm of all its contents, burning what he didn't want and selling anything of value.

'Well, is it yours?' Jones asked.[5]

Ann stared at him, 'No.'

'What's it got to do with you then?' he asked irritably.

With that, they were dismissed. Ann was deeply frustrated: 'I really felt that the police were working against us and not with us.' Robert was equally disappointed: 'We both realized that the investigation was stagnant and getting nowhere. We both felt very dejected and I felt that the police had made a muck up of the whole case.'[6]

On Brett's invitation, the owner of Vale Antiques called at Sheila's flat to view the items Jeremy wanted to sell, mostly bric-a-brac and several small tables. He offered £250 for the lot. Brett helped load everything into the dealer's yellow Datsun, asking him to call again later that day when Jeremy would have some more silver and glassware to sell.

Julie had arranged to meet Jeremy at the flat that Wednesday afternoon, 4 September, but no one answered when she pressed the buzzer. She sat on the steps and eventually the silver Astra appeared. Spotting Brett in the passenger seat, she asked to speak to Jeremy alone.

The two of them crossed the broad avenue to a cafe and sat down. 'I asked him what was going on in respect of our relationship,' Julie recalled. 'He said it had already been sorted out. I told him he was selfish and that I couldn't let him get away with hurting people anymore. He said, "You mean I either confess or I carry on the relationship with you." He thought I was giving him an ultimatum. He discussed our relationship further and basically he wanted his freedom.'[7]

Brett called at the cafe to remind Jeremy that the antiques dealer was due, so they all returned to the flat. While the dealer was looking through the items from the farm, the telephone rang. Jeremy answered, speaking 'in a friendly manner' to the caller.

'Who is it?' Julie asked, growing suspicious.

'Virginia,' he said.

Julie knew at once that he meant Virginia Greaves, and asked him to put the phone down. When he carried on talking, she cut the call herself. They then began to argue and Jeremy admitted he was seeing Virginia. When the telephone rang again and he answered it, Julie stormed through to Sheila's bedroom.

'I was so angry,' she remembered. 'I picked up a Chinese box of Jeremy's and threw it against a mirror, which smashed.'

Still on the line, Virginia heard the splintering glass. 'What's that?' she asked.[8]

Jeremy replied, 'Oh, Julie just smashing some plates up.'

There was another crash.

'What's that?' asked Virginia again.

'Julie's just put her wrists through the window.'

Shocked, Virginia told him definitely, 'I don't want anything to do with that and I'll speak to you some time.'

Curiously, the crash had triggered Jeremy's memory of Sheila's reaction to Colin's infidelity. Entering the bedroom he saw the mirrored shards glittering on the carpet.

'He asked me why I did it,' Julie recalled. 'I said I thought it was a cruel thing to do, to ask out another woman whilst I was there. He became very cross because he said there was an excusable reason and I slapped his face. He then got hold of my right arm and twisted it up my back, pushed me on the bed and then he raised his arm as if to hit me.'

Brett emerged from the lounge, saw the splintered glass on the floor, and heard Julie shout: 'Go on then. If you do, I'll go straight to the police.'[9] Releasing her arm, Jeremy sank onto the bed. Brett returned to the antique dealer, who paid him £300 cash for the items and departed.

Jeremy later gave his version of the incident to Essex Police: 'After smashing the mirror I came in the room, thinking that she'd put her hand through the window or something like that, and I was concerned. She stood by the window and I sat on the dressing table. We talked for a couple of minutes about the phone call from Virginia and she thought I was being unfaithful. She then just flared up and hit me around the face a couple of times. I grabbed her by the arms to restrain her and in anger pushed her down on the bed.'[10] He stated that her threat to call the police was because 'she could see I was angry about being hit round the face'.

Julie recalled that she had then 'asked him why he was so quiet. He got upset and looked troubled and I felt sorry for him.' She apologized and told him again that he could trust her: 'I wouldn't say anything.' Jeremy gave her a second cheque for

£400 towards the holiday she and Liz were planning, then drove her home.

'In the car he told me he didn't like being threatened and that I scared him,' Julie remembered. She picked up an envelope from the cassette compartment but he took it off her: 'He told me that it was from his mother June and was to be opened in the event of her death. He told me it had been written recently and was a letter apologizing for the way his mother had sometimes treated him. He said that his mother loved him, but he said that it didn't make any difference about the way he felt about her.'[11]

After saying goodbye to Jeremy at the Bishops' flat, Julie told Karen that he had 'terminated' their relationship and showed her the cheque. She then mentioned the letter from June, stating that Jeremy had laughed and was glad his mother was dead. She told Karen that he had offered to pay her off with her own wine bar. 'I understood her to mean that she was being paid off for the trauma and emotion that she had suffered because of the murders and Jeremy's treatment of her,' Karen recalled. 'I had no reason to think otherwise.'

Jeremy and Brett returned to Goldhanger the following day. When Charles Marsden joined them for dinner Jeremy told him that he had broken up with Julie, implying that her dislike of Brett was a factor. Charles recalled that the main topic of conversation 'was that Brett and Jeremy were going to live in his sister's flat in Maida Vale and they were going to sell the cottage. Jeremy spoke of a girl, Virginia, who was going to move in with him.'[12]

Having planned to spend the weekend with Brett at Sheila's flat, Jeremy called at White House Farm early on Friday morning to collect a dinner service and the rest of the glassware, telling Jean that he was taking them away for safekeeping because the alarm had been removed.

Julie telephoned him later to ask if he was still willing to help her move into new digs in Hither Green. He agreed, then asked if she'd seen *Fatal Vision*, a two part NBC series based on the case of US army officer Jeffrey MacDonald, convicted in 1979 of murdering his pregnant wife and two young daughters nine years before. 'I told him I had seen part of the first episode on Monday evening,' Julie recalled. 'He said he could not bear to watch it as it freaked him out. I assumed that as it was a murder case where one of the family was left and everyone was supportive to him, Jeremy felt it was an uncanny coincidence for something like that to be on the television.'[13]

Julie broke down that morning while talking to Karen Bishop about the Bambers: 'She said that she still could not believe that they were dead and that she was really sad about their deaths, particularly the two boys. She said she had had a much closer relationship with all the family than Jeremy had.' Julie told her that Jeremy had 'the devil in him' and had 'hated his mother, sister and the two children'. She spoke bitterly about Brett and declared that she no longer loved Jeremy but pitied him. She then left to meet Liz. Because the bank were unable to cash the cheque Jeremy had given her, Liz footed the bill for their holiday to Malta. They were due to leave on Monday.

The two girls returned to Caterham Road to wait for Jeremy, who arrived with Brett. Julie had asked if she could have June's bicycle for travelling to college, but he hadn't brought it with him. After moving her belongings to the new digs, Jeremy and Brett gave the two girls a lift to Piccadilly, where they were going nightclubbing.

'We left on a reasonably happy note,' Julie remembered. 'I haven't seen him since.'

On the advice of James Carr, the manager of Osea Road, Robert Boutflour had written to the Chief Constable of Essex to complain about the police investigation. On Thursday, 5 September, he was invited to meet Assistant Chief Constable Peter Simpson. 'He listened to me for three quarters of an hour,' Robert remembered, 'then said I had said enough; he would appoint a senior detective to investigate the case from the very beginning to see where, if anywhere, things had gone wrong.'

Simpson called in Acting Chief Superintendent Mike Ainsley, whose career began in 1958. By 1985 Ainsley was head of Essex CID. 'Although I didn't really want to be in the CID, to be honest,' he reflects. 'It's not me. I'm not an administrator, I didn't want to sit on my arse doing nothing in an office all day long and going to meetings with self-opinionated chief officers.'[14]

Ainsley instructed Detective Superintendent James Kenneally,

responsible for Chelmsford Division, to carry out a full assessment of the case. Kenneally spoke to Taff Jones, a personal friend
of his, and Stan Jones, with whom he had served as a young
constable at Witham. Together they scrutinized all the existing
information, including the witness statements, and discussed the
relatives' suspicions. Kenneally also made preliminary enquiries
with the Huntingdon laboratory, on the basis that further questions needed to be asked about Sheila's mental health and her
ability to use firearms.

At 6pm on Friday, 6 September he presented his conclusions
to Mike Ainsley, Peter Simpson and Chief Constable Robert Bunyard. He informed them that, based on what he had seen, 'it
appeared the murder-suicide theory was correct'.[15] Kenneally
affirmed that he would continue to re-assess the situation, 'but
did not hold out too much hope of arriving at a different conclusion'.[16]

Aware that Colin and Heather had returned from Norway on
Friday, Jeremy called at Maygrove Road. Colin was out; he had
agreed to meet Sheila's birth mother Christine at Heathrow Airport before she flew on to Europe.

But Heather and her friend Judy were at the flat, though
Jeremy explained he couldn't stay long because he was meeting
someone for lunch. He suggested that Colin should call at Morshead Mansions that evening to collect the twins' belongings, then
began talking about finances, stating that after capital gains tax
and death duties he would be left with about 30 per cent of the
estate's total value, though he would have a steady income from
the caravan site. He mentioned the solicitor's letter from Jacqueline, in which she enquired about the items she and her brother
Anthony had been left at White House Farm, adding that family
pressures and the need to sell his house in Goldhanger had
resulted in him living at Sheila's flat.

He also spoke about the breakdown of his relationship with
Julie and said that he was looking forward to a motoring holiday
in Europe with Brett. Judy recalled: 'He said that he was taking
Valium tablets and also drinking. I advised him that if he could
do without the Valium, he should slowly stop taking them. He
kept looking at his watch and kept saying he mustn't miss his

engagement.'[17] Heather suggested going out that night, but he told her: 'We'll have to see how we get on this afternoon.'[18] He then left in a taxi bound for Covent Garden, where Virginia Greaves was waiting for him.

Liz and Julie, meanwhile, were on the train bound for Colchester. Having persuaded Julie to speak to Malcolm Waters about the murders, Liz hoped she would listen to his advice. At Malcolm's home in Colchester, they spent two hours cloistered in the lounge, emerging only for a drink or to use the toilet, while his girlfriend sat in the kitchen wondering what was going on.

Julie began by telling Malcolm: 'I don't know how to put this, but those murders – I'm sure Jeremy was involved.'[19] Before she went any further, he asked whether she was 'saying these things because of her split with Jeremy'. Starting to cry, Julie swore that she wasn't, then told him that Jeremy had 'employed Matthew' to kill his family and was selling things from the farm to raise cash to pay him off.

Malcolm sat back, speechless, as Julie reiterated everything she had told Liz and Susan. She brought her story to a close by stating that Jeremy had enjoyed goading her with 'how it had been done and that he had got away with it'. She was also frightened for her own safety.

Trying to marshal his thoughts into order, Malcolm decided that Julie was telling the truth. He told her that she must go to the police.

Julie broke down again, asking Liz to make the call on her behalf.

It was four o'clock when Liz telephoned Witham and asked to speak to Stan Jones. He was at home, but rang Liz on the number she left with the duty sergeant.

'Have you got Julie with you?' he asked.[20]

She said she had.

'I'll be right over.'

When Colin and Heather called at Sheila's apartment that evening, the first thing they noticed was the painting propped against the wall in the hallway; it was the portrait of Beatrice Bamber from the stairs at White House Farm. Jeremy told them a valuer was coming to look at it on Monday.

The lounge had been stripped of everything belonging to Sheila and the twins and most of the furniture was gone. In the empty dining room boxes of glassware were stacked with another painting from the farm. For a while the three of them made small talk, but Jeremy seemed impatient for them to leave, explaining that he and Brett were going to the Mud Club, one of London's hippest nightspots. He led them through to the twins' starkly empty bedroom. Everything the boys had owned was either piled up in the cupboard or in black bin bags near the entrance to the flat. Colin stared at the blank walls, reeling inside.

Sheila's photo albums of the twins were also in the cupboard, each picture meticulously captioned. When Colin asked about her modelling portfolio, Jeremy replied that it was at Bourtree Cottage and he intended to keep any photographs that had already appeared in the press. He showed them a small heap of modelling shots, some contact sheets and a box of twenty-four slides. Glancing through the latter, Colin saw that they were the explicit shots taken in the paddling pool and asked if he could take them away to destroy. Jeremy agreed, grinning that he had more slides at home which showed everything 'right down to the last detail'.[1] He added that the nude photographs Colin had taken of Sheila when June caught them together in the field were in his mother's bureau.

Colin picked up the slides, saying he would call the following day for the rest. Jeremy explained that he would be out but gave him a key to the flat. Then they said goodbye, unaware that the next time they met would be in a crowded courtroom.

Stan Jones had just one question for Julie, who automatically rose to her feet when he appeared: 'Did Jeremy do it?'[2]

'Yes.'

'Right,' said Stan, 'let's go.'

In an interview twenty-five years later, Jeremy declared: 'I certainly didn't deserve what she did to me. She should never have gone to the police, but she had no idea what she was doing.'[3] He insisted that 'Julie, Lizzie, and Malcolm hatched a plot that night to stitch me up.' Three years later he changed his stance, asserting that Julie 'did not go of her own volition' but was 'grassed up' by Liz for 'hiding evidence' after the two girls had a serious argument.[4] He questioned 'if, as the court was led to believe, that Julie had voluntarily gone to the police on the 7th September', why she had 'spent all that money' booking a holiday the day before. But Liz had paid for the holiday and did her utmost to convince Julie to call the police; she may have believed that the physical and emotional distance of the holiday would give her friend the strength she needed. Ultimately, it was Malcolm who proved the most persuasive.

Arriving at Witham Police Station with Julie and Liz in tow, Jones telephoned DI Miller, who recalls: 'When the phone rang, I turned to my wife Maureen and said, "This is going to be Stan Jones."'[5]

He picked up the phone. 'Hello guv,' Jones said.

'Hello Stan, what you got?' Miller asked.

'Julie's come in – wants to tell us all about it.'

'I'll be over,' Miller replied. He nods at the memory: 'I just knew.'

At 7pm, Julie was shown into an interviewing suite. She was no longer nervous, but calm, open and very straightforward. 'It was just me, her and Stan in a little room,' Miller remembers. 'I sat her down and said, "Right, no one's going to interrupt you. Just tell us everything you know." And away she went. Everything started falling into place. Stuff like how he'd got into the house and left it secure. Things where we were a bit backward, she said, "No, this is how he did it . . ." It was a brilliant account – like a jigsaw slotting together.'

Julie's interview lasted three-and-a-half hours. Miller then telephoned Chief Superintendent Harris.

'George, sorry to bother you . . .' he began.

'What is it?' Harris asked.

'I thought you'd like to know we've got Julie Mugford in. *Jeremy's done it.* Are you going to come down and see us?'

'No, I've got guests here, I'm at dinner. Call out the detective superintendent who's on call.'

Miller remembers: 'I had to ring Mike Ainsley then. I only knew him by reputation. He was supposed to be a bit of an ayatollah but he was the best bloke I ever worked with, very direct.'[6]

Ainsley was at home when the telephone rang. 'I think you ought to come over, guv,' Miller said after introducing himself. 'I've got Jeremy Bamber's girlfriend here. She's told me that he did the murders. I've been over it with her a couple of times and I believe her.'

'I will be over,' Ainsley replied tersely.[7] He called Taff Jones immediately and by 11pm the two men were sitting down with Julie at Witham.

Over the ensuing weeks, Julie Mugford made a number of statements to the police. At their suggestion, she also compiled a concise 'diary' to assist her memory on salient points. What follows is a chronological summary of everything pertaining to the murders, as recounted by Julie.

After explaining how her relationship with Jeremy had developed, she declared that 'the conversations about Jeremy killing his family must have been said between July 1984 and October 1984,' seven months after she began dating him.[8] Complaining that he didn't think his parents had done enough for him, 'like buying carpets and furniture for his house', he became 'very angry about the way he was treated by his parents, and in talking he stated he wished that he could get rid of them and all the family so he could live his own life. I told him he shouldn't say such horrible things and I dismissed it as idle talk.' Following that first conversation, 'Jeremy would often complain about his parents and would occasionally mention the fact that he wished they were dead.'

He swiftly graduated to expounding 'on how he could kill the whole family. We were talking round the house and he stated that he would like to kill his parents. He also said that he would have to kill Sheila and the twins as well. I asked him why, as I could understand him talking about his parents like that, not about Sheila and the twins. I asked him why kill Sheila and the twins as they had done nothing to him. He told me that he deserved everything and Sheila had done nothing on the farm so she didn't deserve anything. He also said she was crazy and he would be getting her out of her misery and by killing the twins it would be doing them a favour as they would grow up disturbed because of the way they were being brought up.'

Julie had asked him how Colin might react to his sons' deaths: 'He told me that the twins were a burden to Colin and were like a millstone round his neck . . . because [Colin] was looking after the twins more and more he could not get regular work. Jeremy stated that he would be doing Colin a favour if the twins were dead. During the conversation I believed that Jeremy meant what he had said, although I didn't really believe he would do it.'

She was privy to his first murder plot, which involved him staying at the farm for drinks and leaving his car in Goldhanger: 'Whilst with his family he would slip sleeping pills into their drinks then when they retired for the night he would go home, returning a short while later. He would then enter the house by opening a sash window. Then he would set fire to the house using alcohol spirit as this would not have been traceable. That plan was shelved as it had too many flaws.'[9]

Jeremy 'would frequently mention the fact that he would like to kill the whole family so he could have everything to himself. He said he would like to commit the perfect murder.' His initial idea evolved: 'He would have to do it when all the family were there, that is Sheila, the twins and Mr and Mrs Bamber. He said he would go there for supper in the evening and put something in their drinks to make them sleep well and would then shoot them all and afterwards set fire to the house using gin or vodka. He said that he would make it look as if his father was in the lounge with the rest asleep in bed and that his father had accidentally set the house on fire with a cigarette end when he had fallen to sleep in the chair. The fire would destroy all the evidence. He said that he would have left the house saying goodnight to everyone, taking the car back to Goldhanger and either walking or cycling back to the farm via the back road. He told me that he knew of a way of getting in and out of the house without anyone knowing, as the front and back doors were always locked. I remember that he said that he would use his mother's sleeping pills to put in the drinks as she was taking them at this time. At this time I was besotted by him and really didn't believe what he said. I frequently told him that I didn't like what he said.'

Coincidentally, on 29 October 1984, Julie was prescribed ten days' worth of temazepam tablets by the doctor at Goldsmiths College's Medical Centre. Recommended for short term treatment of insomnia, the tablets were to calm Julie during a stressful time during her work placement at a primary school in Kent. She showed Jeremy the pills when she brought them with her to Goldhanger the following weekend, leaving them at the cottage without having taken any.[10] A few days later he telephoned her: 'He was going to take some of the pills I had bought him. For some reason or another he had it in his mind that I had bought the pills especially for him so he could use them on his parents.' This is not true and I had no idea why he should think this. He told me that he was going to take some of the pills to see what effect they had on him and if they tasted in drink.' He told her the pills were 'useless and didn't have the desired effect. I told Jeremy that I didn't like him talking about stupid things and I suppose for about six weeks up to late November 1984 he did not mention about killing his family.'

That Christmas, Jeremy had asked her to marry him but swiftly retracted his proposal when his parents gave their blessing to the relationship at last: 'At this time it appeared as if Jeremy was getting on worse with his parents. He constantly told me that they were nagging him about not working hard enough on the farm or caravan site and that he wasn't seeing them enough.'

During the first few weeks of the new year, until March 1985, 'Jeremy appeared to be more content and appeared by what he said to be getting on better with his parents.' But as Easter neared, Jeremy began to talk about murder again: 'He said that his original plan was not fool proof because of the drugs, and he

---

* The wording 'bought' must have been transcribed wrongly, since Julie's statements to the police make it plain that she was prescribed the pills by her doctor.

didn't know how to administer it. He said he thought about getting cyanide but wherever he got it would be recorded. He then said that as they lived on a farm it might be acceptable but then he dismissed that idea. I remember that I made a joke about the house, saying that he couldn't burn it down because it was so beautiful. He said he had changed his mind about burning it down because it might have been seen too quickly and the evidence would not have been destroyed. He also dismissed the fire because there were valuables in the house which would be lost. He told me the house insurance was low. He mentioned a Myson [sic] clock and china and silver which he thought were valuable. He said that the only other way that he could do it was to shoot them . . . I still didn't believe he would carry it through.'

Julie declared that Jeremy 'was going to make it look as if Sheila was responsible and the grounds would be that she was mad, having been in a mental hospital. He also told me that there would be a phone call made from the house because the last phone call made would be recorded. He said the call would be made from the White House to his house. He didn't say who would make it or why. I know there was a portable phone in the house with a memory key which when pressed would phone back to the last number called.'

A few weeks prior to the shootings, 'Jeremy returned from work one day and told me that he had killed several rats with his bare hands to see if he had the ability to kill things. He then told me that he had done it for a test to see if he could kill his family. He then said that as a result of this he couldn't kill his family. I believed what he said to be true. In another conversation prior to the murders he told me that it was society that led us to believe that murder was the ultimate sin. He told me he did not believe this.'[11]

In June, while she and Jeremy were out in his car, 'he told me that he was being pressurised by his parents and he hoped Sheila was coming to stay. He said that he would use a cycle to do it and would do a trial run to see how long it would take. He thought it would take about 15 minutes one way.' He intended to enter through a downstairs window: 'He said they would all be shot. He told me he could get out of the house through a window which the latch would close when the window was

closed. He said as you closed the window the latch closed,
making it look as if the window had never been opened. I got
very upset and cried and insisted he did not mention it again.
Jeremy did not mention to me about killing his family until Tuesday, 6th August 1985.'

Julie was at Caterham Road that evening, watching television
with Susan and Doug when the telephone rang. It was 10pm and
she had smoked some marijuana, which made her 'quite flippant'
while talking to Jeremy.

'I've had a wonderful day at work,' she told him. 'How was
your day?'

'As best as can be expected,' he replied, explaining that he
had spent the entire day inside the tractor with the sun beating
down.

'You sound pissed off,' she said.

Jeremy told her, 'I've been thinking on the tractor and the
crime will have to be tonight or never.'

'I told him not to be so stupid,' Julie recounted, 'and that he
was only saying this because he had had a bad day on the tractor. He also told me that he had only just got back from work
and had had supper with his parents and Sheila and the twins
and that was why he was late in phoning me. I then continued
telling him about my day and dropped the matter concerning his
family. I was aware that when he said the word "crime" he was
referring to the killing of his family. I did not believe he would
carry it out. I remember that he told me that he had been on the
phone seventeen minutes and I said words to the effect, "Oh, I
am sorry, do you want me to go now?" He just said that he
hadn't got anything else to say. We both said goodbye and put
the phone down. I remember now that he said words to the
effect that I might be hearing from him later. I thought nothing
of this.'

Julie went to bed about quarter past eleven, sleeping until the
telephone rang in the early hours: 'I got out of bed and went to
the phone on the landing and said, "Hello." I felt very dozy and
I suppose I was only half awake. He said, "Everything is going
well, not to worry, there is something wrong at the farm."' He
told her he hadn't been to bed all night. 'I told him simply to go
to bed and he said, "Bye honey, I love you lots." I then put the

Nevill at White House Farm with Nicholas and Daniel. He was a fun-loving and patient grandfather to the boys.

Sheila and June in the garden at White House Farm around the time of Sheila's second breakdown in March 1985. To help manage her illness Sheila was given monthly injections of haloperidol, but suffered several side effects and was keen to lower the dose.

June and Sheila with Nicholas and Daniel in the fields
at White House Farm, 1985.

Sheila with her sons shortly before the murders in 1985.

Morshead Mansions, Maida Vale. Sheila's flat was on the ground floor, to the right of the main door.

Jeremy's home, Bourtree Cottage in Goldhanger.

Aerial photograph of White House Farm taken on 6 August 1985, just hours before the murders. The farm cottages can be seen in the upper right corner.

White House Farm from the kitchen yard. The back door was replaced following the police raid. Ground floor windows, from left to right: scullery, kitchen, sitting room. First floor windows, from left to right: office, store room, bathroom, twins' bedroom, box room.

Funeral of Nevill and June Bamber and Sheila Caffell at Tolleshunt D'Arcy, 16 August 1985. Jeremy and Julie lead the mourners. Behind them are Reg Caffell, Colin Caffell, Robert Boutflour, Ann Eaton and David Boutflour.

Jeremy Bamber at magistrates' court, October 1985.

Jeremy's close friend
Brett Collins and new girlfriend
Anji Greaves supported him
during his appearances at
magistrates' court.

Detective Sergeant Stan Jones (left) and Acting Chief Superintendent
Mike Ainsley (first from left) leave Chelmsford Crown Court. Both men
were convinced that Jeremy Bamber was guilty of killing his family.

Julie Mugford, Jeremy's girlfriend from late 1983 until September 1985, arrives at court to give evidence. With her is Detective Sergeant Stan Jones. Julie's mother, Mary Mugford, is in the background.

Jeremy Bamber arrives at the Appeal Court in 2002, hoping to have his conviction overturned.

The headstone of Nevill and June Bamber, Tolleshunt D'Arcy.

Jeremy Bamber today, thirty years after the murders of his family.

phone down. I particularly remember the phrase "everything is going well." I then got into bed and laid there for, I suppose, five minutes, when I suddenly came to my senses and realized what he had said. In my view he was telling me they were all dead.'

She then got out of bed and spoke to Susan, who was 'very cross and complained about Jerry phoning at a stupid time. She asked me what was wrong as apparently I looked worried. I told her that I didn't know, but there was something wrong at the farm. She said again, "what was wrong" and I just said, "I don't know."'

The two girls went back to their bedrooms. Julie 'lay in bed but did not go to sleep as I knew that Jerry had murdered his family.' At 5.40am he rang to say that the police would collect her. Arriving at Bourtree Cottage, the situation was explained to her 'although I already knew. Detective Sergeant Jones allowed me a few minutes with Jerry in the dining room when we hugged and kissed. Whilst we were kissing he whispered in my ear and said, "I should have been an actor." He then gave a slight chuckle.' As the house filled with devastated relatives, she and Jeremy escaped to the bathroom occasionally because she found it difficult to behave normally in front of other people.

Twenty-five years later, David Boutflour reflected: '[Julie] was obviously putting on a fantastic act because she knew – she'd had the phone call earlier on that night. And actually I remember saying to her, "He's going to need a lot of love, you know, to get through this. He'll really need to lean on you." And she didn't say a thing. She had a chance to tell me what had really happened because we both left the house to get some fish and chips, or something to eat. So we went to the pub. We walked up the road to where the Chequers is and we got some food from there, and then we brought [it] back to the house. She had all that time to tell me that something was wrong. And she didn't. She had every opportunity at that point to say: "Well, David, you know, it isn't true. Jeremy actually has killed them." And she didn't say that. Didn't say a thing. Nothing.'[12]

Julie recalled that, when everyone had gone from the cottage that first evening after the murders, Jeremy remarked that he was glad the day was over: 'I then said to Jeremy, "Did you do it?"

He said, "No, I couldn't have done it, Matthew did it." I knew to whom he was referring.'

For the benefit of the detectives, Julie then described how 'Matthew' had committed the murders in an account that was identical to the story she had related to Susan and Liz. She added a single detail: that 'Matthew' had lost a glove while carrying out the murders and as a result, Jeremy was 'worried in case [Sheila's] fingerprints didn't come out on the gun properly. The reason for the flaw in the fingerprinting was that during the fight with Mr Bamber a glove might have come off or been dropped and it might have rubbed Sheila's fingerprints off or have extra fingerprints on the gun which were fresher than Sheila's and would show up.' Afterwards, Jeremy told her not to talk about 'it' indoors in case the cottage had been bugged by police.

She explained why she had volunteered to identify the bodies: 'For some unknown reason I felt I had to see the bodies. Probably because I could not believe what Jeremy had told me he was going to do and because I needed to know if they had suffered, especially the twins.'[13] She wanted to touch them 'to see if they could give me guidance on what I should do, but I could not summon up the courage to do it. I left and once outside made up my mind to go back and seek guidance from the bodies. However I thought that if I requested to see the bodies again someone may have started asking questions which I could not answer.'[14]

In giving her first witness statement the day after the murders, she had 'omitted some things' because she was trying to protect Jeremy, and didn't want to say too much because she didn't know what he had told police. He assured her she had nothing to worry about if she kept 'as near to the truth as possible. He was in fact saying that when he telephoned me in the early hours of the morning and said about there is something wrong at the farm, that is what he wanted me to say to the police. I told Jeremy exactly what I said in my statement.'

Telling her that the crime had been 'fool proof', Jeremy warned that if she spoke out against him she would be regarded as an accessory 'and would suffer the same punishment as him. This obviously worried me and made me feel responsible for what had happened.'[15]

Later she recalled that they had looked through the newspapers together and she commented that it was awful to see Sheila blamed: 'This didn't bother Jeremy, he was only bothered by the fact that he was the only one in the Jubilee photograph of his parents, Colin and Sheila who was unrecognized and, I think unnamed, although he was in the photograph.'[16] She was also upset by a sympathy card from Matthew and his girlfriend Christine, still apparently believing that Matthew had committed the murders at Jeremy's behest. She told Jeremy that it was 'horrible', but he reassured her that Christine would have sent it without Matthew's knowledge.[17] It was never made explicit exactly when Julie stopped believing the story of Matthew's involvement, only that it occurred gradually.

She recalled spending the first weekend after the murders with Colin: 'On the way there I was very quiet and [Jeremy] kept on asking me what was wrong. I told him he knew what was wrong and during the journey I was quiet and kept on thinking.' When she told him at the pizza restaurant that she 'couldn't take the pretence anymore', he replied that 'he had done it because he had convinced himself that there was a valid reason for doing it.'

Visiting White House Farm the following Monday, Jeremy pretended to be upset 'for the benefit of Ann. He held my hand and he pretended that he felt sick and ill. He told Ann that he didn't like being in the house and didn't really want to look in the rooms. At one point we went in the hallway next to the kitchen when Jeremy said words to the effect that the police hadn't been very thorough as there wasn't much finger dust powder around. He also told me that on one of the windows there was a layer of dust or dirt and that hadn't got finger dust powder on it either. He said the police had been careless about that.'

Prior to buying outfits for the funeral, 'Jeremy had gone to the bank to get wages for the farm workers and he kept some money back for himself. It therefore meant that some of the workers didn't get their full amount.' He then reprised his role as a grieving son, asking Julie after the funeral if he had acted well enough. She recalled: 'Throughout the whole affair he has persistently asked me if he acted alright and I kept telling him he was too happy. I found it difficult to believe he could keep up a charade to people who thought so much of his family.'[18]

On the day they left for Pevensey, 'I told Jeremy I couldn't understand him betraying people in that he had known what he had done and was still accepting their love. He said as far as he was concerned it had been done and he had worked it all out and weighed up the pros and cons and it was finalised. I believe on that occasion I said to him, I can't believe £2,000 for five lives. He just dismissed me.'

On 27 August, after three weeks of keeping his secret, Julie departed Goldhanger 'due to the fact that I could no longer handle the situation which had arisen, ie., the killings. I still loved Jeremy and I still do but I just wanted to get away from the area.' Their relationship finally collapsed after his infidelity with Virginia Greaves and the row at Sheila's flat.

Julie's story ended there. It was not until May 1986, five months before the trial, that she was asked to address the question of why it had taken her exactly one month to the day since the murders to come forward: 'In my subconscious I believed what Jeremy had said was true, and I would qualify this by stating that I believed Jeremy when he said he had hired Matthew to kill the family. However, I did not wish to accept the truth of the situation. Also, I was frightened of the consequences, since Jeremy had told me that I also would be an accessory to the murders.'[19] But as time went on, it dawned on her that Matthew's involvement was a lie invented by Jeremy because he knew that she 'could not have withheld the information' if she suspected him of actually killing his family. There was a second reason she had not spoken out sooner: 'I felt frightened as I might be harmed as well.'

'I realised that I was listening to the horrific truth,' Acting Chief Superintendent Mike Ainsley said of Julie's interview. He was in no doubt that Jeremy had carried out the murders himself, 'but in view of what had occurred in the previous month, including the findings of the coroner's court, it was essential to establish the veracity of what Julie Mugford was now saying.'[1] She and Liz were taken into protective custody at the force training school in Chelmsford. 'I was encouraged not to talk to anyone outside while I was there,' Julie remembered, 'and that included my mum.'[2]

Ainsley called DCI Jones, DS Jones and DI Miller into his office. 'Mike heads up the four of us in a circle and asks, "Who's done it?"' Miller recounts. 'Stan says, "Jeremy." Then he asked me. I felt a bit sorry for Taff then. I said, "Well, this girl does sound very plausible. There's a lot that we didn't know about and it's definitely put a different complexion on the inquiry." Taff said, "It's the sister." He'd got himself into a corner. I'm convinced of that.'[3]

Aware that Jeremy was due to leave the country within the next forty-eight hours, Ainsley decided to arrest him and Brett, while property found at Sheila's flat relating to 'any of the deceased' was also to be seized.[4]

At 7.45am on Sunday, 8 September, Jeremy answered the buzzer at Morshead Mansions. Bleary-eyed from his night out and dressed in jeans and a green shirt, he looked dazed as nine officers crowded into the hall: DCI Jones, DI Miller, DC Barlow, three uniformed officers, a Scenes of Crime officer and two CID officers. DCI Jones asked if he might have a word. Jeremy led him into the front room, whereupon Jones declared, 'I'm arresting you on suspicion of murdering your mother, father, sister and her two children.'[5]

Jeremy gaped: 'I don't believe what I'm hearing . . . you're not serious are you?'

'Yes, you're now under arrest. It's my intention to search this flat. Where's your clothing kept?'

Brett's shouts of protest at being woken where he lay sprawled naked in the twins' bedroom reached them. 'All my clothes are at Head Street except what's in that bag,' Jeremy said, reaching for a canvas hold-all. He unzipped it and rummaged through the clothing for a wooden box containing banknotes and a substance in a small plastic bag.

'What is it?' Jones asked, taking the plastic bag from him.

'Marijuana, there's a bit more at Head Street.' Jeremy handed him a pipe. 'You'll want this as well.' He explained that the marijuana was bought during a trip to Holland with Brett and Julie 'but it's got nothing to do with them'.

Brett stumbled into the room, looking tense and exhausted while DCI Jones asked about property removed from White House Farm. Jeremy replied that he'd made £1,000 from items already sold, while other valuables were being held at Sotheby's. Then he asked, 'You're not serious about this, are you? It must be something else you want me for, not murder.'

DCI Jones replied, 'You're wanted in connection with the murders and I also want to speak to you about other matters, including a burglary at the caravan site earlier this year when £1,000 was stolen.' He paused. 'We'll do all this at Chelmsford.'

Jeremy shook his head slowly: 'I don't believe it, you *must* be joking.' But Jones told him to get dressed. Pulling on socks and baseball boots, Jeremy lifted the bag onto his shoulder and followed the team of officers out to the empty, sunlit street.

He was divested of his possessions at Chelmsford Police Station, including his Cartier wristwatch, the wooden box containing £1,460 in notes and a cheque for £589. He and Brett were then led away to separate detention rooms. Told that he was suspected of withholding information about the Bamber killings, Brett responded in disgust: 'You don't have a clue what you're talking about.'[6]

Ainsley had managed to grab a couple of hours' sleep before meeting Assistant Chief Constable Peter Simpson, who agreed he should replace Taff Jones as Senior Investigating Officer. Assembling his team, Ainsley established a Major Incident Office into which all information for 'Operation Raleigh' would be fed, recalling: 'My duty was to oversee the whole process and examine every word and decision, sifting the information that would be required to formulate an evidence file. Everything was to be made available to Bamber's defence should he be charged.'

DI Miller began interviewing Brett Collins shortly after 11am. Detective Sergeant Mark Hughes kept notes throughout. Interviews in custody were not tape recorded until 1988 following the Police and Criminal Evidence Act; it became standard practice in 1991.

Miller was interested in Brett's arrival in Essex three months earlier.

Brett recalled meeting Nevill 'three or four times', finding him a 'quite nice, very astute man'.[7]

'How did Jeremy get on with him?' Miller asked.

'Didn't seem to be any love lost between them,' Brett answered. 'Not close, more like a business relationship, he got his instructions from his dad in the morning and got on with it.'

'Did Jeremy talk about his relationship with his father?'

'No, not really.' Brett found June 'quite strange. Jeremy had discussed her, about her giving her money away, she had depressions.'

'Jeremy mentioned her giving money away?' Miller asked.

'Yes, to the church.'

'Did that concern Jeremy?'

'Yes.'

'Why?'

Brett shrugged, 'He didn't think it was right, her giving so much to the church when the farm needed so much. It was apparently out of her own income so Jeremy couldn't ask her to stop.'

'Jeremy likes money, doesn't he?'

'Yes, like all young people.'

Miller asked if it was true that Jeremy hated his mother.

'Yeah, at times. I'd say so. Apparently there is two sides to her.'

'Did he hate her enough to kill her?'

Brett shook his head. 'No. I don't think he has it in him to kill anyone. I don't think he has the guts. I can't imagine it, to be honest.' When Miller switched the subject to 'drugs Jeremy might have sold in New Zealand', Brett told him: 'Not while at my place. He always seemed ok financially. I don't know what he did in Australia.'

Miller asked if Jeremy had ever discussed the shootings. Brett replied, 'Yes, but only that he just couldn't believe what had happened – that the sister was unstable at times, but he couldn't believe it.' As far as he could remember, Jeremy had brought up the shootings on just one occasion when he mentioned 'Colin sending her round the bend'.

Miller returned to the subject of drugs. Brett told him that the marijuana came from Amsterdam and there was a man in Scotland 'who Jeremy sometimes sent some dope to', but he knew no more than that. As for Jeremy's character: 'I haven't seen a nasty side of him. He's always been straight up with me.' He knew that Jeremy had gone shooting with his father but otherwise had no knowledge of Jeremy's experience with fire-arms. The interview concluded with Brett insisting that his friend wasn't capable of murder: 'I couldn't see him doing anything like that at all.'

Jeremy was questioned by DCI Jones and DC Barlow shortly after midday.

'What was your relationship like with your mother?' Jones launched in.[8]

'Rough and smooth.'

'Did you antagonize your mother by speaking to her about religion?'

Jeremy frowned. 'It's not really fair, the way you angle your question. About eighteen months ago, we'd have heated argu-ments through a lack of understanding for each other's views, and due in part to mother's strong character and to some extent my immaturity. Over the last couple of years – eighteen months – we've found much more common ground, due somewhat to mature discussion and all of us giving a little and trying to be more understanding.'

'Was your relationship then over the last six months quite amicable?'

'Yes, it was quite amicable but every now and then we would have our moments. But in general things were more loving towards each other.'

Jones questioned him about the day of the murders, asking: 'I believe you took the .22 rifle out to shoot a rabbit. Where did you get it from?'

'The gun? Out of the study, I think.'

'Was the silencer on it?'

'No, I don't think so.'

'Did you put the silencer or telescopic sights on the gun?' Jones asked.

'No.'

'Do you know where they are kept in the house?'

'No. In the study, I should think.'

'Did you use the gun?'

'Did I fire a shot?'

'Yes.'

'No.'

'What did you do with the gun when you returned home?' Jones asked.

'I put it down by the seat thing – the bench – unclipped the magazine, and put it down on the side.' Jeremy told them again about the conversation around the supper table. When asked how Sheila had reacted to the idea of someone else taking care of her children, he replied: 'She didn't, really. Although I wasn't paying much attention to the conversation. She didn't really express any reaction.'

'Were you at the house when your mother spoke on the phone to Pam?'

'No – if I was I didn't hear it.'

'Did you see anyone on your way home that you knew?'

'No, I don't think so. I didn't see any of the neighbours.'

'Tell me what you did between arriving home and going to bed.'

'I phoned Julie,' Jeremy said. 'We spoke about what we had done during the day and I watched the TV. I probably had a cup of coffee or a coke and possibly a sandwich, then I went to bed about eleven thirty to eleven forty. Then I turned the light out and went to sleep. It was a normal evening after a day at work.'

Jones asked, 'When you spoke to Julie on the phone, did you not say to her words to the effect of "Tonight's the night"?'

'No.'

'Are you sure?'

'Certain.'

'Have you not planned over a number of months to get rid of your parents, Sheila and the children?'

'No.'

'Did you go back to the farmhouse and shoot all five of them?'

'No.'

'Have you discussed with anyone getting rid of your parents?'

'No. Never.'

Earlier that afternoon, accompanied by the two officers responsible for taking the bulk of witness statements, senior investigating officer Mike Ainsley had driven out to Vaulty, where he broke the news that Jeremy had been arrested. He reflects: 'I will never forget the words spoken to me by Robert on that sunny Sunday afternoon. Having generally chatted and made me aware of his feelings about the whole matter, including the way he felt the police had been misled, I told Robert that I would leave no stone unturned in order to discover the truth of what took place that night.

'"I am 68 years old," said Robert, "and if you cannot see that justice is done, I have enough time left to see that it is."'

Ainsley returned to the Incident Office, demanding a full Scenes of Crime and scientific search at White House Farm and Bourtree Cottage. The search at the farm would include a finger-print examination and search for blood, with particular attention paid to entry and exit marks. Jeremy's clothing and all vehicles owned by the family were to be examined. As executor of the estate, Basil Cock was invited to be present but he declined, promising total cooperation.

Officers led by DI Cook arrived at Bourtree Cottage that same Sunday afternoon. 'A whole squad of Scenes of Crime offi-cers were employed,' he recalls. 'I was involved in that second leg of the investigation but different teams of people came on board and Geordie Wright [DCI Charles Wright] took charge of that side of it.'[9] They took possession of Jeremy's marijuana books and equipment, a wooden box containing marijuana, the sympa-thy card from Matthew McDonald and June's bicycle.

DC Hammersley conducted a fingerprint examination of Sheila's flat while other officers swarmed over White House

Farm. Carpet fibres and two bottles of tablets were removed from the master bedroom and the side window in the lounge was examined and photographed. DS Davidson scrutinized Jeremy's Vauxhall Astra in the kitchen yard and took possession of several items, including June's letter. Around 140 fingerprint marks were found at White House Farm. 'They could have been in situ for years,' Ainsley explains. 'It would have been a mammoth task to even attempt to trace every person who had been in the house.'[10]

During the search, officers slid open the doors of the white, built-in wardrobe in the twins' bedroom. A photograph taken after fingerprinting shows the inside of the wardrobe. Scratched into the wood in tall, condemnatory letters were the words: 'I HATE THIS PLACE.'

Brett was interviewed briefly again in the late afternoon regarding the trip to Amsterdam, the sale of his restaurant in New Zealand and his intention to remain in England until Christmas. 'They were telling us we had plotted the murders,' Brett declared in the *Star* some months later. 'They said to me, "Okay, we know you were both in on it, but we can't prove it." Fortunately, I was able to convince them I was in Greece at the time of the killings. I still had the plane ticket stubs. So they let me go.'[11]

Both he and Jeremy were questioned extensively on their sexual relationships. Brett was adamant that he and Jeremy had never been attracted to each other, but was less circumspect when talking afterwards to the *Daily Mail*: 'I have known Jeremy for a very long time. He is the gentlest of men. Are we having an affair? I would rather not say anything about that. We are very close.'[12] Essex Police tried to establish whether their relationship was sexual, presumably because it gave greater weight to the idea that they had either colluded in the killings or that Jeremy had confided in Brett.

Jeremy's interview resumed at half-past five after an hour's break. He admitted to DCI Jones that he was responsible for the burglary at Osea Road: 'Julie and I went down there and broke in as she has said. I was working down there at weekends with my father. We took a couple of caravan rentals, about £600, and I thought if things went right the safe key was on the wall. I knew I would be number one suspect but that they couldn't prove it. The money would come in handy, buying drinks and things for the house.'[13]

'How did you get into the office?' Jones asked.

'With the key.'

'How did you get the key?'

'It was in the letter box. I just reached through the letter box and got it. I've done it before in order to get in.'

'How much money was in there?'

'There was two caravan rentals and some cash in the safe. I thought it was under £900.'

'Why did you do it?'

'To bring home to the other directors and people involved in the caravan site that we were too lackadaisical and the reasons why we were always getting done. It was to prove a point.'

Jones asked again whether he had rung Julie and declared, 'Tonight's the night.' Jeremy denied it, but agreed that he had received a phone call from his father 'some time' after three: 'I can't remember the exact time now but I put it in my original statement.'

'When the phone was cut off did you ring back immediately?' Jones queried.

'Yes, twenty or thirty seconds later.'

'And you tried a couple of times?'

'Yes, my phone has a memory redial. I normally use it when a number I try is engaged.'

'Did you then phone your girlfriend?' Jones asked.

'Yes.'

'And how long were you on the phone to her?'

'A minute, two minutes. Not very long as I had to ring the police.'

'Did you then ring the Chelmsford police?'

'Yes.'

'Did you know the number?'

'No, I had to look it up.'

'Approximately how long would it have taken you to find the number and get through?'

'Ten minutes at the outside.'

Jones let that sink in, then asked whether the phone calls

were made 'to give the appearance it was not you involved in the shooting of your parents'.

Jeremy shook his head. 'No.'

'Sure about that?'

'Yes.'

'Have you discussed with your girlfriend getting rid of your parents?'

'No.'

With the interview over, Jeremy was led back to a cell. At half-past six, he called out to DC Barlow: 'Could you hand this to Julie, please?'[14]

Barlow walked away, unfolding the piece of paper. It read: 'Hi, darling. Hope this gets to you from Stalag 13. Thinking about you. Sorry we're splitting up. I love you, Stinker.'[15] Later, Jeremy explained: 'I had been told by the police about the allegations Julie was making against me and I believed she was doing that out of spite because of splitting up. I wrote the note believing she would take everything back.'[16]

At 6.30am on Monday, 9 September, Matthew McDonald's girl-friend Christine Bacon was taken into custody. While officers searched her home, Christine was interviewed by DI Miller at Witham. Divorced and free to pursue a relationship with Matthew, the father of her youngest child, Christine knew surprisingly little about her lover's life. She was unable to say whether he was still married, what work he did or even where he lived.

She was on firmer ground when discussing Jeremy, declaring that there 'wasn't a lot of love lost' between him and his family, and that he had often spoken of his parents favouring his sister 'a great deal financially'.[1] He resented the fact that he was adopted and had talked about 'what he could do if his parents weren't around', which included buying 'a nice, fast car, running the business, and not [having] all the hassle with his father.' She believed him to be 'callous and aggressive enough' to have killed his family. Matthew hadn't spoken to him since Christmas, and Christine had sent the condolence card herself.

In Chelmsford at 8.30am, Assistant Chief Constable Peter Simpson chaired a conference attended by Chief Superintendent George Harris, DCI Charles Wright, Acting Chief Superintendent Mike Ainsley, DCI Taff Jones, and DS Stan Jones. Simpson asked each man in turn to give him the name of the killer. All answered 'Jeremy', apart from Taff, who maintained that he had seen nothing to dissuade him from his original theory. Nor was he convinced by Julie Mugford's testimony, since she had only come forward after being discarded by Jeremy. 'Taff would never, ever have admitted he was wrong,' Ainsley reflects. 'Not even if he'd lived to be a thousand. It's how he was. But George Harris was the Chief Superintendent Divisional Commander and present at White House Farm on the morning of the murders. Now, Harris had been a detective superintendent for fifteen years. And on that first morning he *and* Taff Jones decided Bamber was telling the truth.'[2]

At 9am, David Boutflour dialled Colin's number by mistake,

blurting out that the family had made statements to the police and that they were 'sure that Sheila couldn't have pulled the trigger'.[3] He couldn't say more, but warned Colin about 'a bombshell' in tomorrow's press. Asked if Jeremy knew about it, David replied grimly that he did, then ended the call.

Colin had already begun to question the official account of the murders, finding it too difficult to accept that Sheila had committed suicide in the room where her mother lay dead, rather than near the twins. But it had never occurred to him that Jeremy might be the killer and he suspected that the family were ganging up on his former brother-in-law because of financial matters. He telephoned Witham, where DI Miller denied any developments, then rang Heather. She called Witham and spoke to Stan Jones, who told her to be patient. Colin's calls to Jeremy went unanswered.

Colin and Heather had visited Sheila's flat a few hours after Jeremy's arrest the day before, without realizing that he had been taken into police custody. The detectives left behind to search the flat had gone; Colin entered using the key Jeremy had given him. It was obvious that anything valuable owned by Sheila had been removed from the premises. Although the police had also been issued with instructions to retain property belonging to the deceased, Colin found the photographs Jeremy had shown him. He binned the nude slides of his ex-wife but took home the albums of Nicholas and Daniel growing up.

A photograph of the twins found at the flat some time after Jeremy's arrest showed one of them pointing directly at the camera; it had been torn to pieces, as if someone saw the child's gesture not as a playful act, but an accusation.

At 11.26am on 9 September, Jeremy was formally charged with the Osea Road burglary.

His interview resumed around one o'clock. After questioning his behaviour at the funeral in Tolleshunt D'Arcy, which Jeremy attributed to 'manic depression', DCI Jones moved on to the Cartier watches brought back from Australia, asking whether they were stolen.[4]

'Stealing's the wrong word,' Jeremy replied.

'Was there an incident in Australia involving some Cartier watches you want to tell me about?'

'No comment.'

'Were you involved in stealing some diamonds in Australia?'

'Australia or New Zealand? I had some in New Zealand.'

'Did you steal them?'

'No comment.'

'Did you get involved dealing with hard drugs such as heroin whilst you were in Australia or New Zealand?'

'Never ever came across them.'

'We have received some information concerning the diamonds and Cartier watches. Why is it you don't want to tell me about those?'

'Because you have the wrong end of the stick.'

Jones then asked about the wills, which Jeremy had read out of 'inquisitiveness'. Barlow questioned him about his friendship with Matthew McDonald and whether he had ever been violent towards Suzette Ford, which Jeremy denied. He admitted that during the row with Julie at Sheila's flat he had 'grabbed her arms and put her on the bed' after she had broken the mirror and slapped his face.

'Did you say to her that the police wouldn't believe anything she said because you had just broken up?' Jones asked.

Jeremy shook his head. 'No, that was never talked about at all. I had no idea what she was scheming in her mind. I've told you the truth about having no involvement with regard to my parents' deaths. I've never spoken to anybody with regard to wanting to kill them.'

'What about arranging to have them killed?'

'No, I've never had anything to do with anyone with regard to arranging their deaths.' He paused. 'With regard to my involvement with the Cartier watches and diamonds, I've told a lot of people a lot of different stories to make me seem a bit of a Jack the Lad. But the truth is, that there was never any criminal activity or skullduggery. To explain the truth would just be simply embarrassing.'

Ainsley decided that Stan Jones and Mick Clark should conduct the next round of interviews. 'Jeremy had sized us up,' DC Barlow admitted. 'He knew we were making no headway.'[5]

When DS Davidson arrived to fingerprint him after the interview, Jeremy seemed in good spirits, remarking that the officer was wearing the same shirt last time they met. At 7pm, he appeared at Chelmsford Magistrates' Court in a specially convened hearing and was remanded in custody for three days, ostensibly to allow Essex Police to investigate him for possession and supply of drugs.

Christine Bacon was given accommodation for the night; Matthew had no idea that she had been taken into custody. When he let himself into her house that evening, Constables Collins and Delgado were waiting. Told that he was under arrest on suspicion of committing offences against the Firearms Act, Matthew was too stunned to respond. At Witham he learned he was a suspect in the Bamber murders and exclaimed: 'What – Jeremy?' before being seen by the Duty Sergeant and placed in a cell.[6]

Charles Marsden gave a statement that was of particular interest to detectives. He asserted that Jeremy had never 'made mention either in a jocular fashion or otherwise of doing harm to his family', except obliquely on one occasion in December 1984.[7] The two of them were in a Maldon wine bar when Jeremy commented that the whole family was getting together and that 'if the house were to burn down at Christmas everything would be his.' Charles thought it 'a strange thing to say' but dismissed it as typical Jeremy, trying to shock. Essex Police did not dismiss it: his statement chimed with what Julie had already told them about Jeremy's original plan – to raze White House Farm to the ground with his family trapped inside.

Colin awoke the next morning to find the newspapers saturated with stories about the murders. The *Sun* announced: 'Bambi: New Sensation – Model May Not Have Massacred Her Family', while the *Daily Mail* revealed that police were questioning a number of people including Jeremy, who had been charged with 'theft from a caravan site'. Aghast and sickened, Colin telephoned Witham, where Stan Jones confirmed that Jeremy and Brett had been arrested.

At 11am, officers headed back to White House Farm and Bourtree Cottage. DC Bird took a series of photographs of the farm, outbuildings, gardens and incinerators. At Bourtree Cottage, DC Sweeney fingerprinted Nevill's blue Citroen Pallas and took sweepings from it. At Witham, Matthew McDonald was questioned by DI Miller, who began by asking if he understood why he had been arrested. Matthew replied that he did, then drew his hands over his face, saying, 'I can't handle this, I really can't.'[8]

'Do you know a man called Jeremy Bamber?'

'I do.'

'Tell me about your relationship with him.'

'I met him about four and a half years ago in a wine bar, the Frog and Beans, and he was dressed bizarrely. He was wearing make up and bright red jeans . . .' Matthew described Jeremy as 'a cold fish. He may have hit Suzette, I don't know, it's only an opinion.' Asked if Jeremy had ever mentioned wanting to kill his parents, Matthew reacted: 'No! Christ no.' He vigorously denied any involvement in the shootings, stating that if Jeremy had approached him about murder, 'I would have grassed him up straight away.'

Jeremy's interview had also resumed, with DS Stan Jones questioning him in the presence of DC Clark and solicitor Bruce Bowler. Earlier, while escorting Jeremy to the interview room, Jones had been unable to resist sniping: 'You did it, didn't you? I knew you did it from the second day. You won't get away with this. You're sick, you need help.'[9] Confident that he would get a confession out of Jeremy, he intended to put the two days spent working with Julie on her statement to good use. After covering the early stages of the couple's relationship, he declared: 'Julie has made a thirty page statement outlining her association with you and she states that you told her you arranged the murders of your family. Is that right?'[10]

'No. She's lying on that particular point.'

'Is it correct that you didn't like Sheila, who you thought was crazy?'

'That's untrue. I loved my sister but could not understand, in the last few years, her mental illness.'

'Did you dislike your parents?'

'No.'

After questioning Jeremy about his income, Jones asserted:

'Julie says that some time in 1984 you mentioned about killing your whole family.'

'She's lying,' Jeremy repeated. Jones asked him what he stood to gain in the event of his parents' deaths.

'Nothing.'

'Surely if your mum and dad died you would be left something.'

'True.'

'What would you be left?'

'You can see the wills. Look at the wills.'

'Would you and Sheila be left half shares, basically?'

'Yes.'

'What about the twins?'

'I don't remember if they're mentioned in the wills. I think they are but I'm not sure. Certainly not in name.'

'So if Sheila and your parents died, you would basically get everything.'

'Understandably so.'

Jones spent some time going over his inheritance before breaking for lunch. When they reconvened at half-past two, Jeremy insisted that he had never discussed killing his family with Julie, but there were 'many reasons' why she would lie about it, particularly 'jilted love'.

Jones asked: 'If she was jilted and accused you of murder and you were charged, she would have lost you anyway. So how can you say jilted?'

'Yes, she has lost me, but if she could put me behind bars, then nobody else could have me either,' Jeremy reasoned.

'She states that some time last year you told her that you would like to kill all the family, which included Sheila and the twins. Do you remember that?'

'I never said anything of the sort.'

'She states that she said to you, "I can understand you talking like that about your parents, but why kill Sheila and the twins, as they have done nothing to you?" Do you remember her saying that?'

'It was never spoken about, ever.'

Jones turned to the matter of June's bicycle. Jeremy said that he had transported it to the cottage in his car for Julie's use and denied using it to travel home after murdering his family. Asked whether he had a key to the farmhouse, Jeremy replied that he had one to the door that the police had broken down and received a key to the new door about a week after it was fitted.

'When Julie and you have gone to the house have you got into the house other than through doors?' Jones queried.

'I can't remember doing so with Julie.'

'Do you know of a way of getting in and out of the house other than by the door?'

'There are many ways to get into the house, ie., windows.'

'What do you mean? Insecure windows?'

'Insecure windows, secure windows, it makes no difference,' Jeremy replied. 'With sash windows you can flick the catch with any thin metal object and open the window, but you can't close them from the outside.'

Jones asked again if he knew of a clandestine way in and out of the house. Jeremy replied, 'I know ways in, and one can always climb out of the pane window, but you can't close catches or lock bolts or turn keys.'

Jones nodded. 'Only, you see, Julie states that there was a window in the house with a catch on it: you can open the window and close it, bang on the frame from the outside and the catch will close, giving the appearance that the window is secure and *is* in fact secure. Furthermore, she states that you told her of such a window. Did you tell her?'

'I don't think so.'

Jones frowned. 'Surely the answer should be no, shouldn't it? Because you have just said you don't know of such a window in the White House.'

'"I don't think so" is another way of saying no,' Jeremy answered. He added that Julie might have spotted such a window while she was at the house.

'Are you telling me that she's in your parents' house and she's going round trying to find a way in and out without anybody knowing?'

'She might do, to make her story look better.'

'What story?'

'The allegations against me having involvement in my family's deaths.'

'When are you saying she's done this then?'

'I'm not suggesting she has or hasn't but she has had opportunity in the last six weeks.'

Jones pointed out that he and Julie had 'parted company' around 1 September.

'Our relationship has been unsteady for a long time,' Jeremy responded.

Asked about the sleeping pills Julie had been prescribed by her doctor, Jeremy stated that he hadn't touched them and didn't pay much attention to them.

Jones persevered, 'But she did bring the pills down?'

'They were her medication that she brought with her.'

'It is true she brought them down?'

'They were her medication and she brought them with her.'

'So she is telling the truth when she says that she brought the pills down to your house when she was doing her teaching practice last year?'

'She needed the tranquillisers so she brought them with her.'

'So she is telling the truth about the pills, that she brought them down to Goldhanger?'

'She brought her medication down with her, yes.'

'Yes what?'

'Yes, she brought her medication to Goldhanger.'

Jones shook his head: 'You don't like to tell me that Julie tells the truth. It's quite obvious to me that she's telling the truth when she says she brought the pills down to Goldhanger. She says she did and you confirmed it. That is the truth which you try to deny. It's obviously true what she said and I feel the reason you won't admit she is telling the truth is because I might believe her when she says you told her the story of trying the pills out to use them on murder. What do you say to that?'

'She did bring her medication down to Goldhanger for her tension or whatever and not for me.'

'Did you ask Julie to marry you?'

For the first time, Jeremy seemed nonplussed, asking if he could have a word with his solicitor in private. Jones refused: 'I'm conducting an interview. I'd like you to answer the question.'

'Marriage was talked about,' Jeremy conceded.

'Julie states that prior to Christmas 1984 you asked her to marry you. Is that true?'

'I can't answer that question without having a word with my solicitor but marriage was talked about.'

'Did you discuss going to a registry office to get married at some time?'

Jeremy hesitated again. 'A registry office was discussed.'

'So Julie is telling the truth when she says marriage was discussed and the registry office was discussed?'

Bruce Bowler interjected: 'I suggest you answer "no reply" to that question. You obviously don't want to discuss it.'

After ascertaining that June had offered to buy Julie a flat in order to prevent her living at Bourtree Cottage, Jones moved on to the day of the shootings, asking Jeremy to describe his activities. He related them as before.

'Did you sleep?' Jones asked.

'Like a log.'

'You were woken by a telephone call from your father, is that right?'

'Yes.'

'As a result of that phone call I understand you tried to phone him back but got an engaged tone?'

'Yes.'

'You then phoned Chelmsford police station and told them what had happened. Is that right?'

'No, I think I phoned Julie before them.'

'Why phone Julie before phoning the police?'

'I don't remember my reasons.'

Jones persisted with the same line of questioning until Jeremy eventually snapped in exasperation: 'My *first* statement is the true one and it shows how easy it is to muddle events . . .'

Sensing that his energy was flagging, Jones said, 'So to finalise this: your first statement states you phoned the police first and then Julie. Is that the correct and honest version?'

'Yes.'

Jones called a halt to the interview for something to eat. Half an hour later, the war of nerves began again.

Matthew McDonald's interview resumed at 3.10pm that day. He admitted that on the night of the murders he was neither with Christine nor his wife, but with another woman. When DI Miller told him that Jeremy had been planning the murders for a long time, Matthew responded: 'Has he? Well, he's an evil bastard then and he's even more evil for involving other people.'[1] After providing a blood sample he was led back to a detention room for the night.

At five past six, Stan Jones sat down again with Jeremy, who refused to be tied on the order of the calls. 'I am asking you a straightforward, simple question. Did you phone the police first and Julie after?' Jones demanded.[2]

'If I reply how I want to, which is yes, I think so, you will just ask me again and again and again.'

'So you're answering "yes" to my questions?'

Bruce Bowler interjected: 'I would advise you not to make any further reply.'

Jones ignored him: 'You see, Mr Bamber, we know that at about 3.26am that morning you phoned the police. We know that at 3.15am you phoned Julie up. What have you got to say about this?'

'You are very clever men to prove both clocks were accurate,' Jeremy replied.

'I will tell you the police clock on Control is always accurate. I will tell you that the clock in the house where you phoned Julie showed 3.15am, and might even have been minutes fast. In view of this it looks as if you received a phone call from your father who said something like, "Sheila's gone crazy, she has got a gun." The next thing you do is to phone your girlfriend up and then about ten minutes after, you phone the police up. I think that most people having received the message you received from your father would have phoned up the police straight away. Why didn't you?'

'What you have just written is your opinion. No comment.'

'What did you say to your girlfriend when you phoned her up?'

'I cannot remember. You tell me.'

When Jones asked why he had called Julie at all, Jeremy replied, 'I probably felt pissed off by the reaction from the police and needed a friendly ear.'

'But we know you made the phone call to Julie before you phoned the police.'

'That's your opinion – no comment.'

'What happens if it's proven that it's fact?'

'Hypothetical question. Can I have a cup of tea?'

Jeremy had his cup of tea and a toilet break. He was calm for the remainder of the interview, but tested the officers' patience. Jones recalled: 'Bamber frequently stared at me and quite often had what I would describe as a sly grin on his face. He frequently pulled pieces of fibres off his jumper which he chewed and constantly wound round his tongue and pulled in his teeth with his fingers. He would occasionally hook a piece of fibre to his teeth and pluck the fibre with his other hand.'[3]

Clark found him equally disagreeable: 'He occasionally answered a question with the words "Yes," which was said with a musical tone, giving the appearance of sounding sarcastic.'[4] He rarely gave a straightforward reply; asked how long he had spent on the tractor in the hours before the murders, he responded that it was 'impossible to say' even approximately, and repeatedly denied telling Julie that the crime would have to be that night.

'So she made that bit up?' Jones asked.

'Yes,' Jeremy replied.

Jones told him: 'You had discussed with her so many times killing your parents and family that she knew what you were saying. "Tonight is the night, or never." What do you say about that?'

'She has a fertile imagination.'

'But they did get killed a few hours later. Do you agree?'

Jeremy said slowly, 'My parents and family did die on the morning of the seventh of August . . .'

At 9pm, Jones brought the interview to a close and Jeremy was led back to his cell.

A few hours earlier, Susan Battersby had been taken into protective custody after returning from Ibiza. Julie was in the same building, but they were kept apart. Interviewed at length, Susan confessed to the cheque fraud she and Julie had committed and was told that a report would be sent to the Director of Public Prosecutions to ascertain what action should be taken. She was then released without charge.

Julie had not previously mentioned the matter of the cheques 'because I wasn't really talking about me', but while continuing her statement that evening she too admitted the illicit spending spree.[5]

Later, she recalled feeling terrified that 'no one would believe me and they would put me in a mental institution. I believed the police would find out everything.' Her fears were unfounded; senior investigating officer Mike Ainsley observed that during her 'extremely long and arduous sessions of interview' with various officers, Julie 'never faltered in what she had to say'.[6] Her evidence was 'thoroughly investigated and tested' and he had 'no doubts whatsoever' that she spoke the truth.[7]

The headlines on Wednesday, 11 September focused again on the Bamber murders. The *Mirror* and the *Sun* declared that 'Bambi Owed Drug Barons £40,000' while the *Daily Mail* ran a story about the 'Drugs Ring Riddle of Farm Massacre Model', following the discovery of the registered letter from Scotland, which led to wild speculation that Sheila 'could have played a part in a drugs chain stretching from Essex to London's wealthy society'.

A team of officers began carrying out house-to-house enquiries in Tolleshunt D'Arcy and Goldhanger, while at White House Farm and Bourtree Cottage the Scenes of Crime operation continued. A local man handed in two torches he had found in the field immediately opposite the farm and a polythene bag containing Marigold gloves was recovered near a ditch. Together with some items of clothing from the burning pit, the polythene bag was sent for further examination. Forensic scientist John Hayward discovered three small bloodstains on the front seat of Nevill's blue Citroen Pallas but tests to determine whether they were of human origin were unsuccessful. He examined June's bicycle at Chelmsford police station but was unable to detect any blood. Following a call from David Boutflour, the telescopic sight and ammunition were finally collected from Oak Farm.

Two fingerprints had been identified on the Anschütz: the

mark on the butt belonged to Sheila, while the mark on the barrel was from Jeremy's right forefinger. DI Cook stated that there were actually a number of fingerprints on the gun, including three on the barrel, but these contained insufficient detail for identification. He had 'expected to find more of Sheila Caffell's fingerprints on the gun . . . Had she extensively and firmly handled the gun with unprotected hands prior to her death, I would have expected to see more evidence of finger marks or ridge detail on the gun, especially those areas associated with the normal gripping or holding of the gun when firing, loading etc.'[8] Assuming that Sheila was the killer, he could only surmise that 'she could have worn some form of protection on her hands or possibly that she did not handle the gun that extensively.'

Ballistics expert Malcolm Fletcher compiled a report on all the bullets recovered from the bodies, noting that the majority were 'suggestive', 'strongly suggestive' or 'very strongly suggestive' of having been fired from the Anschütz.[9] There was no evidence that they had been fired from any other weapon; it was simply that the bullets were too badly contorted to allow for absolutes. For instance, Fletcher found that bullet PV/20, the non-fatal neck shot from Sheila, was 'extensively damaged – probably hit bone', while PV/19, the fatal chin shot, was also 'badly damaged' with its nose 'mushroomed and one side flattened.' A bullet recovered from the base of Nevill's skull was 'flattened', 'mushroomed' and its 'nose chewed and gouged', leaving not enough 'detail for matching'. The cartridge cases were in good condition generally and could be positively linked with the Anschütz.

Miller and Clark commenced interviewing Matthew McDonald again at 9.25am on Wednesday. They covered the same ground as before, but in more depth. Asked why Jeremy had pointed the finger at him, Matthew floundered: 'I don't know what to say. It's all fabrication . . . He must be a monster, involving all these people.'[10]

Jeremy's interview resumed at 11am, with solicitor Richard Pirie joining them in place of Bruce Bowler. Jones began by announcing: 'I will tell you now that it has been proved that your sister Sheila did not kill herself and in fact she was murdered along with your parents and the twins. Is there anything you wish to say about this?'[11] When Pirie reminded Jeremy that he was under no obligation to reply, Jones continued: 'In view of this, what you have told us about your father phoning you in the early hours of the seventh of August, saying words to the effect, "Sheila has gone crazy, she has got a gun," cannot be true, can it?'

Jeremy replied, 'As in my first statement and on talking to the police on the night, I was unsure whether he said, "Sheila" or "she" has—'

'You have told and put in writing to us that you said, "Sheila's gone crazy", you told police officers who came to the scene with you it was Sheila, and you have repeated to us and to your girlfriend it was Sheila that had gone crazy. Are you now changing Sheila to "she has" for the first time?'

'No. I'm just saying . . . I've got to get my words right . . .' Jeremy hesitated. 'I'm just trying to remember the question. It's easy to make conclusions as to what was going on and at the time until now I have been told that Sheila did it.'

They argued back and forth, with Jones suggesting that he was changing his story, which Jeremy denied. When Jones declared that he didn't believe there was any call from Nevill, Jeremy replied, 'Telecom must be able to tell you the times or phone calls on my parents' phone.'

'What do you mean by that?'

'It would be proof that I received a phone call from my father.'

BT experts had examined the telephones at the farm and found them to be working normally. They explained that if Nevill had ended a call to Jeremy without replacing the receiver or pressing the cradle buttons, the line would have remained open, preventing Jeremy dialling out on his own telephone. Picking up his receiver, he would find himself still connected to White House Farm. The difficulty was in determining how long the line would remain open until the 'forced release' of the equipment, dependent on time elements called meter pulses, which determined the cost of a call. The first meter pulse was activated when the phone was answered and occurred at regular intervals afterwards. A call from Tolleshunt D'Arcy to Goldhanger overnight would result in meter pulses every eight minutes. If it was simply abandoned, then the force release would activate somewhere between eight to sixteen minutes, and Jeremy could not have used his own telephone until that point. However, the situation was straightforward enough if the call had been deliberately ended.[12]

Jones abandoned the subject of telephones to ask whether the socks found beside Sheila's body were his. 'If you show me the socks, I might be able to identify them,' Jeremy answered. 'But to my knowledge, I have very few clothes at my parents' house and I'm pretty certain that my father didn't have any of my socks.'

They discussed ownership of the Anschütz and when Jeremy had last handled it before that night. He was unable to answer. Jones quizzed him on why he'd wanted a shotgun and his ability with firearms generally. Following a brief lunch break, Jones asked a series of rapid, unrelated questions, before suddenly querying when he last saw Charles Marsden prior to the shootings.

'It could be weeks,' Jeremy replied.

'Do you remember me yesterday putting to you that Julie had said that you intended to drug the family and burn the farm down when they were all in it?'

'You did say something like that yesterday.'

'You said she was telling lies,' Jones prompted.

'I think my reply was that.'

'You see, Charles Marsden also says the same thing. He says that around Christmas time last year when all the family – ie., your parents, Sheila and the twins – were there, you told him that if you burnt the house down with them all in it you would get everything. Is he telling lies as well?'

'I do not remember ever discussing that and my conclusion is that he is.'

'Julie is telling lies and he is telling lies. For what reason?'

'No comment.'

Jones asked again about his movements before bed. Jeremy told him he had watched a programme called *Recovery* and described it in general terms. Jones explained that *Recovery* started ten minutes after Jeremy said he had gone to bed. Jeremy replied that he must have got his timings wrong. He gave permission for the police to inspect his bank and building society accounts and answered several questions about the insurance on the contents of White House Farm.

At quarter to five, the interview was paused for two hours. Returning, Jones asked: 'Did you decide not to burn the house down because of the valuables in it? Because Julie says you did.'

'You are implying that I planned to burn the house, which is lies,' Jeremy responded.

'She has said it and Charles Marsden also says you said it to him. Are they both lying?'

'Yes.'

'What for?'

'Matter of opinion.'

'You could say she is lying perhaps because of a broken down romance, but what reason would he have for saying such things about you?'

'Who knows.'

After another series of rapid, seemingly random questions, Jones asked, 'Do you still love Julie?'

'No comment.'

'Didn't you give DC Barlow a piece of paper with a message on it to be delivered to her since you have been in custody?'

'That was personal and you had no right to read it.'

'What did it say in the letter or note?'

'No comment.'

'Do you love Julie?'

'No comment.'

After a pause, Jones asked: 'Was Sheila a good shot with a rifle?'

'Don't know. I hadn't been with her shooting targets.'

'Have you ever seen her shoot?'

'Can't remember.'

Jones took a breath. 'I will tell you that no one I have spoken to has ever seen her fire a gun, and you say you can't remember, so it could well be she has never fired a gun in her life. Would you agree?'

'No.'

'You say you can't remember her ever firing a gun. Why say no to my question?'

'Because she might have.'

'I will tell you this, in excess of over 20 bullets were fired into the bodies of your family. I won't tell you the exact amount but I will tell you every one apart from one hit the target.'[13]

Jeremy's face whitened. 'You're a hard bastard – I don't want to know about things like that.'

'Would you agree that it would take a very good shot to achieve that?'

'No comment.'

DC Clark remembered that moment with curiosity. Jeremy's evident boredom and mild irritation had turned to something more tangible – even vulnerable. But the interview concluded at 8.35pm and 'almost immediately Bamber changed from appearing upset to being quite jovial.'[14] Humming while signing his contemporaneous notes, Jeremy then scraped back his chair, nodding: 'Goodnight Stan, goodnight Mick, I'll see you in the morning,' and smiled.

By Thursday, 12 September, Mike Ainsley was 'totally satisfied' that Matthew McDonald was not involved in the Bamber murders 'and, in fact, would not know one end of a firearm from the other'.[1] With his alibi confirmed, Matthew was released.

DS Jones began questioning Jeremy again shortly before noon. Asked about the silencer, Jeremy stated that the Anschütz was too long for its case with it attached, 'so most times it was used without'.[2] He had taken the silencer off the weapon 'many times' and it was 'so simple, a five year old could do it'.

'Do you think Sheila killed herself?' Jones asked.

'Yes, I do,' Jeremy replied.

'Why?'

'I don't know . . . I think one would want to kill oneself after what happened.'

'Will you accept from me that she did not kill herself?'

'Not really.'

'I will tell you she has two shots fired into her and I understand that either or both would have been fatal. Now what do you have to say?'

Jeremy gave a small shrug, 'I can't really comment, can I?'

'You must agree that if the first bullet wound was fatal, she could not have shot another one into herself,' Jones persisted. 'Is that right?'

'No, I don't believe that.'

'Why don't you believe?'

'Automatic gun, nerves, anything could have triggered the gun again,' Jeremy said vaguely. 'The dog . . . I think you're right, but you sound so one hundred percent.'

'What do you mean – one hundred percent?'

'You say it's impossible.'

'You're not saying *the dog* pulled the trigger for the second one, are you?' Jones gave him an incredulous look.

'I'm not saying anything, but nothing's impossible,' Jeremy replied.

'You said anything could have triggered the second shot off

and you mentioned the dog,' Jones insisted. 'Are you saying that after Sheila had been shot once, the dog came along and pulled the trigger for the second shot?'

'It was only an idea. The dog was in the house.'

'I suggest you knew where the dog was that night,' Jones said. 'That's why you mentioned the dog. It was found in the room that morning near the bodies. Did you know that?'

'You told me that.'

'Do you accept that Sheila couldn't have shot herself two times?'

'No.'

Jones then discussed the grey hair, blood and paint on the silencer, demanding: 'Did you fake a suicide and four murders, Mr Bamber?'

'No,' said Jeremy.

After a long lunch break, Jones asked whether he had recently handled the Bible found next to Sheila's body. 'I could have handled it,' Jeremy conceded.

'For what reason could you have handled it?'

'To threaten the dog.'

'When would this have been?'

'No comment.'

'During the morning of the murder?'

'No.'

'How long before?'

'You asked me for any reason. I gave you one of many possibilities.'

'Have you read that bible recently – prior to the murders?'

'I can't say whether I have ever read that particular bible, but my mother's I had handled, but not read.'

'If you was to pick that bible up purely to frighten off the dog, your fingers wouldn't be inside it, would they?' Jones asked.

'That's your opinion,' Jeremy replied. 'Depends on how it was picked up.'

Jones went over the telephone calls to Julie again, asking Jeremy why he insisted on splitting hairs. 'Splitting hairs is the wrong word,' Jeremy retorted. 'This is not a friendly chat, it's important for the truth to be said and for me to feel satisfied with my answers.'

Jones then told him that only one fingerprint belonging to Sheila had been found on the gun, potentially giving credence to Julie's statement that he had been worried about fingerprints. Asked for a response, Jeremy answered: 'I can't really make any comment, other than I had nothing to do with the murders and that fingerprints is your department.'

After a further two hour break, questioning recommenced at 7.30pm. Jones asked Jeremy to look at a photograph of the telephone on the kitchen worktop with the ammunition beside it.

'Before I see the photograph is it in any way disturbing?'

'No, it is not.'

Jones pushed the image across the table. Jeremy pointed to a photograph on the worktop. 'Picture of my mum,' he said quietly.

'Is that where you left the cartridges, as far as you can remember?'

'I left them on the side there [the kitchen worktop].'

Jones told him: 'That phone, if we are to believe you, should have been handled by your father. There is no sign of any blood on it, which is remarkable considering your dad was injured upstairs and eventually killed downstairs. I suggest that you killed your father, lifted the phone off the hook to substantiate your astonishing story about not being able to phone him back. Did you do what I have just said?'

'No.'

Jones asked if he had entered the house via any windows recently. Jeremy nodded: 'Kitchen windows, scullery windows, downstairs toilet window and sitting room window. In the last six months, I can't say how many times I've done it.'

'Have you ever got in a window by putting something in between the window frames, like a knife to move the catch, so you could slide a window open?'

'Yes.'

'Which window in the White House have you done that to?'

'Downstairs toilet and the lounge window.'

Jones pulled out a photograph of the shower room: 'You've been into that room by using a knife, moving the catch and then getting in at some time or another?'

'Yes,' Jeremy said.

Jones asked about the conversation with Sheila in the rape field hours before the murders, but Jeremy couldn't remember what was said.

Jones then told him: 'I put it to you that over a period of time you were obsessed with the idea of killing your family so you could have the benefits of everything your parents had worked for. I believe that you murdered your family and made it look as if Sheila had done it and then committed suicide. Julie's said this, and some of the things she said you told her have in fact been true.' He gave Jeremy a penetrating look. 'Did you kill the members of your family?'

Jeremy returned the detective's clear gaze: 'No, I did not. And I did not have any plans to do so, or any involvement in their deaths.'

It was 9.55pm. Three days of intense questioning were over. Senior investigating officer Mike Ainsley regarded Jeremy's replies throughout as 'an exercise in avoiding the issue. Bamber proved himself to be a very shrewd subject, but at the same time painting a picture of himself as a very devious character indeed, leaving the interviewing officers in no doubt that he was directly responsible for the five murders.'[3]

Jeremy states that after he was led down to his cell for the night, DCI Taff Jones paid him a visit:

> He looked at me and he said: 'We're letting you out.' I went: 'Great.' He said, 'That Julie's full of shit.' Those were his words: 'That Julie's full of shit.' And off I went. In my own mind I knew that she was just angry about things. And I actually thought that I would be able to go and see her and say to her: 'What's all that about? I'm sorry. I didn't realise that my behaviour would so upset you that you'd be [prepared] to lie.' And I genuinely thought I was going to go and see her, after getting out of the police station. She was put in police protective custody from then on.[4]

Jeremy appeared the following morning, Friday 13 September, at Chelmsford Magistrates' Court, where he was granted bail until 16 October. His Uncle Robert was astounded to receive a telephone call from Betty Howie, who declared that she and her husband intended to stand bail: 'I told her there was enough in my file to hang him.'⁵ Colin had his own reservations as he departed for a few days' escape in Cornwall: 'Everything was going crazy but I still wasn't completely satisfied that it wasn't just his relations ganging up on him.'⁶

After the hearing, Jeremy was met by Rodney Brown, owner of the Caribbean Cottage, who had borrowed a white Jaguar for the occasion. Sitting beside him was Angela Greaves, Virginia's older sister. A beautician six years Jeremy's senior, 'Anji' had quickly grown close to Jeremy following his visits with Virginia: 'The poor chap was on Valium and he was drinking. He had nobody to turn to. His relatives were fighting over everything. It was awful, absolutely awful.'⁷ Anji later told the *Sun* that she and Jeremy became lovers before his arrest and that it was their affair, rather than his with her sister, that had led to Julie being so inflamed with jealousy that she named him as the murderer.

Regardless of what lay behind Julie's motivation, Anji was there to meet Jeremy upon his release. Rodney drove to Witham Police Station, where grim-faced detectives including Mike Ainsley watched their arrival. 'The court bailed him knowing full well why we'd taken him there,' Ainsley remembers. 'He turned up in a Jaguar with this guy who owned a restaurant in Burnham-on-Crouch and sat there smirking. I said to him, "We'll see who's smirking at the end of all this, shall we?"'⁸ He left Jeremy at the reception desk and walked up to the first floor. Gathering his belongings, Jeremy looked up and gave the detective a final glance before leaving for a wine bar in town. Rodney and Anji saw him onto the London train later that afternoon.

Jeremy spent the evening with Brett at Peppermint Park, a cocktail bar and restaurant in Covent Garden. He telephoned Michael Deckers around 1am, slurring: 'The police think that I've committed a murder.'⁹ Michael asked if he had a solicitor. Jeremy replied that he did. 'He also said that he had been told by the police not to contact certain people,' Michael recalled. 'He was adamant he was not involved and he said there was no evidence.' Jeremy continued his night out with Brett, heading to Stringfellow's and the Sunrise Café, returning to Sheila's flat at daybreak.

The two of them spent Sunday shopping and eating out,

aware that their movements were being monitored by the police, who continued to observe them until the early hours of Monday morning. Ainsley called off the exercise because 'I couldn't in all honesty justify watching Mr Bamber enjoying himself in London.'[10]

Although displeased by the magistrates' decision, Ainsley acknowledges that it gave him 'sufficient time to muster a team of detectives who, in turn, would have time to carry out the tasks allotted to them without the pressure that can apply when they have remanded prisoners in custody'. He recalls being 'very, very aware that the reputation of the police service, to which I had given the whole of my working life, was at stake. I knew, in spite of what was being said, that we had made a mistake. I use the singular because the one big mistake which then set the course for all of the subsequent action prior to 7th September, was the belief in Jeremy's story.'

Forensic work continued: DC Bird visited White House Farm the day before Jeremy's release with DI Cook to photograph the scratches on the mantelpiece above the Aga. He also collected a number of items, including the socks found next to Sheila, which were thought to have been removed by Nevill when he climbed into bed earlier that evening and were of interest only because of the blood spots on them.[11] At the laboratory in Huntingdon, Malcolm Fletcher examined the Anschütz, noting its measurements and any damage before checking the mechanism. 'In terms of blood, viewing it externally, there was very little visible,' he recalls.[12] The Anschütz test fired normally, but he observed: 'The magazine is progressively harder to load as the number of cartridges in the magazine increases; loading the tenth cartridge is exceptionally difficult.'[13] Today he reflects: 'You had to really press the last few hard and slide them into the magazine.'

Fletcher also discovered a fault with the reloading mechanism: 'The slide that you pulled back to release a cartridge from the magazine into the chamber sometimes didn't go back far enough to let the cartridge case be drawn out, fire one and throw it out to the side of the weapon as normal. The cartridge case would be partially out and the slide would fly forward again, trapping the case in the chamber. This happened when I was doing my tests and again later, when the jury asked for a demonstration of the gun being fired: part way through the sequence of firing a full magazine, the cartridge case jammed in the chamber and the ejection port.' The fault provided one explanation for the cartridge case found on the stairs, although cartridge cases 'bounce and roll, and it's just as possible that they get picked up on clothing or kicked by someone walking past. The ejection pattern on this gun was to the right and [it was] a matter of two or three feet where the case would normally fall. But that was certainly one possibility.'

The test firings, together with Fletcher's study of the crime scene photographs, victims' clothing and X-rays, and statements from Vanezis, Hayward and Elliott, enabled him to estimate the range from which the bullets were fired. Several were contact or close contact wounds; the furthest was little more than three feet away. Firearms discharge residues were present on the cloth pull-through from the barrel of the rifle, but he was unable to determine whether any of the bullets had passed through the silencer.

Fletcher recalls that 'the biologist wanted to examine the baffles inside the silencer for blood. I assisted John Hayward in dismantling it. Very simply, that was done by unscrewing the front of the silencer and then sliding out the baffles. We tried to keep them in the same order and the same positions. I vaguely recall paint deposits and talk about the silencer having struck the mantelpiece.'

Hayward recorded 'a considerable amount of blood inside the muzzle end of the baffles'.[14] The blood in the silencer was due to a phenomenon known as 'back-spatter', whereby the expansion of gases generated by a bullet being discharged creates back pressure, which in turn propels blood from the wound back towards the gun. The effect is only seen when the muzzle of the gun is either in contact with or in very close contact to the victim. Further tests were needed to establish whether the blood was human in origin and, if so, to whom it belonged.

On the evening of Jeremy's release from custody, DS Davidson was dispatched to Bourtree Cottage to locate the grey jogging bottoms Jeremy had worn on the day of the murders. After finding two pairs, Davidson walked about the place. It was a typical bachelor pad, nicely decorated with a smart kitchen and all the latest gadgets and technology, including a top-of-the-range stereo. Curious to find out what Jeremy had been listening to before his arrest, Davidson switched the stereo on and the distinctive, jangling bars of Tears for Fears' recent summer hit 'Everybody Wants To Rule The World' filled the house.

On Monday 16 September, Jeremy and Brett lunched in a Chelmsford pub with *Sun* journalist Michael Fielder. Brett had met Fielder the previous week, when he rang the newspaper to offer them a story on Jeremy in return for a lift back to Chelmsford. 'Bambi Police Blaming My Pal Jeremy' had appeared in Friday's paper.

Fielder later gave a detailed account of their Monday meeting, stating that Jeremy wanted £20,000 for twenty nude photographs of Sheila and a large fee for his life story. Fielder agreed to view the photographs at Morshead Mansions but his editor vetoed it, sensing that a story about Jeremy's attempts to sell the photographs would make for more explosive headlines than explicit shots they couldn't publish anyway. The *Sun* ran the piece the following day, telling its readers: 'The brother of farmhouse massacre model Bambi Caffell was trying to cash in on the horror yesterday – by peddling soft-porn pictures of her. Smiling Jeremy Bamber, 24, offered topless and full frontal nude pictures of Bambi for "a substantial sum."' Jeremy was quoted as saying, 'Unless the offer is really good, I'm not interested.'

An affiliate website to Jeremy's campaign pages today denounces Fielder's account, insisting that Jeremy met the *Sun* reporter against his better judgment and that Fielder repeatedly pressed for any nude shots of Sheila which were 'never obtained' because 'they didn't exist'.[15] But Sheila's friend has spoken at length about helping her prepare for the photo session, and Colin saw the resulting slides for himself, discussing them both in his witness statements and his memoir. He recalls that Jeremy's description of the photographs to Fielder – 'They show everything, right down to the last detail' – was identical to the words Jeremy had used to him.

The *Evening Standard* ran a follow up story that day, after one of their journalists spoke to Jeremy at Sheila's flat. Peter Gruner recalled that Jeremy hadn't denied the *Sun's* claims, responding, 'That is interesting, but I have yet to read the papers today,' although he did confirm, 'I want a lot of money for my story, about £100,000. I think newspapers tend to make up stories about me.' Colin saw the headlines in Cornwall only moments after posting a letter to Jeremy in which he expressed concern about the photographs. He immediately wrote a second letter expressing anger that Jeremy had tried to sell the images. He then regretted it, fearing he had placed himself in danger, and left to stay with friends in Somerset.

Jeremy and Brett departed for the south of France after the story broke, travelling to Dover in the silver Astra. They enjoyed a week of sun, sea and relaxation during a caravan holiday in St Tropez. In a 1986 interview with the *Star*, Brett declared that Jeremy 'fell in love with a millionairess. She fell for him. There weren't many girls he couldn't pull. He was an absolute charmer. He had a great time making love to her, sunbathing and drinking. I warned him he was suspect number one on the police list for the killings, but he wasn't bothered. He just wanted to enjoy himself while he could. But I knew a storm was brewing for him at home.'

While the number one suspect departed for France, a round table conference took place at the laboratory in Huntingdon. Present were senior investigating officer Mike Ainsley, DCI Taff Jones, DCI Charles Wright, DI Miller, DI Cook, DI Wilkinson, DS Jones, Branch Crown Prosecutor David Adams, Dr Peter Vanezis and a number of scientific staff. Among the issues raised was Sheila's hand swabs, taken at the mortuary. Ainsley insisted that they should be examined irrespective of cost to detect any residue from the gun and cartridges.

Ballistics expert Malcolm Fletcher recalls: 'The ammunition used to carry out the murders was Eley Subsonic. The bullets themselves were coated with beeswax, which was quite unusual. When you handled them you got a sort of black grease on your hands and when they were discharged, small specks of grease or wax were emitted, not just with the bullet but from the ejection port as well. It would have been very visible.'[1] Forensic scientist Brian Elliot recorded 'very low levels of lead' from Sheila's hand swabs.[2] Comparison tests with two members of laboratory staff who loaded a total of eighteen cartridges into the magazine from the rifle, showed significantly higher levels of lead. Elliot concluded: 'I would expect the hands of a person loading cartridges into the rifle to bear appreciable deposits of lead. No such deposits have been found on the hand swabs from Sheila Caffell.'

The lack of damage to her fingernails appeared to support his findings. Varying in length from long to very long, Sheila's nails were real rather than synthetic. DC Bird recalls 'being in the studio with Ainsley and the technician, enlarging the mortuary photographs of her hands and fixing them to the walls for examination. Sheila's long nails were unbroken.'[3] The original images show her scarlet nail polish only very slightly worn at the tips – not chipped – indicating that she had painted them some days earlier. The matching varnish on her toenails has the same slight wearing.

Her feet were clean, save for a couple of minor bloodspots on the soles, suggesting that she hadn't walked through the kitchen, where the floor into the hallway was stippled with blood, but creating a puzzle regarding the blood-streaked bedroom carpet. Pathologist Dr Vanezis explains that the area of marking and porousness of the carpet should be taken into account: 'An expert on blood spatter might tell you that small spots of blood on the carpet won't transfer so easily, particularly if it's more or less dried. If she'd been carried, would that have been willingly? No, I can't see that. The other thing is: if a gun had been held to her head, she would have been led there and told to lie down. Jeremy would then have to get round this blood, thinking he mustn't touch it. I think it was just small amounts of blood on the carpet and it was the luck of the draw whether she got any on her feet or not.'[4]

Sheila's turquoise nightdress was also tested for firearm residue and oil. None was detected, although the 1986 internal review stated that 'the significance of this would depend on the position of the gun in relation to her body and the nightdress at the time it was fired.' But Fletcher remains confident that wax discharged from the fired bullets would have resulted in 'some of that material ending up on the shooter. I tested the surface of Sheila's nightdress and I got no indication, either visual or chemical, of lead or wax material. I would have expected to find it, especially with the number of shots that were fired. I tested it thoroughly and there was no evidence of the spots of waxy material that showed up on the test fires.' The blood on the nightdress was Sheila's own; both Fletcher and Vanezis agree that had she been the killer, blood from the other victims would have been detected on the garment.

The human blood found on the outside of the silencer was insufficient for grouping purposes, but inside there was a considerable amount of blood on the four or five baffles nearest the end from which the bullet would exit. Comparing the test results to blood samples from the five deceased and one from Jeremy, Hayward confirmed that it belonged to the same groups as Sheila's blood sample. Since she was the only one to have the blood grouping A, EAP, BA, AK 1, Hp 2-1, the finding was consistent with Sheila 'having been shot with a gun which was fitted with the sound moderator'.[5] Blood from the stock and near the breech of the rifle was also tested and found to be human but further tests to determine grouping were unsuccessful. The lack of blood on the pull-through from the rifle barrel led Hayward to conclude that Sheila had been shot 'whilst the sound moderator was fitted to the rifle'. Ballistics expert Malcolm Fletcher agreed.

Hayward subsequently clarified that in view of the grouping results, he could not 'totally exclude the possibility' that the blood inside the silencer was a mixture of blood from June and Nevill but 'in my view the possibility is remote because I would expect to detect June Bamber's AK 2-1 group in such a mixture. In addition, the distribution of the blood suggested that the blood has come from a single individual.'[6] He later stated in court that he would be 'very surprised' to find blood from someone who hadn't received a contact or very close contact shot inside the silencer.

Experiments conducted using scientist Glynis Howard, who was two inches taller than Sheila, established that it was 'physically impossible' for a woman of Sheila's height and reach to have operated the trigger and shot herself with the silencer attached: 'She simply could not have reached it. Thus she could only have committed suicide if the sound moderator had been removed from the rifle.'[7]

The blood on the bedroom carpet and socks found next to Sheila was found to belong to June's blood group and was therefore consistent with blood having dripped from her injuries. The blood smear on the wall into the kitchen matched the blood group of Nevill and the twins, but since Nicholas and Daniel had been murdered in their sleep, it could only belong to Nevill. The blood on his watch, discovered near the kitchen sink, and on a jacket and bathrobe found at Jeremy's cottage, was human in origin but insufficient for grouping purposes.

DI Cook confirmed that the Bible which had lain next to Sheila's body was 'subjected to chemical fingerprint treatment, resulting in the development of a large number of impressions. All of these impressions with the exception of one have either been identified as those of June Bamber, or were insufficient for identification purposes. The outstanding impression gives the appearance of not being that of an adult but is more consistent with that of a child, possibly under the age of 10 years. The fingers and palm prints were not taken from the two boys Daniel and Nicholas Caffell.'[8]

Further tests conducted on June's bicycle proved negative for blood and fingerprints. DI Robert Wilkinson trialled various cycle, foot and vehicle routes from Goldhanger to White House Farm, concluding that the shortest and quickest practicable route was the Brook House Farm track. Ainsley came to believe that Jeremy had used that path on the night of the murders, particularly given Julie's testimony that he had estimated his journey would take fifteen minutes by bike and Wilkinson timed the Brook House Farm route as sixteen minutes.

In order to test the idea that Jeremy had left the scene of the massacre via the kitchen window, photographs of the kitchen on the morning of the murders were shown to Jean Bouttell. She stated that items in and around the sink had been moved from their usual positions. Police also discovered the top and bottoms of Jeremy's wetsuit in his bedroom at the farm and the head-piece at Bourtree Cottage. Since Robert Boutflour had already put forward the theory that Jeremy might have worn his wetsuit to commit the murders, they consulted Julie, who stated that Jeremy had planned to wear a mask and dark clothing so he would not be recognized during the shootings. She was aware that he had a wetsuit with jacket, hat and flippers and a mask for diving and thought the discovery of part of the wetsuit at the farm strange since, to her knowledge, it was all kept together at Goldhanger.

As forensic tests continued, lurid stories about the murders appeared in the press. Sheila's fictitious links with an international drug cartel had merged with the discovery of the broken torches to produce tales of 'a dropping zone for a light plane carrying drugs', while 'a mystery figure was seen creeping away from the farmhouse' on the night of the murders.[9]

When the stories proved impossible to sustain, the focus switched to the investigation itself. Public faith in the police was low during the mid-1980s. Inner city riots, the notorious 'Sus' law, and violent clashes between police and picketers during the miners' strike fuelled hostility, together with a number of controversial convictions from the previous decade. Stefan Kiszko,

Stephen Downing, the Birmingham Six, the Guildford Four and the Maguire Seven – all were eventually exposed as appalling miscarriages of justice. Two documentaries in 1982 caused further outrage: a *World in Action* report exposed corruption in the Met, and the BBC series *Police* showed a Thames Valley officer dismissing the testimony of a rape victim as 'the biggest bollocks I've ever heard'. In Essex, the failure to obtain a conviction for the brutal killing of pregnant Diane Jones, who vanished from Coggeshall in July 1983 after a row with her husband, continued to rankle, although the investigation was handled by Suffolk constabulary.

The Jones murder was cited in an editorial about the Bamber case in the *Evening Gazette* on 16 September, which called for 'reassurance about the way the inquiry into the Bamber massacre is going'. Other newspapers followed suit; on 18 September the *Daily Mirror* described the investigation as 'disgracefully mishandled', marred by mistakes that even Inspector Clouseau would have avoided. Assistant Chief Constable Peter Simpson responded directly to the criticism. Disregarding previous press releases, he declared: 'There was always a possibility that all five victims were murdered and that remains the position. We never regarded it as an open and shut case of murder and suicide.'[10] Although admitting it might be several weeks before they reached a decision, he was satisfied with the way the investigation had progressed, reminding the press that Essex Police held a 95 per cent murder detection rate since 1969.

During the Ainsley-led stage of the enquiry, a further 228 exhibits were collected and an additional 100 photographs taken, while statements from material witnesses exceeded 1,000 pages, together with the same number from non-material witnesses.

Not all evidence could be verified, including Robert Boutflour's recollection of a conversation with his sister-in-law on 16 June 1985: 'She said, "What would you think if you'd seen Jeremy trying to persuade Sheila to load bullets into the thing that goes on his rifle?" I was quite shocked by this and said, "You don't want to encourage that." I presume she had meant the magazine. I then asked June if Sheila had done it and she replied, "No, she didn't want to have anything to do with it."'[11]

Pamela had no memory of the conversation although she was present, and Robert's account was therefore designated hearsay, along with a remark Nevill was said to have passed about Jeremy, which Barbara Wilson repeated to Colin: 'I must never turn my back on that young man.'[12] Today, Barbara muses: 'I think that came about because they'd had a row and Jeremy had threatened him. I can easily imagine him after a row, telling Mr Bamber, "You want to watch your back, Dad, when you're out shooting."'[13]

But senior investigating officer Mike Ainsley was satisfied that there was enough evidence to charge Jeremy. On 25 September, he presented Branch Crown Prosecutor David Adams with an extensive report. In a covering letter, Assistant Chief Constable Peter Simpson drew particular attention to how 'Bamber's account of the events of that night are entirely negated by the evidence of the blood found in the silencer, coupled with the evidence of the pathologist that two bullet wounds in the mouth would have made it physically impossible for Ralph Nevill Bamber to have made the phone call to which Jeremy Bamber refers.'[14]

John Walker, Principal Assistant Director of Public Prosecutions, wrote to inform Essex Police the following day: 'There is sufficient evidence to justify charging Bamber with the murders of his father, mother, sister and two nephews. In the light of this advice the Director does not consider that Bamber should now be further interviewed.'[15]

The ferry carrying Jeremy and Brett docked at Dover on the afternoon of Sunday, 29 September. At half-past four, Detective Constable Ian Davidson and Detective Sergeant Harry Hutchison apprehended them in the HM Customs and Excise Car Hall. Looking fit and tanned in a jumper, jeans and his favourite white baseball boots, Jeremy seemed stoic when Davidson declared that he was being arrested on suspicion of murder. 'Okay,' he replied after being cautioned, adding, 'I knew the police would be waiting for me. I should have come in a different way.'[16]

The call about Jeremy's arrest galvanized DI Miller into action. He rounded up Stan Jones and Mick Clark: 'We jumped

in the old Ford Mondeo, the CID car, and belted down to Folke-
stone. Micky drove.'[17] They reached Dover at half-past five,
colliding with a car full of French holidaymakers. No one was
injured, and after a pantomime in which the three officers tried
to explain their urgency in lamentable French, they headed to the
police office at the dock, where they found Jeremy sitting calmly
in handcuffs. Brett departed after Jeremy gave him his £200
share of their holiday expenses, driving the silver Astra back to
London.

DS Jones told Jeremy that he would be charged at Chelmsford Police Station. 'I want you to understand that you're still
under caution,' he said. 'Do you understand that?'[18]

'Yes, I do,' Jeremy answered, before closing his eyes and resting his head against the wall.

'Do you want a cup of tea?'

'Two sugars please,' said Jeremy, sitting up again. When teas
were handed round, he eyed DC Clark over the rim of his cup:
'Was it your day off today, Mick?'

Clark gave a slight frown. 'No.'

Jeremy turned to Stan Jones: 'Is it alright if I ask some
questions?'

'Whatever you say will be recorded.'

'I understand.' He said no more until Jones left the room,
then shifted in his chair and smiled at Clark: 'Have you ever been
to St Tropez?'

'Yes.'

'When do I get to see my solicitor?'

Returning to the room, Jones answered: 'It'll be arranged at
Chelmsford.'

'Are you telling the truth?' Jeremy asked in a polite voice.

Jones looked at him. 'I have personally made a phone call
arranging for your solicitor to be at Chelmsford when we get
back there.'

Jeremy started to hum tunelessly, pulling fibres from his
jumper and putting them in his mouth, using a finger to wind
them around his tongue and teeth. After ten minutes, he said:
'Please record I have got food poisoning. I've driven 1,800 miles
and I'm taking medication.'

In the hour that passed before their departure, he remained

seated, occasionally shutting his eyes, frequently humming to himself and chewing the fibres from his jumper.

At 7.20pm, he was led out to the car. Clark took the wheel again, with Miller at his side. Jones sat in the back next to Jeremy, who leaned forward: 'I thought you would have sent a better car to pick me up.'[19]

'It's the best we could do,' Miller replied evenly.

Jeremy sat back and closed his eyes: 'I suppose it's what's inside that counts.'

Miller glanced at him through the wing mirror. 'Precisely.'

The car pulled away from the docks and Jeremy slept for the better part of an hour. Waking, he commented on what a lovely place St Tropez was, adding that there wasn't the same road congestion in France. After that, he said nothing.

Shortly before 9pm, they arrived at the Essex side of the Dartford Tunnel, where Clark and Miller got out of the car for five minutes. Jones recalled: 'During this time Bamber continually stared at me. After a couple of minutes I said to him, "I don't like you continually staring at me but if you get some satisfaction out of it carry on." He made no reply but continued staring at me.' Jeremy promptly fell asleep again when Miller and Clark returned, then woke for the last half hour of the journey and was taken to the Charge Room at Chelmsford Police Station.

At 10.15pm, in the presence of Jeremy's solicitor and DC Clark, Stan Jones charged him with the murders of his parents, sister and two young nephews.

Jeremy made no reply.

4: WINTER

30 September 1985 to July 2015

During the ten minute hearing at Maldon Magistrates' Court on Monday, 30 September, Jeremy spoke only to acknowledge his details and confirm that he understood the charges. His solicitor Bruce Bowler hadn't had time to prepare an application for bail, intending to do so during the two days he asked for his client to be remanded in custody. Despite being told he was to be held for ten days, Jeremy managed a smile for a couple of friends as he climbed into the van bound for Norwich Prison. Bowler told the waiting media that his client wished it be known that he was 'completely innocent of all five charges of murder'.[1]

Robert Boutflour left the court without comment, face pinched with emotion. Barbara Wilson felt an overwhelming sense of relief: 'I had no compunctions – Jeremy killed them. I knew it in my heart and he knew it too. But that's why I still didn't dare say a word against him, even when the police and later Jeremy's defence came to see me. Because I thought, "If I say something, and he gets off . . ." I was terrified. Jean Bouttell was different, she refused to believe it was Jeremy *or* Sheila. She thought it was someone from outside.'[2]

On the steps of Morshead Mansions, Brett Collins told the *Evening Standard* that Jeremy maintained his innocence 'and I believe him. There is no love lost between Jeremy and his immediate relatives. But his friends, including his girlfriend Angela, will be standing by him and we hope that the truth will finally prevail in what is a most confusing series of events.' He flew back to New Zealand on 3 November 1985, following proceedings from afar.

Sue Ford visited Jeremy 'two or three times' on remand: 'He always told me he didn't do it. I said to him directly, "To have been capable of that, you would have to have been a cold-blooded murderer" and he said, "Yes, I know and I'm not." Maybe he changed after we split up – or maybe he just hid it very well.'[3]

After being told that his former brother-in-law had been charged with the murders, Colin Caffell immersed himself in art as a means of 'expressing something that was so traumatic I could never put it into words. It was the beginning of releasing myself from the past and facing the future as a different person. The first sculpture I ever made was of me holding Nicholas and Daniel. I was filled with regret that I hadn't seen my children's bodies before they were buried – that I hadn't said goodbye properly.'[4] He suffered from nightmares, 'not about the massacre but that Nicholas and Daniel were being taken away from me – or I'd wake up thinking that I'd heard their voices'.

On 1 October 1985, DI Cook and DS Davidson accompanied forensic scientist Brian Elliot to White House Farm. Elliot had already compared the paint sample from the Aga surround with that recovered from the knurled end of the silencer; each contained an identical fifteen layers of paint and varnish. In the farmhouse kitchen, he noted 'several marks and impressions' in the paintwork of the Aga surround and made two casts of the damage.[5] His subsequent examination confirmed 'features consistent with being caused by the knurled end of the sound moderator'.

Elliot also scrutinized the downstairs shower room window, observing scratches to the brass catch and marks on the adjacent paintwork. He was confident that the damage was 'consistent with a thin blade having been inserted between the closely fitting sashes of the window in an effort to force the catch open' and that it had occurred after the window was painted earlier that summer. Outside the shower room, DS Davidson spotted 'a broken, rusty hacksaw blade' bearing 'smears of brass' among old lengths of wood and weeds. The space between the blade's teeth matched two notches on the brass catch, while paint on the blade corresponded with paint on the catch. Elliot concluded that the blade had been used to force the catch but conceded it was unlikely he would have noticed the marks without being previously informed of the window's significance. The blade was 'proved to have been one used by [Jeremy] Bamber in repairing his vehicles'.[6]

Jeremy had an explanation for the scratch marks on the window catch. During the weekend after his release from custody, he had realized the car documents he needed for his holiday were at the farm, but having no key, got in through the shower room window. He shrugged off the idea that it had been unwise under the circumstances. No one checked the dates he mentioned – 15 and 16 September – but the records of the surveillance team place him squarely in London on both evenings. The discrepancy didn't come to light until some while afterwards, sparing Jeremy and his defence at trial a troubling cross-examination.[7]

Julie Mugford visited Colin in October at his request. With Liz Rimington at her side and visibly trembling, she gave him an edited version of her testimony to the police, who had briefed her on how much she was able to say. Although Colin thanked her for coming forward, he asked why she hadn't done so sooner, and Julie wept that she hadn't wanted to believe Jeremy was the killer. The hardest part for Colin was hearing from her that he had justified the murders as mercy killings: his father was old, his mother and sister were mad, and Nicholas and Daniel would have grown up as disturbed as their mother. 'I began to feel sick and didn't take much notice of anything that was said after that,' Colin recalls. 'My only thought was that *he* had to be completely mad.'[8]

According to the local *Evening Gazette*, seven of Jeremy's friends, relatives and neighbours made individual offers of around £1,000 for bail, but he remained in custody, making regular appearances at Maldon Magistrates' Court. Knowing that his solicitor was unused to high profile criminal cases, Jeremy asked Anji to approach Sir David Napley, who had famously defended former Liberal Party leader Jeremy Thorpe at committal proceedings in 1978. Napley was unable to accept on a Legal Aid basis and suggested his partner Paul Terzeon instead. Jeremy's case was one in which Terzeon 'personally invested a great deal' of his professional time, working 'extremely closely with the counsel instructed, namely Edmund Lawson QC (as Junior) and Geoffrey Rivlin QC (as Leader).'[9] Rivlin had a solid background in murder trials, mostly as prosecutor, while Lawson was hailed by *Chambers Guide to the Legal Profession* as 'the cleverest of the clever'.[10] Terzeon also frequently visited Jeremy in the run up to the trial, finding him polite, determined and controlled.

He broke down only once, when Terzeon showed him a crime scene photograph of his father.

Once the case had been accepted for trial, all decisions on disclosure were made by the Director of Public Prosecutions and the Prosecuting Counsel. In the years since, Jeremy and his lawyers have consistently argued that vital evidence was deliberately suppressed beforehand. Senior investigating officer Mike Ainsley categorically denies that the police excluded evidence, insisting that Lawson, the barrister, and a female solicitor from Napleys were given unrestricted access to everything and allowed as much time as they wanted. If evidence wasn't found at the time, he believes it was not due to police obstruction.[11]

The defence solicitors visited White House Farm and its environs, and viewed the 'master bundle' of photographs which contained every image taken at the scene and in the mortuary. DI Cook recalls: 'I personally made all these available at Mike Ainsley's instructions. I also accompanied Mr Rivlin to the Huntingdon Forensic Laboratory, where we went through every bit of the prosecution forensic evidence. The respective scientists showed and disclosed to Mr Rivlin whatever he wanted to see.'[12]

On 7 November, Mike Ainsley submitted his final report to the Director of Public Prosecutions, fully setting out the case. He recommended dropping the burglary charges against Jeremy and the drug offences admitted by him. Nor did he see any justification for prosecuting Julie, having no doubt that she became 'morally and criminally corrupted' as a result of her relationship with Jeremy, including the fact that she had 'withheld information relating to the murders'.[13]

He was forthright about problems with the investigation, stating:

> Although the scene was treated as a major crime scene, there was without doubt a certain lack of urgency in submission of articles to the laboratory and a mistake was made in advising the coroner that the bodies of the victims could be disposed of. Also, as will be seen from the statements of the Eatons and Boutflours, the police search of the premises failed to reveal a vital piece of evidence, namely the sound moderator. Additionally, the police failed to realise the sig-

nificance of Sheila's appearance, ie., relatively clean hands and nails immaculate, feet clear of blood. Also the failure to realise that Sheila, in her nightdress, had no means readily available to enable her to carry around the necessary cartridges to reload the rifle at least twice. I make these points at this stage of the report as I feel strongly that the prosecution will receive justifiable criticism from the defence on these points and it would be foolish for us not to agree that this was the case.

Officers had been 'temporarily fooled by what amounted to a very carefully premeditated and executed murder plot'.

The Director of Public Prosecutions agreed with Essex Police that Julie Mugford should not be prosecuted for any offence. There would be no charges brought against Susan Battersby, either, for her part in the cheque fraud. Jeremy maintains that his former girlfriend 'won complete immunity from prosecution in return for giving evidence against me', but as part of a wider investigation into matters pertaining to the case in 1991, the City of London Police declared that they had found 'no evidence' to suggest such a deal.[14] The jury at his trial were to be fully informed about the admissions Julie and Susan had made to the police and the fact that neither girl had been prosecuted.

In early January, June's will was read. Her estate was valued at approximately £230,000 (£646,000 today). Within a fortnight, Nevill's will was published; his estate was valued at around £380,000 (£1,067,000 today). The family business, N. & J. Bamber Ltd, was estimated to be worth £400,000. Jeremy was now the major beneficiary.

Committal proceedings had been due to be held in February, but were delayed until May. Before then, Colin met Sheila's relatives over a meal at the Pargeters' home. Conversation revolved around Mabel Speakman, whose recent passing had left another irreplaceable hollow in their lives. The family were also uncharacteristically superstitious, filled with trepidation at the thought of the trial. Searching for solace, Colin visited medium Betty Shine, who wrote about their encounter in her bestseller *Mind to Mind* (1989). She assured him that the twins were 'well and

happy' and had 'made the transition in their sleep', while Sheila
had been 'put in a state of rest' and was 'being looked after'.[15]

Julie Mugford had nightmares as the trial loomed: 'I used to
dream I was in court and could see nothing but eyes staring at
me. Then there'd be Jeremy in the dock, laughing at me. I was
terrified of going to sleep.'[16] She continued with her studies but
was suspended from the primary school where she worked until
after the trial.

Anji Greaves visited Jeremy regularly in Brixton Prison,
where he had been transferred in early 1986. In a constant
stream of letters, Jeremy told her that he felt 'very close to the
edge . . . If I hadn't had your love and knowledge that soonish I
would be out to give some of myself back to you I would have
called it a day.'[17] In another he wrote of his fear of being harmed:
'You know how sensitive and non-violent I am, but what can
you do. I told the governor and he laughed at me.'

On 29 April, defence firearms expert Freddie Mead asked to
examine the rifle, silencer, bullets, cartridge cases, clothing,
X-rays and photographs at the laboratory in Huntingdon.
Malcolm Fletcher recalls: 'What they did was they got Freddie
Meade to load cartridges into the magazine without touching the
bullet, which is all fine and good – yes, you can do it, but it's
contrived. You've got to put the base of the cartridge case in and
then press it and slide it down without touching the bullet itself,
which isn't easy. Once you get up to the ninth and tenth cartridge
it's damn near impossible.'[18]

The defence also commissioned Dr Patrick Lincoln to examine the prosecution evidence about the blood in the silencer.
Visiting the laboratory, he carried out his own tests, which indicated weak or very weak positive reactions for blood on the
first eight baffles.[19] He was keen to pursue the possibility that
the blood grouping result that provided a match for Sheila might
be a combination of blood from more than one person. But he
abandoned his theory after a meeting with John Hayward,
believing that Hayward had used a single flake of blood 'trapped
under the first or second baffle to produce a solution from which
he was able to determine the groups'.[20]

Malcolm Fletcher recalls that he and other laboratory staff
visited White House Farm 'probably a month or two before the

trial. Anthony Arlidge from the prosecution and his junior and a few hangers-on were also present. We were doing what we should have done on day one – getting a feel of the scene. You can't beat actually standing there and looking at it all, rather than being told what happened and going through photographs. What struck me was how confined some of the spaces were – for instance, the distance round the bed, where you had mum on one side, Sheila on the other. And the two single beds where the boys were with a little narrow space between them. Things like that joined the disconnected dots. Had we been able to go in sooner, I would have been drawing diagrams showing where the bodies were found, where the cartridge cases were, the pillows with the bullets in – everything would have been measured up and photographed with our eyes, rather than through SOCO. Which isn't to say they didn't do an exceptionally good job, but even so, it would have made all the difference.'

On 7 May, Jeremy was committed for trial. His solicitors unsuccessfully argued against the choice of venue, insisting that it would be impossible for him to have a fair hearing anywhere in Essex. But the place and date were set: Chelmsford Crown Court on 2 October 1986.

Four days after the committal, on 11 May 1986, Detective Chief Inspector Taff Jones passed away at the age of forty-six. While painting the upper floor of the outside of his house, the ladder on which he was standing broke unexpectedly. He died of 'multiple injuries including a fractured skull' at Broomfield Hospital in Chelmsford.[21] An official inquest held on 20 June 1986 found that his death was the result of a tragic accident. Chief Constable Robert Bunyard declared him 'a hard-working and able detective of whom Essex Police are justly proud'.[22]

One month before the trial was due to begin, leading defence counsel Geoffrey Rivlin told Jeremy that while they were not ruling out the theory that Sheila had killed her family before committing suicide, there were 'many difficulties' with it.[23] He admitted there were 'even more difficulties' when they turned away from the murder-suicide theory, particularly the blood in the silencer, 'which was Sheila Caffell's blood'. Jeremy's suggestion that the blood had been planted by a relative was dismissed by Rivlin as too far-fetched to pursue.

The psychiatrist engaged by the defence failed to provide any cause for optimism, announcing to the team that Jeremy displayed a number of classic psychopathic symptoms, chief of which was his very real belief that he had not committed the murders. Although disparate from the recognized psychopathic tendency of refusing to accept any guilt for wrong-doing, the psychiatrist cited it as his prime reason for diagnosing Jeremy as a psychopath, adding that in such cases, the memory of events is pushed into the recesses of the mind where it is eventually forgotten. The psychiatrist was of the opinion that Jeremy did kill his family and had successfully suppressed the knowledge until it no longer existed.

'If ever there was a psychopath,' he concluded, 'it's Jeremy Bamber.'[24]

Chelmsford Crown Court sits on New Street like a squat brown toad, a modern monolith containing six courts on its first floor. Court Number One is the largest, a brightly lit, windowless box in beige and oak. It was filled to capacity on day one of the trial, with journalists and members of the public jostling for seats.

'The "devil incarnate" had good taste,' recalled reporter David Connett, who was among those watching curiously as Jeremy was led into the courtroom. 'His fondness for fine tailoring was obvious from the first moment I set eyes on him. Immaculately dressed, he was handsome and knew it.'[1] Stan Jones's daughter informed her father that some of her school friends had crushes on Jeremy, and the media reported that he appeared to be revelling in the female attention. Garbed each day in the same smart blue suit, white shirt and tie, his neatly cut hair still dyed black, he sometimes looked schoolboyish himself. The *Independent* noted: 'He had a trick of putting his head to one side, raising his eyebrows and opening his eyes wide.'[2]

Jeremy's letters to Anji Greaves had an occasional adolescent tone. Chivvying, 'Remember Non illegitimi [sic] carborundum, which is schoolboy Latin for don't let the bastards grind you down,' he also added an end-of-term mantra: 'Three more weeks to go, three more weeks of sorrow, three more weeks in this old dump, and I'll be home tomorrow.'[3] The 'almost supernatural calmness' emanating from him was due to his unswerving belief in an acquittal.[4] 'I am depressed but know 100% I am not guilty,' Jeremy wrote to Anji. 'So why should they convict an innocent man of such a terrible charge? It will not happen.'[5] The same determined ebullience reached Brett Collins: 'He wrote to me many times and it was always when – not if – he would be found not guilty. He had everything planned. He was going to sell up, have a good holiday and he would then probably settle in Australia, where I am living at the moment. His confidence was on such a high, he was even planning to sue the police for wrongful arrest.'[6]

The case was heard before Maurice Drake, a wartime navigator in the RAF who had been called to the bar at Lincoln's Inn
in 1950, and appointed to the Queen's Bench Division of the
High Court in 1978. Surveying the court from his seat on a platform below the coat of arms, he had a reputation as a stickler for
detail and distributor of tough sentences.

After Jeremy had answered each charge of murder with a
quiet but steady 'not guilty', Anthony Arlidge QC, leading Crown
counsel, rose to set out the prosecution evidence. In a measured
speech to the seven men and five women of the jury, he declared
that 'on the face of things', it was 'most credible' that Sheila had
shot herself after killing her parents and children, given that the
house was locked from the inside. But Jeremy's behaviour in the
aftermath, together with the discovery of the silencer containing
Sheila's blood, had raised suspicions.[7]

He told the court: 'If Sheila Caffell had shot herself, it must
mean that she had shot herself once, injured herself, decided that
she did not want to have the sound moderator on, gone and put
it inside a wrapping in a box at the back of the gun cupboard,
then walked upstairs and shot herself again. In human terms,
that wouldn't make any sense, would it?'

He reminded them that Sheila had no experience with firearms, yet twenty-five shots were fired and 'all hit their target'.
Eventually, despite being 'besotted' with Jeremy, Julie Mugford
had come forward to inform police that he was responsible for
the murders. Although Jeremy denied it, 'other bits of evidence
became available and the plot thickened.'

He summarized the 'bits of evidence':

i. Jeremy's expressed dislike of his family;

ii. His plans to kill his family and thereafter his confessions to his
girlfriend;

iii. The discovery of his mother's bicycle at Goldhanger;

iv. Jeremy's self-confessed ability to enter and exit the farmhouse
undetected and the finding of the hacksaw blade outside the
shower room window. His claim to have entered the house
that way *after* his first arrest was an attempt to cover his
tracks;

v. Given the facts of the case, it could only have been Jeremy or Sheila who carried out the killings, but the following details proved her innocence:

a) Although mentally ill, there had been no indication of any deterioration in Sheila's mental health in the days before the killings. Neither had she expressed any recent suicidal thoughts and expert evidence told that she would not have harmed her children or her father;

b) Apart from Jeremy, nobody had seen Sheila use a gun and she had no interest in them. Due to very poor co-ordination she would not have been capable of loading and operating the rifle, nor would she have had the required knowledge to do so;

c) She would not have been physically able to overcome her father (who was fit, strong and six feet four inches tall) during the struggle which took place before his death in the kitchen;

d) Her hands and feet were clean;

e) Hand swabs from her body did not reveal the levels of lead expected in someone who had re-loaded the magazine of the rifle on at least two occasions;

f) Her clothing was relatively clean and she was not injured in the way that might be expected of someone involved in a struggle. Her long fingernails were undamaged.

vi. The red paint on the silencer matched the paint of the Aga surround and indicated that the silencer had been attached to the rifle during the fight in the kitchen. But if Sheila had committed suicide, it must have been removed before she shot herself. The following factors established that it was still on the gun when she was murdered:

a) The blood grouping analysis proved that Sheila's blood was inside the silencer;

b) Had she murdered the other members of her family with the silencer attached to the gun and then discovered she could not reach the trigger to kill herself, the silencer would have been found next to her body. There would have been no reason for her to have returned it to the cupboard before going upstairs to commit suicide in her parents' room.

vii. Jeremy's account of the telephone call from his father could be shown to be false because:

a) His father was too badly injured to have spoken to anybody;

b) The telephone in the kitchen was not obviously bloodstained;

c) Nevill would have called the police before ringing his son;

d) Had Jeremy truly received such a call, he would have dialled 999, alerted the farm workers who lived near the farmhouse, and driven at speed to his parents' home;

e) Instead he had spoken to Julie first. When he subsequently contacted the police, it was not by way of the emergency system.

viii. He stood to inherit considerable sums of money.[8] Arlidge explained that Jeremy had seen draft wills made by his parents and 'certainly in his mind he knew that if his parents, sister and her twins died, he would benefit from the estate.'

Most of those present, including the defendant himself, had settled back into their seats during Arlidge's long address. Hearing that the prosecution witnesses would be called created a small surge of activity.

Constable Michael West was first to take the stand, explaining his work in the control room at Chelmsford Police Station, where he had answered Jeremy's call in the early hours of 7 August 1985. There was some discussion over the timing of the call, which both prosecution and defence were keen to determine in order to prove whether Jeremy had telephoned Julie first or the police. West had recorded his call as 3.36am from the digital clock on the control room wall, following the usual practice of recording the time as the call came in, then filled out a report form as conversation ensued.

During cross-examination, Rivlin asked: 'Is it right that you may have misread the clock and the time may have been 3.26?'

West replied: 'I was informed I actually spoke to the Information Room at a time prior to the one that I recorded, so I can only assume that I have wrote – I actually recorded the wrong time, as it were.'

Rivlin read from West's 9 August 1985 statement, in which he had given the time as 3.26am. He referred to the same statement regarding Jeremy's initial request for help, illustrating that he had been more panicked than West's previous description in the witness box ('He seemed very "laconic" . . . the message he gave to me was neither hurried nor appeared to give any sense of urgency'). Rivlin pointed out that in his statement, West had recalled Jeremy twice pleading, 'You've got to help me', and that he was unable to remember his sister's surname, indicating that he was not calm at all.

Next into the witness box was Malcolm Bonnett, the civilian employee working in the Information Room at Essex Police headquarters that night and to whom West had spoken after receiving Jeremy's call. He confirmed that he had recorded West's call at 3.26am and had arranged for a police vehicle to be dispatched at 3.35am, indicating that Jeremy must have telephoned for assistance some time before 3.26am.

After Bonnett stepped down, two witness statements were read to the court before Sergeant Chris Bews took the stand to relate the conversations he had had with Jeremy during the siege at White House Farm. Rivlin asked about the 'window sighting', which none of those present that night, including Jeremy himself, had mentioned in their statements. Bews declared firmly that it was 'a trick of the light'. His was the last evidence of the day.

Constable Stephen Myall was the first witness to be sworn in the following morning. Much of his testimony echoed that of his colleague, but Rivlin pounced on his reference to Jeremy seeming 'very well dressed' when he met them in Pages Lane. Myall conceded that 'adequately dressed' was another way of phrasing it. Rivlin was less successful in persuading him that Jeremy hadn't said he had left the rifle on the kitchen table; Myall insisted that he had.

Several officers, including firearms team leader Sergeant Douglas Adams, then took the stand to relate their experiences at

White House Farm. Dr Craig explained how difficult it was to
establish a time of death: 'It could have been any time during
that night.' He described Jeremy's shock, tears and nausea, and
that he had mentioned the family's discussion about having the
twins fostered.

Next into the witness box was Julie Foakes, followed by her
parents. Julie told the court that Sheila was 'a loving mother' who
had been skipping down Pages Lane with her sons on the afternoon before their deaths. Len Foakes also thought Sheila looked
'happy enough' when he saw her with one of the boys just hours
before the murders. He hadn't noticed anything unusual in
Jeremy's manner that day, but some months earlier the young
man had told the farm workers that 'if anything happened to his
parents he would just sell the whole lot and pack up.' In cross-
examination Len agreed that Jeremy seemed to have 'settled down
quite well' recently. His wife Dorothy remembered an occasion
the previous autumn when Jeremy declared that he didn't get on
with Sheila and had no intention of sharing his inheritance with
her. She had heard his car speed away from the farm at 9.30pm
on the night of the murders.

Constable Golding gave evidence about the security of the
farmhouse windows, after which Detective Constable David Bird
was sworn in. 'I was in the box for forty-five minutes,' Bird
reflects. 'They asked me if I'd taken the photographs and if I
could have a look at them. I'd put my photographic album into
sequence according to each negative I'd taken and numbered the
pages, but I nearly had a heart attack when I opened the album
and had to explain: "Excuse me, these aren't in the order I put
them in." It took virtually all my time in the witness box to
put them right.'[9]

Queried about the different positions of Sheila's hand in the
crime scene shots, he clarified that both photographs were taken
at the same time, but Detective Inspector Cook had moved her
hand 'because he wanted to show the mark on the nightdress'.
He was also questioned about a photograph in which the rifle
could be seen leaning against the master bedroom window. Bird
told the court: 'I had finished taking photographs in the main
bedroom. I had come out and photographed the top landing, and
I stood on the middle of the upper set of stairs and took that

photograph up there.' He hadn't been present when the gun was moved from Sheila's body.

Detective Inspector Ron Cook was next into the witness box. He described arriving at the scene and directing his team, adding that he himself was under DCI Jones's directive. He agreed that he was responsible for moving Sheila's hand in order to view 'the blood marks which were not readily visible under the wrist'. When Junior Crown Counsel Andrew Munday asked him about the rifle photographed in the master bedroom window, Cook replied: 'When we commenced work, I instructed Detective Constable Bird to commence taking a series of photographs. This is normal procedure. Before anything was moved in the main bedroom, I asked him to photograph it first, and then to continue to photograph the remaining parts of the house. This photograph would have been taken after he had taken his original photographs of the main bedroom.'

'Who moved the gun to that position?'

'I did sir.'

'Would that be before or after it had been checked by a firearms officer?'

'It was checked as we removed it from the body, and then stood there having been given a safety check.'

Before the court adjourned for the weekend, Munday ascertained that none of the officers present had made a detailed examination of the cupboard in the den.

Among those due to give evidence on Monday was Barbara Wilson. On Saturday afternoon, her husband reported her missing. Barbara shakes her head at the memory: 'That was a big mix up. Keith, my husband, had had a serious accident and was having a difficult time. My sons were both teenagers and there was a lot going on with them, and then the trial loomed. I just thought, "I've had enough, I need to get out." I was going to visit a friend, but decided to park in a country lane and get my thoughts together. I read a book for a while and had a good cry. I felt calm and clear again, so went to visit my friend. When I got there, I found that Keith had rung the police and my friend had called Stan Jones. I couldn't believe it – I was so cross. Someone had given Stan Jones a lift to my friend's house, but I took him back to mine. He reckoned it was the most hair-raising drive he'd ever had! I didn't drive fast on purpose, I was just exasperated that they'd called the police when there was no need. All I wanted was a bit of breathing space.'[10]

Detective Sergeant Winston Bernard accompanied Barbara to court with Jean Bouttell. 'I was petrified,' Barbara recalls. 'I was shaking so much my teeth were chattering. In the lift up to the court Winston said, "Barbara, you're making the lift shake with your trembling." But I was in such a state I couldn't help it.'

DI Cook was re-called to finish giving his evidence first. Munday asked him about receiving the silencer from Stan Jones, the makeshift packaging in which it was enclosed, and the loss of the grey hair during transportation to the laboratory, whose staff were not informed of its existence. Mr Justice Drake admonished: 'They should have been told, shouldn't they? You know they should.'

Cook then told the court that he had identified two fingerprints on the murder weapon, one from Jeremy, the other from Sheila. The media pounced on the fact that he had not worn gloves while handling the rifle at the crime scene. Today, Cook shrugs: 'You have to take all that sort of thing as part of the job. Whatever you do is never going to be right in the eyes of some, especially the press. All I can say is that we did what we perceived as right at the time under the circumstances.'[11]

Jean Bouttell followed him into the witness box. She described her years working for the Bambers and how she had never heard Jeremy speak ill of his family in all that time. Several statements were read to the court before Barbara took the stand, still trembling. She recalled that Nevill had not been himself when she spoke to him on the telephone a few hours before the murders and how Jeremy's behaviour after the funeral had been 'arrogant and nasty. He came up to the office and said he wanted everything thrown out and didn't want anything left.' Rivlin queried whether she might have misconstrued his mood but she shook her head: 'He didn't have a farming heart. He didn't really want to be there.' Barbara also spoke about Sheila's illness during spring 1985, when she believed 'the devil was after her' but declared that she had been 'better' before the murders.

Pamela Boutflour was sworn in next, the first of the relatives to address the court. She described Sheila as withdrawn on the telephone just hours before the shootings but was adamant that her niece would have had no knowledge of how to use a rifle, since she had never shown any interest in guns.

David Boutflour gave evidence after his mother, explaining that his suspicions of Jeremy had mounted while listening to him giving his first witness statement. David's testimony spilled over into the following day, when he admitted to having had little recent contact with Sheila. He concurred with his mother that Sheila had had no interest in firearms, then told the court about finding the silencer and examining it in his sister's kitchen, where they all noticed the paint, scratch and 'blob' of blood. David later admitted to the *Daily Mail* that, when asked to look at the rifle while standing in the witness box, 'I could have turned it towards Jeremy in the dock and had there been a bullet in the breech, I would have willingly shot him.'[12]

The family's undisguised hostility towards Jeremy was apparent to all those present, particularly when Ann and her father each took the stand. Ann echoed her brother's evidence about being troubled by Jeremy's statement and finding the silencer with 'something red, jam-like on the end'. Rivlin took her to task over her assumption that it was rabbit's blood on the silencer and their exchange became fractious as he suggested that she was exaggerating Sheila's impractical nature. Ann conceded that she had found Sheila's behaviour strange on occasion and that her aunt and uncle kept their daughter's illness to themselves. She then described the day at the caravan show with Jeremy, when she had been distraught about his revelations concerning Vaulty and the land at Little Renters Farm.

Rivlin was swift to question her account, declaring: 'The last two matters you have told the court are things you have never mentioned before, Mrs Eaton.'

'Which things?' Ann asked.

'The matter about you and him having a caravan site within two years and the matter about "if you say anything convincingly enough you will be believed." These are matters you have never mentioned before. Have you?'

'To whom?' Ann asked, looking bewildered.

'To anyone at all?" Mr Justice Drake offered helpfully.

'Yes, I have,' she said. 'I have mentioned it to people.'

Rivlin gave her a scornful look: 'Certainly not to the police.'

'I *have*,' Ann insisted. 'They probably did not want it in my statement. They would say it was hearsay or something.'

'Even though this was something that Jeremy said to you?' Rivlin asked. 'They said it was hearsay, did they?'

'Jeremy said a lot of things to me,' she retorted. 'He also told me he had won some money on the premium bonds, which I was completely taken in by until I asked his mother and she said, "Of course he hasn't."'

Rivlin asked, 'Can I take it, Mrs Eaton, there was not very much love lost between you and Jeremy?'

Ann hesitated. Having made his point, Rivlin moved on. Ann stepped down from the witness box following Munday's re-examination, and her mother briefly took the stand again before Peter Eaton was sworn in to discuss examining the silencer and its collection by DS Jones.

Robert Boutflour followed his son-in-law into the witness box. He grew agitated when Rivlin asked whether he might have cut himself at any stage after the discovery of the silencer, implying that the blood within the baffles was his rather than Sheila's, since by pure coincidence they had the exact same blood grouping. He became irate when Rivlin questioned his memory of Jeremy declaring: 'I could kill anybody, I could even kill my parents.' In response to Rivlin's suggestion that Jeremy 'didn't say anything at all about killing his parents', Robert thundered: 'You can suggest it, but I was there and I heard it!' He was hustled, red-faced and protesting, out of court while the judge discussed a point of law with both counsels. Colin Caffell was in the witness waiting room at the time, and sensed that the relatives risked turning the jury against them, such was their obvious revulsion towards Jeremy.

Anthony Pargeter was a more unruffled witness, outlining his last visit to the farm before the murders, when he and Jeremy had had a shooting competition and he had seen the Anschütz standing in the gun cupboard with scope and silencer attached. Rivlin asked him about a formal shooting party at which Sheila was thought to have been present. Anthony answered that he couldn't recollect seeing her there, but was quite willing to go through photographs taken that day in order to resolve the issue.

Colin was sworn in towards the end of the court session. It was over a year since he had seen Jeremy, who sat in his direct line of vision. Struggling to quell his emotions, he was even more disturbed than he had expected to be. He told Arlidge that Sheila's 'very hot Latin temper' was 'usually towards inanimate objects' and that where their sons were concerned 'she was always very kind and very gentle'. He described her breakdowns and the fact that Nicholas and Daniel had been living with him in the last few months before their deaths.

Colin completed his evidence the following morning. He was aware of a palpable sense of expectation in the court as he returned to the waiting room and murmured 'good luck' to the next witness: Julie Mugford.

41

'Keep your spirits up and fingers crossed for Wednesday when Julie goes into the witness box,' wrote Jeremy to Anji Greaves ahead of his ex-girlfriend's appearance in court. 'Hope she tells the truth.'[1]

Julie was the lynchpin of the prosecution case in terms of witnesses. Until then, the evidence had largely amounted to observations and theories, some of it by the family whom the jury suspected of having a vested interest in Jeremy's conviction. Both prosecution and defence knew that a great deal rested on Julie's performance. Only four months earlier, she had graduated from Goldsmiths with a degree in education.

Accompanied to court by her mother, Julie looked smart in a white printed blouse and navy fishtail skirt. Sworn in, she described how her relationship with Jeremy had developed, then told the court that his resentment and anger towards his parents had swiftly developed into declarations of wishing them dead. Repeatedly clasping and unclasping her hands, she explained that she had dismissed such outbursts as 'idle chit-chat because on occasions I have been angry and said I wished I could be rid of somebody'. When Jeremy's hatred spiralled into a plot to kill them and his sister and her children, Julie had 'told him that I'd rather he didn't mention it':

As Arlidge led her through the calls she had received from Jeremy on the night of the shootings, followed by her arrival at Bourtree Cottage and Jeremy telling her, 'Matthew did it,' Julie gripped the edge of the witness box. Mr Justice Drake invited her to sit if she preferred. Accepting a chair, she composed herself but gulped for breath as she outlined how the murders had been committed and that Jeremy had told her he had offered Matthew £2,000 to kill his family.

When Arlidge asked her why she hadn't gone to the police, Julie answered: 'Initially, I didn't want to believe what I thought I was thinking and I wanted to ask Jeremy about it first. I was scared myself to believe it and Jeremy said that if anything happened, it would also happen to me because I knew about it. He said that if I ever said anything, I could be implicated in the crime as well as he could, because I knew about it.' She had struggled to keep up the pretence during the funerals and visits to Colin, but argued with Jeremy about his behaviour.

Occasionally choking on her words, she told the court about the night at Caterham Road, when she had begged him to remain with her, and the angry confrontation at Sheila's flat when she discovered that Jeremy had begun dating a former girlfriend.

Rivlin rose to his feet. In cross-examination, he established that Julie had been very much in love with Jeremy and hoped to marry him. She agreed that she was still smitten with him even after the murders: 'I loved him, but didn't know whether I could live with him or be with him. But my emotion towards him didn't change, apart from the fact that I found it difficult to be physically close to him.'

Rivlin suggested that she had destroyed the mirror at Sheila's flat out of jealousy.

Julie shook her head: 'It was because I was hurt.'

'You were jealous.'

'I was *hurt*.'

She accepted that Jeremy's feelings towards her had changed, telling Rivlin that she no longer felt the same either.

'But you knew by that time that a future relationship with him was unlikely,' Rivlin said.

'It was unlikely because I couldn't get close to him.'

'You knew that he didn't want a future relationship with you, did you not?'

'He wanted me to still be there, but he wanted the relationship terms to change,' Julie argued, her eyes welling.

'He didn't want you to still be his girlfriend, did he though? That is, his full time girlfriend.'

'No,' she admitted. Rejecting Rivlin's suggestion that she had gone to the police because Jeremy had jilted her, she acknowledged having 'omitted a few points' in her first witness statement to protect him.

Rivlin asked: 'You were trying to protect him after, according to you, he had planned the killing of five people, including two small children?'

Julie stammered: 'Yes . . . I . . . didn't know what else to do.

I didn't want to believe it – I didn't know whether I *could* believe it.' She told him that in order to convince herself, she had volunteered to identify the bodies, simultaneously intending to ask Sheila and June for their advice.

A collective intake of breath went round the court. Rivlin allowed it to settle, then asked: 'When you say "the advice of Sheila and her mother", you are talking about the *dead* Sheila and the *dead* mother?'

Julie looked back at him, her chin jutting. 'Yes, that's correct. I believe in the spiritual world. I believe you can talk to people and help them reason. I believe there is a God.' She hesitated, then said: 'I had no other option. They would know what happened. Nobody else would.'

Rivlin turned to the telephone call from Jeremy at 10pm on 6 August, comparing her later description with her first witness statement.

Julie responded defiantly: 'I am not a liar. He said, "It's tonight or never", as simple as that. He told me, and I didn't say it to the police initially because I was scared.' Then she burst out: 'Is that okay? Is it excusable for somebody to be scared?'

She began to cry violently and covered her face, mumbling, 'I'm sorry, my lord.'

Rivlin waited with pursed lips while she brought her emotions under control. He asked about the second call from Jeremy, which she said had frightened her but she was unable to act upon it because the telephone at Caterham Road was for incoming calls only. She had fallen asleep until his third call at 5.40am, when he told her that a police car was on its way.

'I didn't know what the truth was,' Julie said. 'I wanted to ask him, but it was too horrible to believe. My subconscious believed it but I didn't really want to believe that anyone could do that, let alone anyone close to me. It's something beyond my powers of reasoning. I didn't want to, but at the same time, I did.'

Rivlin queried her knowledge of the murders in order to ascertain whether anything she had told the police could have been gleaned from the press. He then returned to her visit to the mortuary, asking her to explain again how she intended to canvas Sheila and June for their views.

Taking another deep breath, Julie told him: 'I wanted to talk to Sheila, but I didn't know how I could talk to her. I just wanted her to be able to communicate with me.' She paused. 'I suppose I prayed a lot and I was asking God for things, but they didn't say anything back.'

Rivlin asked about the clarity of her thoughts at that stage: 'You say you were in two minds. Will you tell the court what were the two minds?'

Julie replied: 'In my subconscious I believed something – because I could *not* believe it. Everything was there, and in my consciousness I didn't want to believe what my subconscious was telling me.' She paused again: 'I didn't want to believe it, but I did at the same count. I didn't know what to do about it.'

'Then does it all boil down to this: in your subconscious you say you believed that Jeremy was involved but in your conscious-ness you did not?'

'That is incorrect. What I said was my subconscious was telling me something that my consciousness didn't want to be-lieve. But I had no option. *That* is what I said – not wanting to believe something and believing are different.'

Leaving the obfuscating exchange aside, Rivlin moved on to her continued relationship with Jeremy.

Julie asserted that towards the end: 'Jeremy knew what I knew. I was scared for him. I was scared for me. The only person I could be with who knew why I was behaving in a neurotic way – something I am not – was Jeremy. I had no option, but I couldn't handle it anyway.'

Rivlin rejected her explanation: 'What upset you, apart from this terrible tragedy, was that it was apparent to you that you were losing Jeremy Bamber. That is why you became neurotic.'

'No, I *wasn't* neurotic,' she responded. 'I didn't think that. The reason why I went to the police was that I couldn't cope with the guilt I felt for Jeremy. That's the only reason I went to the police. Not because I felt he was slipping away from me, but because I couldn't cope with such a hideous thing.'

'You had coped with it for some time,' Rivlin remarked.

'I was . . . sorting out in my mind what to do. I didn't know what to do, I didn't want to believe it, I thought maybe it was a nightmare which would go away. But it didn't go away, so as soon as I could I got out of Jeremy's company and I left. He asked me to stay but I didn't say I wanted to.' Julie paused. '*He* asked *me*. Maybe he was scared as well. He asked me to stay in his company and I left, and as soon as I was away from Jeremy I could say something.'

'He told you he wanted time to sort himself out?'

'Not before I left, not before I told Susan Battersby how I felt. No, he didn't. He told me that *after* he came to see me.'

'In fact, the whole thing blew up and you went to the police when you realised you had lost the man.'

Julie began to cry again: 'No . . .'

As Julie's five hours in the witness box drew to a close, Rivlin asked: 'Miss Mugford, are you an honest person?'

'Yes, I am an honest person.'

'Really?'

'Yes, really.'

'Completely?'

Julie blinked at him: 'What do you mean by "completely"?'

'Well, you know of one or two incidents in the past, do you not?' Rivlin asked in a dangerously light voice.

Grasping the implications, Julie glanced down. After a moment, she said: 'Yes, I do. But everyone in their lives makes mistakes. Honesty is doing something about them, realising where you've done wrong. If you make a mistake you correct it and from that you can become a more honest person.'

Rivlin then informed the court that she had witnessed the Osea Road burglary five months earlier and had participated in a cheque book fraud the previous year. Julie acknowledged both while adding that she had been truthful with the police and had repaid the funds owed to the bank. But Rivlin contended: 'Each time you were involved in one of those offences you were telling lies, were you not?'

'Yes . . .'

'And you're pretty good at it, are you not, Miss Mugford? You can do it all right, can you not?'

'No, I *cannot*,' she answered vehemently. 'I'm not good at telling lies, I made *one* mistake. That was my biggest mistake. I've done my best to get over it. Just because I did that doesn't mean that I lie about everything else, because I don't. As far as

I'm concerned, I'm more honest than a lot of people I know, because I had the courage to admit that I'd done it. I didn't have to.'

The court then adjourned for the day.

When Julie returned to the witness box the following morning, a small pile of photocopied newspaper articles were stacked neatly before her. Rivlin took her back to her insistence that nothing she had told the police came from the press: 'I'm not suggesting you spent an hour by the fireside reading, but what I am suggesting is that this was all information that was available to almost everyone in the land at that time.'

Julie disagreed, shaking her head as he quoted from the articles: 'Jeremy read them, not me. I know what I know, because of him.'

Rivlin went over other parts of her testimony again. When she stated that Jeremy had prepared for the murders by strangling rats which had eaten his marijuana plants, he seized his chance: 'Well, Miss Mugford, I wasn't going to ask you about marijuana at all . . .'

Julie's gaze strayed to Jeremy, whose face remained impassive. She hesitated, then said: 'I feel it's of relevance because Jeremy was saying that the rats had slowed down because of it. That may have been how he caught them. He didn't tell me.'

'But why did you mention that? Was it an effort to make life more difficult for Jeremy?'

'No, it wasn't.'

Rivlin inclined his head: 'Did *you* smoke marijuana?'

'I smoked Jeremy's marijuana, yes.'

'Jeremy's marijuana?'

'Yes, that's correct.'

'Hmm. He smoked occasionally and you did – occasionally?'

Julie steeled herself: 'No. Jeremy smoked *frequently.* I smoked occasionally.' She glanced towards her former boyfriend again. 'He will verify that himself.'

'Miss Mugford, you are of course a bright, intelligent young lady. You don't wish to miss any opportunity do you, to make your evidence sound as black as possible for Jeremy?'

Julie shook her head. 'No, I'd like to correct you there. I'm telling you only what he told me. The evidence is black without me adding anything, he knows that and I know that. But he knows that he can't admit it. He's told me, I believe him. I don't need to add anything.'

Despite her assured response, when Rivlin turned again to the end of her relationship with Jeremy, she began to cry. He declared that Jeremy had wanted to leave her and she had clung to him, afterwards painting an 'untrue picture' of what had passed between them. Tears coursed down Julie's face as she declared: 'I've painted a picture only by what Jeremy has said to me. I don't like doing it. I've never wanted to do it. But don't you understand what it's like to know something like that and not know what to do? He knew what it was doing to me.'

'An untrue picture,' Rivlin repeated firmly.

'No, it's not untrue.' She wiped the tears away with a tissue, her hands trembling.

'Just listen to me please,' Rivlin said, determined to try and elicit an admission from Julie that she was lying, 'because this is the last question that I hope I will have to ask you: an untrue picture of your feelings and the way you were behaving – in contrast to his feelings and the way he was behaving?'

In a barely audible voice, Julie told him: 'No, that's untrue.'

Arlidge's cross-examination lasted less than ten minutes, leaving a plainly exhausted Julie finally free to step down from the witness box.

'Her evidence was controversial,' reporter David Connett recalled, 'punctuated frequently by tearful outbursts and upset to the point that Bamber's defence counsel, Geoffrey Rivlin QC, suggested it was almost impossible to cross-examine her. He did establish that she went to the police after Bamber had upset her by ending the relationship. Personally, I couldn't understand how she could be relied upon as a witness, but others, particularly women, thought the contradictions in her evidence made her more compelling.'[2]

Mary Mugford then took the stand, describing the relationship between her daughter and Jeremy, and his pronouncements on the 'lack of affection' from his mother, a 'religious maniac' who drove Sheila to madness: 'Jeremy disliked his mother immensely and I felt he was more affectionate to me.' She told the court that he had confided in her that June was thinking of changing her will in favour of the twins, and that after the murders he had begun getting rid of 'everything' except Sheila's portfolio, asking whether she wanted to buy his mother's car before he advertised it.

Julie's student housemates then filed into the witness box, each offering their recollection of the time of Jeremy's second call. Susan Battersby gave further evidence of Julie confiding in her that the murders were committed by Matthew McDonald, who was next to take the stand. His turn as a witness was restricted to a solid rebuttal of the hit man story. Christine Bacon gave a similarly concise testimony, followed by Liz Rimington, who discussed Jeremy's reliance on Valium and his intention to buy a Porsche after the estate was settled.

Following evidence from DI Robert Wilkinson and DC Oakey, DS Neil Davidson was sworn in but scarcely had time to begin answering questions before the court adjourned for the day. When it reconvened the following morning, he described spotting the hacksaw blade outside the shower room window and agreed that senior officers had decided almost immediately that 'Mrs Caffell had carried out the murders before committing suicide.'

Davidson was followed into the witness box by Julie's friend James Richards, who recalled Jeremy stating 'I hate my fucking parents' several times with 'a great deal of vehemence'.

Dennis Wager briefly gave evidence before Basil Cock told the court about finding June's letter in the drawer of the kitchen dresser. As it was read aloud, Jeremy shifted in his seat and shut his eyes tightly, then buried his head in his hands. The accountant stated that he knew nothing of any plans June might have had to alter her will and explained Nevill's purchase of the land at Little Renters Farm. He added that £2,000 had been discovered at the farmhouse since the murders and that Jeremy had trebled the contents insurance to £150,000.

Gun seller Robert Radcliffe took the stand regarding the sale of the Anschütz, clarifying that it was not quite as simple as Jeremy claimed to detach the sight from the weapon. Radcliffe was followed by several forensic experts, beginning with John

Hayward, who testified that the 'considerable quantity' of blood found inside the silencer belonged to Sheila and that there was only a 'very remote possibility' that it was a mixture of Nevill and June's blood.

Rivlin asked whether the lost grey hair – assuming it originated from Nevill – could be said to indicate that the silencer had been in contact with Nevill's head.

Hayward replied: 'It could have, sir, but I understand the moderator was in fact found in the house, in the gun cupboard on the ground floor. Of course, Ralph [Nevill] Bamber and all of the deceased could be regarded as resident, if only temporarily, in the house, so there could be hairs of theirs about the house anyway. The significance of it, I would have thought, was relatively low.' As he gave evidence regarding blood tests, Jeremy betrayed no emotion while his family's heavily stained nightwear was exhibited.

Vanezis was next to be called. 'It was reasonably straightforward really, from my point of view,' he reflects. 'I had a fair cross-examination from Mr Rivlin, who was a very mild-mannered man, although he asked quite searching questions. But he realized it could all go against Bamber if he tested the water too much, because there was no way that Sheila could have got up and gone downstairs to put the silencer away.'[3]

The blood distribution on Sheila's nightdress supported Vanezis's evidence in that regard; he also explained that the staining on the garment and on her right arm indicated that both shots to her throat were produced 'when she was slightly on her right side and partially sitting up', although after the second wound 'she would have immediately gone back'. He then outlined the injuries sustained by her parents and sons before court adjourned for the weekend.

On Monday, 13 October, Rivlin elicited an agreement from Vanezis that there was 'nothing whatsoever on Sheila to suggest that she tried to fight anyone else off.' Pressed as to whether her wounds were consistent with committing suicide, he replied: 'I could not be certain one way or the other whether she had taken her own life or someone else had done.'

'But from the pathological evidence which you are concerned

with you agree the wounds she sustained are quite consistent with her having taken her own life?'

'They are, yes.'

Mr Justice Drake interjected to ask whether the same might be said about the injuries being inflicted on Sheila by someone else. Vanezis stated that was also the case.

Before Vanezis stepped down, Rivlin put forward the possibility of 'ritual cleansing' to explain the absence of other blood and debris on Sheila's hands, feet and nightdress. Vanezis responded firmly: 'I'm not a psychiatrist and I cannot dwell on that, I'm afraid.' He agreed that there was often an element of 'overkill' when a parent suffering mental illness killed their own children.

Ballistics expert Malcolm Fletcher was sworn in next, discussing the tests he had conducted, including those with the faulty magazine release mechanism on the rifle, during the course of which he had broken a thumbnail. He explained the phenomenon of 'backspatter', declaring: 'My opinion on this is that the blood in the sound moderator was due to the contact shot to the neck of Sheila Caffell.' He confirmed that there was no substantial residue on Sheila's hands or nightdress from the rifle or bullets to indicate that she was the killer, and that experiments had shown it was only a very 'remote possibility' that she had committed suicide with the silencer attached to the Anschütz.

Under Edmund Lawson's cross-examination the following morning, Fletcher acknowledged that not all gun experts were convinced by backspatter. To that end, Lawson pointed out that Nicholas had received at least one wound thought to have been caused when the weapon was against his skin, yet 'there's no forensic scientific evidence to suggest that anything attributable to the body of young Nicholas was found in the moderator *or* the gun.'

Fletcher explained that it might have been that the shot was inflicted after a fatal wound, when the blood was no longer pumping around his body. He added: 'You have to take into account the position of the actual wounds themselves, and the amount of blood available at those particular points that could come out.' Today, he ruminates that 'the most awkward questions that you can be asked come from people who don't know anything about it – they have a right to ask those questions but they often ask them with the wrong phraseology and in such a way that makes it very difficult to answer. But there was no real evidence that Sheila had ever carried or fired a gun in her life. There are countless instances where the police themselves have fired at somebody and if you get even a third of the shots hitting the target, that's something. Yet this young woman was alleged to have fired twenty-five shots with the rifle, re-loaded it twice and hit her target every time.'[4]

Fletcher's colleague Glynis Howard gave evidence next, followed by Brian Elliot, who told the court about the very low levels of lead detected from Sheila's hand swabs. Rivlin counteracted his testimony by referring to ritualistic washing again and drawing Elliot's attention to traces of other elements, iron and copper, in the test results. The scientist responded that these were no higher than might be ordinarily obtained from the atmosphere.

Dr Ann Wilkinson then confirmed that she had reduced Sheila's final dosage of haloperidol from 200mg to 100mg. DC Hammersley described collecting bullet cases at the scene and how the rifle was handled, stating that he didn't always wear gloves when handling items to be fingerprinted in the normal course of examining a scene. He had worn gloves when taking possession of the Bible because it was bloodstained, but it hadn't been necessary to do so with the Anschütz 'because of the provisions of the places for a strap. You would be able to handle it in those two places without causing the loss of fingerprints evidence.' He hadn't seen the silencer and was unaware of the existence of the den cupboard until 'some weeks afterward'.

Sergeant Woodcock was re-called to the stand on Wednesday 15 October, conceding that the silencer had escaped his notice when he looked inside the cupboard that first morning.

'If you had seen a sound moderator anywhere in the house, you wouldn't have been interested, would you?' Rivlin demanded.

'No, my lord.'

'Why not?'

'At that stage of the initial search, all I was concerned with was looking for people who were armed,' Woodcock replied.

'The secondary consideration was if we came across any weapon.'

DC Michael Clark gave evidence about Jeremy's behaviour during 7 August, both at the farm and Bourtree Cottage, asserting that by the end of the evening Jeremy was 'in a bit of a jovial mood'.

DS Stan Jones provided a similar account and mentioned the incident when Julie first arrived at Bourtree Cottage and he had heard 'either a cough or chuckle' from Jeremy. He told the court that his suspicions of Jeremy had multiplied from there. After describing taking possession of the silencer from Peter Eaton, Jones stood down but was re-called. Rivlin cross-examined him about his experiments with the kitchen window at White House Farm just prior to the trial, and took issue with his depiction of Jeremy as 'very happy' on the evening after his family were murdered.

Jones's final exit from the witness box marked the conclusion of the prosecution case. It was late afternoon and Mr Justice Drake asked the jury whether they would prefer to continue or reconvene the following day. The twelve jurors opted to adjourn.

Jeremy was next to give evidence.

42

Before Jeremy took the stand, Geoffrey Rivlin presented the case for the defence, describing Sheila as 'a very sick girl'. Urging the jury to seriously consider her state of mind on the night of the murders, he told them that Sheila 'increasingly thought she was being taken over by the devil. She had become involved in a complex of ideas with regard to her children. She had visions of having sex with them and suffering violence at their hands. These were little titches of five . . . She expressed certain morbid thoughts that she was capable of murdering the boys. She had fears that they were able to become evil and murderers themselves.'

Among her delusions was a belief that she was a white witch whose mission was 'to rid the world of evil'. She had told her psychiatrist that she and her mother needed some form of exorcism and ignored his exhortations to avoid cannabis. There was a tendency for her to relapse into psychosis without external influence, and it was for the jury to decide if anything had happened on the night she and her family died to 'trigger that catastrophe'.

Concluding, Rivlin vowed to illustrate how 'badly flawed' Julie's testimony had been, while witnesses would confirm that the real Jeremy bore little resemblance to the person presented by the prosecution.

The defence case was built upon the following considerations:

i. The witnesses who spoke of Jeremy's hatred of his family were lying or had misinterpreted his words;

ii. Julie had lied to prevent anybody else being with the man she loved;

iii. Nobody had seen Jeremy arriving at or leaving the farm that night;

iv. Because Jeremy had, on several occasions before and after the murders, entered the house by its ground floor windows, there was no evidential value in the discovery of the hacksaw blade or the marks on the catch and paintwork of the shower room window;

v. Sheila had killed her parents and children and then taken her own life because:

a) She had a very serious mental illness and it was known that even those with no previous history of violence had killed. She had expressed thoughts of killing her children;

b) Those who carried out 'altruistic' killings had been known to indulge in ritualistic behaviour before committing suicide. Sheila might have replaced the silencer, changed and washed before killing herself, thus explaining the absence of blood-staining, the minimum traces of lead on her hands, and lack of sugar on her feet;

c) Having lived on a farm and attended shoots, Sheila would have understood how to load and operate the rifle;

d) The gun, magazine and rounds of ammunition had been left by Jeremy in the room where he had heard an argument about placing the children in foster care;

e) Jeremy bore no obvious signs of injury;

f) No bloodstained clothing of his had been recovered by the police;

g) Dr Craig and the first senior investigating officer had proceeded on the basis that Sheila was responsible for the killings.

vi. There was a possibility, however remote, that the blood in the silencer was not from Sheila, but a mixture of Nevill and June's blood;

vii. Regarding the telephone call from his father, Jeremy had not initially appreciated the seriousness of the situation and had then become frightened to go to the farm alone.[1]

Jeremy entered the witness box. Much of his evidence was given in a voice so quiet that he was repeatedly asked to speak up, but he maintained his self-control at all times. In that sense, his testimony was less compelling than his former girlfriend's far more emotional declarations and outbursts to court. On the surface at least, he was cool and calm, with measured replies to every question. In the charged atmosphere of a multiple murder trial in which he stood accused, his detached bearing did him no favours at all.

Sipping water constantly, Jeremy agreed with Rivlin that he had experience of guns and had used the Anschütz previously. He also accepted that Sheila was less knowledgeable but stated that she had sometimes joined shooting parties.

He described how, hours before the murders, his parents had raised the idea of fostering Nicholas and Daniel because Sheila's mental health 'was causing us worry, because of the lack of interest in herself, lack of interest in anything, really'. He had found her reaction hard to judge: 'It was as if she was just concentrating. She was just sitting there and occasionally she would just say something like, "I want to stay in London", or a few words. But she didn't really seem to be paying much attention.'

Jeremy told the court that his relationship with both parents had been 'very loving', although his mother's religiosity caused some friction. He and Sheila had got on well, but for the past couple of years he had found the symptoms of her mental illness difficult. He was aware that she had considered suicide several times: 'She wanted to be with God, she wanted to go to heaven. She wanted to take people with her and she wanted to save the world.'

His eyes filled with tears as he described the telephone ringing in the early hours of 7 August: 'It was dad. He said something like, "Come quickly, Sheila's gone crazy, she's got a gun." It ended and there was no more. I didn't get a chance to say a single word.'

The line was engaged when he tried to call back and it didn't cross his mind to dial 999; the local police seemed a better option, but when there was no response he called Chelmsford, who didn't take him seriously at first.

He then telephoned Julie because 'I needed a friendly ear. I told her there was trouble on the farm. She told me to go back to bed, as if she thought the whole thing was a practical joke.'

He had driven slowly to the farm because he was afraid of

what awaited him. Upon arrival, he had told the police about his father's call, Sheila's schizophrenia and where he had left the gun. While creeping towards the front of the property, 'we thought we saw something and we ducked down behind a hedge.' They then returned to the police vehicle.

'I was trying to explain,' he declared. 'I didn't think the police understood the nature of Sheila's illness. I was trying to convince them that she was very unpredictable.' When they asked him about firearms inside the property, he told them 'there were lots of guns in the house and she could have used any of them.'

Rivlin covered several further points. Jeremy stated that he had entered and exited the house 'many times' using the shower room window and had personally witnessed Sheila punching one of her young children. Julie's destruction of the mirror at Sheila's flat was entirely due to her being 'really jealous'.

Rivlin then sat as Arlidge rose to cross-examine.

Jeremy reached for the glass of water. He sipped it steadily, replying frankly to the prosecution's question about breaking into Osea Road, conceding that he could have affected entry to demonstrate how poor security was at the site without stealing, but the money was 'important'.

'Why was the money important to you?' Arlidge asked.

'Greed,' said Jeremy.

He admitted there were arguments between himself and his mother, and that he felt her personality had been 'a contributory factor' in his sister's illness. When Arlidge asked him to comment on James Richards' recollection that he 'fucking hated' his parents, Jeremy responded that he had never said it.

'Can you explain to the jury why you think that young man should come along and give that evidence to this court if it isn't true?' queried Mr Justice Drake.

'I can only surmise, my lord, that people's recollections of such events have been changed because of the way I have been portrayed in the newspapers, because he is a friend of Julie's and he doesn't know me that well.' He gave the faintest of shrugs: 'Really, I don't know the reasons why people do this. I wish I did.'

Arlidge asked about his desire for a Porsche. Jeremy replied that he had looked into buying a kit model manufactured by Covan Turbo for a fraction of the price. Questioned about his parents' estates, he hadn't known there was a clause in his father's will binding him to the farm in order to claim his inheritance until the relevant section was read to court.

Mindful that Jeremy had spent a full day in the witness box, Mr Justice Drake then decided to adjourn proceedings slightly earlier than usual.

The following day, Arlidge returned to the assertion that witnesses who had spoken out against him were dishonest. Jeremy stated that James Richards was probably genuinely mistaken, but it would be 'very dangerous' to speculate about Robert Boutflour's motive for lying.

Arlidge then asked about the foolishness of leaving the Anschütz in the scullery.

'I didn't know what was going to happen, did I?' Jeremy responded.

Arlidge said sternly: 'You're not telling the truth about it, are you?'

Jeremy gazed at him. 'That is what you have got to try and establish.'

A low murmur went around the court. Mike Ainsley recalls: 'I'll never forget that moment. The defence had objected to me being in court, but I snuck back in that day and when I heard him say that, I thought: "You've just convicted yourself."'[2]

Arlidge rattled through the afternoon's cross-examination, eliciting an admission from Jeremy that his interest in Julie had begun to wane after Christmas 1984 and that he had been unfaithful to her on several occasions. Jeremy disputed her claims about having plotted the murders. He denied having killed his family and removing the silencer from the weapon after realizing that Sheila couldn't have committed suicide with it attached.

Arlidge asked one last time: 'You killed them all, didn't you?'

Jeremy stood very straight and said in a clear voice: 'No, I did not.'

The witnesses called to give evidence on Jeremy's behalf were an uneven collection of people who didn't know him particularly well. They included Paul Osborne, manager of Cues snooker club, and a couple of businessmen who had dealt with Jeremy at Osea Road and White House Farm. All testified that he was pleasant, approachable and appeared to have a good relationship with his father, yet were little more than acquaintances. The absence of those close to him who had spoken well of him in their witness statements – such as Sue Ford, Brett Collins, Michael Deckers, Rodney Brown and Virginia Greaves – didn't help his case.

On Monday, 20 October, the focus turned to Sheila's mental health as statements were read from Sandra Elston, Barbara Babic, Farhad Emami (Freddie), Caroline Heath, Judy Salvage (Heather's flatmate), Barry Parker and Doris Tweed. At fifteen years old, Helen Grimster was the youngest witness to take the stand. She recounted her strange conversation with Sheila at White House Farm in March 1985, when her relative had declared herself to be a white witch whose mission was to rid the world of evil.

Dr Hugh Ferguson followed her into the witness box, recounting his first meeting with Sheila in August 1983, when she was 'very agitated and in a psychotic state'. He discussed her admission to St Andrew's and how she had become 'completely caught up in the themes of good and evil and, more specifically, her ability to project evil onto others'.

Led by Rivlin, Dr Ferguson confirmed the most distressing aspects of her illness but was adamant that he had never seen any signs of actual violence during his two years as her psychiatrist. He told the court about her occasional use of cannabis and cocaine, and explained the medication she had been prescribed to help manage her illness: first Stelazine, then haloperidol. Between 1983 and 1985 she had developed an obsession with her cervix. The psychotic episode in March 1985 was a period in which she was 'more acutely disturbed, very agitated and highly suspicious and bewildered'. Thoughts of good and evil had continued to preoccupy her; she believed Freddie to be the devil and stated that she wanted to be 'by Jesus' side', although she didn't appear suicidal.

The jury asked for clarification on two issues. The first concerned whether Sheila's moods were unduly affected by menstruation. Dr Ferguson responded that to the best of his knowledge they were not. The second query was whether her illness was hereditary. He explained that there was no 'clear cut' answer, reminding them that she and June were not genetically related and their illnesses were quite different.

Dr Ferguson declared himself unable to judge the precise effect of halving Sheila's haloperidol dosage, but after hearing witness accounts of her 'lapsing into moods' where she seemed vacant, he replied: 'Indeed, that was rather the Sheila I knew. Even at the time that she left hospital in March, she was prone at times to look quite distracted, vague, somewhat distanced, somewhat withdrawn.'

Prompted for his reaction to the news that Sheila had killed her family before committing suicide, he declared: 'Shock and horror, and I have to say, a great deal of dismay that such a thing could have happened because it did not fit my concept of Sheila Caffell. I did not feel that she was someone who would be violent to her children or to her father, although I was very aware that she was a highly disturbed woman and had disturbed feelings towards her mother.' However, he agreed that she was likely to have reacted 'very strongly' to any perceived threat of losing her sons.

When Dr Ferguson stood down, Mr Justice Drake, the lawyers, and the jury were driven to the firing range at Fingringhoe, south of Colchester, to hear the murder weapon fired with and without a silencer attached. Malcolm Fletcher handled the demonstration, during which the magazine release mechanism jammed.

The first witness called the following morning was John Jennery Bradley, consultant psychiatrist and honorary senior lecturer at the Royal Free Hospital School of Medicine and University of London. He had never met Sheila and gave evidence from his reading of the case reports. The defence then called forensic pathologist Professor Bernard Knight, who spoke about ritualistic murders and suicides, telling the court: 'Sheila's is the only shooting of the five where the bullets have gone upwards, and to shoot upwards one must put the gun under the chin. For a third person to do this seems extraordinary. It would be difficult for someone else to have done it without her objecting.' His final comment encapsulated the difficulty he had in determining whether Sheila or Jeremy was the killer: 'In all this, the supposition exceeds the evidence.'

His was the last evidence to be given. It was now a matter of closing speeches before Mr Justice Drake summarized proceedings and the jury retired to consider their verdict. But two issues had to be addressed first.

The first was a note from the jury, who wanted to know: 'If Jeremy Bamber was found guilty and imprisoned for many years, who would be the beneficiarys [sic] of the Bamber estate and monies. Could it be his uncle and family? A possible reason or mottiff [sic] from Robert Boutflour's statement about Jeremy being able to kill his own parents.'

Arlidge consulted Basil Cock and the jury were duly informed that Jeremy would not inherit his parents' fortune if convicted; in that event, civil proceedings might be necessary to establish the distribution of the estates. Robert would not be a direct beneficiary, but his wife would probably inherit a substantial sum.

The jury also requested an opportunity to see for themselves how much oil and other residues might be left on the hands of someone loading bullets into the Anschütz magazine. They were permitted to conduct their own experiment in a nearby room.

Arlidge then rose to deliver his closing speech.

Announcing that the trial was 'a two horse race', he declared that the alleged call from Nevill precluded a third suspect: 'It was Sheila running amok with the gun if Nevill made that telephone call. If, on the other hand, Bamber didn't get that call, if that's a lie – and I'm going to suggest that it is – there can only be one reason for his lying.'

Accepting that Sheila suffered mental health problems, Arlidge stated that her vacant manner may have been due not to an imminent psychotic episode, but to the haloperidol. Although she was known to have some fixation with religion, he asserted that the Bible found at her side had been placed there by Jeremy to set the scene. It was ridiculous to suggest that she could have overpowered her father; the absence of defence marks on her did not imply a willing death but rather a paralysing terror when her brother appeared in the dead of night with a gun.

It was regrettable, Arlidge admitted, that certain officers had accepted Jeremy's account of events so readily. A little more caution might have led to a different conclusion at a much earlier stage. But as the investigation went on it became obvious that Sheila could not have removed the silencer from the gun 'because she would have been dead after the second shot. It's far more likely that someone had shot everyone with the silencer on, then when he tried to fake the suicide by placing the rifle on the body, realised she couldn't have shot herself. So he removes it.' But while the silencer was at the forefront of the forensic evidence, it was by no means the most crucial aspect: 'You can throw the sound moderator out of the window and still the prosecution say they have an overwhelming case.'

Jeremy's explanation for not dialling 999 was untenable, as was his claim that he had called Julie because he needed a friendly ear. Arlidge demanded: 'If you realise your family is in danger, what are you doing ringing up your girlfriend in Lewisham in the middle of the night for some moral support?' As for all the prosecution witnesses lying on oath, whatever their apparent motive that 'would be a pretty incredible thing to do'.

He agreed that the veracity of Julie's testimony was paramount because 'somebody in this case is lying, and lying their heads off. Either Julie Mugford is lying or Jeremy Bamber is lying. It is something you've got to face.'

Rivlin then stood to address the jury. He stressed that they must be absolutely certain of Jeremy's guilt to convict him. A great deal of the prosecution case relied on the performance of Julie Mugford, with her carefully timed 'droplets of poison' and tears that vanished 'as if by magic' when no longer faced with a defence lawyer. She was free to manipulate the court with her weeping; Jeremy, on the other hand, would be accused of 'crocodile tears' if he cried and of being 'cold-blooded' if he did not. There was nothing in Julie's account of the injuries suffered by the victims that hadn't already been published in the press and therefore the jury must decide whether they were dealing with a skilled actress or a consummate actor.

Court then adjourned for the day, but Rivlin continued his speech the following morning, damning the forensic evidence as non-existent. There was nothing to link Jeremy to the murders; the blood in the silencer could be a mixture belonging to Sheila's parents, rather than hers. And why hadn't the police found the silencer? Four officers had looked into the 'tiny' den cupboard, yet none of them noticed 'the silencer propped up against a box'.

Nor was it 'a grouse or a grumble' to ask why only eleven of the approximately forty officers present that day had been called to give evidence.

Rivlin asked the jury to consider how different Sheila might have been in the grip of psychosis: 'If you had seen her when she was having one of her fits, would you have said, "Just a slip of a girl, just a chit of a girl"?'

Discharged from hospital on 29 March 1985 after being diagnosed with schizophrenia, the very next day Sheila was discussing thoughts of suicide and getting rid of the world's evil. Her state of mind had deteriorated until 31 July, when she 'looked a mess, was fidgety and appeared frightened and paranoid'. At a friend's home on 1 August, she seemed out of sorts and two days later at her ex-husband's party, several guests noticed that she was vacant.

'Things were building up,' warned Rivlin.

By the time Sheila spoke to her aunt on the evening of the murders, she was 'a zombie'. The evidence revealed that Sheila, that very night, was heading for 'a state of schizophrenic relapse'. Hence the 'overkill' murders of her children, and the ritualistic washing which removed blood and debris from her hands and feet.

Rivlin declared that Jeremy had told the truth about his father's call. To do otherwise would have been too perilous, since it fixed a time on the killings, and if the police had burst into the farmhouse immediately, their suspicions would have been raised by the warmth of the victims' bodies. Nor would he have risked ringing Julie and sending the police to collect her: 'How was he to know when she was met with the catastrophic news that five people had been killed in a house, including two children, she's not going to immediately break down and say, "My God, he's done it!"'

Rivlin paused, then said simply: 'It just doesn't add up.'

43

'I kept an open mind until the evidence was building up and there came a time when I came to the conclusion Julie Mugford was telling the truth,' recalled Maurice Drake years later.[1] The judge asked the jury to consider the same in his summing up: 'Quite simply, do you believe Jeremy Bamber or do you believe Julie Mugford? If you are sure that Julie Mugford told the truth, then it means you are sure that the defendant told her that he had planned the killings and had, in fact, carried them out.'

He reminded them that 'we are not concerned with any fanciful imaginations of some mysterious third party having appeared on the scene', and that it was not for the defence to prove Sheila guilty, but for the prosecution to show that she was as much a victim as her parents and children. The jurors should approach the evidence of each witness impartially, including the defendant: 'He starts equally with everybody else.'

The judge turned again to Julie, asking them to consider whether her testimony had 'the ring of truth'. If not, 'then you reject her evidence and that is the end of it'. Even if they were convinced that her story was sustainable, they should bear in mind 'the possible motive she might have to tell lies' and look to see whether there was other evidence, 'entirely independent of hers', which would lead them to the conclusion that Jeremy was guilty.

He then precised the evidence, highlighting the issue of whether the silencer was on the gun when Sheila was shot. Jeremy had testified that the rifle was minus its silencer when he left it out that evening; therefore Sheila must have looked for it and fixed it to the weapon herself. 'Why on earth should she take the trouble?' the judge queried.

There was also the question of the blood found inside the baffles, which scientific analysis had shown to almost certainly belong to Sheila. The forensic evidence relating to the silencer could, 'on its own', lead them to conclude that Jeremy was guilty. But equally, they could set it aside and it would still be possible 'to find the defendant guilty on a number of different approaches from the prosecution evidence'.

The judge concurred with the prosecution that Jeremy's explanation for the marks on the shower room window was 'too much of a coincidence to be credible' and was just 'one of many examples in this case of there being too many curious coincidences'.

The court adjoined for the weekend.

On Monday 27 October, the judge took the jury through Julie's testimony again, asking: 'Is that whole story a complete pack of lies, a complete fabrication? If she had made it all up, every bit of it a deliberate lie, could she then repeat it at such length and in such detail, and stick to her story under the skilled cross-examination of an experienced advocate? Mr Rivlin complained to you bitterly that she was an impossible witness to cross-examine. Was she? If she showed some degree of emotion when giving evidence, is that a drawback to a skilled Queen's Counsel in cross-examination, or is it something that can be exploited to see whether she maintains her story in the face of persistent skilled questioning?'

He advised them to consider Jeremy's calls that night, 'not only on variations in what he has said that his father said to him, but on those timings which the prosecution say could lead you to the conclusion that the story of the telephone call is a false one'.

Although there were episodes in Sheila's life when her behaviour and thoughts were deeply disturbing, and she was clearly liable to relapse, the only evidence to support the theory that she had killed her family before committing suicide was that she was found in an ostensibly locked house with the gun laid across her body. There were no marks on Sheila to indicate that she had carried out the murders, and though the same might also be said of Jeremy, circumstance and the dearth of police suspicion had allowed him time to clean himself up and hide any marks on his person.

Finally, Mr Justice Drake declared: 'If you believe that he may have been telling you the truth when he gave evidence, then he is not guilty. If you are driven to the conclusion that, by a number of approaches, the evidence against him is conclusive, then it is your duty to find him guilty.'

The jury left the courtroom at 12.49pm. The judge departed and Jeremy was led from the dock, causing a bustle in the public seats as people stretched, reached for sandwiches and went outside for air.

The defence team fumed at the judge's summing up, feeling that the balance was unfairly tipped in the prosecution's favour. But among the journalists scribbling copy was David Connett, who reflects: 'In all honesty I would not have convicted Bamber on the evidence I heard. Admittedly, I didn't attend every day of the trial, but the evidence I heard left me far from certain that Bamber's guilt had been established beyond reasonable doubt. And yet I believe Bamber was guilty. I remember thinking later that I now understood the benefit enjoyed by Scottish juries of being able to return a verdict of "not proven".'[2]

Jeremy's lawyer Edmund Lawson recalled that in the cells underneath the court, his client appeared 'disconcertingly composed' and talked 'somewhat unattractively about how much money he would make from selling his story to Fleet Street'.[3] Jeremy admits regretting his behaviour: 'Looking back, I wouldn't have acted in the way I did. I thought all you had to do was to be innocent. It wasn't until it was too late that I found out that wasn't the case.'[4]

The jury returned at 5.59pm, unable to reach a unanimous verdict on any of the murder indictments and doubtful they would do so that day. They were directed to a nearby hotel for the night. When Mr Justice Drake arrived in court the following morning, the clerk handed him a note from the jury: 'We need to hear blood expert's evidence regarding the blood in the silencer (a) a perfect match of Sheila's blood (b) what was the chance of the blood group being June and Ralph's mixing together.'

Since Arlidge was not in court that day, the judge asked Munday and Rivlin if they would read John Hayward's evidence again, while he repeated his own explanation to the jury on the matter. Rivlin had two points to make. First, that while giving evidence, Hayward had stated that his deductions were based to some extent on passages from the witness statements of Dr Peter Vanezis and Malcolm Fletcher, but had nonetheless acknowledged the possibility that the blood could be a mixture from June and Nevill. Secondly, that Hayward had conceded it might also be possible to get the blood distribution he had found as a result of the entry wounds to Nevill Bamber, which if inflicted at close range might have caused his blood to enter the silencer.

Munday countered that by reading from Hayward's statement on the blood groupings: 'I did not detect June's AK 2, and if there was sufficient blood to detect the A group, there would have been a similar chance to detect the AK 2-1 amongst it, which I did not detect.' Therefore, the most likely conclusion was that the blood inside the silencer was specific to Sheila.

Mr Justice Drake nodded: 'I've got that. Very well, let us have the jury back in.'

For the benefit of the jurors, he then recounted his conversation with Munday and Rivlin regarding the blood. In addition, he told them that John Hayward 'said that he had been blood testing for nineteen years and in addition to the scientific tests, it is possible by experience to form an opinion from the *appearance* of the blood that you are grouping, and he said that nothing in the appearance of the blood inside the moderator suggested to him that there was the blood of more than one person.'

It was a small but appreciable error; Hayward certainly had not said that he was able to form an opinion from the appearance of blood.

The jury once more retired.

When they returned two-and-a-half hours later, Jeremy was led up into the dock from a door at the back of the court. He stood, pale but calm, clasping his hands behind his back. The judge declared: 'Mr Rivlin, Mr Munday, I have received a note from the jury, the effect of which will be that I shall give them a majority direction, so I propose to do that.' He then explained the process. There were murmurs of frustration around the court as the jury trooped out again. Jeremy sat down heavily in his seat.

Less than twenty minutes later, at 2.35pm on Tuesday, 28 October 1986, the door opened and the jury filed back in. Two of the five female jurors were crying.

Jeremy rose, swaying slightly and swallowing hard.

'Would the foreman please stand,' announced the clerk. He waited a moment, then asked: 'Mr Foreman, to the question I am about to put to you please answer yes or no. Have the jury reached a verdict in respect of each count on which at least ten of you are agreed?'

'Yes.'

'On count one of this indictment do you find the defendant guilty or not guilty?'

'Guilty.'

'Is that the verdict of you all or by a majority?'

'By a majority.'

'How many of you agreed and how many dissented?'

'Ten agreed, two dissented.'

The exchange was repeated word for word four more times.

Jeremy Bamber, twenty-five years old, had been convicted of the murders of his mother, father, sister and two six-year-old nephews. In the eyes of the law, he was no longer 'the defendant', but a mass murderer who had committed matricide, patricide, fratricide and was twice a child killer. In prison terms, he would be the lowest of the low: a nonce, a nothing.

The airless room was silent, save for the scratching of the judge's pen and the weeping female jurors.

Jeremy sank into his seat. He felt 'stunned as if hit by a 10 ton truck. It was as if I'd been knocked unconscious yet, still being awake, I just couldn't believe it.'[5]

Suddenly Mr Justice Drake stopped writing. 'Stand up, Jeremy Bamber.'

Jeremy stood, his face a white, immobile mask. He stared straight ahead as the judge pronounced: 'When, in about March 1985 you stole nearly £1000 from the caravan site owned by other members of your family, you told your girlfriend Julie Mugford: "I shall be the prime suspect, but they will never be able to prove it against me." When you planned the killings of five members of your family, you went one better. You used the mental illness of your sister and planned matters so she became the prime suspect.'

He went on: 'Your conduct in planning and carrying out the killing of five members of your family was evil, almost beyond belief. It shows that you, young man that you are, have a warped and callous and evil mind behind an outwardly presentable and civilized appearance and manner. You killed your mother, you killed your father, you killed your sister. Each alone would have been a dreadful crime. But you killed all of them. You fired shot after shot into them, and also into two little boys aged six whom you murdered in cold blood while they were asleep in their beds. I believe you did so partly out of greed, but I take the view you also killed out of an arrogance in your character which made you resent any form of parental restriction or criticism of your behaviour.'

He paused, then declared: 'In passing on you the five sentences which are fixed by law for murder I have to consider when I think it likely it will be safe for you to be released from prison to live in the community. And I find it difficult to foresee whether it will *ever* be safe to release into the community someone who could plan to kill five members of their family, and shoot two little boys aged six while they lay asleep in their beds. First of all, I pass sentence on you of life imprisonment on each of the counts. And the recommendation I make is that you serve a minimum – and I repeat a *minimum* – of 25 years.'

Jeremy closed his eyes momentarily. Flanked by two prison officers, he moved of his own volition towards the door behind the dock, slowly descending the stairs to the corridor below. He was stopped at the entrance to the cell and ordered to remove his silk tie.

In a flutter of black robes, his legal team appeared. Jeremy sat down, murmuring about an appeal; Lawson assured him they would be in touch. Then the lawyers left, the heavy door closing behind them with a resounding bang.

Jeremy crumpled, dropping his head to his hands: 'No, no, no . . .' When they came for him, he was still sobbing.

David Boutflour recalls: 'When the verdict came in, I went into a vestibule and I howled.'[6] He told the jostling reporters and camera crews outside the court: 'I'm very sad. I have feelings of relief and a lot of sadness. No one wins and everybody loses. It can't bring them back.'[7]

On behalf of the family, Robert Boutflour had prepared a statement which he read to the media, taking particular care to defend June and speaking of her many acts of kindness. He was at pains to point out that Sheila's illness was only recent and until then she had been 'an extrovert, fun-loving girl who gave great joy to her parents.'[8] He left it to the judge and jury to pass comment on Jeremy, but expressed gratitude to senior investigating officer Mike Ainsley and his team for the 'painstaking and diligent manner in which I believe they set out to achieve the task that was assigned to them. I consider it was to the highest standards of their profession.' Colin was interviewed by *ITV News* at home, surrounded by the sculptures he had begun working on of the twins, 'happy, vibrant children', and Sheila, their 'very loving and caring mother'.[9]

Stan Jones felt vindicated when the verdict was announced, recalling that Jeremy's face showed 'absolutely nothing. An innocent man would have been shouting about lies and rubbish.'[10] Mike Ainsley was relieved: 'You just never know with juries. But Mr Justice Drake got it right when he said Bamber was evil beyond belief. Bamber got twenty-five years, which works out at five years for each murder. Five years – you get that for burglary.'[11] Malcolm Fletcher thought the defence had miscalculated 'by deciding to run with this story that it was Sheila and not Jeremy – that she'd done it. That removed every other explanation.'[12] Watching the news on television, Dr Ferguson was 'glad that it wasn't Sheila after all. But the whole thing was a tragic loss of lives.'[13]

One former member of the investigation team who does not wish to be named asked the jury foreman afterwards if there had been a deciding factor. He was told: 'It was all down to the judge's summing up. He directed us to find Jeremy guilty and that's why we did, in the end. If it hadn't been for the judge telling us what we should do, he would have walked free.'[14]

In Australia, Brett gave an interview to the press, declaring that he was 'absolutely shattered' by the verdict and would continue to believe in Jeremy's innocence until he heard otherwise from him.[15] In Jersey, Sue Ford told the media that she, too, was in shock, remembering how Jeremy 'couldn't bear to hurt [even] the smallest animal'.[16]

Anji Greaves had waited for the verdict in a hotel not far from Chelmsford with two friends and a journalist. Her room was decorated with 'Welcome Home, Jeremy!' banners, and she wore her glitziest outfit, with a bag packed; the journalist intended to write Jeremy's story when he was acquitted and then hustle the couple off on holiday. But when the television news delivered the outcome, Anji walked out in a daze, narrowly avoiding being run over. She told the journalist: 'I feel so much loyalty for Jeremy but I do not know if I can bring myself to go on visiting now. It could be a life sentence for both of us.'[17]

Stan Jones broke the news to Julie at the Holiday Inn on Sloane Square in London. The venue was chosen by the *News of the World*, whose reporters Rosalie Shann and Polly Hepburn were poised to record Julie's story for a two-part serialization. Jeremy has always insisted there was a contract in place before the verdict was passed but no evidence has been found to support his claim. Julie recalled that her solicitor arranged the deal in order to stop the press harassment she and her family had endured since Jeremy's first arrest. The *News of the World* was the highest bidder for her story, leaving her with a 'moral dilemma' about accepting the £25,000 fee. She used it to pay legal expenses and put the rest towards the purchase of a flat.[18]

Julie was unhappy with the serialization and its accompanying photographs. In a bid to counteract it, she spoke to *She* magazine in 1987 as part of a feature titled: 'Violent Men: Why Do Women Shield Them?' Since then, she has refused all offers – many of them extremely lucrative – for further interviews. There is more than a touch of hypocrisy in Jeremy complaining about Julie selling her story, since he had hoped to do the same for a higher sum. If, as claimed, his defence counsel were aware at the time of the trial that Julie was in talks with a newspaper, they could have raised the matter in court – but to do so would have exposed them to questions about Jeremy's equivalent intentions.

Instead of the celebration he had anticipated, Jeremy was hand-cuffed and driven in the sweatbox to Wormwood Scrubs. Although the prison was regarded as a model of reform when it was built a century ago, the Scrubs' governor quit in 1982, calling it a 'penal dustbin'.[19]

Like all lifers, Jeremy was initially assigned to the hospital wing, where the newly convicted were assumed to be in a state of shock, watched closely and sedated. After several days he moved onto D Wing, described by writer-in-residence Ken Smith as 'paranoia central. Here some 250 long-sentence prisoners live their cloistered lives, for years together . . . In single occupancy, they each live in cells 8 feet by 12, minimally furnished, poorly ventilated by one small window, hot in summer and cold in winter.'[20] Jeremy joined Smith's literacy classes as he began to adjust. His tutor found that he had 'a sharp, reptilian business-man's brain, considerable self-control, and somewhere still a sense of humour'. He habitually brought every conversation round to his appeal and his determination to clear his name. Sometimes he talked of his family and once Smith saw tears well-ing up, but there seemed to be 'an absence in his grief', perhaps because he was by necessity so focused on himself.

As the months lumbered on, Jeremy moved upstairs and Smith would see him 'greyer, hanging out, rocking on the twos' landing rail. He'd grin, and saunter down, but as time went by, he had less and less writing to show, and spoke only of his business.'

A year or so passed and Jeremy 'drifted off, into the crowd. He grew greyer, yellower, more withdrawn, turning into the colour of old newspapers. Prison was beginning to drown him in its silence. With less and less to say for himself, he began fading into the paintwork and bricks, increasingly absorbed in the time-consuming business of his appeal.'

Within an hour of the verdict, Essex Police had called a news conference. Clearly tense, Deputy Chief Constable Ronald Stone told journalists that although 'with the benefit of that perfect science – hindsight – it could be said that the judgment of senior officers was misdirected' he didn't consider an enquiry necessary.[1]

Home Secretary Douglas Hurd disagreed. Less than an hour later, he called for a report from Stone's superior, Essex Chief Constable Robert Bunyard, adding that he would make a statement to Parliament after discussing the case with HM Chief Inspector of Constabulary, Sir Lawrence Byford.

The media were vociferous in their condemnation of Essex Police. 'Blunders, omissions and ineptitude' proclaimed *The Times*, while the *Daily Mail* referred to 'the Clouseau squad who let the evil murderer stay at large for too long'. The *News of the World* featured a cartoon corpse dragged from a river, its feet encased in cement, arms bound and an axe in its mouth, while a watching detective announced, 'It's an open-and-shut case – suicide.' Former DC David Bird laughs ruefully at the memory: 'That cartoon was horrible. You did get the bung taken out of you something terrible.'[2]

Detective Chief Superintendent James Dickinson led the internal review, examining the evidence file and conducting interviews with a number of officers, forensic staff and the Bamber relatives. His report ran to over 300 pages, expressing regret that DCI Jones was no longer able to account for his decisions, which were 'the focal point of accountability in respect of any inadequacies' albeit as a result of honest actions and 'mistaken judgment'.[3] Several officers were singled out for criticism, as was the investigation's lack of structure, but there was praise for the comprehensive scene of crime photography and the 'very thorough nature' of the Ainsley-led enquiry. Some surprising concessions were made, such as it being 'apparent that without the evidence of Julie Mugford or the discovery of the blood on the sound moderator, there was very little substantiated fact to implicate Jeremy Bamber with the murders'. But there would be no disciplinary action against any officer since the errors, 'whilst not excusable, were in all cases honest mistakes'.

Following Dickinson's report and the subsequent inquiry by the Chief Inspector of Constabulary (Byford's replacement, Sir Richard Barrett), the Home Secretary issued a statement that 'errors were made in the early stages of the police investigation contrary to existing Force practice' and there had been 'inadequate supervision of the senior investigating officer', but 'prompt and effective action to remedy these shortcomings was taken once the Chief Constable and senior officers were made aware of the misgivings which relatives of the Bamber family expressed.'[4] A comprehensive list of guidelines for future investigations were subsequently adopted throughout the police service.

Pathologist Peter Vanezis reflects: 'I guess there are a lot of cases that fall into this category that don't go wrong like that and turn out to be exactly what they seem. To be fair to Essex Police, it's not the sort of thing they came across every day. I think probably even the Met would be out of their comfort zone. Obviously, now we have procedures in place where things like this are extremely unlikely to happen. For example, all firearms injuries and all stabbings, as far as I'm aware, are treated as homicide until proven otherwise. It's the classic hypothesis in science: "Prove to me it's not what it looks like."'[5]

But the shadows cast across the force were long and painful. In 1989 the Chief Constable of Essex Police ended his response to a letter from Robert Boutflour regarding Jeremy's appeal: 'If the system had operated correctly we would have had the benefit of a detective superintendent's objective professional judgment which would have shown up the flaws in the investigation before they actually came to light. I hope now that we can put this terrible case behind us personally and professionally.'[6]

But there would be little chance of that for any of those involved.

Jeremy's first application for appeal, lodged in November 1986, was based on the claim that the judge's address to the jury had been misleading and predisposed towards the prosecution. It was refused by a single judge of the Court of Appeal in March 1988 and again by the full Court of Appeal in March 1989.

A new approach was necessary, and Jeremy began poring over the papers in his case file for any discrepancies, ambiguities and irregularities. In December 1990 he made a statement to the Police Complaints Authority listing twenty-six grievances against Essex Police. As a result, the PCA instructed the City of London Police (COLP) to conduct an independent investigation. The Crown Prosecution Service contacted the Chief Constable of Essex Police in March 1991, observing: 'It is clear from his previous letters that Bamber is looking for every opportunity to make complaints about the handling of his case and the evidence presented by officers of the Essex Police.'[7]

The COLP inquiry was exhaustive and methodical, producing 136 witness statements, lengthy transcripts of interviews and detailed forensic reports. None of Jeremy's allegations, from his accusation that witness statements had been tampered with to the deliberate contamination of the blood inside the silencer, were upheld. Nor was any evidence of criminal action by any police officer produced or of any officer being neglectful in his duties 'in the manner alleged'.[8] Jeremy was informed of COLP's findings and the PCA's decision not to bring disciplinary action in August 1992. He recalls his enraged response at Frankland Prison where he was being held: 'I covered myself in shit and [thought]: "I'll fucking show you". . . losing my marbles.'[9]

It was a rare breach in his normally peaceable behaviour. His categorization had been downgraded from A to B status the previous year on recommendations from the governor and wing governor, with reports that he was cooperative and showed no sign of mental illness. When the *News of the World* announced his downgrading, Essex Police and his relatives made representations to the effect that the family would be at grave risk if he were to escape or be released. His security category was consequently reviewed again and reinstated as Category A. Challenges from his legal representatives about the ruling were rejected; in April 1988, the High Court decreed that he would remain a Category A prisoner until he accepted his guilt and participated in offence-related work.

A new appeal was painstakingly constructed, although a

report commissioned from America's foremost expert in forensic ballistics, Professor Herbert Leon MacDonell, proved disappointing. After studying the crime scene photographs and a wealth of documentation, MacDonell concluded: 'There is no question as to the manner of death of Sheila Caffell. She did not commit suicide but, like the other four victims, was shot to death by someone else.'[10]

More encouraging news came for Jeremy from forensic scientist Mark Webster, who suggested that John Hayward's conclusion about the blood inside the silencer was potentially flawed. Questioning how the original blood grouping tests had been conducted, Webster stated that the method of testing could influence the result. He also queried the assumption that there was no blood left inside the silencer for further tests and drew attention to Mr Justice Drake's statement regarding the ability of scientists to deduce whether blood belonged to a single or multiple individuals simply from its appearance. Webster's views formed part of Jeremy's petition for a referral to the Court of Appeal, submitted to the Home Secretary in September 1993.

'Fresh Clues Could Set Bamber Free' announced the *East Anglian Daily Times* on 28 September 1993. The news quickly went nationwide. In November, John Hayward wrote to the Home Office pointing out that he had 'never excluded' the possibility that the blood came from more than one individual, although he had regarded it as remote.[11] He explained that the judge's remark was taken out of context; a transcript of the speech revealed that he had preceded his words with 'in addition to the scientific tests'. Regarding Webster's theory that the flake of blood taken from the silencer was a heterogeneous mixture of blood from Ralph and June Bamber, Hayward stated: 'I cannot accept that this is a real possibility. I shall, of course, be pleased to revise this opinion in the light of any concrete evidence derived from proper experimental investigation.'

The Home Secretary refused the petition in July 1994. Five months later, Jeremy was informed in writing that his sentence had been extended to whole life by Douglas Hurd in 1988, while it was still the practice to do so without the prisoner's knowledge. He lost his first attempt to challenge the decision in April 1995, despite his counsel pointing out that other prisoners convicted of equally violent crimes had not been subjected to the same ruling.

Jeremy had made no secret of his revulsion at the media during the early days of his imprisonment, but soon came to realize that the press were invaluable if his case was to be kept in the public eye. In April 1995, Gary Jacobs, solicitor and host of Talk Radio's legal phone-in, was surprised to receive a call from Jeremy live on air, politely protesting his tariff and stating that there was 'fresh forensic evidence of such a substantial nature that the Home Secretary should be compelled to refer my case back'.[12]

Occasionally, Jeremy found an ally among journalists, but there were instances when his cooperation failed to produce the desired results, such as his meeting with the *Daily Express* at Long Lartin prison in autumn 1995: 'Bearded Jeremy Bamber bounces in with the air of a man who does not have a care in the world and smiles broadly . . .'[13] The article described a 'pampered, privileged lifestyle', which included a key to his 'room', studying for O levels rather than working, daily badminton sessions, an agent who sold his pictures of supermodels, handsome compensation fees for injuries sustained during a prison van accident and again when his Gameboy was stolen, and at least fifty letters a week from admiring women.

While kiss-and-tells from various young women, claiming to have had relationships with him in prison, were a feature of his first few years in captivity, Jeremy explains the reality behind the other claims: 'Everyone had a key to their cells – not the main lock, they were electronic – it was a privacy lock so that you could lock your own door when you went to work. Education was instead of prison workshops and I was treated exactly like the 100 or so others that went to education every day. I used the gym like other prisoners, and attended when I was allocated to attend, that just so happened to be 5 sessions a week from 8am to 9am. I did do art – but did not have an agent – I donated a series of pictures of supermodels to a charity auction . . . I have had as many as 50 letters a week, but as part of my campaign . . . I received £1,800 for whiplash and other injuries – four of the officers injured with me received the same . . . re: items stolen from me – two prisoners stole the master key from the office and while we were all at work, they robbed all the cells, the prison governor admitted liability and paid everyone for the items they lost.'[14]

In April 1997, his case was transferred to the newly established Criminal Cases Review Commission. Further tests were conducted on the silencer using recent DNA technology: a profile was obtained from the baffle plates. Scientists agreed to wait a year until the latest supersensitive tests, DNA Low Copy Number (DNA LCN) became available. When the baffle plates were swabbed, a strong female profile was obtained, along with minor male contributions. The CCRC made enquiries regarding other blood-based exhibits from the case for direct comparison purposes and were astonished to learn that Essex Police had destroyed most of the original exhibits in February 1996, without notifying Jeremy's legal team. The officer instructed to sort the items into waste bags and transport them to an incineration facility in London had expressed concern about the order from a DCI at Special Branch, who stated that he had been unaware of any judicial consideration in the case.

Despite the destruction of so much evidence, comparison tests with a DNA sample from Sheila's birth mother led to scientists stating that the DNA in the silencer could not have come from Sheila. Deciding that the DNA results began 'to support the theory put forward by the defence at trial', in March 2001 the CCRC referred the case to the Appeal Court on the basis that 'if the evidence about the blood in the sound moderator could not be viewed as having the significance attached to it at trial, then the rest of the evidence would not be sufficient to maintain a conviction.'[15]

Jeremy was ecstatic: 'I am now 40 and as I have been told, life begins at 40. I am looking forward to freedom and getting on with my life.'[16] His Aunt Pamela was lost for words: 'We are just stunned. The whole family is completely stunned.'[17]

In July, a team of Metropolitan Police officers began a four-month investigation into the case, which included visiting White House Farm, then home to Ann Eaton and her family, to take samples from areas of bloodstaining in the master bedroom for further DNA tests. Two areas of staining, one on the underlay by the door to the landing and another on the floorboards near the box room, tested positive for blood. They also took possession of a bedside lamp which the officer in charge recognized from the original crime scene photographs, the rings June had been wearing on the night of her murder, and Sheila's jewellery box, containing a piece of her fingernail.

The hearing opened at the Royal Courts of Justice in London on 17 October 2002. *The Times* reported: 'Jeremy Bamber's hair is now greying and cut shapelessly. He wore a white shirt, unbuttoned to expose a thick, muscular neck and the outline of a strong chest.' Eyed by his relatives and flanked by four prison officers, Jeremy stood to confirm his name, sounding bright and eager. He sat down again, looking up repeatedly 'through the bars of his cage' to the packed public gallery and spent most of the proceedings writing notes for his defence team. Representing him, Michael Turner QC stated there were fourteen grounds for believing the conviction unsafe. That evidence was examined, but the three judges focused on the issue of the DNA inside the silencer.

Jeremy's defence argued that statistical tests on a DNA profile from Pamela Boutflour supported the assertion that the unidentified female DNA inside the silencer belonged to June. But as the case unfolded, the court heard that it wasn't possible to ascertain whether the DNA originated from blood or other cellular material, or how it got there and when. During the course of the forensic examinations, the rifle and silencer had been disassembled and put back together, risking trace evidence being transferred from one area to another. Several other areas inside the silencer had also been subjected to DNA LCN tests and complex mixtures were obtained.

Forensic scientists for both prosecution and defence admitted they couldn't exclude Sheila as a contributor to the mixtures, but the complexity of the mixed profiles meant that it wasn't feasible to statistically evaluate the significance of the findings. Experiments had been conducted involving computer simulation to determine the average number of bands that might be shared by chance in a three-person mixture; these indicated that as many as thirteen could be shared by chance. In this case, all but three of the twenty bands from Sheila's profile were represented, providing positive evidence to support the view that DNA from Sheila was in fact present. But since it could not be determined whether this DNA came from blood, the evidence was not beneficial to prosecution or defence. The Appeal Court accepted Mark Webster's assertion – ironically on behalf of the defence – that in view of all the evidence presented, the DNA testing results were 'completely meaningless' and therefore could not be said to render the verdict unsafe.[18]

Jeremy's conviction was upheld. His relatives were filmed leaving the court looking both relieved and victorious. Recognizing that his best chance of freedom to date was in tatters, Jeremy posted a notice on the nascent website run by his supporters: 'Important News . . . One Million Pounds Reward Guaranteed . . . Do you have or do you know someone who has information that could lead to my release? If you have then I can guarantee one million pounds upon my release from prison.'[19]

By March 2004, his legal team had submitted another request for his case to be referred to the Court of Appeal, on the basis of evidence which they asserted was not available to them previously. The CCRC made a provisional decision to reject the application due to its limited scope. Jeremy devoted hour after hour to studying the crime scene photographs and police logs, resulting in extensive further submissions. In 2005 Andrew Hunter, then MP for Basingstoke, became a staunch vocal supporter, raising questions in the House of Commons about Jeremy's conviction, 'one of the worst miscarriages of justice in recent times'.[20]

The CCRC made a second provisional decision not to refer his case in March 2007. The following month, Jeremy passed a polygraph examination at HMP Full Sutton after years of petitioning the Home Secretary for permission to sit the test. 'I am absolutely convinced he is innocent,' examiner Terence Mullins stated. 'He did not show any sign of a reaction, not a flicker which would have shown up guilt.'[21] Because the test is not regarded as conclusive – it measures physiological reactions to questions in order to determine whether a subject is telling the truth – the results were not admissible in court. Nonetheless, in 2014 mandatory polygraph tests began being carried out on UK sex offenders.

In 2008, Jeremy applied to the High Court for a review of his tariff. Mr Justice Tugendhat acknowledged the reports of good behaviour and absence of mental disorder, but placed greater emphasis on the nature of the murders themselves and victim impact statements. He declared: 'In my judgment you ought to spend the whole of the rest of your life in prison, and I so order.'[22] Jeremy's subsequent application to the Court of Appeal regarding his tariff was dismissed, likewise his submission that the judgment concerned a point of law of general public importance which ought to be considered by the House of Lords.

2010 marked the passing of twenty-five years since the murders at White House Farm. David James Smith interviewed Jeremy in person at Full Sutton for a balanced article in the *Sunday Times*. Expecting to be 'confronted by a demented psychopath', Smith remembers finding Jeremy:

> . . . very human and understandable. But what did strike me was that there was something 'missing' in him. I can't be more precise than that except to say that there was a certain coldness to his eyes. It's a cliché, but it's the truth. Bearing that in mind, he has been examined umpteen times by psychologists and there are no glaring personality disorders. There were times when his eyes welled up. Did I think it was genuine? Yes, I did. But then again, who am I to judge because obviously some people are very adept at lying and he has had a long time to practise, if that's what he *is* doing. I also felt he was very good at hiding his true feelings, as most people are who have been in prison for that length of time.[23]

The then latest submissions to the CCRC were voluminous, presented over a long period by Jeremy, his legal representatives, his fiancée and a dedicated supporter who was himself a former fellow prisoner. Ultimately they sought to advance three distinct arguments: evidence not disclosed at trial would support the contention that someone other than Jeremy or Sheila had committed the murders; fresh evidence supported the argument that Sheila had committed the murders before killing herself; and fresh evidence generally supported either of the former and demonstrated that Jeremy did not commit the murders. Under the latter, several scenarios were constructed around the 'one dead male, one dead female' confusion in the radio log, including that the police had discovered Sheila's body in the kitchen and repositioned it upstairs; or that she was alive but appeared dead in the kitchen when the raid team entered, escaping upstairs under her own volition only to be killed by a police officer.

In February 2011, the CCRC informed Jeremy that they had provisionally decided not to refer his case to the Court of Appeal, but if he wished to make further submissions he should do so within the year. Simon McKay, a Leeds-based lawyer specializing in judicial review and human rights, agreed to represent him. Experts were commissioned to study the photographs and documentation regarding the marks on Nevill's back and wounds to Sheila, with a view to establishing whether they had been inflicted while the silencer was attached to the weapon. Ballistics expert Philip Boyce conducted experiments on pigskin, asserting that Nevill's back injuries were caused by the end of the rifle barrel and that at least one of Sheila's wounds was consistent with the rifle being fired without a silencer.

Boyce's findings were highlighted in *Bamber: The New Evidence*, which aired in a prime-time slot on ITV in March 2012. Despite the considerable publicity boost to Jeremy's campaign, one month later the CCRC informed him that 'despite a lengthy and complex investigation' into his claims that he was wrongly convicted of his family's murders, they would not be referring his case to the Court of Appeal. Rebutting all the points made in the submissions and dismissing Boyce's findings, the CCRC observed that 'matters of pure speculation or unsubstantiated allegation constitute neither new evidence nor new argument.' Noting that Jeremy had been represented by five different lawyers during the course of their review, they concluded: 'This is a final decision and brings to a close the Commission's current longest running case.'[24] Jeremy's reaction was to immediately instruct McKay Law to issue proceedings for a judicial review of the decision.

By summer, he was excited by a new possibility: 'We now have the key to the gate – I sent it to my solicitor, my office and the IPCC yesterday. If we can find verifiable proof of life in the house when I'm outside with the coppers then the case has to collapse immediately – it has to be confirmed proof of life to be a slam dunk point – well, I have found that evidence.'[25] To that end, he spent the summer probing the police logs and assessing material on the 'window sighting'. He also applied for permission to be interviewed for television in order to argue his case before a national audience and gave thought to the autobiography he would write if he won his liberty.

The High Court refused permission for a judicial review of the CCRC decision on 29 November 2012. Disappointed but unbowed, Jeremy began putting documents together for a disclosure application and gathering evidence for a final CCRC submission. At the time of writing (May 2015), the CCRC has no current application from him.

In July 2013, he and two other prisoners serving whole life sentences took an appeal against their tariff to the Grand Chamber of the European Court of Human Rights. Judges voted by a majority of sixteen to one that 'whole life sentences without any prospect of release amount to inhuman and degrading treatment.'[26] Two years later, in February 2015, the European Court of Human Rights ruled that existing legislation was in fact consistent with the principle of life meaning life in the most serious criminal cases. Nonetheless, the Secretary of State retains the power to release a whole life prisoner in exceptional circumstances at his or her discretion, thereby giving those inmates the possibility of review after all, in principle.

Thirty years after the murders at White House Farm, Jeremy Bamber's determination to overturn his conviction shows no signs of abating. One issue more than any other has been the focus of his repeated attempts to reach the Court of Appeal: the silencer, which remains a sticking point in any discussion about the case.

Post-trial controversy about its provenance began in April 1987, when the press office of Essex Police took a call from a *Sunday Express* reporter. He wanted to know if they would comment on Jeremy's claim that a statement dated 7 August 1985 from DCI Jones revealed that he had found the silencer that day under the bed and placed it in the gun cupboard for safety.

Former senior investigating officer Mike Ainsley derided the claim as 'total nonsense' in a letter to the Crown Prosecution Service, adding that if such a document ever appeared, it would be forged.[1] He had also spoken to Jeremy's solicitor Paul Terzeon who hadn't seen the statement but was assured by his client that he had posted it to his office. It didn't arrive, but Jeremy's defence team admitted they were 'always suspicious of the circumstances in which the moderator came to be found', although they assured their client that the evidence, as it was known, had been investigated thoroughly.[2] They warned him that even if that was shown to be untrue, 'it would have to be of such a falsehood that it went to the core of that which the prosecution was trying to prove'.[3]

Jeremy's arguments about the silencer are by necessity circuitous, stemming from a muddle over the reference number attached to it by Essex Police. Because exhibits are given the initials of the person finding the item, when DI Ron Cook was handed the silencer by DS Stan Jones in August 1985, he gave it the reference SBJ/1. Upon learning that David Boutflour had found it and Jones had merely collected it from the family, he changed the initials accordingly to DB/1. Realizing that could lead to confusion with exhibits located by DC David Bird, he included David Boutflour's middle initial. Thus the silencer was given the final reference DRB/1.

So far, so straightforward. But Essex Police were not always consistent in recording the correct reference. For instance, DI Cook's typed and signed statement of 24 October 1985 bore the exhibit number DRB/1 while an identical version refers to the silencer as DB/1. Furthermore, some statements were modified to reflect the change in exhibit reference without the witness being informed: in her original statement dated 13 November 1985, forensic scientist Glynis Howard referred to the silencer as DB/1; the exhibit number had been changed in pencil to DRB/1, while a typed version of the statement included the final exhibit number. Howard recalled: 'I never received any contact from Essex Police informing me that my statement had been altered in this respect.'[4] She accepted that it was an administrative matter, but 'would have expected to have been informed in writing' in order to prepare a new statement reflecting the alteration, 'which I would have signed'.[5]

The COLP enquiry of 1991 explored five allegations from Jeremy regarding the silencer. Their subsequent observations were scathing, noting that ever since his trial, he had 'attempted to throw doubt on the circumstances surrounding the silencer' by a combination of 'suggestion, implication and a general clouding of the issues', and had attempted to reinforce his claims 'by discrediting the police officers concerned and, to some extent, the scientists'.[6] Among his allegations was the deliberate contamination of the silencer by the police. Asked if he had any evidence to support his theory, he replied: 'No, but it would be unlikely that I would have such evidence.'

The investigating officers were especially critical of his assertion that a hair was placed on the silencer to implicate him in the murders. Aware that a grey hair had been lost from the silencer in transit to the laboratory, and despite not having any grey himself, Jeremy alleged that the hair was lifted from his brush by the police, who were obliged to lose it when Julie revealed that he had dyed his hair some time before the murders. COLP stated: 'Bamber has created a totally malicious argument from the same facts. He has manufactured a "red herring" and made a complaint from totally incomprehensible conclusions.' They found no evidence that there was any other silencer at White House Farm, save the silencer found by David Boutflour on 10 August

1985, and described the oversights in recording the correct silencer reference as 'simple and logical and without sinister implications'. It was regrettable that Essex Police's 'failure to adhere to certain principles' had allowed such errors to creep into the documentary administration of exhibits.

In the intervening years, Jeremy has put forward a number of other scenarios involving the silencer. In one he alleges that DS Jones found Anthony Pargeter's silencer at the scene while relatives found a second silencer in September; the evidence for both was then amalgamated, implying that only one silencer had been found. In 2010, reporter David James Smith told him that the prosecution would always argue he had woven a complex conspiracy around simple confusion over a tag number. Jeremy responded by asking why, if David Boutflour had found the silencer on 10 August, he would 'then go and phone on 11 September and say, "I've just been to White House Farm and I've found a sound moderator with blood on, can you come and get it from me?"'[7] But the message report of David's call shows that he rang regarding the collection of other items and confirms that the silencer had already been submitted for forensic examination.

In 2011, Jeremy announced on his blog: 'We can now prove 100% that there were two sound moderators obtained by police at different times and that the City of London Police enquiry knew this back in 1991', stating that it had been established 'through a number of different means, including witness testimony'.[8] David Boutflour had confirmed at the trial that he had shown Essex Police two of his own silencers, which were identical to the one belonging to the Anschütz. Asked by Rivlin if these were taken into police possession, he replied that they were not. In a 2010 interview, David stated that at some point his silencers were collected by the police, who wanted 'to make sure that there couldn't be any possibility that I had actually involved my silencer'.[9] Although Jeremy acknowledged that there was 'no documented record of David handing in two additional sound moderators in September 1985', he insisted that this was the case.[10] But the exhibits officer recalls that David's silencers were taken into police possession during the trial, not before.

After investigating Jeremy's submissions for a referral to the Court of Appeal in 2011, the CCRC stated that his claims about the silencer were 'not supported by the material that exists, and in some instances appear to be based on a misinterpretation of that material'.[11] Again, they saw nothing to support the contention that the silencer was found at any time other than 10 August 1985 and no evidence that there was more than one silencer discovered. But in March 2013, Jeremy vowed: 'I can now prove with 100% certainty that Essex Police seized one Parker Hale (MM1 type) suppressor from the house on 7 August 1985.'[12] He had 'official documents referring to all of the six forensic reference numbers relating to either sound moderators or silencers, they are not various typing mistakes but refer to different police officers who were exhibiting these items either during the investigation or at trial – except for DB/1 or DRB/2 which refers to Boutflour.'

The Times took up the story closer to the latest CCRC decision: 'He will cite documents suggesting that police and forensic experts on the case had in their possession at least *five* silencers of the same make. Bamber's lawyer, Simon McKay, will argue that a range of different items was examined by scientists, raising fears that the results were merged ... Documents released to Bamber are now said to have cast doubt on the silencer's provenance. They show that, as well as the device found in the gun cupboard, investigators collected three other silencers belonging to family members. There was also one kept in the forensic science laboratory for testing.'[13]

All the former police officers interviewed for the purposes of this book echo retired ballistics expert Malcolm Fletcher who, when asked how many silencers he had examined, responded: 'One sound moderator which had its number changed, purely down to the fact that the exhibit number on that would have been the person who initially found it.'[14]

A statement from Jeremy on his website explains his current position: 'I left the rifle without the sound moderator attached, so Sheila would not have gone to the gun cupboard to look for it, attached it to the gun, used it, removed it and put it back in the gun cupboard. The sound moderator is a total red herring. It was never part of the defence case and we can now prove that it was not even on the gun, it was tampered with, swapped around, contaminated and all of its paper work faked so it cannot form part of the Crown's case, not any more.'[15]

Many of Jeremy's assertions are contradictory, particularly when scrutinized against earlier claims. He has a ready answer for that – namely, that new material keeps emerging – while the repeated production of 'fresh' evidence creates doubt and confusion about several core issues. Undeniably, there are inconsistencies, some of which have been more satisfactorily resolved than others, but it is apparent that the police and courts are weary of dealing with his case. In 2002, his lawyer's request for information was met with an exasperated response by the detective inspector in charge: 'The police will spend all their time responding to your requests if you continue with this.'[16]

David James Smith, the last journalist to publish an interview with Jeremy in prison, muses: 'The CCRC have bent over backwards to be fair to him. He's had free access to all the papers, but ultimately nothing has so far emerged that makes it likely he didn't do it. And it's incredibly easy to pick away at inconsistencies – which there are bound to be in a case as tragic, complex and far-reaching as this one. But it's no good focusing on little details, you have got to look at the whole picture. It's not enough to pull out this and that – everything has to be examined in context. That's been done, but it hasn't made any difference to his incarceration. Plus, for him to be innocent, the scale of the conspiracy would have to be huge. Some of what he argues does sound, on one level, plausible. The relatives planting the silencer – you can weigh that up. Julie Mugford's part in it all is very hazy as well – I find it odd that she acted as she did and no charges were brought against her. But even then, for him to have been fitted up as he claims, that's really a *mountain* of conspiracy. Is it possible? Perhaps, but very unlikely.'[17]

Nonetheless, largely through the efforts of Jeremy's campaign team, on the anniversary of the shootings in August 2013, over 104,000 British citizens used social media to create a 'Thunderclap' declaring their belief in his innocence. The figure is negligible in terms of the population as a whole, but no other prisoner serving a life sentence can reasonably claim to have even that level of support.

The campaign website maintains that Essex Police are still withholding 175 photographs along with 340,000 pages of documents, many of them under Public Interest Immunity. However, in a letter dated 13 October 2013, Jeremy stated that he had now in fact seen '320,000 pages of the 340,000 pages that attracted PII'. In a second letter on 25 December 2013 he wrote that the entire 340,000 pages had been made available and could be used 'in any way I so choose, but for the moment it is not going to assist me in having my appeal heard any sooner and actually it'll muck up any future prosecution of those who deserve to be in jail'.

The police position on his previous claims of withheld material is encapsulated in the declaration of former senior investigating officer Mike Ainsley: 'Bamber was tried on an abundance of evidence and properly convicted. There was no mis-carriage of justice. There were no grave errors in my investigation. No witness for the prosecution gave false or misleading evidence. There were no 'paper' errors. The defence lawyers had full and unencumbered access to ALL of the police statements, documents and exhibits at any time.'[18]

Until recently, it was difficult to think of a constabulary who were more publicly pilloried than Essex Police for their work on the Bamber case. None of the retired officers interviewed for this book were unaffected by the investigation; some have written private memoirs in an attempt to make sense of what happened.

In March 1994, when Essex Police newsletter *The Law* referred unfavourably to the investigation, the criticism from their own particularly rankled. DS Neil Davidson responded in a letter that 'a thorough job was done, based on the facts available at the time. As later facts became known, the enquiry took a different course. Success or failure of an inquiry can depend on many things, not just the thoroughness of an inquiry team . . . A certain amount of luck can play its part.' DS Winston Bernard was also stirred into a defence of those officers who attended the scene, 'affected by what they saw, confronted by a supposedly grieving sole survivor, having to live by decisions made on the day. We are human and have human reactions. Those reactions (no matter how professional we are) may affect our performance . . . They have been made to feel ashamed of being involved in a successful court case. They worked for nearly a year in securing a conviction of one of the most evil men ever to come to the notice of the Essex Police.'

Journalist and author Bob Woffinden, who changed his stance on Jeremy from innocent to guilty over a period of several years, points out that Jeremy has 'a valid argument about the length of time he's serving in prison. He was sentenced to twenty-five years and the Home Secretary increased that some while afterwards. He has served his original sentence, and irrespective of whether or not you think the judge handed out a sufficient punishment, he has done the time allotted to him by the court. So I think that's more the path Jeremy should be pursuing, because that's a more viable route and one which he does have a valid argument about, in my opinion. The fact is that he's now being convicted by the CCRC and that's unconstitutional. In those respects, I wouldn't necessarily be opposed to the idea of Jeremy being granted a re-trial. But it's absolutely certain that he would be found guilty again.'[19]

During his almost thirty years in captivity, Jeremy has been housed in 122 different prison cells. For the most part, he has avoided the violent confrontations with other inmates that are endemic to prison life. One notable exception is an unprovoked attack eleven years ago, when an inmate stabbed him in the neck while he was speaking to a friend on the telephone. Rushed to hospital, he received twenty-eight stitches for the wound.

Before his trial, Jeremy had been reluctant to submit to medical examination, resulting in limited reports that concluded, as far as it was possible to do so, that he was not suffering from any discernible mental illness. Reports prepared by HMP Full Sutton six years later confirmed the same, variously describing him as 'personable, intelligent and cunning . . . inwardly cold and unfeeling'.[20] Over the years, he has become more cooperative with psychologists and is now keen to highlight the fact that following examination by at least 'twenty-seven different psychologists, not a single one of these experts has concluded that I show any traits consistent with psychopathy.'[21] These are routine assessments conducted within the prison service itself, rather than in-depth psychological examinations from independent experts, with the most recent available report on Jeremy dating from 2009. Professor Vincent Egan, a Chartered Clinical Psychologist and senior lecturer in forensic pathology at Leicester University, was instructed to assess him for possible psychopathy, any putative personality disorder, and to discover whether his impression management – the means by which he sought to control perceptions about himself – negated prior assessments. His future risk of violence was also considered.

Egan was given access to Jeremy's prison medical records, interviewed him at length and set him various psychological tests. These included the PCL-R, a revised psychopathy checklist originally developed by Canadian psychologist Robert D. Hare and widely regarded as the definitive evaluation. Individuals scoring more than 30 out of a possible 40 points are regarded as psychopathic. The PCL-R lists the following symptoms: glib and superficial charm, grandiose self-worth, seeking stimulation or prone to boredom, pathological lying, conning and manipulativeness, lack of remorse or guilt, shallow affect, callousness and lack of empathy, a parasitic lifestyle, poor behavioural controls, promiscuous sexual behaviour, early behaviour problems, lack of realistic long term goals, impulsivity, irresponsibility, failure to accept responsibility for one's own actions, many short term relationships, juvenile delinquency, revocation of condition release (withdrawn probation) and criminal versatility.

Professor Egan found that Jeremy was not suffering 'clinical psychopathy or even mild psychopathy'.[22] Nor did he have any personality disorders. His risk assessment results placed him 'in the "low" band for a final risk of violence judgment' while his impression management calculation showed that he was within the low to normal range and therefore was not presenting himself in an excessively neutral way in order to deceive the assessor. In summary, Egan proclaimed that 'these findings suggest it is hard to sustain the view that Jeremy Bamber is so expert in deceptive self-presentation as to maintain this front over a variety of different assessors, different assessment instruments and different times . . . Dangerous, violent persons tend to be angry, alienated, impulsive and out of control, and none of these qualities appear to reflect Mr Bamber.'

Feeling vindicated by Egan's report, Jeremy was outraged the following year when psychologist Kerry Daynes declared in an interview for Sky Three's *Killing Mum and Dad: The Jeremy Bamber Story* that he 'ticks an awful lot of the boxes for a psychopath'.[23] With the PCL-R in mind, she announced: 'Here is somebody who is grandiose. He's arrogant. He seems to have very little emotion. And what he does is very shallow and rather fake. He manipulates other people and he's quite happy to use people to meet his own ends.' Echoing the psychiatrist hired by Jeremy's defence before the trial, she stated that in the past, Jeremy had 'coped with overwhelming emotions by simply cutting off from them, and really he's done the same thing in response to his offences. Denial of his offences is the biggest form of cutting off you can have. In his mind, he probably believes that he really didn't do it.' Jeremy complained to Ofcom that the programme unfairly and inaccurately portrayed him as a psychopath; Daynes had never met him nor read any of the favourable psychological reports on him. Ofcom rejected his complaints.

In a recent letter, Jeremy reflects on the assessments he has undertaken in prison with a potentially telling phrase: 'I don't tend to cooperate with the psychologist unless . . . well, it's for a whole load of reasons, though for the most part I'm happy for them to probe my mind.'[24] His comment about non-cooperation is a curious one, given the assessment into his impression management, perhaps implying that his replies are not always as genuine as they seem. However, he goes on to refer to the much earlier Gartree analysis of his character: 'I don't believe my personality is cold, though it's hard to judge yourself – I do try to be reserved until I know someone quite well, perhaps that can seem a bit cold sometimes, and unfeeling – the complete opposite, my PCL-R tests prove the point but those who know me will attest to this . . . Mostly I look at how the prison system wanted to find this supposed evil monster inside me, so I was given all kinds of labels and put under so much stress over the first 6–8 years; there was never any monster to find . . . I'd like to hope that if they wrote a report about me now it would be a little more flattering.'

Jeremy turned fifty-four in January 2015, in the confines of HMP Full Sutton where he had been incarcerated for almost fifteen years. Five months later, in June 2015, he was suddenly and unexpectedly transferred to Wakefield Prison. Prior to that, he stated that he did his time as a 'whole life' inmate day by day and took part in various prison activities, making use of the gym and practising yoga, and was studying for an OU degree in Philosophy. He worked in the Braille shop, scanning books and converting them using a computer programme, and taught as a 'peer partner' in Full Sutton's education department, assisting other prisoners with literacy ('what helps is that I'm patient and I empathise – plus I'm well-trained so I know what I'm doing'). He describes himself as:

> ... a normal bloke. I'm sure I've got lots of personality flaws and I can be selfish and I can be kind of nasty, just like everybody else at times. But I'm not cold, I'm a [loving] person, I can make friends. I've always been the same guy. I've never been violent, ever. I don't have that in me. I'm not someone who gets angry, who loses my temper or lashes out, ever. And I'm certainly not a murderer.[25]

Is he sincere or not? Claims of innocence in letter after letter, interview after interview, year after year, coming from a man who is rarely anything other than extremely personable to the media, can be very persuasive. Or is that, too, the mark of a psychopath, who cares nothing for the feelings of those close to his victims as he grows increasingly desperate in his attempts to gain freedom?

Epilogue

Many lives were changed forever by the White House Farm murders.

In the aftermath of the trial, Colin Caffell trained to become a workshop facilitator and trauma counsellor, involving himself with the Parents of Murdered Children support group. His relationship with Heather broke down a few months after the shootings. In 1988, he wrote to the man convicted of killing his sons. The reply was in Jeremy's trademark capital letters, and told Colin that his letter had been 'a touch premature. Your [sic] writing to me hoping, I guess, for the last few pieces of the jigsaw so that you may hold the picture of what happened is not possible. If I could furnish you with what you wanted then I would gladly do so – whatever happened that fateful night will never be fully explained . . .'[1]

When Colin didn't respond and went on to participate in the BBC's *Everyman: As We Forgive Them . . . ?* in February 1989, Jeremy wrote again, raging at his former brother-in-law for publicly disbelieving him:

> You can't imagine how I've suffered since Sheila killed my family – I don't suppose you care and why should you, Colin, with your nice little book and your pretty little sculptures pouring out your grief to any film crew around – nice timing too, eh, with my appeal up soon . . . Maybe you'll be on Wogan next and can advertise your book and sculptures that way – how you can cheapen Daniel and Nicholas and their tragic death I just don't know . . . It was your fault that Sheila went mad and killed everyone.[2]

There was no more communication between them, but in 1994 Colin wrote to the *Guardian* after reading about Jeremy's submissions for an appeal. He urged people to bear in mind that his former brother-in-law 'is an extremely dangerous and seductive individual, so I am not surprised some people are taken in by him when they only hear his side of the story.'[3]

That year, Colin told 'the other side' in his book *In Search of the Rainbow's End: The Inside Story of the Bamber Murders*, and gradually built a career as an outstanding sculptor and ceramicist, exhibiting throughout Europe and South Africa. Today, he is the director of an art gallery in Cornwall, where he lives with his wife and daughter. 'No one around here knows who I am or my background,' he declares. 'I do visit the twins' grave whenever I am in London, but I try not to think about the whole thing. I've re-married and have a new family. I moved to get away from it.'[4]

Jeremy said of Julie Mugford in 2010: 'Once I'd come to jail, I knew that she would never go back.'[5] It didn't stop him trying at first. In April 1987, after reading about his ex-girlfriend in the *Daily Mirror*, Jeremy wrote to her:

> On the one hand I was very pleased to read that you have been reinstated in your dream job with all the advantages such a step entails, such as security, peace of mind and future prospects. On the other hand I am also reminded that I have spent some six months convicted of something I'm not guilty of and all the hardship such as an unjust verdict . . . I could never forgive you if you wrongly abandoned me to a life in prison because you couldn't find the strength and courage to do what's right. A good first step would be to write to me.[6]

But Julie ignored his letter, passing it to the police together with the cards he had sent for Valentine's Day and Christmas. She continued teaching for another two years before deciding to travel. In Australia, she met a Canadian computer salesman, whom she married one year later in Essex. When Jeremy's case was referred to the Court of Appeal in 2002, Julie was living with her husband and children in Canada. Then vice principal of a primary school in Winnipeg, she told journalists: 'Do I stand by my original story? Yes, absolutely. I always assumed he would be in jail for life. And while I fully accept that new forensic techniques could throw new light on the case, I still believe he is guilty.'[7] Julie arrived in London to give evidence at the appeal but wasn't called and returned to her life in Canada.

*

White House Farm stood empty for five years after the murders, virtually unchanged. While Peter Eaton continued to act as manager, Jeremy battled his relatives for the tenancy from prison, pending his first appeal. In 1989, Peter and Ann travelled to York with a representative of the Henry Smith Charity to oppose his bid at a specially-convened hearing at Full Sutton, where Jeremy had been transferred. Looking 'fairly tanned and sporting a designer short-cropped beard', he promptly withdrew his claim.[8]

Twenty individuals applied for the tenancy, which was awarded to the Eatons on 25 March 1990. Ann recalled how, ever since Jeremy's second arrest, 'I had felt responsible for the contents of White House Farm. I did my best to keep them all safe. I visited the house every morning and evening – doing the Aga and keeping the house aired, feeding the cat, drawing the curtains, lights on in the evenings, off in the mornings for five years or there about.'[9] She and her husband and children moved into the house in the summer of 1990. Driving Nevill's blue Sherpa van, Peter and David collected all the effects and furnishings that had languished in a cell at Witham Police Station and returned them to their rightful place.

Barbara Wilson had stopped working for the Eatons the previous year: 'I'd promised Mr Bamber I'd look after the farm so I left at the end of his tenancy. I did four years and haven't been back since. Who could live there knowing what had happened?'[10] Colin, too, found it 'inconceivable' that the family would want to live there.[11] David Boutflour reflects: 'Peter wanted more land, Ann was quite happy to have a bigger house. She liked it there [but] I couldn't do that, although I've had such happy times there. We have been back since and although I've felt reasonably relaxed there, the memories can never go, can they? I do know that the children have had some nightmares.'[12]

A year after moving in, Ann declared that she and her family had 'tried to block out that very unhappy traumatic experience' and for the most part succeeded.[13] She once dreamed of living at Vaulty Manor, but White House Farm became home. She felt an affinity to the place, despite its past – or perhaps because of it, having been its guardian for so long. Even in the immediate aftermath of the murders, when she kept seeing the faces of her aunt and uncle, cousin Sheila and the twins, 'they were all happy, smiling faces', untouched by the horror that had unfolded there.[14]

The Pargeters retrieved the items promised to them at White House Farm, having already informed the Eatons that they intended to contest the wills. Anthony and Jacqueline put in a claim for both Nevill and June's estates after the former decreased in value during the Eatons' running of N. & J. Bamber Ltd. The family were rent apart emotionally and financially by the legal action that followed. With Jeremy disinherited due to his conviction, the courts eventually ruled that the estates should pass to Pamela, working on the principle that in the absence of contrary evidence, the five deceased were assumed to have died in order of seniority. The beneficiary would be the first victim's next of kin. Since June was the eldest by a matter of days and her mother Mabel Speakman had died within months of the murders, all monies and effects passed to Pamela. She handed Nevill's estate to his niece and nephew, and everything from the Speakman side to her son and daughter.

The company set up by Nevill and June, N. & J. Bamber Ltd, was dissolved in 1999. Jeremy's shares in the caravan site were bought by his relatives and split between them. In October 2013, Osea Leisure Park celebrated its eightieth anniversary under the management of Mabel Speakman's great-granddaughter Janie, while Vaulty Manor Farm has served as an exclusive wedding venue for over a decade. Bourtree Cottage, together with Sheila's flat in Maida Vale, was sold after the estates had been settled. The land at Little Renters Farm, which Nevill had purchased in the hope that it would encourage Jeremy to settle into country life, became the property of the Eatons.

Jeremy has had no contact with his relatives for many years. His uncle Robert stopped referring to him by name and until his own death, in 2010, would only mention his nephew by prison number or as 'the evil one'.[15]

Sheila's blood grandfather, Eric Jay, died in February 1989. His wife Margaret passed away four years later. Sheila's mother Christine still lives with her husband in Canada, near their three children and five grandchildren.

Jeremy's birth parents, Major and Mrs Marsham, live out their retirement in a mews house near Hampton Court Palace. 'I cannot be held responsible for his behaviour,' declared Major Marsham after Jeremy was found guilty of the murders. 'We had no part in his upbringing whatsoever. He is a horrible man.'[16] He made it plain there was 'not going to be any reuniting. We have perfectly nice children, who've also been greatly affected by this. Quite frankly he's nothing to do with us.'

Told of his response, Jeremy stated: 'I'd like their support, what son wouldn't? I am sure my life would have been very different if I hadn't been adopted.'

Today, a small headstone marks the spot in the Tolleshunt D'Arcy churchyard where Nevill and June's ashes lie buried. The only indication of the violence of their deaths is in the line: 'Tragically taken from us.' On the church itself, an old-fashioned lamp hangs above the entrance to the porch, where a wooden plaque reads: 'The lantern outside this porch was given in memory of Nevill and June Bamber, former churchwardens, died 1985.' June, especially, would have appreciated the significance of the memorial, whose soft light glows on the path each night, invoking Jesus's phrase: 'I am the light of the world. Whoever follows me will never walk in darkness . . .'

Inspirational quotes were one of June's passions. In 2006, when her blue Bible was returned to her family, they found it crammed with little notes and passages she had underlined. One read: 'Evil only thrives when good men do nothing.' It was this Bible which had been found next to Sheila on the morning of her death, opened at psalms 51–55 with a red smear under the line 'Save me from bloodguiltiness, O God, / the God who saves me.' The note on stiff card that had slipped between Sheila's shoulder and the stained pages of the book bore June's handwriting in her own words: 'Love one another. A determination always to act in the others' best interest, whether we feel good or not, whether we like them or not. It is an act of will, commandment to obey. Be determined to be loving and kind to every person you meet whether you like them or not. Lord Jesus in Thy mercy, teach me to love for Thy name's sake, help me to live and speak as a Christian, no matter what others may think.'[17]

In Highgate Cemetery, the resting place of Sheila and her young sons awaits a new memorial to replace the original wooden one eroded by the elements. Spring flowers from her grandmother's garden on the Blackwater estuary bloom there year after year, near the stone piano marking the grave of music hall entertainer Harry Thornton. On a still, misty afternoon, it suddenly doesn't seem beyond the bounds of possibility that a ghostly melody will play.

'Sheila absolutely loved music,' her close friend Tora recalls. 'She could sing too, and someone once asked her to record a song. I said, "Do you want to do that, Bambi?" and her face lit up, "Oh yeah, I would!" She often had music on at her flat. Nick and Dan would jig about with her.' She pauses for a moment, thinking. 'I know it sounds idyllic, how we talk about her, but she was just such a lovely person, full of sweetness and fun. We saw her almost every day and there was no side to her that wasn't good.'

Tora stops again, then says simply: 'We loved her.'[18]

Appendix I:

A reconstruction of events at
White House Farm on 7 August 1985

The official police account of how Jeremy Bamber killed his family is contained in the report to the Director of Public Prosecutions in November 1985, written with a view to having him committed for trial.

Acknowledging that the order of deaths could not be determined with certainty, the report contends that:

> ... there were probably ten shots fired in the first fusillade [four into Nevill, one into Sheila and five into June] and the remaining three – two into June's head, one into Sheila's head – were inflicted after Ralph Nevill was killed in the kitchen. Eight shots were fired into the boys – eight cases were recovered in their bedroom. Four shots were fired into Ralph Nevill in the kitchen – namely, the two in his temple area and the two in the top of his head. Three cartridge cases were recovered in the kitchen. It is therefore reasonable to assume that the fourth cartridge case was carried on the feet of the killer, or possibly a police officer, and deposited on the stairway.

A potential explanation was given for the extensive bloodspotting leading from June's body and around the bottom of the bed to where Sheila lay: prior to her head wounds, June had sought the telephone which ought to have been on her husband's bedside table. The report also suggests that the burn marks on Nevill's back were caused either by the hot end of the rifle or – presupposing that Jeremy had attempted to force his father to reveal the whereabouts of cash in the house – with a hot poker from the Aga.

For the purposes of this book, those who worked on the original investigation were asked to address some of the more ambiguous aspects of the prosecution case, utilizing their many years of further experience in order to reconstruct a detailed sequence of events at White House Farm on 7 August 1985. But before such an attempt can be made, a number of key points must be borne in mind:

— Twenty-five shots were fired that night. Nevill was wounded eight times, June seven, Daniel five, Nicholas three and Sheila twice. Thirteen cartridge cases were found in the master bedroom, accounting for four shots to Nevill and all of those to June and Sheila. Eight cartridge cases were found in the twins' bedroom, accounting for their injuries. There were three cartridge cases in the kitchen, and one on the stairs. The gun was empty when discovered on Sheila's body.

— Julie Mugford's description of Jeremy's account about how the murders were committed contains a number of factually incorrect details, including that the killer 'fired seven consecutive shots' into Nevill in the kitchen. The forensic evidence shows that Nevill was shot four times in the bedroom and four times in the kitchen; his head wounds could only have been inflicted downstairs.

— There was little or no blood from Nevill in the bed he and June shared, despite the injuries he sustained in that room.

— Sheila was found lying on her mother's blood, yet had little or no blood on her feet. Vanezis's explanation was that the spilled blood may have dried fairly quickly, allowing Sheila to walk across the carpet without contaminating her feet.

— Colin Caffell was adamant that if Sheila had committed suicide, she would never have chosen to die in the same room as her mother. Unable to bear the thought of being parted from her children, she would have killed herself in the twins' bedroom.

— The raid team recorded which lights were on when they forced entry: kitchen light, downstairs hall light, the light in the upstairs corridor at the rear (which shone through the curtains of the twins' room and the bathroom next door), the landing light, and – oddly – the light in the box room above the front door. The switch was inside that room and the half-glazed door was closed.

— There were only three telephones at the farm on the night of the murders; one of the kitchen phones had been removed for repair the day before. On the morning that the murders were discovered, the other kitchen telephone was not in its usual place on the work surface, but found some days later under a pile of magazines nearby. The telephone that usually sat on Nevill's bedside table was off the hook on the kitchen worktop when the raid team arrived. In the upstairs office was another telephone, in perfect working order.

With those points in place, we can now begin to look at a possible scenario for the prosecution case that Jeremy Bamber murdered his family.

On Tuesday, 6 August 1985, Jeremy worked a full day at the farm, from 7.30am until 9.30pm. He took several short breaks, including one that evening when he found his parents and Sheila seated around the table in the kitchen having supper.

Whether the conversation that he claimed to have overheard actually took place can never be known. One former policeman believes that Jeremy instigated a discussion about the twins in order to cause friction between Sheila and her parents. Another suggests that Jeremy was so angered by Nevill and June's idea that Sheila should move into Bourtree Cottage – his home for little more than a year and on which he had lavished considerable expense – that he decided to carry out the murder plot that night.

The story of Jeremy spotting rabbits and loading the gun in the kitchen is regarded as spurious, although he may have prepared the weapon elsewhere. Whether he left it in the scullery as he said, with the magazine on the settle nearby, is also thought unlikely given that Nevill did not normally allow guns there. But certainly the telescopic sight had been removed from the rifle beforehand and the silencer attached.

Jeremy left for home around 9.30pm; Dorothy Foakes heard his car speeding away down the lane. By then, all was not well at the farm. Nevill was uncharacteristically brusque with Barbara Wilson when she telephoned just after 9.30pm, and neither June nor Sheila were themselves when Pamela Boutflour called just before 10pm. Barbara, especially, was under the impression that she had interrupted a row.

Dorothy's husband Len was the last person to see any member of the household that night. At about 10.15pm, he observed Nevill collecting the final load of rape as arranged with Jeremy. After finishing work, Nevill's usual practice was to walk the dogs in the field at the front, then shower downstairs and relax in the sitting room with a drink and cigarette before retiring for bed.

The house was fully secured on the ground floor that night. Two external doors had been bolted internally and the rear door was fastened with a mortise lock; the key was either left in the lock or inserted later by Jeremy. All ground floor windows were fastened, with the exception of the dairy window, which was protected by a metal mesh. Upstairs, the window in Nevill and June's bedroom was slightly open at the top.

Jeremy telephoned Julie from Bourtree Cottage around 10pm. He sounded 'pissed off', telling her: 'I've been thinking on the tractor and the crime will have to be tonight or never.' Aware that he was referring to killing his entire family, Julie told him not to be stupid – he was just fed up because he had been stuck on the tractor all day. They spoke for about twenty minutes. He told her she might hear from him later, although Julie 'thought nothing of this'.

Jeremy later described how, after ending the call, he had something to eat and drink and watched television before going to bed about 11.30pm. None of his neighbours heard anything from him. A local car valet who knew Jeremy by sight took a stroll around the village about midnight after drinking in the Chequers; he noticed a number of cars outside Bourtree Cottage, including Jeremy's Astra, but couldn't remember if any lights were on inside the property.

But some time that night, probably around 11pm or later, Jeremy collected his mother's bicycle – brought home a few days earlier – and headed back to the farm. What he was wearing is anyone's guess, although old clothing is the obvious answer. The police seemed to think the idea of his wetsuit was not without merit, but it would have been extremely uncomfortable when cycling. Whatever he wore, he had time afterwards to get rid of his clothing and footwear.

The route along Maldon Road from Goldhanger to Tolleshunt D'Arcy was easiest, taking no more than ten minutes by bike to the turning at Brook House Farm. It was another five minutes down the track through the fields to White House Farm. An approach from the front of the house was too risky; it was safer for Jeremy to dismount in the back garden, leaving the bicycle there before pulling on gloves and some sort of mask.

Using a hacksaw blade to slip the catch on the downstairs shower room window was easy enough. It was harder to avoid the old wooden slats of the cellar entrance directly below the window, which would have made a loud noise if stepped on in the dead of night. Sash windows do not open silently either, but Jeremy managed to get into the house without alerting either the labrador in the garage or his mother's dog indoors.

After gaining entry, he took the kitchen phone off the hook, thereby disabling all the farmhouse telephones, including the one on Nevill's bedside table. The rifle was where Jeremy had left it earlier that evening; he either loaded it then or had already fully loaded it.

Climbing the stairs, he steeled himself to kill the greatest threats first: his parents. A thin film of moonlight glimmered through the curtains in the master bedroom, where his parents lay sleeping. He stood in the doorway, lifted the rifle, and fired.

The first two shots pierced the right side of June's chest, embedding themselves in the pillow. Another shot hit her in the arm and a third travelled up inside her leg, lodging in her knee. The terrible impact woke Nevill, who lurched out of bed. Jeremy turned the gun on his father, firing four shots that caught him on his left side: two bullets penetrated his forearm and shoulder, and two tore into his lip and jaw.

Jeremy left the room, heading down the first flight of stairs and through the corridor to the twins' bedroom, firing one shot into each slumbering child. With all ten cartridges expended, he made his way down to the kitchen to reload.

He managed to slot four cartridges into the magazine before his father stumbled into the room. A fierce fight for possession of the weapon ensued: they fell against the table, knocking it into the dresser and sending crockery to the floor. The rifle struck the overhead lampshade, shattering it. Jeremy used the gun to beat his father about the arms, head and face; Nevill's watch broke and skittered across the lino. The struggle came to a brutal end near the Aga, where the rifle damaged the underside of the mantel. As Nevill collapsed over a chair, landing at an impossible angle with his pyjamas tangling around his feet, Jeremy brought the gun down on his skull, then fired four shots into his head.

The last produced a stovepipe jam, trapping the empty cartridge case in the ejection port. Jeremy removed the magazine and loaded it to its full capacity, then inserted it into the magazine well. Climbing the stairs again, he cleared the jammed cartridge by working the bolt. It fell out, rolling towards the skirting board on the first landing.

While father and son were fighting in the kitchen, June had managed to force herself up from the bed. The commotion had also woken Sheila, who crossed the landing to her parents' bedroom, drowsy and confused. At the sight of her mother bleeding profusely as she steadied herself on the edge of the bed, Sheila rushed to the other side of the room, where the door to the box room was the quickest route to the twins. June staggered round the bed after her, but before she could reach Sheila, Jeremy returned with the gun.

Sheila froze. June started towards her son, who fired three more shots into her neck, head, and finally between the eyes. June hit her shoulder against the door as she slumped to the floor.

Jeremy then forced Sheila down beside the bed and shot her once in the throat. With six cartridges left in the rifle, he headed back down the corridor where he fired two further shots into Nicholas and four into Daniel, emptying the magazine. The element of 'overkill' would help his story that Sheila, in the grip of psychosis, was the guilty party.

He then retraced his footsteps to the master bedroom, intending to finish setting the scene. To his shock he found his sister incapacitated but still alive. Quickly, he returned to the kitchen, loading a single cartridge into the magazine. Upstairs once more, he crouched down and took aim. The bullet went into Sheila's brain, killing her instantly. He then placed his mother's bible at his sister's side, unscrewed the silencer and positioned the empty rifle on her body.

After showering, he changed into some clothes from his old bedroom, pushing the others into a bag for disposal later. He replaced the silencer in a box in the den cupboard, since to dispose of it might raise questions about its whereabouts. To account for his father's death downstairs and the fact that he hadn't been able to use the bedside telephone, Jeremy hid the kitchen telephone in a pile of magazines, then placed the bedroom telephone on the kitchen work surface. He dialled his own number, pressing the cradle to cut the call, and left the receiver off the hook. Removing all the household paraphernalia from the area around the sink, he then climbed out of the window. He reached back in to return everything more or less to its usual spot, then banged the window shut, causing the lock to fall into place. In the garden, he collected the bicycle and headed home along the same route as before.

Just after 3am he called Julie. He chose his words carefully in case anyone else should overhear but said enough to let the reality of what he had done sink in. Then, to ensure that his version of events was the first, he rang Chelmsford Police Station, telling Constable West: 'You've got to help me, my father has just phoned me saying, "please come over, your sister has gone crazy and has the gun", then the phone went dead. My father sounded terrified, I don't think he was kidding.'

'Where does your father live?' West asked.

'White House Farm, Tolleshunt D'Arcy . . .'

Not all those consulted agree on every point of the above. Ballistics expert Malcolm Fletcher believes that Jeremy fired eight shots into his parents first, and that Nevill escaped to try and raise the alarm using the telephone downstairs, while Jeremy forced Sheila into the master bedroom, where he shot her once; after killing Nevill, he returned to fire the fatal shots at June, and another at Sheila before expending the remaining bullets on Nicholas and Daniel. However, pathologist Peter Vanezis is of the opinion that the twins may have been first to die. And no one is able to satisfactorily explain the burn marks to Nevill's back.

All of which demonstrates that no matter how far-reaching an investigation, and regardless of how many years of experience and hindsight the experts involved possess, there are often questions that cannot be answered – except by the killer.

Appendix II:
A Message from Colin Caffell

I have remained silent through many years of Jeremy Bamber's perennial intrusions into our lives because I have been endeavouring to create a normal life for my new family who have nothing to do with my tragic past. Despite my best endeavours to shield them, however, they have had to live under its shadow. The new ruling by the European Court of Human Rights in Strasbourg, against the setting of 'whole life tariffs' as 'inhumane', not only potentially places the lives of myself, my family and the families of all those who fought for Jeremy's conviction in very real danger (and the public in general in the case of other dangerous 'whole lifers' who are also seeking parole) but undermines our democracy and strikes at the very heart of what is globally recognised as one of the finest and fairest justice systems in the world. It is perhaps a blessing for my family that, despite a fair trial in 1986 and a later appeal before three judges who determined that new evidence made Bamber's original conviction 'even safer', he has refused to admit his guilt and therefore does not meet the Strasbourg court's criteria of 'progressing towards rehabilitation.'

Bamber has proved himself an extremely dangerous and devious man who will clearly remain that way having shown no sign of remorse or contrition for murdering five members of his family for financial gain. *That* is 'inhumane.' Any 'depression and despair' he has said that he feels may be the beginning of him coming to terms with the fact that he has lost his spurious battle with justice; something most 'lifers' begin to accept much earlier on in their sentences. It is *not* inhumane to have to face that, they need to, but it *is* inhumane to make victims and their families live a life sentence of uncertainty. The victims' families have to truly face overwhelming loss, depression and despair.

It is also inhumane that our daughter and a group of her friends at the age of 11, Googled her name only to be confronted with Bamber's website that included photographs of bullet wounds to my former wife's neck. My daughter would understandably like to change her name.

It is inhumane that my career as an artist is tainted every time a potential client Googles my name and is confronted by the same website. No matter what quality the artist, nobody wants to buy a slice of tragedy. I could change my name but that would wipe out the good reputation I have worked many years to establish.

It is also inhumane that my wife is scared for our lives every time an ambitious lawyer, out simply to make a name for themselves, tries to get Bamber freed. *That* is inhumane.

It is a basic human right of every person in this country to be provided protection from known dangers and I would urge all parties of our government to stand firm against this tyranny of the Strasbourg Court. We as a country need to be outraged at this decision and to remain outraged until it is properly dealt with.

Colin Caffell, 19 July 2013[1]

Acknowledgements

A great many people have assisted me during the research and writing of this book. Some have asked not to be named, but I thank them unreservedly nonetheless for sharing their personal and professional memories and for providing source material.

From the beginning, Jeremy Bamber generously shared a vast amount of documentation with me, as well as answering innumerable questions. His campaign team have also been extremely helpful when dealing with my enquiries.

The testimonies of lead figures from the 1985–6 enquiry have helped shed new light on those involved as well as on the investigation itself. I thank especially Mike Ainsley, Ron Cook, Dave Bird, Neil Davidson, Chris Bews and Steve Myall. Sadly, several retired officers have passed away recently, including Bob Miller, whom I interviewed at length.

Professor Peter Vanezis was exceptionally kind in taking time out of a hectic schedule to answer my questions, for which I am deeply grateful; sincere thanks too to his assistant Adam Konstanciak. Malcolm Fletcher patiently and expertly dealt with my queries regarding ballistics and other forensic matters. I spent an incredibly interesting day with him, during which his wife Debbie thoughtfully provided a lovely evening meal. Dr Hugh Ferguson and his wife made me very welcome at their home as we discussed his care of Sheila and June and their treatment at St Andrew's Hospital; I offer them my heartfelt thanks. I must also extend further gratitude to Ron Cook for facilitating some of the interviews; he and his wife Alvina have been extremely generous in ways too numerous to mention, but especially in introducing me to people.

Of those who spoke to me about Sheila, the two who brought her most vividly to life were Tora and David Tomkinson. It was easy, when spending time with them, to picture a much happier, relaxed Bambs/Bambi playing with her children and enjoying the company of those who never judged her, but saw her simply as a very dear friend. I am also deeply grateful to Barbara Wilson, for

sharing her memories of the Bambers with me and for demon-
strating that there is no end to true loyalty.

Journalist and author David James Smith very kindly made
the transcript of his 2010 interviews with Jeremy Bamber and
David and Karen Boutflour available to me. Others who have
contributed to this book in various forms include: Bob Woffinden
for many insights and a possible explanation regarding the movement of telephones at White House Farm; Mrs Alison Standen,
senior librarian, archive and alumni project leader at Moira
House Girls School in Eastbourne; Greg Andrews, clerk and chief
executive at Christ's Hospital Foundation; Mrs Rachel Hill at
Hethersett Old Hall School; Logie Bruce-Lockhart, former headmaster of Gresham's; current and retired staff at Gresham's;
Annette Witheridge, Aysha St Giles, Richard Christmas, Bryan
Fraser, Andrew Kirk and Keith Skinner.

I also thank Simon McKay for providing the initial introduction to Jeremy Bamber; Diane Courtney at Hearst for tracking
down Julie Mugford's 1987 interview in *She* magazine; Dawn
Waters, senior administrator at FANY, and Jennifer Kauntz,
records archivist at FANY (PRVC), for information about June's
wartime service; Essex Record Office for fascinating material on
the Speakman family; RAF Disclosures for supplying Nevill's
record of service; the Children's Society Records and Archive
Centre for general information about adoptions in the 1950s and
early 1960s; and Darren Powell, research manager at Skyviews
Aerial Archives in Leeds for providing the aerial photograph of
White House Farm taken on 6 August 1985. I am also indebted
to the National Archives for agreeing to my FOI request regarding June Bamber's SOE file.

The unceasing wisdom, patience and kindness of my agent
Robert Smith and editor Ingrid Connell at Sidgwick & Jackson
ensured that this book reached completion. Without them, it
would have been a much more difficult process for very many
reasons. Originally commissioned by Bill Campbell and Peter
MacKenzie at Mainstream Publishing, this was to have been
their final title before the company closed down, but due to
serious family illness I was unable to deliver the manuscript on
time. I remain extremely thankful to Bill and Peter and all the
staff at Mainstream for their encouragement and assistance over

the years. Jan Michael's continuing support and advice also helped immeasurably and mean a great deal to me.

I also can't express gratitude enough to my friend Tricia Room, who ferried me about to various interviews, archives, etc., while being brilliant company and completely trustworthy. Finally, I would also like to thank my family and above all – as ever – my son, River, for making every day worthwhile.

Bibliography

BOOKS

Allingham, Margery, *The Oaken Heart: The Story of an English Village at War* (Pleshey: Golden Duck (UK) Ltd, 2011).

Bruce-Lockhart, Logie, *Now and Then, This and That* (Dereham: The Larks Press, 2013).

Caffell, Colin, *In Search of the Rainbow's End: The Inside Story of the Bamber Murders* (London: Hodder & Stoughton, 1994).

Cromwell, Thomas Kitson, *Excursions in the County of Essex* (London: Longman, Hurst, Rees, Orme & Brown, 1818).

D'Cruze, Shani, Walklate, Sandra and Pegg, Samantha, *Murder: Social and Historical Approaches to Understanding Murder and Murderers* (London: Routledge 2011).

DeGroot, Gerard, *The Seventies Unplugged: A Kaleidoscope Look at a Violent Decade* (London: Pan, 2010).

Foot, M. R. D., *SOE in France: An Account of the Work of the British Special Operations Executive in France 1940–1944* (London: Frank Cass Publishers, 2004).

Foss, Arthur and Trick, Kenneth, *St Andrew's Hospital, Northampton: The First One Hundred and Fifty Years 1838–1988* (London: Granta Editions 1989).

Frith, Christopher and Johnstone, Eve, *Schizophrenia: A Very Short Introduction* (Oxford: Oxford University Press, 2003).

Gillet, Louise, *Surviving Schizophrenia: A Memoir* (Twynham Press, 2012).

Haslam, Dave, *Young Hearts Run Free: The Real Story of the 1970s* (London: Harper Perennial, 2005).

Healey, Peter Thomas, *Rough Justice: Essex Murders* (CreateSpace Independent Publishing Platform, 2012).

Howarth-Williams, Martin, *R. D. Laing* (London: Routledge, 2014).

Jones, Julia, *The Adventures of Margery Allingham* (Pleshey: Golden Duck (UK) Ltd, 2013).

Laing, R. D., *The Divided Self: An Existential Study in Sanity and Madness* (London: Penguin Classics, 2010).

Leyton, Elliott, *Sole Survivor: Children Who Murder Their Families* (London: John Blake, 2009).

Loeb Schloss, Carol, *Lucia Joyce: To Dance in the Wake* (London: Bloomsbury, 2004).

Lomax, Scott, *Jeremy Bamber: Evil Beyond Belief?* (Stroud: The History Press, 2008).

McGinniss, Joe, *Fatal Vision* (London: Signet, 2012).

McKay, Sinclair, *The Secret Listeners: The Men and Women Posted Across the World to Intercept the German Codes for Bletchley Park* (London: Aurum Press, 2013).

McSmith, Andy, *No Such Thing As Society: A History of Britain in the 1980s* (London: Constable & Robinson, 2011).

Malcolm, Janet, *Iphigenia in Forest Hills: Anatomy of a Murder Trial* (New York: Yale University Press, 2011).

Malcolm, Janet, *The Crime of Sheila McGough* (London: Papermac, 2000).

Malcolm, Janet, *The Journalist and the Murderer* (London: Granta Books, 2012).

Mandelsberg, Rose G. (ed.), *The Crimes of the Rich and Famous* (New York: Pinnacle, 1992).

Pawley, Margaret, *In Obedience to Instructions: FANY with the SOE in the Mediterranean* (Barnsley: Leo Cooper, 1999).

Plath, Sylvia, *The Bell Jar* (London: Faber & Faber, 2005).

Powell, Claire, *Murder at White House Farm: The Story of Jeremy Bamber* (London: Headline Books, 1994).

Rigden, Dennis, *SOE Syllabus: Lessons in Ungentlemanly Warfare, World War II* (Richmond: National Archives, 2001).

Sandbrook, Dominic, *State of Emergency: The Way We Were: Britain 1970–1974* (London: Penguin, 2011).

Sandbrook, Dominic, *Seasons in the Sun: The Battle for Britain 1974–1979* (London: Penguin 2013).

Schiller, Lori and Bennett, Amanda, *The Quiet Room: A Journey out of the Torment of Madness* (New York: Grand Central Publishing, 2011).

Scollan, Maureen, *Sworn to Serve: Police in Essex 1840–1990* (Chichester: Phillimore & Co. Ltd, 1993).

Shine, Betty, *Mind to Mind: The Secrets of Your Mind Energy Revealed* (London: Corgi Books, 1989).

Smith, Ken, *Inside Time* (London: Mandarin, 1990).

Stewart, Graham, *Bang! A History of Britain in the 1980s*
    (London: Atlantic Books, 2013).

Stroud, John, *13 Penny Stamps: The Story of the Church of
    England Children's Society from its beginnings as 'Waifs and
    Strays'* (London: Hodder & Stoughton, 1971).

Thurlow, David, *The Essex Triangle: Four Decades of Violence
    and Murder* (London: Robert Hale Ltd, 1990).

Turner, Alwyn W., *Rejoice! Rejoice! Britain in the 1980s* (London:
    Aurum Press, 2010).

Verrier, Nancy Newton, *The Primal Wound: Understanding the
    Adopted Child* (London: British Association for Adoption and
    Fostering, 2012).

Vinen, Richard, *Thatcher's Britain: The Politics and Social
    Upheaval of the 1980s* (London: Simon & Schuster, 2009).

Warburton, Eileen, *John Fowles: A Life in Two Worlds* (London:
    Viking, 2004).

Wheen, Francis, *Strange Days Indeed: The Golden Age of Paranoia*
    (London: Fourth Estate, 2010).

Wilkes, Roger, *Blood Relations: Jeremy Bamber and the White
    House Farm Murders* (London: Robinson Publishing, 1994).

DOCUMENTARIES

Clear My Name, 'Jeremy Bamber', Channel 4, May 1998.

Crime Story – The White House Farm Murders, ITV, December
    1993.

Infamous Murders: Inheritance Killers, The History Channel,
    March 2003.

The Amazing Story of Jeremy Bamber, Channel 4, April 2003.

Real Crime, 'Jeremy Bamber', ITV, January 2004.

Killing Mum and Dad: The Jeremy Bamber Story, Sky Three,
    September 2010.

Crimes That Shook Britain, 'Jeremy Bamber', Crime &
    Investigation Network, April 2011.

Tonight, 'Jeremy Bamber: The New Evidence', ITV, March 2012.

Countdown to Murder, 'Slaughter at the Farm', Channel 5,
    November 2013.

ONLINE MEDIA

Jeremy Bamber blog: jeremybamber.blogspot.co.uk
Jeremy Bamber official website: jeremy-bamber.co.uk
Jeremy Bamber Twitter page: twitter.com/bambertweets
Jeremy Bamber campaign for freedom: jeremybamber.org
ITN archive news footage of the case: www.itnsource.com/en/
A detailed explanation of the Court of Appeal's 2002 decision to
    uphold Jeremy Bamber's sentence can be found at: www.
    homepage-link.to/justice/judgements/Bamber/index.html

Notes and References

Prologue

1 Joan Frost, written statement (hereafter w/s), 26 September 1985.
2 Jeremy Bamber, w/s, 7 August 1985.
3 Colin Caffell, w/s, 7 August 1985.
4 Colin Caffell, w/s, 11 September 1985.
5 Caffell, Colin, *In Search of the Rainbow's End: The Inside Story of the Bamber Murders* (London: Hodder & Stoughton, 1994), p. 29.
6 Julie Mugford, w/s, 8–9 September 1985.
7 Julie Mugford, w/s, 8 August 1985.
8 Colin Caffell, w/s, 7 August 1985.
9 Caffell, Colin, *In Search*, p. 30.
10 Ibid., p. 163.

Chapter One

1 *Essex Standard, West Suffolk Gazette & Eastern Counties Advertiser*, 'Death of Mr Benjamin Page', 9 January 1892.
2 Cromwell, Thomas Kitson, *Excursions in the County of Essex* (Oxford: Oxford University Press, 1819), pp. 89–90.
3 *Essex Review* 1955, 'Farm House Tea Party', Bevington Smith, pp. 243–5.
4 Betty Howie, w/s, 18 September 1985.
5 *East Anglian Daily Times*, 'Farming Feature: Janie's Childhood Idyll at Osea Remains a Magical Place', Sarah Chambers, 19 October 2013.
6 National Archives, Ref: HS9/1397/2.
7 Rigden, Dennis, *SOE Syllabus: Lessons in Ungentlemanly Warfare, World War II* (Richmond: National Archives, 2001), p. 2.
8 Margaret Grimster, w/s, 28 September 1985.
9 Robert Boutflour, w/s, 15 August 1991.

Chapter Two

1 Margery Allingham, *The Oaken Heart: The Story of an English Village at War* (Pleshey: Golden Duck (UK) Ltd, 2011), p. 24.
2 Tora Tomkinson, author interviews, 2013.
3 Peter Jay, w/s, 16 September 1985.

4 Ann Eaton, w/s, 8 September 1985. Quotes from Ann Eaton in this chapter are from this source.

5 Verrier, Nancy Newton, *The Primal Wound: Understanding the Adopted Child* (London: British Association for Adoption and Fostering, 2012), p. 38.

6 *Independent*, 'Seeds of Doom in Bamber Family', 29 October 1986.

7 Karen Boutflour, David James Smith full interview transcript, 2010 (hereafter Smith 2010).

8 Hugh Ferguson, author interviews, 2013.

Chapter Three

1 *Daily Mirror*, 'He Went to Lovely People Who Gave Him the Best Start in Life', Garry Jones, 31 January 2004. The remaining quotations in this section are from this source.

2 Agnes Low, w/s, 11 September 1985.

3 Ann Eaton, w/s, 14 August 1991.

4 *Daily Mirror*, 'I Was a Mummy's Boy: Killer Jeremy Bamber . . .', Justin Penrose, 22 July 2012. Unless otherwise stated, quotations from Jeremy Bamber in this chapter are from this source.

5 Inez Bowen, w/s, 25 September 1985.

6 Powell, Claire, *Murder at White House Farm: The Story of Jeremy Bamber* (London: Headline Books, 1994), p. 28.

7 *Evening Gazette*: 'Sheila: A Model Who was Unlucky in Love', Dave Woods and Judith Bastin, 29 October 1986.

8 *Guardian*, 'Murder Family Sued by Killer', John Ezard, 19 August 2003.

9 'Extremely well', Anthony Pargeter, w/s, 8 August 1985; 'Jeremy and Sheila were jealous', Jacqueline Wood (née Pargeter), w/s, 10 September 1985.

10 David Boutflour, Smith 2010. Unless otherwise stated, quotes from David Boutflour in this chapter are from this source.

11 Anne Hunter, w/s, 23 November 1985.

12 Hugh Ferguson, w/s, 18 September 1985.

Chapter Four

1 Jeremy Bamber, Official Blog, 'A Life of Less Liberty', 20 October 2012. http://jeremybamber.blogspot.co.uk/2012/10/second-article-in-series-jeremy-bamber.html. Unless otherwise stated, quotations from Jeremy Bamber in this chapter are from this source.

2 'To make the night . . .' ibid.; 'We'd identify . . .' Jeremy Bamber, letter to author, 7 July 2013.

3 Caffell, Colin, *In Search*, p. 132.
4 Susan Burgess (née Wallace), w/s, 4 November 1985. All quotes from
   Susan Burgess in this chapter are from this source.
5 James Carr, w/s, 10 September 1985.
6 Robert Carr, w/s, 20 September 1985.
7 Rosalind Nockold, w/s, 24 November 1985.
8 Tora Tomkinson, author interviews, 2013.
9 Inez Bowen, w/s, 25 September 1985.
10 John Wilkin, w/s, 26 September 1985.
11 Jeremy Bamber, Smith 2010.
12 *Daily Telegraph*, 'Fear Lay Beneath Bambi's Glamour', Neil
   Derbyshire, 29 October 1986.
13 Bettine Thorp, w/s, 24 September 1985.
14 Dorothy Carr, w/s, 11 October 1985.
15 Karen Boutflour (née Butt), Smith 2010.
16 William Thomas, w/s, 13 September 1985.

Chapter Five

1 *Star*, 'The Man Who Lost Everything', Barry Gardner, 29 October
   1986.
2 Josie Jacobs, w/s, 17 October 1985.
3 Ronald Crowe, w/s, 11 October 1985.
4 John Wilkin, w/s, 26 September 1985.
5 Sandbrook, Dominic, *State of Emergency: The Way We Were: Britain
   1970–1974* (London: Headline Books, 1994), p. 423.
6 Kathleen Whitworth, w/s, 3 October 1985.
7 *Daily Mirror,* 'Torment of Bambi', 29 October 1986.
8 Caffell, Colin, *In Search*, p. 134.
9 Hugh Ferguson, author interviews, 2013.
10 Tora Tomkinson, author interviews, 2013.
11 *Independent*, 'Seeds of Doom in Bamber Family'.
12 *Evening Gazette*, 'Maybe They Were Spoiled', Dave Woods and
   Judith Bastin, 29 October 1986.
13 Caffell, Colin, *In Search*, p. 28.
14 Ibid., p. 132.
15 *East Anglian Daily Times*, 'The Oddball Schoolboy Who Enjoyed
   Attention', 29 October 1986. Quotes from John Fielding in this
   chapter are taken from this source.
16 *Daily Mirror*, 'I Was a Mummy's Boy'.
17 William Thomas, w/s, 13 September 1985.

Chapter Six

1 Tora Tomkinson, author interviews, 2013.
2 Caffell, Colin, *In Search*, pp. 140–41.
3 Sarah Hailey (née Howie), w/s, 17 September–2 October 1985.
4 Josie Jacobs, w/s, 17 October 1985.
5 *East Anglian Daily Times*, 'The Oddball Schoolboy'.
6 Richard Gale, w/s, 24 September 1985.
7 *East Anglian Daily Times*, 'The Oddball Schoolboy'.
8 William Thomas, w/s, 23 September 1985.
9 William Thomas, w/s, 13 September 1985. Unless otherwise indicated, quotes from William Thomas in this chapter are taken from this source.
10 Wilkes, Roger, *Blood Relations: Jeremy Bamber and the White House Farm Murders* (London: Robinson Publishing, 1994), p34.
11 Jeremy Bamber, Smith 2010.
12 Karen Boutflour, w/s, 20 September 1985.
13 *The Times*, 'After the Mourning: Colin Caffell', Julia Llewellyn Smith, 1 August 1994.
14 David Boutflour, Smith 2010. All quotes from David Boutflour in this chapter are taken from this source.
15 John Wilkin, w/s, 26 September 1985.
16 Logie Bruce-Lockhart, letter to author, 4 October 2013.
17 *Guardian*, letters page, 'The Bambi I Married' by Colin Caffell, 27 November 1993.
18 Agnes Low, w/s, 11 September 1985.
19 Kenneth Witts, w/s, 21 October 1985.
20 Barry Hadden, w/s, 28 September 1985.
21 Jeremy Bamber, Official Blog, 'A New Year of Less Liberty', 31 December 2013. http://jeremybamber.blogspot.co.uk/2013/12/a-new-year-of-less-liberty.html.
22 *Daily Mirror*, 'Torment of Bambi'.
23 Sarah Hailey, w/s, 17 September–2 October 1985; Ann Eaton, w/s, 8 September 1985.
24 Caffell, Colin, *In Search*, p. 142.

Chapter Seven

1 Mairead Maguire, w/s, 16 September 1985.
2 Jeremy Bamber, Official Blog, 'A Life of Less Liberty,' 28 October

2012. http://jeremybamber.blogspot.co.uk/2012/10/third-article-in-series-jeremy-bamber.html.

3 Scott Yates, w/s, 27 September 1985.
4 Peter Eaton, w/s, 18–21 September 1985.
5 Michael Leyland, w/s, 3 October 1985.
6 John Seabrook, w/s, 18 September 1985.
7 Barbara Babic, w/s, 11 October 1985.
8 Nicholas Flowers, w/s, 13 September 1985.
9 Ann Eaton, w/s, 8 September 1985.
10 Jeremy Bamber, letter to author, 15 May 2013. Unless otherwise indicated, quotes in this chapter from Jeremy Bamber are from this source.
11 There is some confusion over the date of Jeremy's first trip to Australia and New Zealand. Jeremy believes it was 1979, but family and friends clearly recall his departure as July 1980. Regarding his return, in her 10 September 1985 w/s Jacqueline Wood (née Pargeter) noted: 'I have an entry in my diary dated 15 June 1981, "Jem arrives back."'
12 Louise Carr, w/s, 21 September 1985.
13 Christopher Nevill, w/s, 2 October 1985.
14 Stephanie Kinnersley, w/s, 8 November 1985.
15 Judith Jackson, w/s, 19 October 1985. All quotes from Judith Jackson in this chapter are from this source.
16 Sandra Elston, w/s, 18 September 1985.
17 Farhad Emami, w/s, 8 August 1985.
18 *The Times*, 'Model's Body Tested for Drugs', 9 August 1985.
19 Elsa Reid, w/s, 16 September 1985.
20 Jeremy Bamber, w/s, 7 August 1985.
21 Jeremy Bamber, letter to author, 15 May 2013.
22 'He had read . . .' Louise Rees, w/s, 18 September 1985. See also: *Daily Mirror*, 'He Went to Lovely People'.
23 David Boutflour, Smith 2010. All quotes from David and Karen Boutflour in this chapter are from this source.

Chapter Eight

1 Robert Boutflour, w/s, 10 September 1985.
2 David Boutflour, w/s, 17 September 1985.
3 Robert Boutflour, undated diary notes, 1985.
4 Jeremy Bamber, letter to author, 15 May 2013. Unless otherwise indicated, quotes from Jeremy Bamber in this chapter are from this source.

5 Barbara Wilson, author interviews, 2014.
6 Agnes Low, w/s, 11 September 1985.
7 Colin Caffell, w/s, 11 September 1985.
8 *People*, 'The Secret Babies of Jeremy Bear', Paul Davidson, 2 November 1985. Unless otherwise indicated, quotes from Suzette Ford in this chapter are from this source.
9 *Star*, 'Dream Turned into a Nightmare', 29 October 1986.
10 Malcolm Waters, w/s, 15 September 1985.
11 *Daily Mail*, 'The Two Faces of a Vicious Psychopath', Tim Miles, 29 October 1986.
12 Mark Chard, w/s, 16 September 1985.
13 Matthew McDonald, w/s, 12 September 1985.
14 Suzette Ford, w/s, 19 September 1985.
15 *Daily Mail*, 'The Two Faces'.
16 Henry Frost, w/s, 26 September 1985.
17 Agnes Low, w/s, 15 September 1985.
18 Nevill Bamber, letter, 30 December 1981.
19 Daphne Wilkin, w/s, 26 September 1985.
20 Matthew McDonald, record of police interview, 11 September 1985.

Chapter Nine

1 Peter Jay, w/s, 16 September 1985.
2 Barbara Babic, w/s, 11 October 1985.
3 Michael Abel, w/s, 30 September 1985.
4 Janet Ashcroft, w/s, 24 September 1985.
5 Barbara Wilson, w/s, 12 September 1985.
6 Jeremy Bamber, letter to author, 7 July 2013.
7 http://www.eafa.org.uk/catalogue/214123.
8 Hugh Ferguson, author interviews, 2013. Unless otherwise indicated, quotes from Hugh Ferguson in this chapter are from this source.
9 Robert Boutflour, w/s, 15 August 1991.
10 June Bamber, letter, 20 May 1982.
11 Hugh Ferguson, w/s, 8 August 1985.
12 Daphne Wilkin, w/s, 26 September 1985.
13 Anne Hunter, w/s, 23 November 1985.
14 Barbara Wilson, author interviews, 2014. Unless otherwise indicated, quotes from Barbara Wilson in this chapter are from this source.
15 Jeremy Bamber, w/s, 7 August 1985.
16 Farhad Emami, w/s, 8 August 1985.
17 Jacqueline Wood, w/s, 10 September 1985.

18 Jeremy Bamber, record of police interview, 10–11 September 1985.
19 David Boutflour, w/s, 17 September 1985.
20 Suzette Ford, w/s, 12 September 1985. All quotes from Sue Ford in this chapter are from this source.
21 Brett Collins, w/s, 1 October 1985.
22 Ibid.
23 Julie Mugford, w/s, 10 September 1985. All quotes from Julie Mugford in this chapter are from this source.
24 Brett Collins, w/s, 9 September 1985.
25 Kathleen Whitworth, w/s, 3 October 1985.
26 *Daily Mail*, 'The Two Faces'.

Chapter Ten

1 Lea Wood, w/s, 9 October 1985.
2 Michael Abel, w/s, 30 September 1985.
3 Christopher Nevill, w/s, 2 October 1985.
4 Suzette Ford, w/s, 12 September 1985. All quotes from Sue Ford in this chapter are from this source.
5 Christine Bacon, w/s, 10 September 1985.
6 *People*, 'The Secret Babies'.
7 Barbara Wilson, author interviews, 2014.
8 Paul Osborne, w/s, 21 October 1985.
9 Ann Eaton, trial testimony, October 1986.
10 Robert Boutflour, w/s, 15 August 1991.
11 Ann Eaton, w/s, 14 August 1991.
12 Susan Elliott-Brown, w/s, 4 November 1985.
13 Maria Seabrook, w/s, 24 September 1985.
14 Farhad Emami, w/s, 8 August 1985.
15 Barbara Wilson, w/s, 12 September 1985.
16 Hugh Ferguson, w/s, 8 August 1985.
17 Hugh Ferguson, author interviews, 2013. Unless otherwise indicated, quotes from Hugh Ferguson in this chapter are from this source.
18 Hugh Ferguson, w/s, 8 August 1985.
19 Hugh Ferguson, trial testimony, October 1986.
20 http://www.eafa.org.uk/catalogue/214123.
21 Hugh Ferguson, trial testimony, October 1986.
22 Hugh Ferguson, w/s, 8 August 1985.
23 Hugh Ferguson, trial testimony, October 1986.
24 Hugh Ferguson, trial testimony, October 1986. Other quotes in this paragraph are from the same source.

25 Caffell, Colin, *In Search*, pp. 201–2.
26 Ibid., p. 202.
27 Hugh Ferguson, trial testimony, October 1986. The following quotes until otherwise indicated are from this source.
28 Hugh Ferguson, author interviews, 2013. The following quotes until otherwise indicated are from this source.
29 Hugh Ferguson, trial testimony, October 1986.
30 Hugh Ferguson, author interviews, 2013.
31 Lomax, Scott, *Jeremy Bamber: Evil Beyond Belief?* (Stroud: The History Press, 2012), p. 112.
32 Jeremy Bamber, Smith 2010.

Chapter Eleven

1 Barbara Wilson, author interviews, 2014.
2 Farhad Emami, w/s, 8 August 1985.
3 Tora Tomkinson, author interviews, 2013. All quotes from Tora Tomkinson in this chapter are from this source.
4 David Tomkinson, author interviews, 2013.
5 *Star*, 'Julie was Warned by her Mother', Neil Wallis, 29 October 1986.
6 *Evening Gazette*, 'The Ordeal of Julie Mugford', Dave Woods and Judith Bastin, 29 October 1986.
7 Susan Battersby, w/s, 10 September 1985.
8 *News of the World*, 'I Tried to Smother the Sleeping Bambi Beast', Polly Hepburn and Rosaline Shann, 9 November 1986.
9 Jeremy Bamber, w/s, 7 August 1985.
10 *People*, 'The Secret Babies'.
11 Dennis Wager, w/s, 23 September 1985.
12 Kim Aston, w/s, 11 October 1985.
13 Julie Mugford, w/s, 8–9 September 1985.
14 *The Times*, 'Bamber Strangled Rats to Test Courage, says Girlfriend', Michael Horsnell, 9 October 1986.
15 Powell, Claire, *Murder at*, p. 50.

Chapter Twelve

1 Tora Tomkinson, author interviews, 2013. All quotes from Tora Tomkinson in this chapter are from this source.
2 Powell, Claire, *Murder at*, pp. 62–3.
3 Ibid., pp. 65–6.

4　Tora Tomkinson, author interviews, 2013; Colin Caffell, w/s, 11 September 1985.

5　Hugh Ferguson, trial testimony, October 1986. Quotes from Hugh Ferguson in this chapter are from this source.

6　Elizabeth Rimington, w/s, 8 September 1985.

7　[name withheld], w/s, 22 September 1985.

8　Michael Deckers, w/s, 10 September 1985.

9　[name withheld], w/s, 22 September 1985.

10　Julie Mugford, w/s, 10 September 1985. Unless otherwise indicated, quotes from Julie Mugford in this chapter are from this source.

11　Jeremy Bamber, Smith 2010.

12　Jeremy Bamber, letter to author, 7 July 2013.

13　Edward O'Donoghue, w/s, 9 October 1985.

14　Ann Eaton, w/s, 14 August 1991.

15　Ann Eaton, trial testimony, October 1986.

16　Ann Eaton, w/s, 14 August 1991.

17　Jeremy Bamber, letter to author, 15 May 2013.

18　Peter Jay, w/s, 16 September 1985.

19　Julie Mugford, w/s, 8 August 1985.

20　Julie Mugford, w/s, 8–9 September 1985.

21　Jeremy Bamber, record of police interview, 10–11 September 1985.

22　Sandra Elston, w/s, 18 September 1985.

23　Mary Mugford, w/s, 13 January 1986.

24　Jeremy Bamber, record of police interview, 8 September 1985.

25　Elizabeth Rimington, w/s, 11 September 1985.

26　Susan Battersby, w/s, 10 September 1985. All quotes from Susan Battersby in this chapter are from this source.

27　When Essex Police investigated the incident in 1985, a witness statement from Hamish McTavish (not his real name) told them he had received nothing in response to the first £100 he sent to Jeremy's address and had written it off as a bad experience.

28　Julie Mugford, w/s, 23 September 1985.

29　Jeremy Bamber, record of police interview, 9 September 1985.

30　Andrew Bishop, w/s, 13 December 1985.

31　Julie Smerchanski (née Mugford), w/s, 12 April 2002.

32　Julie Smerchanski, w/s, 12 April 2002; Susan Battersby, w/s, 7 May 2002.

Chapter Thirteen

1 Turner, Alwyn W., *Rejoice! Rejoice! Britain in the 1980s* (London: Aurum Press, 2010), p.x.
2 Jeremy Bamber, record of police interview, 10–12 September 1985: unless otherwise indicated, quotes from Jeremy Bamber in this chapter are from this source; Mary Mugford, w/s, 13 January 1986.
3 Ann Eaton, trial testimony, October 1986.
4 Ann Eaton, w/s, 14 August 1991.
5 Robert Boutflour, undated diary notes, 1985.
6 Robert Boutflour, w/s, 15 August 1991.
7 Michael Deckers, w/s, 10 September 1985.
8 Thomas Howie, w/s, 26 September 1985.
9 Colin Caffell, w/s, 11 September 1985.
10 Julie Mugford, w/s, 8–9 September 1985.
11 Christine Bacon, w/s, 10 September 1985. All quotes from Christine Bacon in this chapter are from this source.
12 Julie Mugford, w/s, 10 September 1985.
13 Agnes Low, w/s, 11 September 1985.
14 Jeremy Bamber, Smith 2010.
15 Michael Ainsley, 'Report on the Bamber Killings'.
16 Keith Dryland, w/s, 16 October 1985.
17 Anthony Pargeter, w/s, 18 December 1985.
18 Anthony Pargeter, w/s, 12 December 1985.
19 Ian Dalgleish, w/s, 28 September 1985.
20 Hugh Ferguson, trial testimony, October 1986.
21 Julie Mugford, w/s, 8–9 September 1985.
22 Jeremy Bamber, official website post, 2002.
23 Christianna (Tora) Tomkinson, w/s, 12 September 1985.
24 Farhad Emami, w/s, 8 August 1985. In his statement, he refers to June as Sheila's stepmother; for reasons of clarity and accuracy, the term has been removed in the main text.

Chapter Fourteen

1 Powell, Claire, *Murder at*, p77.
2 Hugh Ferguson, author interviews, 2013.
3 Barbara Wilson, w/s, 12 September 1985.
4 Farhad Emami, w/s, 8 August 1985. All quotes from Farhad Emami in this chapter are from this source.

5 Dorothy Brencher, w/s, 23 September 1985. All quotes from Dorothy Brencher in this chapter are from this source.

6 Dr Steven Iliffe, w/s, 14 November 1985. All quotes from Steven Iliffe in this chapter are from this source.

7 David Tomkinson, w/s, 20 September 1985.

8 Reginald Caffell, w/s, 8 October 1985.

9 Dr Michael Finnegan, w/s, 24 September 1985.

10 Hugh Ferguson, trial testimony, October 1986.

11 Joan Frost, w/s, 26 September 1985.

12 Hugh Ferguson, trial testimony, October 1986; Hugh Ferguson, author interviews, 2013.

13 Hugh Ferguson, w/s, 8 August 1985.

14 Hugh Ferguson, w/s, 30 September 1986.

15 Hugh Ferguson, author interviews, 31 October 2013.

16 Frith, Christopher and Johnstone, Eve, *Schizophrenia: A Very Short Introduction* (Oxford: Oxford University Press, 2003), p. 30.

17 Ibid., p145.

18 Laing, R. D., *The Divided Self: An Existential Study in Sanity and Madness* (London: Penguin Classics, 2010), p. 38; Howarth-Williams, Martin, *R. D. Laing* (London: Routledge, 2014), p. 127.

19 Colin Caffell, undated letter, thought to be June/July 1985. All quotes in this paragraph are from this source.

20 Colin Caffell, w/s, 11 September 1985.

21 Caffell, Colin, *In Search*, p. 32.

22 Hugh Ferguson, w/s, 30 September 1986.

23 Tora Tomkinson, author interviews, 2013.

Chapter Fifteen

1 Agnes Low, w/s, 11 September 1985.

2 James Richards, w/s, 13 December 1985.

3 Lomax, Scott, *Jeremy Bamber*, p. 111.

4 Michael Deckers, w/s, 10 September 1985.

5 James Carr, w/s, 10 September 1985.

6 Julie Mugford, w/s, 10 September 1985. All quotes in this paragraph are from this source.

7 Jeremy Bamber, Smith 2010. Unless otherwise indicated, quotes from Jeremy Bamber in this chapter are from this source.

8 Jeremy Bamber, record of police interview, 8 September 1985.

9 Barbara Wilson, author interviews, 2014. All quotes from Barbara Wilson in this chapter are from this source.

10 Lomax, Scott, *Jeremy Bamber*, p. 171.
11 Susan Harvey, w/s, 5 November 1985.
12 Donald Hawkins, w/s, 8 October 1985.
13 Sheila's letter quoted in Ann Eaton, trial testimony, October 1986.
14 Ann Eaton, trial testimony, October 1986.
15 Hugh Ferguson, author interviews, 2013. Unless otherwise indicated, quotes from Hugh Ferguson in this chapter are from this source.
16 Hugh Ferguson, trial testimony, October 1986.
17 Helen Grimster, w/s, 28 September 1985.
18 David Boutflour, trial testimony, October 1986.
19 Mary Mugford, trial testimony, October 1986.
20 Julie Mugford, w/s, 14 October 1985.
21 Mary Mugford, w/s, 13 January 1986.
22 Julie Mugford, w/s, 8–9 September 1985.
23 Jeremy Bamber, record of police interview, 9 September 1985.
24 Jeremy Bamber, record of police interview, 10–11 September 1985.
25 Nevill Bamber, last will and testament, 3 August 1979.
26 Michael Ainsley, 'Report'.
27 Jeremy Bamber, trial testimony, October 1986.

Chapter Sixteen

1 Susan Harvey, w/s, 5 November 1985.
2 'Seemed to do things . . .' Farhad Emami, w/s, 24 September 1985; 'very slow and deliberate . . .' Farhad Emami, w/s, 8 August 1985.
3 Jeremy Bamber, letter to author, 15 May 2013.
4 Tora Tomkinson, author interviews, 2013.
5 Hugh Ferguson, author interviews, 2013.
6 Barbara Wilson, w/s, 12 September 1985.
7 Colin Caffell, w/s, 11 September 1985.
8 Caffell, Colin, *In Search*, p. 72.
9 Jeremy Bamber, letter to author, 15 May 2013.
10 Caffell, Colin, *In Search*, p. 73.
11 Elizabeth Rimington, w/s, 8 September 1985.
12 Robert Boutflour, w/s, 15 August 1991.
13 Colin Caffell, w/s, 11 September 1985.
14 George Nicholls, w/s, 27 September 1985.
15 Barbara Wilson, w/s, 5 October 1985.
16 ibid.
17 Barbara Wilson, author interviews, 2014. All remaining quotes from Barbara Wilson in this chapter are from this source.

18 Jeremy Bamber, Official Blog, 'A Life of Less Liberty', 6 October 2012. http://jeremybamber.blogspot.co.uk/2012/10/jeremy-bamber-life-of-less-liberty.html.
19 Thomas Glover, w/s, 3 October 1975.
20 Jeremy Bamber, Smith 2010.
21 Robert Boutflour, w/s, 15 August 1991.
22 Robert Boutflour, w/s, 10 September 1985.
23 Dorothy Brencher, w/s, 23 September 1985.
24 Sarah Hailey, w/s, 17 September–2 October 1985.
25 Ibid.
26 Ethel Taylor, w/s, 26 September 1985.

Chapter Seventeen
1 Ann Eaton, trial testimony, October 1986.
2 Ann Eaton, trial testimony, October 1986. Unless otherwise indicated, the conversation recounted is from this source.
3 Ann Eaton, w/s, 8 September 1985.
4 Andrew Bishop, w/s, 14 September 1985.
5 Ann Wilkinson, w/s, 9 October 1985.
6 Hugh Ferguson, trial testimony, October 1986.
7 Hugh Ferguson, author interviews, 2013. There is some confusion in Dr Ferguson's statements regarding the regularity of the injections, but they were administered monthly.
8 Michael Harvatt, w/s, 26 September 1985.
9 George Gros, w/s, 12 September 1985.
10 Barbara Wilson, w/s, 5 October 1985.
11 Ann Eaton, w/s, 14 August 1991. Ann made no mention of the argument in 1985. Robert could not remember a row on this date and Pamela never referred to it.
12 Pamela Boutflour, w/s, 16 September 1985. All quotes from Pamela Boutflour in this chapter are from this source.
13 Robert Boutflour, w/s, 15 August 1991.
14 Basil Cock, w/s, 17 September 1985.
15 Peter Jay, w/s, 16 September 1985.
16 Colin Caffell, w/s, 7 August 1985.
17 Sandra Elston, w/s, 18 September 1985.
18 Jeremy Bamber, letter to author, 7 July 2013.
19 Jeremy Bamber, w/s, 8 August 1985.
20 Inez Bowen, w/s, 25 September 1985.
21 Hugh Ferguson, w/s, 18 September 1985.

22 Dorothy Brencher, w/s, 23 September 1985.
23 Barbara Wilson, author interviews, 2014.
24 Jeremy Bamber website post, 2002.
25 Tora Tomkinson, author interviews, 2013.
26 Caffell, Colin, *In Search*, p. 152.
27 *The Times,* 'After the Mourning'.

Chapter Eighteen

1 David Boutflour, Smith 2010.
2 Barbara Wilson, author interviews, 2014. All quotes from Barbara Wilson in this chapter are from this source.
3 Anthony Pargeter, w/s, 12 December 1985. Until otherwise indicated, the quotes from Anthony Pargeter in this section are from this source.
4 Regine Pargeter, w/s, 17 September 1985. All quotes from Regine Pargeter in this chapter are from this source.
5 Anthony Pargeter, w/s, 8 August 1985. All quotes in this paragraph are from this source.
6 Reginald Caffell, w/s, 8 October 1985.
7 Martin Williams, w/s, 19 September 1985.
8 Catherine Stone, w/s, 14 September 1985.
9 Caroline Heath, w/s, 11 August 1985. All quotes from Caroline Heath in this chapter are from this source.
10 Tora Tomkinson, author interviews, 2013.
11 Agnes Mennie, w/s, 2 October 1985.
12 Farhad Emami, w/s, 8 August 1985.
13 Agnes Low, w/s, 11 September 1985. All quotes from Agnes Low in this chapter are from this source.
14 Caffell, Colin, *In Search*, p. 26.
15 Judith Salvage, w/s, 30 September 1985.
16 Colin Caffell, w/s, 7 August 1985.
17 Caffell, Colin, *In Search*, p. 27. Jeremy Bamber's conversation is based on this source and also Colin Caffell, w/s, 11 September 1985.
18 Douglas Pike, trial testimony, October 1986.
19 Enid Howe, w/s, 24 September 1985.
20 Philip Wilson, w/s, 15 September 1985.
21 Yvonne Richards, w/s, 13 August 1985.
22 Leyton, Elliott, *Sole Survivor: Children Who Murder Their Families* (London: John Blake, 2009), p. 248.
23 D'Cruze, Shani, Walklate, Sandra and Pegg, Samantha, *Murder*, p. 122.

24 'Statement on Behalf of the Family', Robert Boutflour, 27 October 1986.
25 Karen Boutflour, Smith 2010.
26 Jeremy Bamber, Smith 2010.
27 *Independent*, 'Seeds of Doom in Bamber Family'.
28 Charles Marsden, w/s, 9 September 1985.

Chapter Nineteen

1 Jeremy Bamber, record of police interview, 10–12 September 1985.
2 Laurie Lawrence, w/s, 31 October 1985.
3 Len Foakes, w/s, 11 September 1985. All quotes from Len Foakes in this chapter are from this source.
4 Michael Horsnell, w/s, 23 September 1985.
5 Jeremy Bamber, w/s, 7 August 1985. Unless otherwise indicated, all quotes from Jeremy Bamber in this chapter are from this source.
6 Barbara Wilson, author interviews, 2014. All quotes from Barbara Wilson in this chapter are from this source.
7 Jeremy Bamber, record of police interview, 10–12 September 1985.
8 Barry Parker, w/s, 13 August 1985. All quotes in this section are from this source.
9 Elizabeth Smith, w/s, 14 September 1985.
10 Katherine Golding, w/s, 28 November 1985.
11 Jeremy Bamber, letter to author, 7 July 2013. In her 26 September 1985 w/s, fellow Bible group member Audrey Childs recalled that June's aunt Connie Lugg had informed them all that June wouldn't be attending that night because Sheila and the twins were visiting.
12 Jeremy Bamber, w/s, 8 August 1985.
13 Jeremy Bamber, letter to author, 7 July 2013.
14 Jeremy Bamber, w/s, 8 August 1985.
15 Jeremy Bamber, official website post, 2002; in this post, Jeremy stated that he tried to shoot the rabbits before going into the kitchen and hearing the conversation.
16 Jeremy Bamber, w/s, 8 August 1985.
17 Ibid.
18 Philip Wilson, w/s, 15 September 1985.
19 Jeremy Bamber, official website post, 2002.
20 Dorothy Foakes, w/s, 12 October 1985.
21 Stephen Smith, w/s, 25 September 1985. Contrary to the claim in the Lomax book, Smith states that he heard the gunshot at this time, no later.
22 Pamela Boutflour, w/s, 16 September 1985.

23 Pamela Boutflour, w/s, 12 August 1985. Quotes in this paragraph are from this source.
24 Robert Boutflour, w/s, 10 September 1985.
25 *Guardian*, 'The Bambi I Married'.
26 David Boutflour, trial testimony, October 1986.
27 Julie Mugford, w/s, 18 November 1985; Colin Caffell, w/s, 11 September 1985; Jean Bouttell, w/s, 11 October 1985.
28 Robert Boutflour, w/s, 15 August 1991.
29 Caffell, Colin, *In Search*, p. 68.
30 Caffell, Colin, *In Search*, p. 69.

Chapter Twenty

1 Christopher Bews, author interviews, 2013. Unless otherwise indicated, all quotes from Christopher Bews in this chapter are from this source.
2 Stephen Myall, author interviews, 2014. Unless otherwise indicated, all quotes from Stephen Myall in this chapter are from this source.
3 Stephen Myall, trial testimony, October 1986.
4 Christopher Bews, w/s, 16 August 1985. The following conversation is from this source.
5 Stephen Myall, w/s, 15 August 1985.
6 Michael West, w/s, 13 September 1985.
7 Jean Rowe, w/s, 8 August 1985. All quotes from Jean Rowe in this chapter are from this source.
8 Christopher Bews, w/s, 19 September 1985. Unless otherwise indicated, the following conversation is from this source.
9 Christopher Bews, w/s, 16 August 1985.
10 Ibid.
11 Christopher Bews, trial testimony, October 1986.
12 Stephen Myall, w/s, 15 August 1985. The following conversation is from this source.
13 Paul Cracknell, w/s, 20 September 1985.
14 Christopher Bews, w/s, 16 August 1985.
15 Lomax, Scott, *Jeremy Bamber*, p. 29.
16 Laurence Collins, w/s, 30 September 1985.
17 Nigel Dermott, w/s, 20 September 1985.
18 The following entry appears in the police communications log at 5.26am: 'Firearms team are in conversation with a person from inside the farm.' In 2011, the CCRC rejected the claim put forward by the defence that the firearms team were speaking to Sheila, stating that

the person 'from inside the farm' was Jeremy. Statements from those present confirm that no contact was ever made with any of the victims; in addition, the GPO had an open link with the farmhouse telephone and the only sound was the barking dog.

19 Stephen Myall, w/s, 15 August 1985.
20 Ibid.
21 Douglas Adams, City of London Police, Report Re: Criminal Allegations Made by Jeremy Bamber, 1 February 1991, notes for 7 August 1985. Hereafter COLP (1991). Quotes from Douglas Adams in this chapter are from this source.
22 Stephen Myall, w/s, 15 August 1985.
23 Police Events Log: Operation Stokenchurch Holmes 2 Account A49, Box/Item Number: 1/33, Copy of Original (Form C). 7 August 1985. Ref: AT-1-033. Hereafter Ref: AT-1-033.
24 Peter Woodcock, w/s, 20 September 1985.
25 Michael Mercer, w/s, 20 September 1985.
26 Ref: AT-1-033.

Chapter Twenty-One

1 Robert Lay, w/s, 1 October 1985.
2 Jeremy's defence team at his 2002 appeal asked former DI Ron Cook if the items around Nevill's body had been placed there by police. Cook declared that they had not (Defence interview of Mr Ron Cook by Mr Ewen Smith at the Royal Courts of Justice, 22 October 2002). The matter was brought up again by the CCRC in 2011 who stated that the items' neatly folded appearance suggested they were placed there later to mop up the flow of blood, possibly by police officers, prior to the crime scene photographs being taken. They did not consider the point gave rise to a ground of appeal (Criminal Cases Review Commission Provisional Statement of Reasons in the case of Jeremy Bamber, 10 February 2011).
3 Laurence Collins, w/s, 7 August 1985. Chris Bews explains the problem with the logs: 'Two or three logs were going on simultaneously. I got Bob Saxby to start doing one, there'd have been one running at Information Room, and probably one at Chelmsford Police Station. The firearms unit would possibly have run their own. So those logs are like Chinese whispers, going through two or three people before anything is actually written down.' Chris Bews, author interviews, 2013.
4 Raymond Rozga, w/s, 19 September 1985.

5 Ibid.

6 Peter Woodcock, w/s, 20 September 1985.

7 John Manners, w/s, 23 September 1985.

8 Christopher Bews, author interviews, 2013. The conversation that follows is from this source.

9 Ivor Montgomery, w/s, 26 September 1985.

10 Douglas Adams, COLP (1991), notes for 7 August 1985. All quotes from Douglas Adams in this chapter are from this source.

11 Ian Craig, notes for Essex Police, 'A Review of the Bamber Killings', November 1986. Unless indicated otherwise, all quotes from Ian Craig in this chapter are from this source.

12 Robin Saxby, w/s, 23 September 1985. The conversation that follows is from this source.

13 Ian Craig, w/s, 7 August 1985.

14 Ibid.

15 George Harris, w/s, 19 September 1985. The conversation that follows is from this source.

16 Neil Davidson, COLP interview, 16 October 1991.

17 Essex Police, 'A Review'.

18 Ibid.

19 At 9.16am, PC Chaplin logged DC Henderson rather than DC Hammersley as arriving with DC Davidson. How the error arose is unclear, but DC Davidson is adamant that he arrived with Hammersley and did not see DC Henderson that day.

20 Michael Ainsley, 'Personal Reflections on the Bamber Case', undated manuscript.

21 Neil Davidson, w/s, 11 November 1986.

22 Bob Miller, author interviews, 2013. All quotes from Bob Miller in this chapter are from this source.

23 Ian Craig, w/s, 1 October 1985.

24 David Bird, author interviews, 2014.

25 Ron Cook, w/s, 25 September 1991.

26 Ron Cook, author interviews, 2013.

Chapter Twenty-Two

1 Michael Clark, w/s, 17 September 1985. Unless otherwise indicated, quotes from Michael Clark in this chapter are from this source.

2 Stephen Savage, w/s, 23 September 1985.

3 Stanley Jones, w/s, 3 October 1985. The conversation that follows is from this source.

4 Len Foakes, w/s, 11 September 1985.

5 Michael Clark, w/s, 6 October 1985. Other accounts describe DS Jones leaving with Jeremy and DC Clark, but statements show that Jones remained at the farm until later.

6 Michael Clark, w/s, 17 September 1985.

7 Jeremy Bamber, letter to author, 1 July 2013.

8 Jill Foakes, w/s, 18 September 1985.

9 Ann Eaton, w/s, 14 August 1991.

10 David Boutflour, Smith 2010.

11 Ann Eaton, w/s, 8 September 1985.

12 Pamela Boutflour, w/s, 16 September 1985.

13 Norman Wright, w/s, 24 September 1985.

14 Ibid.

15 Ron Cook, w/s, 25 September 1991. Unless otherwise indicated, quotes from Ron Cook in this chapter are from this source.

16 Ivor Montgomery, w/s, 26 September 1985. Unless otherwise indicated, quotes from Ivor Montgomery in this chapter are from this source.

17 David Bird, trial testimony, October 1986.

18 Ron Cook, 'Bamber: Facts not Fiction', April 1990, unpublished manuscript. All quotes in this paragraph are from this source.

19 David Hammersley, w/s, 27 February 1986.

20 Ibid.

21 Peter Woodcock, w/s, 20 September 1985.

22 Ron Cook, author interviews, 2013.

Chapter Twenty-Three

1 Michael Clark, w/s, 17 September 1985. To avoid repetition in the text, the phrase 'or words to the effect' have been omitted from his and other statements. Ann stated that a police officer (whom she named as Clark in her 14 August 1991 w/s) gave her further details, but much of what she was told was incorrect, i.e., that June and Sheila were found on the bed in the master bedroom, with the gun next to Sheila and the Bible on her chest.

2 Barry Langham, w/s, 15 October 1985.

3 Jonathan Turner, w/s, 4 October 1985. All quotes from Jonathan Turner in this chapter are from this source.

4 Stanley Jones, w/s, 3 October 1985.

5 *Daily Express*, 'We Know Bamber is a Liar – and a Killer', Anna Pukas, 28 April 2007.

6 Ann Eaton, w/s, 14 August 1991.

7 Julie Mugford, w/s, 18 November 1985.

8 Barbara Wilson, author interviews, 2014.

9 Stephen Golding, w/s, 26 September 1985.

10 Thomas Jones, w/s, 7 October 1985.

11 Michael Ainsley, 'Report'.

12 Peter Vanezis, author interviews, 2014. Unless otherwise indicated, quotes from Peter Vanezis are from this source.

13 Malcolm Fletcher, email to author, 28 January 2015. Unless otherwise indicated, quotes from Malcolm Fletcher in this chapter are from this source.

14 Peter Vanezis, trial testimony, October 1986.

15 David Hammersley, w/s, 27 February 1986. No swabs were taken from the other victims.

16 Ron Cook, author interviews, 2013.

17 Peter Vanezis, post-mortem notes, August 1985. Colin Caffell confirmed that Sheila was right-handed in his 11 September 1985 witness statement.

18 Peter Vanezis, trial testimony, October 1986.

19 Ibid.

20 Peter Vanezis, author interviews, 2014.

21 'She did not appear . . .' Hugh Ferguson, trial testimony, October 1986; 'Bambi told me . . .' Christine Finlay, w/s, 18 September 1985.

22 Peter Vanezis, w/s, 30 September 1985.

23 Peter Vanezis, notes, 12 November 1986.

24 Essex Police, 'Appendix to the Report: A Review of the Bamber Killings', November 1986.

25 Ron Cook, w/s, 25 September 1991.

26 Peter Vanezis, notes, 12 November 1986.

27 Ron Cook, w/s, 25 September 1991.

Chapter Twenty-Four

1 Caffell, Colin, *In Search*, pp. 32–3. Until otherwise indicated, the quotes that follow are from this source.

2 Michael Clark, w/s, 17 September 1985.

3 Ann Eaton, w/s, 14 August 1991. Unless otherwise indicated, quotes from Ann Eaton in this chapter are from this source.

4 Colin Caffell, w/s, 25 October 1985.

5 Wilkes, Roger, *Blood Relations*, p. 52.

6 Michael Clark, w/s, 17 September 1985.

7 Caffell, Colin, *In Search*, p. 39.

8 Ann Eaton, w/s, 8 September 1985.

9 Robert Boutflour, w/s, 10 September 1985.

10 Pamela Boutflour, w/s, 16 September 1985.

11 David Boutflour, w/s extracts, 1991.

12 Tora Tomkinson, author interviews, 2013.

13 Mairead Maguire, w/s, 16 September 1985.

14 Donald Hawkins, w/s, 8 October 1985.

15 Sandra Elston, w/s, 18 September 1985.

16 Barbara Babic, w/s, 11 October 1985. Author's italics.

17 Caffell, Colin, *In Search*, p. 12.

18 Jeremy Bamber, w/s, 7 August 1985. Until otherwise indicated, quotes from Jeremy Bamber in this chapter are from this source. In his memoir Colin states that Sheila's entire class was expelled after high spirits on their final day at Hethersett, but the school has no record of this.

19 'Jeremy often . . .' Suzette Ford, w/s, 12 September 1985; 'He had seen . . .' Suzette Ford, w/s, 16 September 1986. Jeremy Bamber's official campaign website states that Freddie told Suzette that Sheila was violent to her children (http://www.jeremy-bamber.co.uk/how-and-why-did-sheila-do-it), yet Freddie made no mention of this to police.

20 *Guardian*, 'The Bambi I Married'.

21 Jeremy Bamber, record of police interview, 10–12 September 1985.

22 Suzette Ford, w/s, 12 September 1985.

23 Jeremy Bamber, official website post, 2002. Author's italics.

24 Barbara Babic, w/s, 11 October 1985.

25 Myrto Angeloglou, w/s, 12 September 1985.

26 Michael Clark, w/s, 5 December 1985.

27 Stephen Myall, w/s, 15 August 1985.

28 Caffell, Colin, *In Search*, p. 54.

29 David Ware, w/s, 5 October 1985.

Chapter Twenty-Five

1 Peter Vanezis, author interviews, 2014. Unless otherwise indicated, quotes in this chapter from Peter Vanezis are from this source.

2 Peter Vanezis, trial testimony, October 1986.

3 Peter Vanezis, notes, 12 November 1986.

4 Julie Mugford, w/s, 18 November 1985.

5 Jeremy Bamber, w/s, 8 August 1985.

6 Ann Eaton, w/s, 8 September 1985. Unless otherwise indicated, quotes in this chapter from Ann Eaton are from this source.
7 Ann Eaton, w/s, 2 October 1985.
8 Bob Miller, author interviews, 2013. All quotes from Bob Miller in this chapter are from this source.
9 Norman Wright, w/s, 24 September 1985.
10 Ann Eaton, w/s, 14 August 1991.
11 Ann Eaton, card notes re: events, 8 August 1985.
12 Hugh Ferguson, author interviews, 2013.
13 Hugh Ferguson, w/s, 8 August 1985.
14 Ron Cook, author interviews, 2013. Unless otherwise indicated, quotes from Ron Cook in this chapter are from this source.
15 Peter Vanezis, notes, 12 November 1986.
16 David Bird, author interviews, 2014.
17 Ron Cook, w/s, 25 September 1991.
18 Julie Mugford, w/s, 8 August 1985. Unless otherwise indicated, quotes from Julie Mugford in this chapter are from this source.
19 In 1991, the City of London Police looked into the decision to have the bodies cremated. Jeremy told them his parents had let it be known that they wished to be cremated and their ashes scattered in the woods near the farm. Family solicitor Thomas Wilson could not specify whether the instructions came from Jeremy or his relatives.
20 Farhad Emami, w/s, 8 August 1985. Freddie referred to June as Sheila's stepmother.

Chapter Twenty-Six

1 Tora Tomkinson, author interviews, 2013.
2 R v. Jeremy Nevill Bamber: Judgment: Approved by the Court for Handing Down (Subject to Editorial Corrections), 12 December 2002. (Hereafter R v. Jeremy Nevill Bamber: Judgment 2002.)
3 R v. Jeremy Nevill Bamber: Judgment 2002.
4 Ron Cook, author interviews, 2013. Unless otherwise indicated, quotes from Ron Cook in this chapter are from this source.
5 Ron Cook, memo, 2 June 1986.
6 David Bird, author interviews, 2014.
7 Essex Police, 'A Review'.
8 Ann Eaton, w/s, 14 August 1991.
9 David Boutflour, Smith 2010.
10 Ann Eaton, w/s, 14 August 1991. Unless otherwise indicated, quotes from Ann Eaton in this chapter are from this source.

11 Peter Eaton, w/s, 18–21 September 1985.
12 Ann Eaton, w/s, 8 September 1985.
13 Thomas Jones, w/s, 7 October 1985.The conversation that follows is from this source.
14 Elizabeth Rimington, w/s, 8 September 1985.
15 Caffell, Colin, *In Search*, pp. 64–5.
16 Ann Eaton, w/s, 8 September 1985. Unless otherwise indicated, the remaining quotes in this chapter are from this source.
17 Crime scene photographs show that the wallpaper was already missing on the morning of the murders.
18 Ann Eaton, w/s, 14 August 1991.

Chapter Twenty-Seven

 1 Ann Eaton, w/s, 14 August 1991. Unless otherwise indicated, all quotes from Ann Eaton in this chapter are from this source.
 2 'This was arranged . . .' Basil Cock, w/s, 16 September 1985; 'We were to remove . . .' Ann Eaton, notes for Michael Ainsley, 11 December 1994 (hereafter Ann Eaton, notes, 1994).
 3 Barbara Wilson, author interviews, 2014. Unless otherwise indicated, quotes from Barbara Wilson in this chapter are from this source.
 4 David Boutflour, w/s, 17 September 1985. In his 2010 interview with David James Smith, David said it was then that he tried to look inside the silencer: 'I was trying to unscrew it because I wanted to look inside myself, but it was too tight. I couldn't undo it. Then we suddenly saw the blood and the hair and I thought, "Oh my God, what am I doing? Leave it alone."'
 5 Jill Bonney, w/s, 8 October 1985.
 6 Ibid.
 7 David Boutflour, Smith 2010.
 8 David Boutflour, w/s extract, 1991.
 9 Ann Eaton, w/s, 8 September 1985.
10 Anthony Pargeter, w/s, 13 May 1991.
11 Ann Eaton, w/s, 8 September 1985.
12 Robert Boutflour, w/s, 10 September 1985.
13 Robert Boutflour, undated diary notes, 1985.
14 David Boutflour, w/s extract, 1991.
15 Susan Battersby, w/s, 10 September 1985.
16 Peter Eaton, w/s, 18–21 September 1985.
17 Ann Eaton, card dated 6 August 1991.
18 Ann Eaton, w/s, 16 September 1985.

19 Robert Boutflour, w/s, 15 August 1991. Unless otherwise indicated, quotes from Robert Boutflour in this chapter are from this source.
20 Ann Eaton, w/s, 16 September 1985.
21 Robert Boutflour, w/s, 10 September 1985.
22 Basil Cock, w/s, 16 September 1985.
23 Peter Vanezis, author interviews, 2014. All quotes from Peter Vanezis in this chapter are from this source.
24 Alexander Allen, w/s, 12 November 1985.
25 Elizabeth Rimington, w/s, 8 September 1985.
26 Stanley Jones, w/s, 3 October 1985.
27 COLP (1991).
28 Ibid.
29 Bob Miller, author interviews, 2013.
30 Ron Cook, w/s, 25 September 1991.
31 Ron Cook, letter, 25 January 1991.
32 Malcolm Fletcher, author interviews, 2013.

Chapter Twenty-Eight

1 Brett Collins, record of police interview, 8 September 1985.
2 Roland Pargeter, w/s, 26 September 1985; Ann Eaton, notes, 1994.
3 Ann Eaton, w/s, 14 August 1991. Unless otherwise indicated, quotes from Ann Eaton in this chapter are from this source.
4 Michael Ainsley, 'Personal Reflections'.
5 Ann Eaton, notes, 1994.
6 In April 2001, the Metropolitan Police took possession of eleven of Sheila's diaries from the family's solicitor Basil Cock. They dated from 1969 until 1985, although 1980–83 were missing. Jeremy's then solicitor Ewan Smith viewed the diaries and was provided with copies which he collected from the CPS.
7 James Carr, letter, 15 August 1985.
8 Ron Cook, w/s, 25 September 1991. Unless otherwise indicated, quotes from Ron Cook in this chapter are from this source.
9 Ron Cook, author interviews, 2013.
10 Stanley Jones, w/s, 3 October 1985.
11 Ron Cook, author interviews, 2013. Ann declared in her 14 June 1991 witness statement: 'Red paint did not immediately make me realise it was mantle. Not until the 14th did it all add up.' David Boutflour gives conflicting accounts of making the connection.
12 Stanley Jones, undated statement, COLP (1991).
13 Ron Cook, author interviews, 2013.

14 Michael Barlow, COLP (1991), notes for 15 August 1985.
15 Essex Police, 'A Review'.
16 Michael Barlow, COLP (1991), notes for 15 August 1985.
17 Elizabeth Rimington, w/s, 11 September 1985. Unless otherwise indicated, quotes from Liz Rimington in this chapter are from this source.
18 Agnes Low, w/s, 11 September 1985.
19 Julie Mugford, w/s, 8–9 September 1985.
20 Elizabeth Rimington, w/s, 8 September 1985. The remaining quotes in this chapter are from this source.

Chapter Twenty-Nine

 1 Brett Collins, w/s, 9 September 1985.
 2 Julie Mugford, w/s, 23 September 1985.
 3 Karen Boutflour, w/s, 20 September 1985.
 4 *Essex Chronicle*, 'Son's Last Farewell', Steve Clow, 16 August 1985.
 5 Caffell, Colin, *In Search*, pp. 75–6.
 6 Bob Miller, author interviews, 2013. Unless otherwise indicated, quotes from Bob Miller in this chapter are from this source.
 7 William Thomas, w/s, 13 September 1985.
 8 Michael Ainsley, author interviews, 2013.
 9 *Daily Express*, 'We Know Bamber'.
10 Bob Miller, w/s, 7 October 1985.
11 *Daily Mail*, 'The Two Faces'.
12 Powell, Claire, *Murder at*, p. 112.
13 Julie Mugford, w/s, 10 September 1985. Unless otherwise indicated, quotes from Julie Mugford in this chapter are from this source.
14 Rodney Brown, w/s, 15 September 1985. All quotes from Rodney Brown in this chapter are from this source.
15 Jacqueline Wood, w/s, 10 September 1985.
16 *Daily Express*, 'Father's Farewell to his Little Angels', Peter Kent, 20 August 1985.
17 Michael Barlow, w/s, 21 November 1985.
18 Barbara Wilson, w/s, 16 December 1985.
19 Michael Ainsley states that the Sceptre 100 was connected in the office and in working order on the morning of 7 August 1985 when it was used by the firearms team 'who were unable to use the kitchen telephone for obvious reasons'. Michael Ainsley, 'Report'.
20 Jean Bouttell, w/s, 30 September 1985. In his 12 September 1985 police interview, Jeremy stated that 'the secretary said we no longer

needed' the Envoy cordless telephone, but Barbara did not recall saying that.

Chapter Thirty

1 Robert Boutflour, notes/observations, 25 August – 9 December 1985.
2 Julie Mugford, w/s, 8–9 September 1985.
3 Wilkes, Roger, *Blood Relations*, p. 99.
4 Ann Eaton, w/s, 16 September 1985. The 'fanlight' window above the sink is mentioned but it was the casement window to which she referred.
5 Robert Boutflour, w/s, 10 September 1985. Unless otherwise indicated, quotes from Robert Boutflour in this chapter are taken from this source.
6 Julie Mugford, w/s, 8–9 September 1985.
7 Susan Battersby, w/s, 10 September 1985. Until otherwise indicated, the quotes that follow are taken from this source.
8 Julie Mugford, w/s, 23 September 1985. Until otherwise indicated, the quotes that follow are taken from this source.
9 Susan Battersby, w/s, 10 September 1985.
10 Julie Mugford, w/s, 23 September 1985.
11 Susan Battersby, w/s, 10 September 1985. Until otherwise indicated, the quotes that follow are taken from this source.
12 Julie Mugford, w/s, 8–9 September 1985.
13 Ann Eaton, notes, 1994.
14 John Stancliffe, w/s, 18 September 1985.
15 Jeremy Bamber, Smith 2010.
16 Robert Boutflour, undated diary notes, 1985.
17 Robert Boutflour, w/s, 15 August 1991.
18 Ann Eaton, w/s, 14 August 1991. Until otherwise indicated, the quotes that follow are taken from this source.
19 Julie Mugford, w/s, 23 September 1985.
20 Susan Battersby, w/s, 23 September 1985. Until otherwise indicated, the conversation that follows is taken from this source.
21 Elizabeth Rimington, w/s, 8 September 1985. Quotes from Liz Rimington in this chapter are taken from this source.
22 Brett Collins, w/s, 1 October 1985.
23 Barbara Wilson, w/s, 5 October 1985.
24 Barbara Wilson, author interviews, 2014.
25 Barbara Wilson, w/s, 27 September 1985.
26 Gerald Wiggins, w/s, 8 October 1985.

Chapter Thirty-One

1 Robert Boutflour, undated diary notes, 1985.
2 Michael Barlow, COLP (1991), notes for 30 August 1985.
3 Ibid.
4 Virginia Greaves, w/s, 12 September 1985. Until otherwise indicated, the quotes that follow are from this source.
5 Pamela Boutflour, w/s, 2 September 1985. The conversation that follows is from this source.
6 Julie Mugford, w/s, 8–9 September 1985. Until otherwise indicated, the quotes that follow are from this source.
7 Julie Mugford, w/s, 18 November 1985.
8 Julie Mugford, w/s, 8–9 September 1985. Unless otherwise indicated, the quotes that follow are from this source.
9 Jeremy Bamber, official website post, 2002.
10 *News of the World*, 'I Tried to Smother'.
11 Julie Mugford, w/s, 8–9 September 1985; Elizabeth Rimington, w/s, 8 September 1985. Unless otherwise indicated, the quotes that follow are from the latter source.
12 Elizabeth Rimington, trial testimony, October 1986.
13 Barbara Wilson, w/s, 17 September 1985. There is some confusion over whether the alarm was the one left there by the police or a new one fitted by Jeremy. It was almost certainly the latter.
14 Ann Eaton, w/s, 14 August 1991. All quotes in this chapter from Ann Eaton are from this source.
15 Robert Boutflour, w/s, 15 August 1991. Unless otherwise indicated, quotes in this chapter from Robert Boutflour are from this source.
16 Caffell, Colin, *In Search*, p. 209.
17 Ibid.

Chapter Thirty-Two

1 Karen Bishop, w/s, 14 September 1985. All quotes from Karen Bishop in this chapter are from this source.
2 June Bamber, undated letter.
3 Robert Boutflour, undated diary notes, 1985. Unless otherwise indicated, quotes from Robert Boutflour in this chapter are from this source.
4 Robert Boutflour, w/s, 15 August 1991.
5 Ann Eaton, w/s, 14 August 1991. All quotes from Ann Eaton in this chapter are from this source.

6 Robert Boutflour, w/s, 10 September 1985.

7 Julie Mugford, w/s, 8–9 September 1985. Unless otherwise indicated, quotes from Julie Mugford in this chapter are from this source. The conversation that follows is also from this source.

8 Virginia Greaves, w/s, 12 September 1985. The conversation that follows is from this source.

9 Brett Collins, record of police interview, 8 September 1985.

10 Jeremy Bamber, record of police interview, 9 September 1985.

11 Julie Mugford, w/s, 14 October 1985.

12 Charles Marsden, w/s, 9 September 1985.

13 Julie Mugford, w/s, 10 September 1985.

14 Michael Ainsley, author interviews, 2013.

15 Michael Ainsley, 'Personal Reflections'.

16 Ibid.

17 Judith Salvage, w/s, 30 September 1985.

18 Heather Amos, w/s, 15 September 1985.

19 Malcolm Waters, w/s, 15 September 1985. The conversation that follows is from this source.

20 Wilkes, Roger, *Blood Relations*, p. 115.

Chapter Thirty-Three

1 Caffell, Colin, *In Search*, p. 93.

2 Wilkes, Roger, *Blood Relations*, p. 115.

3 Jeremy Bamber, Smith 2010.

4 Jeremy Bamber, letter to author, 15 May 2013.

5 Bob Miller, author interviews, 2013. Until otherwise indicated, the quotes that follow are from this source.

6 Ibid.

7 Michael Ainsley, 'Personal Reflections'.

8 Julie Mugford, w/s, 8–9 September 1985. Unless otherwise noted, all quotes by Julie Mugford in this chapter are taken from this statement. Julie originally stated that it was Christmas 1984 when Jeremy began talking about murder.

9 Julie Mugford, w/s, 10 September 1985.

10 Julie declared that she 'took one tablet but didn't take anymore' before correcting herself. In his 10–12 September police interview Jeremy said that he had never taken any tablets; they were either in a drawer at Bourtree Cottage or he had thrown them out.

11 Julie Mugford, w/s, 18 November 1985.

12 David Boutflour, Smith 2010.

13 Julie Mugford, w/s, 10 September 1985.
14 Ibid.
15 Ibid.
16 Julie Mugford, w/s, 18 November 1985.
17 Ibid.
18 Julie Mugford, w/s, 10 September 1985.
19 Julie Mugford, w/s, 8 May 1986.

Chapter Thirty-Four

1 Michael Ainsley, 'Personal Reflections'. Unless otherwise indicated,
  quotes from Michael Ainsley in this chapter are from this source.
2 Julie Smerchanski, w/s, 12 April 2002.
3 Bob Miller, author interviews, 2013.
4 Policy File for Bamber Incident, 7 September 1985 – 31 January
  1986.
5 Michael Barlow, w/s, 16 September 1985. Until otherwise indicated,
  the quotes that follow are from the same source.
6 Powell, Claire, *Murder at*, p. 147.
7 Brett Collins, record of police interview, 8 September 1985.
8 Jeremy Bamber, record of police interview, 8 September 1985.
9 Ron Cook, author interviews, 2013.
10 Michael Ainsley, 'Report'.
11 *Star*, 'Bamber Will Kill Himself', Barry Gardner, 30 October 1986.
12 *Daily Mail*, 'The Two Faces'.
13 Jeremy Bamber, record of police interview, 8 September 1985.
14 Michael Barlow, w/s, 21 November 1985.
15 Wilkes, Roger, *Blood Relations*, p. 229.
16 *The Times*, 'Bamber Denies That He Slaughtered his "Loving"
  Parents', Michael Horsnell, 17 October 1986.

Chapter Thirty-Five

1 Christine Bacon, record of police interview, 9 September 1985.
2 Michael Ainsley, author interviews, 2013.
3 Colin Caffell, w/s, 11 September 1985.
4 Jeremy Bamber, record of police interview, 9 September 1985.
5 Michael Barlow, COLP (1991), notes for 9 September 1985.
6 Laurence Collins, w/s, 9 September 1985.
7 Charles Marsden, w/s, 9 September 1985.
8 Matthew McDonald, record of police interview, 10 September 1985.

9 Wilkes, Roger, *Blood Relations*, p. 132.
10 Jeremy Bamber, record of police interview, 10–11 September 1985.

Chapter Thirty-Six

1 Matthew McDonald, record of police interview, 10 September 1985.
2 Jeremy Bamber, record of police interview, 10–11 September 1985.
3 Stanley Jones, w/s, 3 October 1985.
4 Michael Clark, w/s, 6 October 1985.
5 Julie Smerchanski, w/s, 12 April 2002.
6 Michael Ainsley, 'Personal Reflections'.
7 Michael Ainsley, letter, 18 October 1993.
8 Ron Cook, undated memo, 1985.
9 General Examination Records re: ballistics, Malcolm Fletcher, 10–11 September 1985.
10 Matthew McDonald, record of police interview, 11 September 1985.
11 Jeremy Bamber, record of police interview, 10–11 September 1985.
12 Among the later submissions made by Jeremy's legal team to the CCRC was a police log which they suggested showed Nevill Bamber had, in fact, called the police on the night of his death. The CCRC responded firmly that not only was there was nothing to support the contention that such a call had been made, but there was evidence to show that it had not.
13 Jones appeared to be referring to the cartridge case on the stairs.
14 Michael Clark, w/s, 6 October 1985.

Chapter Thirty-Seven

1 Michael Ainsley, 'Personal Reflections'. Unless otherwise indicated, quotes from Michael Ainsley in this chapter are from this source.
2 Jeremy Bamber, record of police interview, 12 September 1985.
3 Michael Ainsley, 'Report'.
4 Jeremy Bamber, Smith 2010.
5 Robert Boutflour, w/s, 15 August 1991.
6 Caffell, Colin, *In Search*, p. 98.
7 *Evening Gazette*, 'The Blonde Who Stands By Bamber', Dave Woods and Judith Bastin, 29 October 1986.
8 Michael Ainsley, author interviews, 2013.
9 Michael Deckers, w/s, 21 September 1985.
10 Michael Ainsley, record of interview, 29 August 2002. R v. Jeremy Nevill Bamber: Judgment 2002 quotes from a Kingsley Napley

attendance note of 3 September 1986 in which the appellant 'confirmed that he <u>was</u> under surveillance after his release from custody'.

11 David Bird, w/s, 24 October 1985. In a 23 July 2013 letter to the author Jeremy states: 'The house was cleaned and tidied by Jean Bouttell and Ann many times in August/September and they did not leave those socks there on the floor for five weeks so the police could seize them when they searched the house for a second time.' Presumably the socks were put away and the police collected them. In the same letter, he writes of a pair of dark/light blue tights seen draped over the banister on the upper landing, suggesting the tights had been used by police to wipe their hands, after which they had been rinsed out. But the tights were not wet; they are two-tone, with clearly defined stitching between the two colours.

12 Malcolm Fletcher, author interviews, 2013. Unless otherwise indicated, quotes from Malcolm Fletcher in this chapter are from this source.

13 Malcolm Fletcher, w/s, 13 November 1985.

14 John Hayward, w/s, 13 November 1985.

15 http://jeremybamber.org/jeremy-bamber/.

Chapter Thirty-Eight

1 Malcolm Fletcher, author interviews, 2013. All quotes from Malcolm Fletcher in this chapter are from this source.

2 Brian Elliot, w/s, 12 November 1985.

3 David Bird, author interviews, 2014.

4 Peter Vanezis, author interviews, 2014.

5 John Hayward, w/s, 13 November 1985. Unless otherwise indicated, quotes from John Hayward in this chapter are from this source.

6 John Hayward, report on blood groupings, 3 October 1986.

7 R v. Jeremy Nevill Bamber: Judgment 2002.

8 Ron Cook, w/s, 21 March 1986. The police doubted whether the Bible was found in its original position, surmising that it had been moved accidentally by one of the raid team as they searched the house. It is not known what happened to the crocheted cloth or the note visible in the crime scene photographs. In 2002, the Court of Appeal made the point that the pages of the Bible were bloodstained and had been closed while the blood was still wet.

9 'A dropping zone . . .' *Daily Mirror*, Peter Kane, 16 September 1985; 'A mystery figure . . .' *Daily Mail*, 'Mystery Man at Massacre Farmhouse', 16 September 1985.

10 *Daily Mirror*, 'Bambi Police Hit at Critics', 19 September 1985.

11 Robert Boutflour, w/s, 20 September 1985.

12 Caffell, Colin, *In Search*, p. 184.

13 Barbara Wilson, author interviews, 2014.

14 Peter Simpson, letter, 25 September 1985.

15 *Guardian* website, 'Jeremy Bamber: Prosecutor's Correspondence with Police – Full Documents', 29 March 2012. http://www.theguardian.com/uk/interactive/2012/mar/29/jeremy-bamber-prosecutor-police-documents.

16 Ian Davison, w/s, 29 September 1985.

17 Bob Miller, author interviews, 2013.

18 Stanley Jones, w/s, 3 October 1985. The conversation and events that follow are taken from his statement and also Michael Clark's 6 October 1985 w/s, unless otherwise indicated.

19 Bob Miller, w/s, 7 October 1985.

Chapter Thirty-Nine

1 *Sun*, 'I Didn't Kill Poor Bambi', Kieron Saunders, 1 October 1985.

2 Barbara Wilson, author interviews, 2014.

3 *People*, 'The Secret Babies'.

4 *Express*, 'Sculpted in Pain and Murder', Lucy Miller, 20 February 1988.

5 Brian Elliot, w/s, 12 November 1985. Until indicated otherwise, the quotations that follow are from this source.

6 Michael Ainsley, 'Personal Reflections'.

7 Some years after the trial, Jeremy's defence argued that he had been confused with the dates and that if the marks had been there previously, they and the blade would have been discovered. But there was not much margin for error; the surveillance operation in London ended at 1.30am on 16 September, although Jeremy was undoubtedly in Essex by lunchtime on 17 September for a meeting with Michael Fielder in Chelmsford. He had returned to London by the following day.

8 Caffell, Colin, *In Search*, p. 103.

9 Paul Terzeon, w/s, 2 September 2002.

10 *Daily Telegraph*, Edmund Lawson obituary, 11 May 2009.

11 Michael Ainsley, author interviews, 2013.

12 Ron Cook, author interviews, 2013.

13 Michael Ainsley, 'Report'.

14 'Won complete immunity . . .' Jeremy Bamber, letter to author, 15 May 2013; 'There is no . . .' COLP (1991).

15 Betty Shine, *Mind to Mind: The Secrets of Your Mind Energy Revealed* (London: Corgi Books, 1989), pp. 118–19.

16 *News of the World*, 'I Tried to Smother'.

17 *Sun*, 'Bambi Killer Suicide Threat', 30 October 1986.

18 Malcolm Fletcher, author interviews, 2013. All quotes from Malcolm Fletcher in this chapter are from this source.

19 R v. Jeremy Nevill Bamber: Judgment 2002.

20 Ibid. The report states that Dr Lincoln was mistaken in his belief that the 'whole of the blood flake was dissolved and the resulting solution was used for all the tests. In fact what had happened was that the flake had been divided into a number of parts and each part had then been used for a separate group test. Thus the tests were not done on liquid drawn from the same solution made from the whole flake but on separate solutions each made from distinct parts of the flake.'

21 Thomas Emyr Jones, death certificate, 12 June 1986.

22 *Sun*, 'Police Chief Jones', 14 May 1986.

23 Criminal Cases Review Commission Provisional Statement of Reasons in the case of Jeremy Bamber, 10 February 2011.

24 Wilkes, Roger, *Blood Relations*, p. 183.

Chapter Forty

1 *Independent*, 'The Bamber Files', David Connett, 8 August 2010.

2 *Independent*, 'Arrogant Approach Spoiled His Act', 29 October 1985.

3 *Sun*, 'Bambi Killer Suicide Threat'. The correct phrase is 'illegitimi non carborundum'.

4 *Independent*, 'The Bamber Files'.

5 *Sun*, 'Bambi Killer Suicide Threat'.

6 *Star*, 'Bamber Will Kill Himself'.

7 Anthony Arlidge QC, trial testimony, October 1986. Unless otherwise indicated, all quotations are from the trial transcript.

8 Based upon the summary given in R v. Jeremy Nevill Bamber: Judgment 2002.

9 David Bird, author interviews, 2014.

10 Barbara Wilson, author interviews, 2014.

11 Ron Cook, author interviews, 2013.

12 *Daily Mail*, 'The Two Faces'.

Chapter Forty-One

1 *Sun*, 'Bambi Killer Suicide Threat'.
2 *Independent*, 'The Bamber Files'.
3 Peter Vanezis, author interviews, 2014.
4 Malcolm Fletcher, author interviews, 2013.

Chapter Forty-Two

1 Based upon the summary given in R v. Jeremy Nevill Bamber: Judgment 2002.
2 Michael Ainsley, author interviews, 2013.

Chapter Forty-Three

1 *Daily Mail*, 'You Would Even Find Something Good to Say About Guy Fawkes', Martin Delgado, 15 December 2002.
2 *Independent*, 'The Bamber Files'.
3 Ibid.
4 Powell, Claire, *Murder at*, p. 298.
5 Lomax, Scott, *Jeremy Bamber*, p. 14.
6 *Daily Express*, 'We Know Bamber'.
7 David Boutflour, *ITN News* footage, 28 October 1986.
8 'Statement on Behalf of the Family', Robert Boutflour, 27 October 1986.
9 Colin Caffell, *ITN News* footage, 28 October 1986.
10 Wilkes, Roger, *Blood Relations*, p. 279.
11 Michael Ainsley, author interviews, 2013.
12 Malcolm Fletcher, author interviews, 2013.
13 Hugh Ferguson, author interviews, 2013.
14 Name withheld, author interviews, 2014.
15 Powell, Claire, *Murder at*, pp. 262–3.
16 Ibid., p. 292.
17 Ibid., p. 262.
18 In 2002, Julie stated that she was unable to recall the exact date of the contract but was certain that nothing was signed until after the verdict. Rosalie Shann and Polly Hepburn are no longer living, but Annette Witheridge, who also worked for the *News of the World*, declares: 'I'm sure there wouldn't have been a contract in place before the verdict came in. Things were strict at that time. I'm sure

they would have tried to secure something, but not in contract form.'
Annette Witheridge, author interviews, 2013.

19 http://news.bbc.co.uk/1/hi/uk/380347.stm.

20 Ken Smith, *Inside Time* (London: Mandarin, 1990), pp. 175–6. The
quotes that follow are from the same source, pp. 291–6.

Chapter Forty-Four

1 Transcript of Bamber press conference, 28 October 1986.

2 David Bird, author interviews, 2014.

3 Essex Police, 'A Review'.

4 Douglas Hurd, written response, 23 March 1989.

5 Peter Vanezis, author interviews, 2014.

6 John Burrow, letter, 10 April 1989.

7 D. M. Williams, letter, 7 March 1991.

8 COLP (1991).

9 Jeremy Bamber, Smith 2010.

10 Herbert Leon MacDonell, letter, 26 October 1992.

11 John Hayward, letter, 17 November 1993.

12 Jeremy Bamber, Official Blog, 13 April 2010. http://jeremybamber.
blogspot.co.uk/2010/04/jeremy-bamber-speaks-on-talk-radio-22nd.
html.

13 *Daily Express*, 'A Soft Life in Jail for Mass Killer Bamber', Maria
Trkulja, 1 October 1995.

14 Jeremy Bamber, letter to author, 27 August 2013.

15 R v. Jeremy Nevill Bamber: Judgment 2002.

16 *Daily Express*, 'Fear of Lover Who Put Away Bamber', Anthony
Mitchell and Bob McGowan, 14 March 2001.

17 Ibid.

18 R v. Jeremy Nevill Bamber: Judgment 2002.

19 Jeremy Bamber, official website post, 2002.

20 *Daily Mail*, 'Jeremy Bamber: Does This Macabre Picture Prove He Is
Innocent?' Glen Owen, 12 October 2013.

21 Polygraph Report, Terence J. Mullins, YK Polygraph Services, 20
April 2007.

22 High Court Setting of Minimum Terms for Mandatory Life Sentences
under the Criminal Justice Act 2003. Case No. 2005/52/MTR. 16
May 2008.

23 David James Smith, author interviews, 2013.

24 Criminal Cases Review Commission Statement, 26 April 2012.

25 Jeremy Bamber, letter to author, 11 July 2012.

26 *Guardian*: 'Whole-Life Terms Without Review Breach Human Rights – European Court', Owen Bowcott and Eric Allison, 9 July 2013.

Chapter Forty-Five

1 Michael Ainsley, letter, 27 April 1987.
2 Paul Terzeon, letter, 2 January 1991.
3 Ibid.
4 Glynis Howard, w/s, 3 October 1991.
5 Ibid.
6 COLP (1991). Until otherwise indicated, the quotations that follow are from this source.
7 Jeremy Bamber, Smith 2010.
8 Jeremy Bamber, Official Blog, 3 June 2011. http://jeremybamber. blogspot.co.uk/2011/06/when-i-am-free-man-i-will-take-steps-to.html.
9 David Boutflour, Smith 2010.
10 Jeremy Bamber, review of *Tonight* programme, 12 April 2012. http://jeremybamber.blogspot.co.uk/2012/04/jeremys-comments-on-tonight-programme.html.
11 Criminal Cases Review Commission Provisional Statement of Reasons in the case of Jeremy Bamber, 10 February 2011.
12 Jeremy Bamber, letter to author, 5 March 2013.
13 *The Times*, 'Bamber Challenges Murder Conviction Over Gun Evidence', Dominic Kennedy, 2 December 2013.
14 Malcolm Fletcher, author interviews, 2013.
15 http://www.jeremy-bamber.co.uk/silencer.
16 Ewan Smith, phone record, 22 May 2002. Enclosure, Jeremy Bamber, letter to author.
17 David James Smith, author interviews, 2013. David James Smith has asked me to point out that he has joined the CCRC as a Commissioner since this interview, that these observations reflect his personal views prior to joining the Commission, and that should Jeremy Bamber ever reapply to the CCRC, his submissions would be considered by a Commissioner or Commissioners with no previous involvement in the case.
18 Michael Ainsley, letter, 1 October 1998.
19 Bob Woffinden, author interviews, 2013.
20 Category A Committee, 'Jeremy Bamber, Review', 27 June 1991.
21 www.jeremy-bamber.co.uk/psychopathy.
22 Professor Vincent Egan, 'Psychological Report on Jeremy Bamber', 31 August 2009.

23 *Ofcom Broadcast Bulletin*, Issue 190, 26 September 2011. Until otherwise indicated, the quotes that follow are from this source.
24 Jeremy Bamber, letter to author, 23 March 2013.
25 Jeremy Bamber, Smith 2010.

Epilogue

1 Caffell, Colin, *In Search*, pp. 243–4.
2 Caffell, Colin, *In Search*, pp. 245–7.
3 *Guardian*, 'The Bambi I Married'.
4 *Daily Mirror*, 'Jeremy Bamber Took My Little Boys from Me: He Must Never Be Set Free', Don Mackay, 28 October 2006.
5 Jeremy Bamber, Smith 2010.
6 Jeremy Bamber, letter, 6 April 1987.
7 *Sunday Mirror*, 'I Put Bamber in Prison', Annette Witheridge, 1 April 2001.
8 *Evening Gazette*, 'Bamber Gives Up His Claim on Farm', Dave Woods, 9 September 1989.
9 Ann Eaton, notes, 1994.
10 Barbara Wilson, author interviews, 2014.
11 Caffell, Colin, *In Search*, p. 118.
12 David Boutflour, Smith 2010.
13 Ann Eaton, w/s, 14 August 1991.
14 Ibid.
15 Robert Boutflour, letter, 3 April 1989.
16 *Daily Mirror*, 'He Went to Lovely People'. The quotes in this section are from this source.
17 Jeremy Bamber, letter to author, 15 May 2013. Michael Ainsley confirms that the note was in June's handwriting and had been fully studied and examined scientifically, along with another note found in Sheila's bedroom, which appeared to be children's writing.
18 Tora Tomkinson, author interviews, 2013.

Appendix II

1 Colin Caffell, email to author, 19 July 2013.

Index

Adams, David 322, 327
Adams, Douglas, Sergeant 166, 167–8, 169, 170, 176, 345–6
Ainsley, Mike, Acting Chief Superintendent 190, 236, 244, 250, 273–4, 278, 287, 288–9, 292, 293, 296, 298, 307, 313, 316, 317, 318, 322, 325, 326, 327, 336–7, 368, 380, 383, 394, 399
Alexander-Smart, Adrian, Constable 168, 173, 174
Amos, Heather 3, 116, 132, 139, 147, 159–60, 189, 190, 198, 199, 219, 243, 266, 274, 275, 276, 297, 369, 404
Angeloglou, Dr Myrto 81, 94, 113, 127, 135, 136
Anschütz, .22 calibre *see* murder weapon
Arlidge QC, Anthony v, 339, 342–4, 351, 352, 358, 367–8, 371, 372, 376

Babic, Barbara 70, 202, 369
Bacon, Christine 65, 67, 68, 78, 104, 105–6, 296, 299, 305, 359
Bamber (née Nevill), Beatrice Cecilia 16, 29, 50–1, 66, 160, 223, 224, 236, 276
Bamber & Speakman 54
Bamber, Herbert Ralph Munro 16, 137
Bamber, Jeremy: adoption of 2, 24, 25–6, 27–8, 59–60; adoption of sister's twins by grandparents, on possibility of 139–40, 198, 205, 241, 253, 254; Amsterdam trip after murders of family 248, 249, 288, 290; appeals against conviction xv–xvi, xvii, xviii, xix, 384–6, 389–92, 393, 394, 405; appearance 53–4, 341, 345; arrests 287–90, 300–1, 316–21, 327–9; Australia and New Zealand, holidays in 56–7, 61, 62, 297–8; author and xvi–xx; bailed 316–21; behaviour in days following murders 205–13, 215, 216–19, 222, 223, 225, 226, 227, 228–32, 235, 236–8, 239, 240–2, 243, 244–6, 247,

248, 249, 250, 251, 252–8, 259, 260, 261, 262, 263, 264, 265; birth 2, 25, 408; birth parents 25, 59–60; Bourtree Cottage and *see* Bourtree Cottage; burglary at Osea Road and 119–21, 235, 288, 293–4, 297–8, 367, 378; Cartier watches and 75–7, 99, 288, 297–8; case papers and xv, xvii, 385; categorization in prison, changes in 385; charged with murder 329; childhood and schooldays 26, 27–9, 31–2, 33, 35, 36–7, 44–5, 47, 48–9, 50, 54; COLP inquiry into case 385; Criminal Cases Review Commission submissions xv, xvi, xvii, 388, 390, 391–2, 393; day of murders xiii, xiv–xv, 152, 153, 155, 156, 157, 158, 163–71; description of sister to police following murders 164, 165, 167, 168, 170, 202–4, 231; drug taking 43, 44, 65, 75, 86, 91, 93, 98–9, 129, 130, 132, 219, 223, 288, 290, 298; family hatred for 266–7, 349–50, 371; family planting evidence about, possibility of 266–7, 339–40, 398; farm work, interest in 36, 53–5, 79, 86, 103, 104, 125, 129, 144, 152; first visit to farm after murders 228–9; fraud 76–7, 100; funerals of family and 239, 240, 243, 244–6, 297, 353; hired killer story 253, 286, 292, 296, 298, 300, 305, 308, 313, 359; inheritance 65, 101, 102, 103–4, 265–6; jail 381–2; Julie Mugford accuses of murders xiv–xv, 275, 276–86, 287 *see also* Mugford, Julie; legal team and 335–6, 338–40; media, attitude towards xv, 387; Metropolitan Police investigation into case (2001) and 388–9; murder weapon and 105, 106, 143–4, 155–6, 167, 169–70, 207, 208, 218, 318–19; Nevill Bamber and *see* Bamber, Nevill; New Zealand, second trip to 75–7; Osea Road and 79–80, 91, 103, 128–9, 132, 134–5, 137; parents wills

Bamber, Jeremy (*cont.*)
and 124–5, 253, 265–6, 268–9, 298, 301, 367–8; PCC, statement to listing grievances on case (1990) 385; phone call to police on night of murders 158, 163, 164, 165, 294–5, 304, 305, 306, 344, 345, 366; phone call with father on night of murders, disputed xiii, 163, 164, 165, 192, 198, 200, 281, 294–5, 304, 305, 309–10, 315, 327, 344, 365, 366, 367, 371, 373, 375; phone calls with Julie Mugford on night of murders 169, 183, 200, 208, 210, 212, 213, 281, 283, 294–5, 304, 305, 306, 314, 344, 352, 354, 359, 366, 372, 373, 375, 413, 416; photographs of sister and 42, 276, 297, 320; police interviews 290–2, 293–5, 298–9, 300–6, 308–12, 313–16; police siege of White House Farm and 165, 166, 167, 168, 169–70, 171, 172, 175; polygraph test, passes 390; prison life xix, 333, 338, 381–2, 385, 400, 402–3; psychological examinations 340, 400–2; public support for 398–9; reaction to news of family's deaths 175, 176, 177, 178, 179, 181–3, 184, 188, 189, 199, 210, 212, 213, 228–9; reconstruction of events at White House Farm, 7 August 1985 and xvi, 410–16; relationships, first 53, 62–8, 75, 76, 78–9, 94–5; Scotland, shooting trip to 49–50; sell story to *Sun*, attempt to 320–1; sells family antiques after murders xiv, 229, 236–7, 251, 253, 254–5, 257–8, 259, 260, 268, 269–70, 271, 272, 276, 288; sentence 379, 386–7; sexual experience and first relationships 53, 63–8, 75, 78–9, 94–5; sexuality 75, 95, 129, 251, 293; Sheila Bamber and 3, 4, 27, 33, 42, 44, 47, 48, 56, 73, 84, 85, 88, 90, 96–7, 104, 124, 126, 128, 139–40, 147, 153, 164, 165, 238, 278–9, 281, 284, 285, 300, 309, 314, 315, 316, 320, 366, 404; St Tropez holiday whilst on bail 321, 327, 329; *Sunday Times* interview for twenty-fifth anniversary of murders (2010) 391; trial xv, 339–40,

341–82; websites 107, 204, 320, 390, 396, 397–8, 399, 418
Bamber, June xiii, 2, 3, 12–13; adoption of Sheila and Jeremy Bamber 2, 20–1, 22–3, 24, 25–6, 27, 28–9; analysis of body/crime scene and 206, 214, 324, 360, 365, 376, 377, 386; assets 101, 102, 124–5, 265–6, 407; bicycle 5, 136–7, 144, 198, 241, 249, 255, 273, 281, 292, 301–2, 307, 325, 342, 413, 414, 416; birth and childhood 13–14; biscuit tins, collection of 259, 260; courting and marriage 17–18; day of murder and 3, 5, 6, 152, 153–4, 155, 156, 157, 158, 159; discovery of body 173–4, 176, 184; failure to conceive, effect upon 20; family/ancestry 12–13; funeral and burial 243–6, 269, 408; grandchildren and 6, 51–2, 53, 56, 116–17, 124, 139–42, 148–9, 198, 253, 366; handbag and purse 222, 227; Jeremy Bamber and 27, 28–9, 31, 32, 33–4, 35–6, 48–9, 50, 60, 65, 66, 67, 71, 74–5, 78, 79, 80, 82, 86, 88, 92, 95, 96, 97, 103–4, 150, 151, 119, 129, 144, 150, 272, 273, 290, 293, 304, 359, 412; jewellery 217–18, 223, 224, 259, 260, 269, 389; murder of xiii, 3, 5, 6, 152, 153–4, 155, 156, 157, 158, 159, 173–4, 176, 184; 206, 214, 250, 253, 256, 324, 360, 365, 376, 377, 386, 410, 411, 412, 413, 414, 415, 416; nervous breakdowns/depressions/psychiatric treatment 3, 20, 22, 23–4, 28–9, 35–6, 49–50, 57, 66–7, 70–3, 81, 129, 289, 369; politics 26, 101; reconstruction of events at White House Farm, 7 August 1985 and xvi, 410–16; religion and xiii, 3, 23, 26, 27, 35–6, 39–40, 41, 42, 70–1, 72, 80–1, 82, 83, 87–8, 95, 112, 117, 123, 129, 131–2, 133, 140–2, 150, 159, 198, 290, 408; Sheila Bamber and 28–9, 31, 32, 33–4, 35–6, 39–41, 42, 43–4, 46, 48–9, 51–2, 53, 55, 56, 57, 59, 63, 66, 70, 81–5, 87–8, 92, 104, 112, 114, 115, 123, 124, 125, 127, 128, 129, 133, 138, 139–40, 141, 144, 146–7, 148–9, 150, 156, 158,

202, 209, 273, 412; SOE career
14–15; will 124–5, 138, 223, 253,
265–6, 268–9, 337, 359, 407
Bamber, Nevill xiii, xiv, 2, 3, 16;
ancestry 16; assets and will 101–2,
124–5, 223, 253, 265, 266, 337, 359,
407; body discovered xiii, 172, 176,
184, 187; body examined 191–3,
214; burial 243–6, 269, 408;
churchwarden 35, 129; day of
murder 3, 5, 6, 152, 153, 155, 156,
157, 158, 159, 163; death of sister
and 29; failure to conceive and 20;
family and childhood 16–17;
farming and 17–18, 19, 26, 54, 79,
80, 103, 130–1, 132, 135, 149;
firearms and 19, 49–50, 104–5, 137,
200, 223, 224, 360, 412;
grandchildren and 53, 56, 139–40;
grave 408; Jeremy Bamber and 2,
20–1, 22–3, 24, 25–6, 28–9, 31, 33,
36, 48–9, 54–5, 63, 65, 74, 76, 79,
80, 86, 91, 102–3, 119, 120, 121,
125, 129, 130–1, 132, 137, 144, 151,
253–4, 327; marries 17–18; mother
and 65, 66; murder of xiii, xiv, 2–3,
130–1, 172, 176, 184, 187, 191–3,
197, 209, 220, 249, 250, 253–4, 308,
308–10, 318, 324, 327, 344, 348,
360, 365, 371, 376, 377, 392, 410,
411, 412, 413, 414, 415, 416; Osea
Road burglary and 119, 120, 121;
phone call with Jeremy Bamber on
night of murder, disputed xiii, 163,
164, 165, 192, 198, 200, 281, 294–5,
304, 305, 309–10, 315, 327, 344,
365, 366, 367, 371, 373, 375; politics
26, 101; reconstruction of events at
White House Farm, 7 August 1985
and xvi, 410–16; religion and 243,
244; Sheila Bamber and 2, 20–1,
22–3, 24, 25–6, 28–9, 31, 33, 36, 39,
40, 42, 43–4, 47, 48–9, 59, 81, 84,
85, 114, 127, 128, 202; wife and
49–50, 66–7, 73
Bamber, Sheila: abuse of children,
accusations of 80–1, 202–4, 367;
adoption of 2, 20–3, 24, 27–8, 59,
69–70, 96, 123, 127–9, 150, 151;
animals, love of 29, 30; appearance
34, 39, 57, 63, 87, 88, 145, 168;

birth mother and 59, 69–70, 96, 123,
127–9; body discovered 174, 176–7;
body examined/post-mortem/crime
scene 184–6, 187, 193–7, 214, 220,
221, 223, 231, 233, 322–5, 336–7,
338, 339, 348, 350, 354, 355, 360–1,
362, 376, 377, 388–90, 391–2;
childhood and school 26, 27–30,
32–4; children and *see* Caffell, Daniel
and Caffell, Nicholas; Colin Caffell
and *see* Caffell, Colin; day of
murders xiii, 1–7, 145–6, 148–9,
152–6, 158, 159–60, 410–16; drug
use 91, 93–4, 111–12, 114, 124, 136,
199, 207, 211, 231, 237, 307, 325,
357, 369; estate 268–71, 272, 276;
Farhad Emami and 58, 63, 69, 74,
81, 87, 88–9, 90, 93–4, 107, 112, 113,
114, 115, 116, 126, 146, 201, 213,
214, 369; fostering of children by
parents, possibility of 139–41, 198,
205, 240, 241, 253, 254, 287; funeral
and burial 217, 219, 239, 243–6,
409; Jeremy Bamber and 4, 27, 44,
47, 48, 84, 88, 90, 96–7, 104, 128,
153, 164, 165, 238, 278–9, 281, 284,
285, 300, 309, 314, 315, 316, 320,
366, 404; June Bamber and *see*
Bamber, June; medication xiv, 3, 6,
84–5, 106, 111, 116, 117–18, 122,
123, 124, 126–7, 135–6, 231, 259,
362, 369, 370, 371; modelling career
39, 44, 46, 47, 58–9, 63, 78, 90, 111,
138, 276, 320, 359; Morshead
Mansions apartment, Maida Vale
73–4, 78, 102, 104, 117, 214, 237,
261, 270–2, 274, 276, 287, 292–3,
297, 320, 333, 407; murder of xiii,
xiv, xviii, xx, xxi, 2, 49–50, 126–7,
165, 167, 170, 171, 174, 176–7,
184–5, 186, 187, 200, 201–2, 207,
210, 215–16, 220, 222, 255, 259,
292–3, 312, 320, 350–1, 362, 370;
Nevill Bamber and *see* Bamber, Nevill;
photographs of, compromising 41,
111, 276, 297, 320; pregnancies
40–1, 42, 43–4, 45, 46–7, 51; press
portrayal of xiii, 91, 93–4, 214, 299,
307, 320, 325; psychological
problems xx, xxi, xiii, xiv, 3, 6, 46,
49, 55, 57, 63, 70, 71, 78, 82, 81–5,

Bamber, Sheila (*cont.*)
86, 88, 94, 106, 107, 111–18, 121–4, 126–7, 131, 132–3, 135–6, 138–9, 144, 145, 146–7, 150, 168, 169, 179, 201–4, 209, 231, 259, 271, 274, 362, 364, 365, 366, 367, 368, 369, 370, 371, 375, 379–80; reconstruction of events at White House Farm, 7 August 1985 and xvi, 410–16; religion, finds 123, 127; suspect for murders xiii, xiv, xviii, xx, xxi, 2, 49–50, 126–7, 163–9, 172–80, 188, 189, 198, 200, 201–4, 207, 209, 210, 211, 212, 213, 214, 215–16, 226, 230, 231, 233, 237, 238, 240, 241, 253, 259, 260, 274, 281, 284, 285, 287, 297, 305, 307–9, 311, 312, 314, 315, 325, 326, 333, 336–7, 339, 342, 343, 346–7, 348, 349, 350–1, 358, 360–1, 362, 364, 365, 366, 367, 368, 369, 370, 371–2, 373, 374, 375, 376, 377, 379–80, 388–90, 391–2, 397, 404; wedding 43–4
Bamber: The New Evidence 392
Bamber family tree viii–ix
Barker, Dorothy 18, 32
Barlow, Mick, Detective Constable 237, 240, 243, 244, 245, 248, 249, 251, 252, 255, 259, 287, 290, 295, 298, 311
Batchelor, Alan, Constable 167
Battersby, Susan 89, 98, 99–100, 213, 227, 252–3, 254, 256, 262, 264, 268, 275, 282, 283, 284, 306–7, 337, 356, 359
Bernard, Winston, Detective Sergeant 348, 399–400
Bews, Chris, Sergeant 163, 164, 165–7, 170, 175, 178, 179, 182, 345
Bird, David, Detective Constable 179–80, 184, 185, 191, 194, 210, 211, 215, 299–300, 318, 322, 346–7, 383, 394
Bishop (née Napier), Karen 86, 99, 129, 135, 136, 201, 227, 245, 246, 256, 268, 272, 273, 284
Bishop, Andrew 99, 135, 136, 245, 246, 256, 272
Bonnet, Malcolm 165, 345
Bonney, Jill 38–9, 225
Bourtree Cottage 5, 86, 91, 94–5, 97–8, 99, 102, 106, 119, 125, 132, 139,

182, 183, 188, 198, 207, 216, 217, 235, 236, 241, 243, 245, 249, 257, 259, 260, 276, 283, 292, 299–300, 304, 307, 319–20, 325, 352, 363, 407, 412, 413
Boutflour, David 16, 19–20, 22, 28, 33, 34, 36, 47, 48, 50, 59, 61, 66, 74, 76, 105, 124, 143, 149, 150, 158, 183–4, 188–9, 198, 201, 215–16, 217, 222, 223, 224, 225, 226, 227, 244, 283, 296–7, 307, 349, 379, 394, 395–6, 406
Boutflour (née Butt), Karen 36, 48, 59, 60, 150, 201, 227, 243, 245
Boutflour (née Speaking), Pamela 13, 14, 15–16, 17, 18, 22, 24, 26, 27, 29, 36, 39, 44, 48, 57, 66, 70, 72, 79, 103, 128, 137–8, 158, 184, 189, 198, 199–200, 201, 223, 224–5, 227, 228, 229, 230, 255, 256, 260, 261, 265, 266, 269, 291, 327, 349, 388, 389, 407, 412–13
Boutflour, Professor Robert Woodiwiss 15–16, 17, 18, 31–2, 39, 44, 57, 61, 66, 72, 74, 80, 103, 105, 120, 126, 128–9, 132, 137, 149–50, 158, 159, 183, 184, 189, 198, 199, 201, 222–3, 224, 226, 228–9, 230, 235, 237, 252, 255–6, 257, 259, 265–6, 267, 269, 270, 273, 274, 292, 316–17, 325, 326, 327, 333, 350, 368, 371, 379–80, 384, 407
Bouttell, Jean 62, 148, 226, 227, 249, 250, 257, 258, 259, 264, 269, 272, 325, 333, 348
Bowen, Inez 26, 33–4, 35, 140
Bowler, Bruce 300, 304, 305, 308, 333
Boyce, Philip 392
Bradley, John Jennery 370
Braintree & Witham Times 183
Brencher, Bernard 38
Brook House Farm 181, 255, 325, 414
Brown, Rodney 246, 247, 317, 369
Bruce (labrador) 144, 158, 159, 168–9, 181, 205, 217
Bruce-Lockhart, Logie 48
Brunt, Geoff 191
Bunting, Alice (Binks) 13, 14, 269
Bunyard, Robert, Chief Constable 274, 339, 383
Byford, Sir Lawrence 383, 384

Caffell, Colin: arrest of Jeremy Bamber and 299, 333–4; art 333–4, 380, 404, 405; Betty Shine, visits 337–8; burial of twins and 213, 239, 246–7; children and xviii, 3–7, 53, 84, 116–17, 128, 140–2, 146, 147–8, 159–60, 198, 203, 204, 209, 213, 243, 244, 245, 246–7, 279, 337–8, 380, 404; day of murders and 159–60; days leading up to murders 3–7; *Everyman: As We Forgive Them . . . ?*, participates in BBC's 404; first told of murders 189–90, 219; funerals of Bambers and 243, 244–5; Heather Amos and *see* Amos, Heather; *In Search of the Rainbow's End: The Inside Story of the Bamber Murders* 141–2, 404–5; interviewed by *ITV News* 380; Jan Flowers and *see* Flowers, Jan; Jeremy Bamber and 32, 103, 105, 147–8, 198, 202, 203, 204, 225, 244–5, 265, 266–7, 276, 279, 285, 290, 320, 321, 335, 404, 417–18; Julie Mugford visits to explain Jeremy Bamber's guilt 335; June and Nevill Bamber and 3–7, 117, 125, 127, 128, 129, 140–2, 147–8, 198; a message from 417–18; photographs of Sheila Bamber and 41, 111, 276, 297, 320, 321; Sheila Bamber as suspect in murders, reaction to 198, 199, 202, 203, 297, 411; Sheila Bamber, relationship with 3–7, 26, 29, 30, 32, 38, 39, 40, 41, 42–3, 44, 45, 46, 47, 48, 49, 51, 52, 53, 55, 56, 63, 70, 74, 83, 84, 87, 88, 90, 93, 96, 106, 107, 113, 116–17, 124, 126, 127, 132–3, 138–9, 140, 271; Sheila Bamber's ashes and 239; trial of Jeremy Bamber and 350, 351, 404; writes to Jeremy Bamber in jail 404

Caffell, Daniel: birth 51–2; body discovered 174–5, 177; burial 213, 239, 241, 244, 246–8; childhood/upbringing 1–7, 55–6, 57, 63, 70, 74, 78, 82–4, 86, 88, 90, 93, 96, 112, 116, 117, 147; day of the murders and 152, 153, 154–5, 158; days leading up to murder 1–7; drawings 7, 141–2, 220; foreknowledge of

death, possibility of 6, 7; grandparents and 81, 117, 124, 128, 139–42, 148, 366; Jeremy Bamber and 53; mother's illness and 55, 56, 57, 63, 70, 78, 82–4, 116; murder of/wounds xviii, 174–5, 204, 206, 207, 324, 325, 334, 335, 411, 415, 416; parents separation and 55–6; post-mortem 206–7

Caffell, Diane 38, 44, 243, 244

Caffell, Doris 38, 53, 112, 113, 116, 132–3, 141

Caffell, Nicholas: birth 51–2; body discovered 175, 176; burial of 213, 239, 241, 246–8; childhood/upbringing 1–7, 53, 55–6, 70, 74, 78, 80–1, 83, 86, 88, 90, 93, 96, 116, 147, 203–4, 366; days of the murders and 152, 153, 154–5, 158; effect of mother's illness upon 57, 78, 80–4, 83, 96, 116, 147, 203–4, 351, 366; fall out of taxi 80–1, 203–4; foreknowledge of death, possibility of 6, 7; funerals of family and 244; grandparents and 81, 117, 124, 128, 139–42, 147; Jeremy Bamber and 53, 147; lead up to murder of 1–7, 154; murder and wounds of xiii, 3, 175, 206–7, 324, 325, 335, 361, 411, 415, 416; post-mortem 206–7

Caffell, Reg 38, 53, 74, 113, 145, 199

Carbonells Farm 14, 16, 183, 265

Carr, James 32, 56, 102, 119, 120, 235, 237, 252, 273

Carr, Robert 32–3

Chaplin, William, PC 165, 178

Chelmsford Police 163–7, 171, 200, 206, 208, 239, 288, 294, 304, 307, 328, 329, 344, 416

Chequers pub 13, 94, 102, 134, 189, 207–8, 283, 413

Church of England Children's Society 20, 21, 22, 24, 25, 69

City of London Police (COLP) xv, 337, 385, 395–6

Clark, Charles, Chief Inspector 170, 176

Clark, Michael (Mick), Detective Constable 177, 178, 181–3, 188, 189, 199, 200–1, 202, 207–8, 209, 210, 212, 298, 300, 306, 308, 312, 327–8, 329, 363

Clifton House, Guildford 16, 29, 50, 102, 119, 265

Cock, Basil 102, 138, 212, 217, 219, 222, 223, 229, 236, 248, 254, 265, 268, 269, 292, 359, 371

Collins, Brett 32, 75, 76, 129–30, 132, 135, 139, 235, 236, 237, 240, 241, 243, 245, 246, 248, 249, 251, 252, 254, 256, 257, 259, 260, 261, 264, 268, 270, 271, 272, 273, 274, 276, 287, 288, 289–90, 293, 299, 317–18, 320, 321, 327, 328, 333, 341, 369, 380

Collins, Laurence, Constable 168, 170, 171, 172, 173, 174, 175

Connell, Detective Inspector 269

Connett, David 341, 358, 376

Cook, Ron, Detective Inspector 179, 180, 184–7, 191, 194, 197, 210, 211, 214–15, 230–1, 232, 233–4, 236, 237, 238–9, 240, 251, 277, 292, 308, 318, 322, 324, 334, 336, 346, 347, 348, 394, 395

Cotton, Penny 58–9, 63

Court of Appeal xv, xvi, 385, 386, 388, 390, 391, 392, 394, 396–7, 405

Craig, Dr Ian 176–7, 178, 179, 182, 346

Criminal Cases Review Commission (CCRC) xv, xvi, xvii, 388, 390, 391–2, 393, 396–7, 398, 400

Crispy (shih–tzu) 6, 144, 152, 154, 158–9, 168, 181, 188, 189, 207

Cross, Bob 27

Crowe, Ronald 39

Crown Prosecution Service (CPS) 385, 394

Daily Express xiii, xxii, 387

Daily Mail 201, 214, 293, 299, 307, 349, 383

Daily Mirror 21, 22, 25, 239, 307, 326, 405

Daily Star 32, 64, 293, 321

Dale, Doug 263, 282

Davidson, Neil, Detective Sergeant 178, 179, 180, 194, 210, 214, 293, 299, 319–20, 334, 359, 399

Davidson, Ian, Detective Constable 327

Daynes, Kerry 402

Deckers, Michael 64, 67, 86, 95, 103, 119, 264, 317, 369

Delgado, Kenneth, Constable 168, 171, 172, 173, 174, 299

Dermott, Nigel, PC 168, 176

Dickinson, James, Detective Chief Superintendent 383–4

Director of Public Prosecutions (DPP) xvii, 125, 307, 327, 336, 337, 410

Drake, Justice Maurice 342, 348, 350, 352, 361, 363, 367, 368, 370–1, 374, 375, 376, 377, 378, 380, 384–5, 386

Eaton (née Boutflour), Christine Ann 18, 20, 22, 24, 26, 28, 34, 39, 42, 44, 51, 56, 80, 90, 96, 101–3, 119, 120, 121, 122–3, 126, 128–9, 132, 133, 134–5, 137, 149, 183, 184, 188–9, 198, 199, 200–1, 207, 208, 209, 212–13, 215–16, 217, 218, 219–21, 222, 223, 224–5, 226, 227–8, 229, 232, 235, 236–7, 238, 239, 240, 247, 248, 249, 251, 252, 254, 255, 256, 259, 260, 265, 266, 269, 270, 285, 349–50, 388, 406–7

Eaton, Janie 14, 44, 227, 228, 407

Eaton, John 101, 102

Eaton, Peter 34, 44, 54, 101–2, 122–3, 134, 135, 189, 199, 216–17, 219–20, 221, 225, 226, 227, 232, 239, 243, 244, 248, 265, 266, 350, 363, 406

Egan, Professor Vincent 401–2

Elliott, Brian 259, 319, 322, 334, 362

Ellis, Dr 256, 266

Elston, Sandra 38, 57–8, 97, 139, 202, 225, 369

Emami, Farhad 'Freddie' 58, 63, 69, 74, 81, 87, 88–9, 90, 93–4, 107, 112, 113, 114, 115, 116, 126, 146, 201, 213, 214, 369

Essex police xviii–xiv, 61, 74, 75, 76, 94, 97, 102, 105, 107, 125, 139, 163–5, 170, 177, 261–2, 265, 266, 271, 293, 299, 326, 327, 337, 339, 345, 383, 384, 385, 388, 394, 395, 396, 397, 399, 400

European Court of Human Rights 393, 417

Evening Gazette 201, 326, 335

Fatal Vision 272–3

Ferguson, Dr Hugh Cameron xx, 23, 28–9, 41, 71–3, 81–2, 83–5, 86, 94,

106, 111, 112, 114, 115, 116, 117, 123, 126, 127, 135–6, 140, 168, 196, 204, 209, 231, 369, 370, 380

Fielder, Michael 320

Fielding, John 44, 45, 47

fingerprints 185–6, 211–12, 214, 230, 234, 239–40, 251, 284, 292–3, 299, 300, 307–8, 315, 324, 325, 348, 362

Finlay, Christine 78, 196

Finnegan, Dr Michael 114

Fletcher, Malcolm xx, 191, 193, 233–4, 259, 308, 318–19, 322, 323, 324, 338–9, 361–2, 370, 376, 380, 397, 416

Flowers, Herbie 51, 55, 147, 225, 247

Flowers, Jan 51, 53, 55, 56, 63, 89–90, 117, 219

Foakes, Alf 153, 257

Foakes, David 86

Foakes, Dorothy 156–7, 346, 412, 413

Foakes, Jill 86, 183

Foakes, Julie 346

Foakes, Kate 86, 91, 98

Foakes, Len 86, 103, 152, 156, 158, 181, 257, 265, 346

Ford, Geoff 63–4

Ford, Suzette 63–5, 66, 67, 75, 76, 78–9, 90–1, 94, 95, 99, 106, 128, 202–3, 213, 246, 259, 298, 300, 333, 369, 380

Forensic Science Laboratory, Huntingdon 191, 193–4, 214, 231, 274, 318, 322, 336, 338–9

Fraser-Bell, Alan 153, 155

Frog & Beans wine bar, Colchester 64–5, 67, 86, 91

Frost, Joan 2–3, 42, 92, 129

Full Sutton, HMP xix, 390, 391, 400, 402–3, 406

Gardener's Farm 14, 139, 156

Gibbons, Terrie, Chief Inspector 171, 175, 176, 178

Goldhanger 4, 5, 13, 16, 18, 20, 36, 86, 91, 97, 102, 129, 139, 146, 148, 152, 153, 155, 156, 157, 190, 212, 227, 235, 241, 247, 249, 252, 255, 259, 260, 272, 274, 279, 280, 286, 303, 307, 309, 325, 342, 414

Golding, Katherine 154

Golding, Stephen, Sergeant 190, 346

Greaves, Angela (Anji) 317, 333, 335, 338, 341, 352, 380–1

Greaves, Virginia 259–60, 261, 270, 271, 272, 275, 286, 317, 369

Gresham's 31–2, 36, 43, 44, 47–9, 91, 244

Grimster, Helen 124, 369

Grimster, Margaret 17–18, 123–4

Gros, George 127, 136, 145, 146

Gruner, Peter 320–1

Guardian 404

Hadden, Barry 50

Hall, Michael, Constable 172–3, 174

Hammersley, David, Detective Constable 178, 180, 186, 193, 210, 214, 292–3, 362

Hare, Robert D. 401

Harris, George, Chief Superintendent 166, 171, 175, 176, 177, 178, 179, 182, 240, 277–8, 296

Harvey, Susan 121–2, 126

Hawkins, Don 58, 63, 122, 145, 201–2

Hayward, John 259, 307, 319, 323, 324, 338, 359–60, 376–7, 386

Heath, Caroline 145, 146, 369

Henry Smith (Kensington Estate) Charity 12, 18, 54, 216–17, 406

Hepburn, Polly 381

Hinde, Jane 33, 44

Horsnell, Michael 119–20, 152

Howard-Williams (née Bamber), Cecily Diana 16, 17, 29

Howard-Williams, Ernest Leslie 17

Howard, Glynis 233, 236, 324, 362, 395

Howie (née Bunting), Betty 13, 14, 27, 183, 235, 269, 316–17

Howie, Sarah 27, 47, 51, 58, 133, 245

Howie, Thomas 14, 103, 183

Hughes, Mark, Detective Sergeant 289

Hunter, Andrew 390

Hunter, Anne 28, 73

Hunter, David 27, 28

Hurd, Douglas 383, 384, 386

Hutchison, Harry, Detective Sergeant 327

Iliffe, Dr Steven 112–13, 114

Independent 341

Independent Police Complaints Commission (IPCC) xv, 392

Jackson, Judith 57, 58, 70
Jacobs, Gary 387
Jacobs, Josie 39, 47
Jay, Eric George 20, 22, 69, 407
Jay, Peter 69, 78, 96, 123, 138, 243
Jeapes, Sergeant 176
Johnson, Graham 79
Jones, Diane 326
Jones, Stan, Detective Sergeant 178, 179,
    180, 181, 182, 188, 190, 198–9, 201,
    207–8, 210–11, 214–15, 216, 217,
    218–19, 220, 221, 230–1, 232, 235,
    237, 238, 239, 240, 269–70, 274,
    275, 276–7, 283, 287, 296, 297, 298,
    299, 300–4, 305, 306, 308–9, 310–12,
    313–16, 322, 327–8, 329, 341, 347–8,
    350, 363, 380, 381, 394, 396
Jones, Thomas 'Taff', Detective Chief
    Inspector 177–9, 180, 184, 187, 190,
    207, 208, 210, 211, 215, 216, 217,
    218–19, 220, 230, 232, 240, 249,
    251, 266, 269, 274, 278, 287, 288,
    290–2, 293, 294–5, 296, 297–8, 316,
    339, 347, 383, 394
Jones, Trevor 134
Judicial Review xviii, 392, 393

Kenneally, Detective Superintendent
    James 273–4
*Killing Mum and Dad: The Jeremy
    Bamber Story* 402
Knight, Professor Bernard 370

Lawrence, Laurie 152
Lawson QC, Edmund 335, 336, 361,
    376, 379
Lay, Robert, Constable 167, 169, 170,
    172
Leyland, Michael 17, 18, 26–7, 54
Leyland, Patricia 26–7, 42
Lincoln, Dr Patrick 338
Little Renters Farm, Little Totham 34,
    101–2, 134–5, 144, 265, 349–50, 359,
    407
London Evening Standard xiv, 320–1, 333
Low (née Barrie), Agnes 14, 26, 49–50,
    62, 66, 74–5, 104, 119, 146–7, 150,
    241

MacDonald, Jeffrey 272–3
McDonald, Matthew 65, 67–8, 86, 98,

106, 253, 254, 275, 284, 285, 286,
    292, 296, 298, 299, 300, 305, 308,
    313, 352, 359
MacDonell, Professor Herbert Leon 386
McKay, Simon xvi, 392, 397
Maguire, Mairead 53, 201
Manners, John, Acting Sergeant 173,
    174, 176
Marsden, Charles 91, 94–5, 128, 151,
    212, 231, 232, 272, 299, 310, 311
Marsham, Leslie Brian 25, 59–60,
    408
Mead, Freddie 338
Mennie, Agnes 138, 145, 146
Mercer, PC 168, 170–1
Metropolitan Police 237, 388–9
Mildenhall, Timothy, Acting Sergeant
    173, 175
Miller, Robert, Detective Inspector 178,
    179, 180, 191, 199, 208, 210, 230,
    232, 236, 237, 238, 240, 243, 244,
    245, 277, 278, 287, 289, 290, 296,
    297, 300, 305, 308, 322, 327–8, 329
Moira House 29–30, 202
Montgomery, Ivor, Inspector 170, 171,
    176, 184–5, 186, 187
Morgan, John 136
Morshead Mansions apartment, Maida
    Vale 73–4, 78, 102, 104, 117, 214,
    237, 261, 270–2, 274, 276, 287,
    292–3, 297, 320, 333, 407
Mugford, Brian 89
Mugford, Julie: behaviour in days after
    murders 188, 189, 190, 199, 200,
    205, 207, 208–9, 210, 212, 213, 217,
    218, 219, 225, 227, 228, 231, 235,
    236, 240, 363; break up of
    relationship with Jeremy Bamber
    261–4, 270–3, 274, 298, 303, 317,
    364, 366, 367, 368; burglaries,
    reveals Jeremy Bamber's involvement
    in 75, 76; confesses knowledge of
    murders to Liz Rimington 264, 268;
    confesses knowledge of murders to
    Malcolm Waters 275; confesses
    knowledge of murders to police xiv,
    275, 276–86, 287, 296, 299, 300,
    301–2, 303, 306–7, 310, 325, 336;
    confesses knowledge of murders to
    Susan Battersby 252–4, 268, 359;
    days leading up to murders and 3, 4,

5; decision not to prosecute 337, 398; first meets Jeremy Bamber 86, 89; fraud 99–100; funerals of Bamber family and 240, 241, 244–5; Jeremy Bamber proposes to 106–7, 252, 303, 304; Jeremy Bamber's police statements and 288, 291–2, 293–4, 295, 298, 300, 301, 302–4, 310, 311, 314, 315, 316; Osea Road burglary and 120–1, 293–4; phone calls with Jeremy Bamber on night of murder 169, 183, 200, 208, 210, 212, 213, 281, 283, 294–5, 304, 305, 306, 314, 344, 352, 354, 359, 366, 372, 373, 375, 413, 416; police interviews 188, 208, 212, 213, 276–86; post-trial life 405; relationship with Jeremy Bamber 3, 4, 5, 86, 89, 90–1, 92, 94, 95, 96, 97, 98–100, 103–4, 106–7, 119, 120–1, 124, 128, 129, 132, 135, 136, 139, 140, 146, 147, 148, 188, 189, 190, 199, 200, 205, 207, 208–9, 210, 212, 213, 217, 218, 219, 225, 227, 228, 231, 235, 236, 240, 246, 247–8, 249, 251, 252, 256, 257, 260; sells story to media 381; Sheila Bamber and 96, 97; trial of Jeremy Bamber and xv, 338, 342, 344, 351, 352–8, 364, 374, 375, 378, 381, 383; visits Colin Caffell to explain Jeremy Bamber's guilt 335; volunteers to identify bodies 208–9

Mugford, Mary 31, 97, 251, 252, 358–9
Mullins, Terence 390
Munday, Andrew 347, 348, 350, 376, 377
murder weapon: Jeremy Bamber informs police of existence of 167, 169–70; Jeremy Bamber's use of 143–4, 155–6, 207, 310, 313, 350, 366, 368, 412, 414–15; fingerprints on 186, 239–40, 251, 284, 307–8, 315, 348; police examination of 233, 239–40, 251, 259, 307–8, 318–19, 348, 359–60, 361, 363, 370, 371; police take possession of 185, 186; purchase of 105–6, 143, 223, 359; Sheila Bamber's capability of using xiv, 170, 184, 194, 196, 199, 207, 210, 216, 259, 313, 368, 374, 392; silencer/ sound moderator xiv, 105, 143–4,

155–6, 185, 193, 200, 207, 208, 216, 218, 224, 225, 226, 227, 230–4, 236, 237, 238–40, 252, 255, 259, 291, 313, 314, 319, 323, 324, 327, 334, 336, 338, 339, 342, 343, 348, 349, 350, 360, 361, 362, 363, 365, 368, 370, 371–2, 374–5, 376, 377, 383, 385, 386, 388, 389, 392, 394, 395–8, 412, 415, 416; telescopic sight 105, 143–4, 155, 200, 207, 208, 215, 216, 218, 224, 226, 232, 291, 307, 359, 412

Myall, Stephen, Constable 163–4, 165–6, 167, 169, 345

N. & J. Bamber Ltd 54, 91, 101, 258, 337, 407
Napley, Sir David 335
Nevill, Christopher (Chris) 57, 61, 78, 216, 217, 226, 252
News of the World 89, 209, 262–4, 381, 383, 385
Nicholls, George 129, 265
Nockold, Rosalind 33, 44
Norcup, Robin, Constable 167
North Maldon Growers Ltd 36, 79, 102, 103, 157, 189

Oak Farm, Tolleshunt Major 56, 96, 102, 122, 134, 135, 199–200, 224, 225, 226, 232, 235, 238, 239, 307
Oakey, Detective Constable 359
Old Hall School, Hethersett, Norfolk 30, 33, 202
Osborne, Paul 79, 368–9
Osea Road campsite 14, 32, 56, 79–80, 91, 102–3, 104, 119–21, 125, 128–9, 132, 133, 134, 135, 137, 139, 148, 155, 169, 182, 212, 227, 235, 237, 265, 273, 293–4, 297–8, 356, 367, 368, 378, 407

Page, Elizabeth Ann (née Seabrook) 11, 12
Page, Frank 11, 12, 14, 18
Pages Lane 1, 86, 148, 152, 163, 166, 175, 178, 179, 181, 183, 184, 221, 345, 346
Pargeter (née Bamber), Phyllis Audrey 16, 17, 18

Pargeter, Anthony 17, 18, 19, 28, 102, 105, 143–4, 188, 200, 207, 208, 212, 213, 215, 216, 217, 223–4, 226, 245, 247, 265, 268, 274, 350–1, 396, 407
Pargeter, Jacqueline 17, 18, 19, 28, 33, 74, 76, 85, 102, 104, 243, 265, 268, 274, 407
Pargeter, Reginald 17, 19, 28, 35
Pargeter, Regine 102, 144, 148–9, 247
Pargeter, Roland 28, 35, 223, 235, 243, 262
Parker, Barry 153–4, 369
Parker Hale sound moderator *see* murder weapon
Peek, Mr 266
Penny Personnel Management Ltd 58–9
PII (Public Interest Immunity) xix, 399
Pike, Douglas 148, 250
Pirie, Richard 308, 309
police: arrest Jeremy Bamber 287–8; City of London police inquiry into case 385; discovery of bodies 171–7; first respond to scene of crime 163–4; internal review into case (1986) 177, 215, 236, 266, 323, 383–4; interview Jeremy Bamber 290–2, 293–5, 298–9, 300–6, 308–12, 313–16; Jeremy Bamber's phone call to on night of murders 158, 163, 164, 165, 294–5, 304, 305, 306, 344, 345, 366; Jeremy Bamber's reaction to news of murders and 175, 176, 177, 178, 179, 181–3; Julie Mugford interview 275, 276–86, 287; Metropolitan Police investigation of case (1997) 388–9; photographs of crime scene 184, 185, 191, 237, 211–12, 230, 284, 292, 293, 307–8, 315, 336, 339, 346, 386, 390; post-mortems 190–7, 206–7; replacement of Taff Jones 288; Scenes of Crime searches 177–80, 184–7, 191, 211–12, 214, 215, 230, 284, 292–3, 307–8, 315, 336, 339, 346–7, 348, 386, 390; siege of White House Farm 164–71; weapon used for murder and 185–7, 193, 194, 197, 198, 199, 200, 207, 208, 215–16, 218, 220, 223–4, 225–6, 227, 230–4, 235–6, 237, 238, 239–40, 251, 252, 255, 259, 284, 290–1, 307–8, 310, 313–14, 315, 318, 319,

322, 323, 324, 327, 334, 338–9, 342, 343–4, 347, 348, 349, 350–1, 359–60, 361–3, 365, 366, 368, 370, 371–3, 374–5, 376–7, 383–4, 385–6, 388, 389–90, 392, 394–8, 411, 412, 414, 415, 416

Radcliffe, Robert 104–5, 359–60
Radcliffe's Gunmakers 104–5
reconstruction of events at White House Farm, 7 August 1985 xvi, 410–16
Richards, James 119, 359, 367, 368
Rimington, Elizabeth 64–5, 86, 89, 90, 94, 97–8, 128, 140, 213, 219, 231–2, 235, 240, 241, 242, 243, 245, 246, 251, 256–7, 261, 264, 268, 272, 273, 275, 277, 284, 287, 335, 359
Rivlin QC, Geoffrey 335, 336, 339, 340, 344–5, 348, 349, 350, 353, 354, 355, 356, 357, 358, 360, 361, 362, 363, 364, 366, 367, 369, 372–3, 375, 376, 377, 396
Roberts, Yvonne xiii–xiv
Robinson, Jane 127, 138, 145, 146
Robson, Rev. Bernard 3, 243–4
Rowe, Jean 165, 169
Royal Free Hospital 49, 51, 81, 370
Rozga, Raymond, Acting Sergeant 173, 175
Ryan, Sue 149–50

Salvage, Judy 274–5, 369
Saxby, Robin, Constable 100, 163, 165, 176, 182
Seabrook, Mark 50, 54–5
Shann, Rosalie 381
Shine, Betty: *Mind to Mind* 337–8
silencer *see* murder weapon
Simpson, Peter, Assistant Chief Constable 175, 273, 274, 288, 296, 326, 327
Sinclair, Stuart 119, 148
Smith, David James 391, 396, 398
Smith, Ken 381–2
Smith, Stephen 157
Sotheby's 217, 229, 236, 254–5, 257, 288
sound moderator *see* murder weapon
Speakman, Leslie 12–13, 14, 18, 19, 29, 41–2, 62
Speakman, (née Bunting), Mabel 13–14, 29, 79–80, 148, 224–5, 241, 255–6,

260, 261, 265–6, 337, 407
St Andrew's Hospital, Northampton 3,
    23, 71–3, 81–5, 113, 115, 114–16,
    121, 122, 209, 369
St Nicholas Church, Tolleshunt D'Arcy
    12, 27, 35
Stancliffe, John 236, 254–5
Stone, Ronald, Deputy Chief Constable
    383
Sun 214, 239, 299, 307, 317, 320
Sunday Express 394
Sunday Times 6, 391
Sykora (née Jay), Christine 20–1, 69–70,
    96, 123, 127–8, 243, 274, 407
Sykora, Oscar 69

Talk Radio 387
Taylor, Ethel 133
Terzeon, Paul 335–6, 394
Thomas, William 37, 44–5, 47–8, 49,
    244
Thorp, Bettine 35–6, 66
Thorp, Rev. Norman 35, 40, 243
Times, The 383, 389, 397
Today xv, 149–50
Tollesbury 1, 46, 89, 148
Tolleshunt D'Arcy, Essex *see under
    individual area, farm or road name*
Tomkinson, David 87, 88, 107, 112,
    113, 117, 138, 243
Tomkinson, Tora 21, 33, 41, 46, 87–9,
    90, 93, 107, 111, 112, 113, 117–18,
    126, 127, 139, 141, 145–6, 201, 214,
    243, 409
Tompkins, Dr Geoffrey 236
Tugendhat, Mr Justice 391
Turner QC, Michael 389
Turner, Jonathan, Constable 188, 190
Tweed, Basil 44, 146, 147
Tweed, Doris 146, 147, 369

Vale Antiques 261, 270
Vanezis, Peter xx, 191, 192–4, 195–6,
    197, 206–7, 210–11, 231, 319, 322,
    323, 360–1, 376, 384, 411, 416
Vaulty Manor Farm, Goldhanger 13, 14,
    15, 16, 18, 29, 70, 102, 134, 135,
    148, 152, 218, 224–5, 226, 257, 260,
    266, 292, 349, 406, 407

Wager, Dennis 91, 190, 359
Walker, John 327
Walton, John 43
Ware, David, Constable 205
Waters, Malcolm 64, 67–8, 86, 94,
    245–6, 275, 277
Webb, Paul, Constable 173, 174
Webster, Mark 386, 390
West, Michael, Constable 164–5,
    344–5
Wheeler, Juliet Dorothy 25
White House Farm, Tolleshunt D'Arcy,
    Essex: floor plans, 7 August 1985
    x–xi; history of (1891–1984) 11–18;
    history of after night of murders 406;
    location and character of 19; Nevill
    and June Bamber becomes tenants of
    18; reconstruction of events at, 7
    August 1985 410–16; siege of
    163–75
Whitworth, Kathleen 41
Wilkin, Barbara 19, 26, 35
Wilkin, Daphne 67, 73
Wilkin, John 19, 20, 26, 34, 39, 48, 67,
    73
Wilkinson, Robert, Detective Inspector
    322, 325, 359
Wilkinson, Dr Anne 135, 362
Wilson, Barbara 61–2, 71, 73, 76, 79,
    81, 86, 91, 111, 121, 124, 127,
    130–2, 133, 136–7, 140, 141, 143,
    148, 150, 153, 157, 189, 223, 224,
    227–8, 240–1, 249, 250, 254, 257,
    264–5, 327, 333, 347–8, 406,
    412–13
Wilson, Keith 61, 347
Wilson, Philip 148, 153, 155, 156, 189,
    257, 264
Witham Police Station 183, 233, 277,
    317, 406
Woffinden, Bob 400
Woodcock, Peter, Acting Sergeant 171,
    172, 173, 174, 175, 176, 185, 186,
    362–3
Wright, Charles 'Geordie', Detective Chief
    Inspector 179, 214, 292, 296, 322
Wright, Norman, PC 184, 191, 196,
    199, 209
Wycke Cottage 5, 154

Picture credits

All photographs from the author's collection with the exception of those listed below.

Section One

Page 1 – top: © Steve Back/ANL/REX Shutterstock
Page 2 – top: © Anglia Press Agency/SWpix.com
Page 4 – bottom: courtesy of the Pargeter family
Page 5 – bottom: © Mirrorpix
Page 6 – top: © Anglia Press Agency/SWpix.com;
    bottom: © Daily Mail / Solo Syndication
Page 7 – top: © Mirrorpix;
    bottom: © Anglia Press Agency/SWpix.com
Page 8 – top: courtesy of the Pargeter family

Section Two

Page 2 – top: © Mirrorpix
Page 4 – top: © Skyviews Aerial Archives, Leeds;
    bottom: © Anglia Press Agency/SWpix.com
Page 5 – top: © Anglia Press Agency/SWpix.com;
    bottom: © Anglia Press Agency/SWpix.com
Page 6 – top: © PA Archive/Press Association Images;
    bottom: © Anglia Press Agency/SWpix.com
Page 7 – top: © Anglia Press Agency/SWpix.com;
    bottom: © Daily Mail / Solo Syndication